QUR'AN,
LIBERATION & PLURALISM

The demise of apartheid in South Africa in the 1980s followed an unprecedented unity in struggle against oppression from members of different faith traditions. Determined as South African Muslims were to participate with the rest of the oppressed in solidarity against apartheid, this brought them into conflict with interpretations of the Qur'an that denied virtue outside Islam, and left them searching for a theology that would allow them to both co-operate against injustice and be true to their faith.

In this challenging account, Farid Esack reflects on key qur'anic passages used in the context of oppression to rethink the role of Islam in a plural society. He exposes how traditional interpretations of the Qur'an were used to legitimize an unjust order, and demonstrates that those very texts used to support religious intolerance, if interpreted within a contemporary socio-historical context, support active solidarity with the religious Other for change.

Combining social history, politics and theology, this book offers scholars, students and all those concerned with Islam in the modern world a fascinating insight into a contemporary issue, against the backdrop of one of the most exciting periods of world history.

This book by a brilliant young Muslim scholar is important for all of us . . . significant new religious understanding always comes out of new experiences, and in the liberation struggle in South Africa the Qur'an revealed new aspects of its meaning.
John Hick, Danforth Professor of Philosophy of Religion, Claremont Graduate School, California

Esack's Islamic liberation theology is as stunning and challenging as was Gutierrez's Christian liberation theology . . . Esack offers a challenge for all religions: that human liberation and interreligious dialogue cannot be realized without each other . . . an extraordinarily good book.
Paul Knitter, Professor of Theology, Xavier University, Cincinnati

QUR'AN,
LIBERATION
&
PLURALISM

An Islamic Perspective of
Interreligious Solidarity
against Oppression

Farid Esack

ONEWORLD
OXFORD

To the lover of five-minute snoozes

QUR'AN, LIBERATION AND PLURALISM

Oneworld Publications
(Sales and Editorial)
185 Banbury Road
Oxford OX2 7AR
England

Oneworld Publications
(US Marketing Office)
PO Box 830, 21 Broadway
Rockport, MA 01966
USA

© Farid Esack 1997

Reprinted 1998

All rights reserved.
Copyright under Berne Convention
A CIP record for this book is available
from the British Library

ISBN 1-85168-121-3

Cover design by Peter Maguire
Printed and bound by WSOY, Finland

ACKNOWLEDGEMENTS

To my late mother who succumbed to the triple oppression of women under apartheid: racism, capitalism and patriarchy . . . and who insisted that her kids were her only form of entertainment.

To Jill Wenman, my fully human teacher of History and English at school who first lit my candle, alerted me to the pain and joys of critical thinking, and popped her lunch pack into my hand as I was escorted from school by the security police.

To Brother Norman Wray and all those crazy Christian Pakistanis, who compelled me to see the relationship between faith and praxis, and who still refuse to adjust to inhumanness.

To all those who journeyed with me (or suffered journeying with me!) in the Call of Islam and without whose commitment there would have been no South African qur'anic hermeneutic of pluralism for liberation.

To all of those who offered me academic support and friendship during my sojourn in England. I am particularly grateful for the critical insight and loving friendship of my doctoral thesis supervisor, Christian Troll S.J. The editorial insights of Sigvard von Sicard, Chris Hewer, and Toby Howarth, were also invaluable.

To the Woodbrook community who survived my sojourn. I am particularly grateful to Claire Chamberlain for all the comforts of home and to John Wyatt for his friendship.

To C. Aid who funded my rather expensive PhD programme. Many thanks for the monthly cheque, Alex, and sorry that I did not get to make it to a single one of the annual get-togethers.

To Patrice Brodeur, for crucial and invaluable editorial assistance, an even more invaluable friendship and for remembering the distance between Nynashamn and Oskarshamn.

To Pfarrerin Frau Gisela Eggler, for a supporting friendship, challenging solidarity *und auch für die (oder 'der'? vielleicht 'das'?) Waschmaschine.*

To all left of the road Claremont Main Roaders for the sense of community. Particularly to the *imam*, Abdul Rashied Omar for his courage and comradely support in developing a theology of disgruntlement and compassion as well as a hermeneutic of suspicion and faith; to its secretary, Fahmi Gamildien, for the wonderfully supportive role he played in my interminable word-processing and printing problems and to Dr Abdul Kader Tayob for having read through the manuscript and offering valuable, albeit unheeded, advice.

To Riffat Muhammad for considerable and tireless, well, sort of, last-minute location of sources and bibliographical details, assistance with proof-reading and a great cup of coffee.

To Novin Doostdar and Juliet Mabey of Oneworld Publications for succumbing to the idea that friendship and business can mix, and to their dog Tess, for offering me some welcome, otherwise entirely withheld, whenever I stay over at my publishers' house.

To the de Smidts, for a piece of sunny Cape Town in the heart of London's East End.

To Helen Coward of Oneworld for her interminable hassling on editorial detail and a great midwifing of this work.

And to my family in Cape Town and Port Shepstone, for always being there.

CONTENTS

LIST *of* ABBREVIATIONS

AMP	African Muslim Party
ANB	Afrikaner National Bond
ANC	African National Congress
APO	African People's Organization
Azapo	Azanian People's Organization
BC	Black Consciousness
CA	Constitutional Assembly
CAD	Coloured Affairs Department
Call	Call of Islam
CIF	Cape Islamic Federation
CMA	Cape Malay Association
CMYA	Claremont Muslim Youth Association
CMYM	Cape Muslim Youth Movement
Codesa	Convention for a Democratic South Africa
Contralesa	Congress of Traditional Leaders
Cosatu	Congress of South African Trade Unions
CPA	Coloured People's Association
DRC	Dutch Reformed Church
ER	*Encyclopaedia of Religion*
EI	*Encyclopaedia of Islam*
ICT	Institute of Contextual Theology
IFP	Inkatha Freedom Party
IP	Islamic Party
IPC	Islamic Propagation Centre
MJC	Muslim Judicial Council
MPL	Muslim Personal Law
MPLB	Muslim Personal Law Board
MSA	Muslim Students Association
MYM	Muslim Youth Movement
NEUM	Non-European Unity Movement
NLL	National Liberation League
NMC	National Muslim Conference
NP	National Party
NUM	New Unity Movement
PAC	Pan-Africanist Congress
Pagad	People Against Drugs and Gangsterism
SEI	*Shorter Encyclopaedia of Islam*
SABSA	South African Black Scholars Association
SACC	South African Council of Churches
UDF	United Democratic Front
UWC	University of the Western Cape
WCRP	World Conference of Religion and Peace

NOTES *on* LANGUAGE

Transliteration

A simplified form of transliteration from Arabic has been followed to facilitate things for the non-specialist reader, with the exception of words such as Qur'an, Islam and Muslim, which, through frequent usage, are part of the English language.

Proper names and titles have been transliterated according to the practice of the organization or individual. Transliteration in quotations is unchanged.

An apostrophe and inverted comma are used for the Arabic letters *hamzah* and *'ayn* respectively. These letters are disregarded in the alphabetical ordering of the Glossary.

Translations

All the translations from foreign languages into English are my own, with the exception of qur'anic texts where, in the main, Muhammad Asad's *The Message of the Qur'an* (Gibraltar: Dar al-Andalus, 1980) was adopted. Citations of the Qur'an are in the form 'chapter (*surah*): verse'.

Local Usage

The following words with a peculiarly, though not exclusively, South African usage are retained: 'motivate' (to account for, to explain, to justify) and 'engage' (to encounter in a deliberate and conscious manner).

In the cases where the local usage of an ideological category differs markedly from that employed elsewhere, I chose the local usage and supply an explanatory note where the term first appears.

Terminology

The following key terms are used throughout the book:

The term *accommodationist* is used in this book in the sense of willingly coexisting in harmony with the structures of political power, whatever their ideological nature. The use of the term is discussed further in chapter 6.

Hermeneutics are discussed in detail in chapter 2, but may be defined briefly as the science of interpretation which deals with the relationship between the author (or speaker), reader (or listener) and text, and the conditions under which one understands a text.

The term *Islamist* is usually employed interchangeably with 'Muslim fundamentalist' in the current discourse of political Islam, which uses an essentialist theology to influence and eventually achieve political power. In South Africa the term 'Islamist' refers to those who are committed to Islam in a comprehensive manner, with particular emphasis on actualizing its ideals in the socio-political sphere. The term is used in this sense throughout this study. Some of these Islamists were committed to what was referred to as 'a South African expression of Islam' (Esack 1988b, p. 48). By this they meant an approach to Islam that made a conscious effort to relate to the struggle for an undivided, non-racial and non-sexist South Africa. In common with growing practice in South Africa, this group is referred to as 'progressive Islamists' in the present work.

Islamic fundamentalism, as popularized in much of the Western media, represents a stereotype with pejorative and disparaging connotations. It is often sweeping in its generalization and insensitive to the many nuances in the world of contemporary Islam. Furthermore, 'fundamentalism', in a religious context, has a peculiarly Christian basis in attitudes to the Bible as scripture (ER, see 'evangelical and fundamental religion'). However, in contemporary Islamic discourse there is a tendency that can appropriately be described as fundamentalism. In brief, this tendency has the following characteristics: 1) a commitment to strict religious practice; 2) a commitment to observance of the text; 3) an ahistorical view of Islam as capable of permanently solving all the problems of humankind; 4) a belief in the necessity of enforcing the *shari'ah* as fundamentalists understand it to have been practised in the Muhammadan era in Medina; 5) a commitment to the establishment of an Islamic state wherein the sovereignty of God, juxtaposed against popular sovereignty, would be supreme; 6) enmity towards all who reject fundamentalist views as people who have chosen Evil against Good and 7) a denial of any virtue in non-Islam.

Liberation, I consider to be the freedom of all people from all those laws, social norms and economic practices that militate against them developing their potential to be fully human and fully alive. In the context of apartheid South Africa, this essentially meant freedom from apartheid and economic exploitation, the right of all its inhabitants freely to elect a government of their choice and to participate on an ongoing basis in the various decision-making processes that would shape their lives.

Pluralism can be described as the acknowledgement and acceptance, rather than tolerance, of Otherness and diversity, both within the Self and within the Other. In the context of religion it means the acceptance of diverse ways of responding to the impulse, which may be both innate and socialized, within each human being towards the Transcendent.

Prophetic is used in the sense of pertaining to the prophets, ranging from Adam to Muhammad, as understood by Muslims.

Other terms are defined briefly in the text as they arise and are also listed in the glossary. Arabic words preceded by the article *al-* (the) are listed in the glossary under the first letter of the following word.

INTRODUCTION

In HUMBLE SUBMISSION to the ALMIGHTY GOD

It is not uncommon for religious believers in the struggle to discover that they have more in common, theologically speaking, with comrades from very different religious traditions than they have with members of their own communities who are not involved in the struggle. This religious commonalty in the struggle demands a theological framework which can give it expression and explain it.

(Gross 1990, p. 2)

What Baggage does this Interpreter Carry?

'God's word is revealed to the searcher'. Which comes first, the word or the searcher? At first glance this is a seemingly innocuous question. Not so when dealing with a text such as the Qur'an which most Muslims believe to be co-eternal with God (in other words, it has existed as long as God has). So where does one commence a work on qur'anic hermeneutics, the text or the context? Alas, the slip will show right from the beginning. Given that every literary production is inescapably autobiographical, I shall locate the birth of my ideas in my personal, social, and ideological history.

I have always been deeply moved by humankind's seemingly inexhaustible capacity to inflict injustice upon the 'Other' – religious, racial or sexual – and for long have I estimated my own humanity – or lack thereof – in terms of my willingness to react against it or my inability, unwillingness or refusal to do so.

My father abandoned our family when I was three weeks old. My mother was left with six sons of whom three were from a previous marriage where her first husband had abandoned her when the third son was three months old. (Enough to drive anyone to Trinitarianism!) I was raised in Bonteheuwel, a coloured township on the Cape Flats to which our family was forcibly moved under the Group Areas Act. This apartheid law, promulgated in 1952, set aside the most barren parts of the country for Blacks, Indians and Coloureds.[1] Long periods passed during which we had no shoes and I recall running across frost-covered fields to school so that the frost could not really bite into my feet. Slightly more painful were the many times when my brother and I went around knocking on the doors of neighbours to ask for a piece of bread or scavenging in the gutters for discarded apple cores and the like.

This poverty was but one manifestation of apartheid South Africa. Here, in the 1980s, Whites, who constituted one-sixth of the total population, earned almost two-thirds of the national income while Blacks, who made up nearly three-quarters, earned only one quarter (Wilson and Ramphele 1989, p. 20). As for the millions who did not even fall in the category of wage earners, the unemployed: 'We just sleep in the wilderness. You sleep without having eaten and you get up without having eaten. Tomorrow you go and look for a job. If you don't get it, you come back. When you come back, you go about uncovering rubbish bins thinking: "Could it be there is something that has been thrown in here, just a little something that I can chew?"' (ibid., p. 100)

My mother was an underpaid worker in a factory where she slogged from can't see to can't see – from early in the morning when it was still dark until late when it was dark already. My early life as a victim of apartheid and poverty, seeing my mother finally succumb under the burden of economic exploitation and patriarchy, filled me with an abiding commitment to a comprehensive sense of justice.

A Land of Many Faiths

In both Wynberg and Bonteheuwel we had Christian neighbours on both sides of our house and in our school we were subjected to Christian National Education, a conservative religious ideology meant to make us obedient and God-fearing citizens of the apartheid state. Besides Christians, the only recollection I have of the religious Other are of Mr Frank, a kind debt collector who was a jew and of Tahirah, a Bahá'í girl at primary school whose parents prohibited her discussing her faith with anyone.

South African society has for long been multi-religious. The now virtually decimated Khoikhoin, the Nguni, the San and other indigenous groups are known to have held diverse religious beliefs and practices. The arrival of Dutch Christian settlers, Muslim slaves and political exiles from the Indonesian Archipelago in the middle of the seventeenth century accentuated this religious diversity. More recent numerically significant additions to this diversity are the Hindus who arrived in the second half of the nineteenth century from India and the East European Jews who made their way to South Africa at the turn of this century.[2]

On our Christian neighbours we depended for 'a cup of sugar', 'a rand until Friday', and a shoulder to cry on – and on the kindness of Mr Frank we depended for extensions on the repayment of the never-ending hire-purchase agreements. The fact that our oppression was made bearable by the solidarity, humanity and laughter of our Christian neighbours made me suspicious of all religious ideas that claimed salvation only for their own and imbued me with a deep awareness of the intrinsic worth of the religious Other. How could I possibly look Mrs Batista and Aunty Katie in the eye while believing that, despite the kindness that shone from every dealing which they had with us, they were destined for the fire of hell? This acceptance of the Other, the core of religious pluralism, did not come naturally however, to the township dwellers. Even as people suffered together they upheld notions of exclusive paradises for Christians or Muslims; even as they shared their humble meals with each other, they did so serving the religious Other out of specially reserved marked plates and cups.

Religion plays a major role among all classes in South African society. In the ghettoes the first community project is invariably the building of a mosque or a church. In the face of dislocation from a stable community under the Group Areas Act, religion or alcohol – more often than not, both – became important factors in the struggle for survival. In my family Islam as a cultural anchor was an important tool in the struggle for survival among the sandy dunes and Port Jackson trees of Bonteheuwel. We bonded quickly with our Muslim neighbours – and 'neighbours' could conceivably include those living thirty or forty houses away from ours. While my family was not unusually religious, the mosque-in-progress was, nevertheless, an important focal point. Here I played after school and weekends, pushed wheelbarrows of sand as a child and ended up as secretary of the society that controlled the mosque and as *madrassah* teacher when I was still a kid at school.

Service in Return for Justice

I was strangely and deeply religious as a child, with a deep concern for the suffering which I experienced and witnessed all around me. I dealt with these two impulses by holding on to an indomitable belief that for God to be God, God had to be just and on the side of the marginalized. More curious was a logic, based on a text in the Qur'an, 'If you assist Allah then He will assist you and make your feet firm' (47:7). For me this meant that I had to participate in a struggle for freedom and justice and, if I wanted God's help in this, then I had to assist Him.[3] 'Him' was interpreted as 'His religion' and so I persisted with the Tablighi Jama'ah, an international Muslim revivalist movement, that I had joined at the age of nine.

I was still at school when I was first detained by the Special Branch, as the security police were then known, as a result of my work in National Youth Action and the South African Black Scholars Association. Both of these organizations were committed to radical socio-political change and were housed in the buildings of the Christian Institute before its banning in 1973. There we enjoyed the warm hospitality and solidarity of its director, the Reverend Theo Kotze, and his staff. Theo offered the Muslims in these organizations prayer facilities and came to visit our families after our release from detention, to console them and to assure them that 'getting mixed up' with the police was actually a privilege. (A poster on the wall of the Christian Institute read: 'Where there's growth there's a branch; where there's special growth, there's bound to be a special branch'.)

Pakistani Women and Christians as Black South Africans

After school I spent eight years on a scholarship in Pakistan doing my theological training, much of it in a frightfully conservative institute where everything 'this-worldly' was frowned upon. I remember a twelve-year-old, Abdul Khaliq Allie, being rushed to hospital one night and undergoing an emergency operation lasting a couple of hours. Adil Johaar stayed with him the morning, while I trod along to classes after having spent the night in hospital. In class the following morning Mawlana Baksh enquired where Adil was. Upon being told that Adil was watching over Abdul Khaliq in hospital, he said: 'Did you people come here to study or to look after sick people?'

I marvel at how I survived the place; a combination of courage, cunning and the Grace of God I suppose.

Much as I came to love Pakistan, my coming from a Muslim family in a minority situation alerted me to the religious and social persecution of the Christian and Hindu minority communities. Derrick Dean, a young Christian activist, was visiting me one night in the *madrassah* room I shared with six others. Haji Bhai Padia, the South African leader of the Tablighi Jama'ah, put in a surprise appearance. Upon discovering that Derrick was not a Muslim he asked him to recite the *kalimah*, the Muslim formula of faith. I had a deep respect for Derrick as he was, and much love for Bhai Padia, and felt somewhat embarrassed. What was happening here was that my simplistic logic of 'If you help God, He will help you' was becoming unstuck. The gap between my inherently conservative theology and progressive praxis was becoming exposed and choices had to be made.

I frequented the discussions of the Student Christian Movement, later renamed Breakthrough and witnessed how they tried to make sense of living as Christians in a fundamentally unjust and exploitative society. The most inspirational figure of the group, Brother Norman Wray, a La Salle brother, invited me to come and teach Islamic Studies at a school where he was the principal. I subsequently worked with him and the group on a number of different projects, which included para-medical work in the Karachi Central Prison, teaching in Hindu and Christian ghettoes for sweepers, and working in a home for abandoned children. Later I was to repeat all of the lessons of marrying belief and praxis in South Africa.

In Pakistan I also became vividly aware of the many similarities between the oppression of women in Muslim society and that of Blacks in apartheid South Africa. The inescapable convergence between sexist and racist discourse has, consequently, come to form a permanent backdrop to my own concerns and commitment.

As if all of this were not enough.

Soon after my return to South Africa in 1982 I was called into a room by Omar, one of my brothers and the door was closed. 'Farid, we have a sister; she's the eldest of all of us'. My mother had had a daughter before marrying her first husband and the baby was handed over to her father seven days later. The pain of living an entire life carrying this secret must have been unbearable. Society stigmatizes women who fall pregnant outside marriage, as if these pregnancies were all phantom-induced, with no men ever involved. Later I learnt from Sharifah, my sister, now sixty years old, of the unbearably sad spectacle of an utterly lonely woman standing on the side of the road, watching from a safe distance the funeral procession of her mother – whom she had never known – passing, not daring to go near in fear of rejection by six brothers.

In 1983 resistance to a new constitution began. The preamble of this widely rejected tricameral constitution commenced with 'In humble submission to the Almighty God' and then proceeded with the details of an elaborate system of entrenching the racial divisions among God's people. While the then state president, P. W. Botha, invoked the biblical narrative of the prodigal son to plead for apartheid South Africa's re-entry into the community of nations, the vast majority of South Africans of diverse religious persuasion were making plans, in the name of the same Almighty God, to intensify that isolation and to destroy that same constitution as the first step of the last stage in the liberation struggle.

Religion as Contested Territory

South Africa was entering the beginning of the last stage of our struggle against apartheid and I could not bear being safely tucked away in a seminary. The discomfort first experienced when Bhai Padia wanted Derrick to recite the *kalimah* had turned full circle. Along with three friends, I spearheaded the founding of the Call of Islam in 1984. This affiliate of the United Democratic Front (UDF, established in 1983), the major internal liberation movement, soon became the most active Muslim movement, mobilizing nationally against apartheid, gender inequality, threats to the environment and to interfaith work. In the UDF itself, the Call was one of many religiously based organizations engaged in 'the struggle'. For these organizations, religion had always been contested terrain and the struggle was as much about regaining ideological territory from religious conservatism and obscurantism as it was about political freedom.

Much of the suffering inflicted on the people of South Africa was committed in the name of, and sometimes with, the scriptural support of a religious tradition, more specifically, that of Christianity. However, the subjugation and oppression of South Africa's people did not proceed with the general support of all Christians. Organizations such as the Christian Institute and individuals such as Beyers Naudé and Theo Kotze show that, even among Christians who came from privileged backgrounds, there were always dissident voices calling for justice and human rights. These voices were often marginalized and smothered, but always coherent and principled. They invoked the same sacred scriptures, often even the same textual references to sustain their arguments, as their fellow Christians to denounce the exploitation and suffering of black people.

Religion and scripture as contested territory were also evident in the responses among the exploited and oppressed. The vast majority of Blacks and a small, but significant, number of Whites viewed the entire social structure of South Africa as irredeemably racist, exploitative and desperately in need of radical changes. Given the significance of religion in the lives of South Africans, it was not surprising that many made a connection between religion and liberation. (Even if some did it rather simplistically, wanting to help God's religion if He helped them bring about freedom!) There were, however, also many who argued that politics should be kept apart from religion. Among Blacks, the 'apolitical' Zionist Christian Church, with a membership numbering a few millions, attracted hundreds of thousands to their annual gathering at Moria. The Charismatic and Pentecostal churches, which claimed to confine themselves to 'spiritual' concerns, attracted people from all race groups and experienced tremendous growth in the urban areas during the 1980s (Gifford 1988; 1989).[4]

All the main political players in South Africa invoked religion as the ultimate proof of self-correctness. In 1985, from his prison cell on Robben Island, Nelson Mandela wrote a moving letter to the Muslim Judicial Council (MJC, established in 1945), wherein he spoke about the spiritual solace he derived from his visits to the shrine of Shaikh Madura, a Muslim saint imprisoned on the island until his death in 1742 (see Appendix One). In that letter he also reaffirmed his commitment to his Methodist roots and spoke glowingly about the role of religion, not just Christianity, in shaping the ideals of the African National Congress (ANC, established in 1912). Meanwhile, in the KwaZulu Bantustan capital of Ulundi, Gatsha Buthelezi, the Bantustan's leader, at his annual prayer breakfasts, lamented the political role which religious leaders were increasingly playing against homeland governments.

In the 1980s especially, the conflict between two expressions of religion, accommodationist and liberatory was increasingly evident. In a context of oppression, it seems that theology, across religious divisions, fulfils one of two tasks: it either underpins and supports the structures and institutions of oppression or it performs this function in relation to the struggle for liberation. Accommodation theology tries to accommodate and justify the dominant status quo 'with its racism, capitalism and totalitarianism. It blesses injustice, canonizes the will of the powerful and reduces the poor to passivity, obedience and apathy' (*The Kairos Document* 1985, p. 13). It focuses on questions of personal conversion and salvation while it ignores or denies the role which socio-economic structures play in the shaping of personal values. In a sociological investigation into this model of religiousness conducted in

1969, Milton Rokeach reported that

> the general picture that emerges is that those who place a high value on salvation are conservative, anxious to maintain the status quo and unsympathetic or indifferent to the plight of the black or the poor. Considered all together, the data suggest a portrait of the religious minded as a person having a self-centred preoccupation with saving his own soul, an other worldly orientation, coupled with indifference toward or even a tacit endorsement of a social system that would perpetuate social inequality and injustice. (Cited in Stott 1984, p. 8)

In South Africa manifestations of this theological model were witnessed both in the so-called mainstream religious structures such as the Anglican and Dutch Reformed Churches and the Majlisul Ulama, and in numerous groups such as Christians for Peace, Christ for All Nations, the Zionist Christian Council, the United Christian Reconciliation Council, the Tablighi Jama'ah and the Islamic Propagation Centre.

In contrast to accommodation theology, liberation theology is the process of praxis for comprehensive justice, the theological reflection that emerges from it and the reshaping of praxis based on that reflection. In South Africa, liberation theology was manifested in the growing numbers of religious figures and organizations who confessed the sin of silence in the face of oppression, acquiescence in the face of exploitation and power in the face of want. They sought a God who is active in history, who desires freedom for all people and the simultaneous conversion of hearts and social structures, a God whose own unity was reflected in the oneness of people.

The tension between these two expressions of theology was not confined to Christianity; Islam, Hinduism, Judaism and African Traditional Religion, in various degrees, saw new forms of contextual theology and religious structures emerging to challenge apartheid. In resisting the ideology of apartheid and its resulting injustices, adherents of all faiths increasingly discovered each other as companions in the struggle for justice. In the Muslim community the most significant area where this battle over interpretations of religion was being waged was the discourse of solidarity with the religious Other in the struggle against apartheid.

When the Self Engages the Other

Interfaith solidarity, particularly during the 1980s, was an intrinsic part of the South African struggle for justice. It also remains an important dimension of the vision for a just and non-racial society held by all of those who were a part of that struggle. The often bitter debate around interfaith solidarity against apartheid featured prominently in Muslim discourse in the 1980s. With the emergence of a non-racial and democratic South Africa, it is timely to examine some of the theological dimensions of this debate and their wider hermeneutical implications.

How did political activism, or the lack of it, shape the Muslim community's understanding of the Qur'an and their perception of the Other? How did a conscious desire to recognize and respect righteousness in religiously Other comrades compel progressive Islamists to reinterpret qur'anic texts which, at a superficial glance, may be regarded as uncharitable, even unjust, to the Other? What led these Islamists regularly to invoke some 'revolutionary texts' while quietly passing over other texts? And what led the accommodationist clerics[5] to invoke the 'spiritual texts' while ignoring other texts? How was Islam affected by its use as a means of liberation? What does this question of Islam being 'affected' say about deeply held beliefs in the Muslim community of a faith which has a timeless essence and which transcends history? These were some of the questions confronting, and being confronted, by progressive Islamists who have been engaged in what has cryptically been known as 'the struggle'.

My present search for a South African qur'anic hermeneutic of pluralism for liberation was rooted in the fusion of our nation's crucible and in my own commitment to comprehensive justice. While this work primarily focuses on rethinking approaches to the Qur'an and to the theological categories of exclusion and inclusion rooted in a struggle for freedom from economic exploitation and racial discrimination, its application is intended to be broader than these two forms of injustice. I believe that the ideas I put forward can have a wider application to all categories of social and political injustice, ranging from the obvious oppression of women in Muslim society to discrimination against left-handed people.

Whose Justice? Which Morality?

But 'whose "injustice"?', one may well ask. In the same way, in the expression 'In humble submission to the Almighty God', one may also ask: 'but which God?'. More than most societies, South Africans have a particularly acute sense of the consequences of living with competing realities and, consequently, rival in-/justices. The task of judging between competing and incompatible rationalities and justices is exceptionally difficult, because one cannot pose a point of view which is free from any one particular conception of rationality or justice (MacIntyre 1988, pp. 1–18).

Contemporary hermeneutics alerts us to the false pretensions of objectivity or neutrality and the need to rehabilitate 'the concept of prejudice and a recognition of the fact that there are legitimate prejudices' (Gadamer 1992, p. 261). The present work, like all literary productions, takes sides. While not denying my personal commitment to the struggle against injustice and the public role I have played in this regard, I strive to make the best use of some contemporary developments in the human sciences to explain the phenomenon of qur'anic interpretation among contemporary South African progressive Islamists.

People with a religious commitment may choose to believe that truth is exclusively an eternal and pre-existing reality beyond history. However, people also make truth. Modernity has increased our awareness that the human mind is not a blank slate covered with facts entirely imported through cognitive or spiritual senses, or through the authority of religio-intellectual traditions. Increasingly, we are beginning to understand that, whatever else it may be, the essential awareness of one's mind is as 'the tissues of contingent relations in language' (Aitken 1991, p. 1). Language, we now know, plays a significant role in shaping us and our consciousness. Language though, much as it shapes history, is also a prisoner of history. Yet, according to Muslims, God is utterly beyond history. It is this utter beyondness and its use of an inevitably history-bound mechanism, language, which provides a central dilemma for the Muslim who also seeks to live contemporaneously and in complete awareness of the baggage of prejudices. More than the elaboration of intellectual modernity and post-modernity in the West, it was the South African crucible that confronted progressive Islamists with the 'truth' that people bring their indispensable baggage of race, class, gender and personal history along when they engage the qur'anic text.

My Baggage of Theological Assumptions

I believe that the Transcendent, God, has intervened and is intervening in history. This intervention, however, can make no sense other than within the framework of humankind's existence here on earth. The religious legacy of South African Muslims, and our ongoing commitment to that legacy, compel us to find new ways of describing the way God may address a world in which human beings constantly change.

In South Africa the world in which Muslims live is also being shaped by others who struggle to survive, who suffer, despair and hope; by others who do not share their religious beliefs. The progressive Islamists could not deny the joys of a shared existence and the moral compulsion of a common struggle against apartheid. Yet we had to live in faithfulness to a text – the Qur'an – that seemed to be harsh towards the Other, suffering along with us in the quest for liberation and justice. To become creatively engaged alongside the Other, risked being transformed. Given that religiosity was an intrinsic part of the identity of progressive Islamists, it was inevitable that our understanding of religious tradition and scripture would also be transformed.

What was, in effect, happening among us closely resembles the use of the 'hermeneutic circle' in liberation theology. Juan Luis Segundo, a liberation theologian from Uruguay, defines the hermeneutic circle as 'the continuing change in our interpretation of the Bible which is dictated by the continuing changes in our present-day reality, both individual and societal' (Segundo 1991, p. 9).[6] He suggests two preconditions for creating a hermeneutic circle. First, profound and enriching questions and suspicion about one's real situation. Second, a new interpretation of scripture that is equally profound and enriching.

The fundamental difference between Segundo's circle and the methodology proposed by Fazlur Rahman (d. 1988), one of this century's most profound modernist Islamic scholars, whose ideas are examined in some detail in the second chapter, is the conscious decision to enter the circle from the point of liberative praxis which is decidedly political. 'The hermeneutic circle', says Segundo, 'is based on the fact that a political option in favour of liberative change is an intrinsic element of faith' (ibid., p. 97).

I believe that a Muslim's task of understanding the Qur'an within a context of oppression is twofold. First, it is to expose the way traditional interpretation and beliefs about a text function as ideology in order to legitimize an unjust order. A text dealing with *fitnah* – (literally, 'disorder') would, for example, be critically re-examined in order to see how the word has come to be broadly interpreted as challenges to the dominant political status quo, however unjust that status quo may be. Second, it is to acknowledge the wholeness of the human being, to extract the religious dimensions within that situation of injustice from the text and utilize these for the cause of liberation. (One would, for example, ask questions about the relationship of God to hunger and exploitation.) These theological dimensions simultaneously shape and are being shaped by the activity of those Islamists engaged in a struggle for justice and freedom.

To search for the religious dimensions of a particular socio-economic situation and to highlight them may open one to charges of the selective and arbitrary appropriation of certain texts, to the exclusion of others. There are two responses to this problem. First, freedom from starvation and exploitation paves the way for a more authentic popular embrace of a comprehensive theology. You cannot truly submit to God when you are under the yoke of hunger. Such submission is a form of coercion. The *hadith* (saying of Muhammad) 'I am in the hands of Allah with regards to poverty and *kufr* (rejection/ denial/ ingratitude)' (Ibn Hanbal 1978, 2, p. 101) is a significant indicator of the relationship between lack of faith and hunger. The Qur'an, in dealing with the encounter of the Israelites and Pharaoh, does not refer to sins of 'personal morality' which may have occurred among the Israelites because their dominant reality was that of oppression; nor does the Qur'an dwell at length on the feebleness of their faith in God; it deals with Pharaoh's claims to divinity and emphasizes the political consequences of those claims for the enslaved Israelites (10:83–5, 90). This is not to suggest that belief in the unity of God was not an important requirement of the Israelites when they were enslaved; it is only to argue that all dimensions of faith do not have to enjoy an equal measure of attention at all times. Furthermore, if socio-political burdens serve as obstacles to faith, then in the present historical circumstances, the struggle for their removal must be the dominant aspect of a believer's activity. The second response is that a search for the theological dimensions in a particular political context does not imply that one views politics as the only dimension of faith and that the text is valuable only in so far as it addresses immediate political concerns. It only emphasizes this dimension as the most crucial one in the here and now 'where people are crushed under the weight of oppression and wandering in search of bread and human dignity' (Boff 1985, p. 104). That the Qur'an does, in fact, deal with these socio-political burdens on numerous occasions is undisputed. These qur'anic texts have, however, been used to legitimize the burden and to provide comfort to those responsible for its imposition. Accommodationist Islam's use of these texts has done nothing to enhance the dignity of the victims of structural injustice, nor to facilitate their freedom.

The beliefs outlined above lead to a number of ideas that both underpin my investigation and are confirmed by it. They also support my advocacy of a South African qur'anic hermeneutic of religious pluralism for liberation.

1. One cannot escape from the personal or social experiences which make up the sum of one's existence. Therefore, any person reading a text or viewing any situation does so through the lenses of his or her experiences.
2. Anyone's attempts to make sense of anything read or experienced take place in a particular context. Because every reader approaches the Qur'an within a particular context it is impossible to speak of an

interpretation of the qur'anic text applicable to the whole world. Meaning is always tentative and biased.

3. According to the Qur'an, one arrives at correct beliefs (orthodoxy) through correct actions (orthopraxis) (29:69). The latter is the criterion by which the former is decided. In a society where injustice and poverty drive people to say 'Even God has left, no one cares anymore', orthopraxis really means activity which supports justice, i.e., liberative praxis. A qur'anic hermeneutic of liberation therefore emerges within concrete struggles for justice and derives its authenticity from that engagement.

4. Formal statements of doctrine, whether 'true' or not, and no matter how intensely the believer clings to them, are, in the first instance, the results of intellectual labour that has often endured for centuries. This labour is invariably accompanied by religio-political disputes, which inevitably impact upon theological developments and the way these statements are shaped.

5. Islamic theology in general, and qur'anic studies specifically, have consistently become increasingly rigid in a process that followed the systematization of theology. Accompanying this process was the growing inability to deal with all forms of Otherness, within the historical community of Muslims and outside it.

6. Both the revelation of the Qur'an within specific contexts, as well as acceptance of the righteous and just Other are intrinsic to the Qur'an (2:281; 3:23–4; 16:111; 4:40, 85; 10:44; 12:56 etc.). It is Muslim conservatism[7] that persistently narrowed the theological base for defining *iman*, *islam* and widened the base for *kufr*.[8] As the basis of conservatism gradually narrowed, the categories of the Other widened so that fewer and fewer were regarded as believers and more and more as *kafir*.

7. Muslims are confronted with a variety of urgent questions: What is an 'authentic' appreciation of the qur'anic message today? What makes and shapes 'authenticity'? How legitimate is it to produce meaning, rather than extracting meaning, from qur'anic texts? These are some of the issues, which hermeneutics does not create (they have always been with us) but which demand to be addressed. They are part and parcel of the search for a qur'anic response to the challenges confronting humankind today.

This Work and its Objectives

This search referred to above is located within a broader, universal struggle for justice and religious pluralism and the need to rethink and reshape the nature and role of religion so that it facilitates such a struggle. The thinking of others who have a similar frame of reference, such as Gustavo Gutierrez, Asghar Ali Engineer, Juan Luis Segundo, Amina Wadud-Muhsin, Clodovis and Leonardo Boff, Hassan Hanafi, Paul Knitter, 'Abdullahi al-Na'im, or Fatima Mernissi, even when not cited, forms a permanent backdrop to this study. In South Africa itself, this work is part of a growing trend among Muslim scholars and thinkers such as Ebrahim Moosa, Abdul Rashied Omar, Ebrahim Rasool, Sa'diyya Shaikh and Abdulkader Tayob to rethink creatively the role of Islam in a religiously plural and patriarchal society.

My objectives in the present work are fourfold. First, to show that it is possible to live in faithfulness to both the Qur'an and to one's present context alongside people of other faiths, working with them to establish a more humane society. Second, to advance the idea of qur'anic hermeneutics as a contribution to the development of theological pluralism within Islam. Third, to re-examine the way the Qur'an defines Self and Other (believer and non-believer) in order to make space for the righteous and just Other in a theology of pluralism for liberation. Fourth, to explore the relationship between religious exclusivism and one form of political conservatism (support for apartheid) on the one hand, and religious inclusivism and one form of progressive politics (support for the liberation struggle) on the other, and to supply a qur'anic rationale for the latter.

Methodology; What About Methodology?

Any discussion on hermeneutics is bound to draw upon a number of different disciplines. Furthermore, while many of the disciplines from which such a discourse for a South African context may be drawn (e.g., history, politics, qur'anic studies, linguistics) are well developed, the idea of bringing them together in an interdisciplinary fashion is rather novel.

This overlapping also accounts for the absence of a chapter specifically devoted to a survey and evaluation of literature on the subject. The second chapter does, however, deal at some length with previous writings on hermeneutics by some Muslims, as well as the limitations of traditional qur'anic scholarship with regard to the emergence of qur'anic hermeneutics as a discipline. For other overlapping themes, such as Muslims in South Africa, Muslim–Other relations or liberation theology in Islam, I supply an overview of the relevant literature in notes, as they are discussed.

While the chapters of this work are clearly focused on particular aspects of this study and follow a logical path, the work is, nevertheless, characterized by a continuous criss-crossing of temporal, geographical and disciplinary boundaries. There is a constant reference to the text, the context wherein it was revealed and the way it was received by the earliest Muslims in the South African context. This criss-crossing of boundaries also applies to my use of sources. The old, seemingly neat, divisions between 'traditionalism', 'modernity', 'western scholarship' and 'orientalism' are no longer tenable, if, indeed, they ever were. As I point out later in another context, Otherness is a condition of Selfhood. A sign on a church in Offenbach on the outskirts of Frankfurt is instructive for those who still believe that there is a solitary path to anything:

> The pizzas you eat come from Italy, your numerical system from the Arabs, your script from the Romans, your toys from Hong Kong, your electronic equipment from Japan, your clothes from Taiwan, your wealth from trade with the rest of the world. And then you still shout 'Foreigners out!'?

The Self cannot walk away from any meaningful encounter with the Other without carrying some of that Otherness along, and leaving some of the Self behind. I have thus made equal use of Muslim and Other, confessional and critical, traditional and contemporary sources. (And I do not assume that a source is either one or the other, for indeed, it is possible to be simultaneously critical and confessional.) The constraints of language ability, though, have compelled me to confine myself to English and to pre-modern Arabic theological sources.[9]

Despite my views on the uncertainty and flexibility of categories, it is, nonetheless, true that some approaches to life and to various ideological responses are sufficiently coherent to warrant demarcation and definition. While I question the present basis for exclusion and inclusion in Islamic theological categories of Self and Other, I do not deny the usefulness of definitions. Besides the categories of *muslim, mu'min* and *kafir*, which I examine in detail in chapter 5, other terms describing ideological or theological persuasions are defined when they are first used, and in the glossary. In the later interpretative chapters, where I apply the ideas developed in the earlier ones, I confine myself mainly to the Qur'an for text-proof. It is the only scripture of Islam that all Muslims believe to be absolutely authentic. Where I do cite a *hadith* in support of a particular opinion, it is not because I believe that it is authentically the word of Muhammad, although that may indeed be the case; I cite a *hadith* because it reflects the presence of, and support for, the idea among earlier Muslims.

Summary of Chapters

Chapter 1 introduces the community from which the qur'anic re-interpretative ideas and redefinition of Self and Other emerged. This historical overview of the Muslim community in the Western Cape up to 1989 seeks to introduce a central notion of this study, that is, however else the discourse on Islam is viewed, it is also an ideology informed by socio-historical circumstances. The various shifts in the community's relationship with the ruling class and the oppressed are examined and we see how these shifts are shaped by socio-political developments rather than belief in an unchanging qur'anic worldview. In this chapter the emphasis is primarily on the post–1970 period, when it appeared as if those opposed to apartheid gradually secured overwhelming community support. This atmosphere saw the rise of both interfaith solidarity against apartheid and resistance to such solidarity. The emergence of crucial qur'anic hermeneutical questions is located within this context.

The second chapter focuses on the relationship between revelation and context. I argue that the process of revelation itself was never independent of the community's context but consisted of a dynamic interaction between the two. The principle of *tadrij*, (literally, 'gradualism' and meaning 'progressive revelation') as reflected in the disciplines of *naskh* (abrogation) and of *asbab al-nuzul* (occasions of revelation), are examined as proof of this assertion. After discussing the definition of hermeneutics, I look at its relationship with traditional *'ulum al-Qur'an* (qur'anic studies) and reflect on the possibilities of the emergence of qur'anic hermeneutics. The relevant writings of Mohammed Arkoun and Fazlur Rahman, among the rare exceptions who deal with qur'anic hermeneutics, are examined. This chapter concludes with an argument for the inevitability of bias and the need to define, clarify and motivate the biases of the interpreter.

Chapter 3 deals with the South African struggle for the right of non-clerics to approach the Qur'an and with 'hermeneutical notions emerging out of the volatile crucible of the interaction between Islam and the liberative praxis' (Le Roux 1989, p. 48). The following hermeneutical keys are defined, contextualized and advocated as indispensable tools for understanding the Qur'an in a society characterized by oppression and a struggle for freedom: *taqwa* (integrity in relation to God), *tawhid* (divine holism and unity), *al-nas* (the people), *al-mustad'afun fi'l-ard* (the oppressed and marginalized on the earth), *'adl wa qist* (balance and justice) and *jihad wa 'amal* (struggle and praxis).

In chapter 4, I examine the three key qur'anic ethical terms whereby Self and Other are defined. The terms *islam*, *iman* and *kufr* are critically examined in the light of the keys defined and motivated in the previous chapter, their etymological meanings and use in the Qur'an. Their use in contemporary Muslim discourse is examined within the context of the contending ideologies and theologies of fundamentalism and liberation and a case is made for their re-appropriation for a progressive Islam.

Using the same hermeneutical keys and the methodological principles elaborated upon and motivated earlier, in chapter 5 I broaden the scope of my enquiry to look at the Qur'an's attitude towards the Other. This is preceded by some introductory comments regarding the terms the Qur'an employs for the various groups, with particular attention to the categories of *ahl al-kitab* and *mushrikun*, and the significance of dealing with these texts within the context of their immediate and overall background. This is followed by a detailed discussion of what I view as the fundamental principles determining the qur'anic attitude towards the Other. These are the linkage between praxis and doctrine, a rejection of religious arrogance and an acknowledgement of the diversity of religions as emanating from God, who is above all forms of service to Him. The chapter concludes with some reflections on the prophetic responsibility in the face of this religious diversity.

Chapter 6 looks at the theme of a theology of religious pluralism and that of liberation. The interreligious co-operation which forms the basis of the previous chapters assumed conscious and dynamic dimensions within the framework of a liberative praxis. The inverse of this is also true: opposition to it came from those who advocated political quietism which, in a situation of manifest injustice, is tantamount to collaboration. This theme is reflected upon as the various sub-themes are drawn together with the overall theme of the study. The influence of cross-cultural interfaith solidarity within liberative praxis on Islamic theology is discussed.

In the final chapter I look at the dramatic political changes occurring in the country from 1990 until the adoption of the country's new constitution in 1996. With this background, I examine how far the Muslim discourse on liberation and pluralism has travelled since the days of the 'struggle' against apartheid. Muslim responses to a very limited sense of morality, and the new terrain of struggle such as Muslim Personal Law and gender equality, are discussed in the light of the success or failure of key anti-apartheid entities to make credible connections between all forms of injustice. The challenges of a liberatory and progressive qur'anic discourse confined to conference halls and a particular mosque rather than among the poor are also discussed.

The book concludes with a summary of the inevitable contextualization of all attempts at understanding; the purpose of understanding scripture in an unjust society; the means of understanding in such a society and the accompanying liberation of the text and of theology through this process. Some final remarks deal with the fact that this liberation takes one into other, unexplored, theological areas. These are raised, but left open for exploration by others at another occasion.

Notes

1. It should be noted that ethnic descriptions in South Africa often bear little or no resemblance to reality. The term 'Arab', for example, was used to describe some Indians in Natal during the late nineteenth century, European Jews were described as 'Peruvians' between 1888 and 1914 and in the 1850s even white converts to Islam were referred to as 'Malays' (Chidester 1991, p. 14). In the case of the description 'African', absurd as it may sound, the Khoikhoin, the earliest known inhabitants of South Africa, would be excluded. 'Blacks' is an ethnic description employed for those usually referred to as 'Africans'. The word 'black' may also be a political description referring to all non-Caucasians in this area. 'Coloureds' refers to those of 'mixed parentage' – and aren't all of humankind? – while 'Whites' refers to people of Caucasian origin.

2. According to the 1991 population census, 70.4% of South Africans indicated a religious affiliation: 66.5% regarded themselves as Christians, 1.3% as Hindus, 1.1% as Muslims and 1.2% indicated that they had no religion, while 29.6% did not answer the question or objected to doing so. Christianity is the dominant religion among all 'racial' groups except the Indians.

3. I do not believe in a masculine Deity and endeavour to use gender-inclusive language wherever possible. In some cases though, particularly when dealing with a text such as the Qur'an, one is constrained to employ the masculine form.

4. Recently revealed information indicates that these groups were the recipients of substantial state funds from the apartheid regime in order to counter the influence of liberation theology.

5. In theory, Sunni Islam does not have an *ecclesia* and has therefore no clerics. In practice though, the *'ulama'* (literally, 'scholars'), to all intents and purposes, fulfil a similar function and are often organized as a formal and institutionalized body. A secondary reason why I prefer the term 'clerics' to *'ulama'* in the South African context is that the group which exercises religious leadership in South Africa comprises individuals with both scholarly and non-scholarly backgrounds. It is, for example, not uncommon for the *mu'adhdhin* (caller to prayer) to succeed the *imam* upon the latter's demise.

6. I am unaware of any of the progressive Islamists, including myself, having read any work on liberation theology during the 1980s. A vague awareness of it and its significance in Latin America and some parts of Asia was, however, common in liberation struggle circles.

7. I use the word 'conservative' to refer to 'those who wish and think that it is possible to preserve society substantially as it is and who deprecate the significance of social change' (Cantwell-Smith 1963, p. 377).

8. Aware that all translation is also a form of interpretation, I prefer using the Arabic terms throughout until the act of interpretation is conscious and intentional. These categories are examined in some detail in chapter 4.

9. This is generally speaking. However, where the occasional work in German, Urdu, Afrikaans or Dutch is cited, unless otherwise stated, the work was studied in the original language and the translation is mine. The language constraint with regards to pre-modern Arabic was particularly an impediment in so far as one had to bypass the contemporary discussions by critical scholars in the Arab world on the Qur'an. The very important contemporary writings on linguistics, hermeneutics and qur'anic studies by the contemporary Egyptian scholar, Nasr Hamid Abu Zaid, with which a casual acquaintance was made, are thus omitted from this book.

1

THE CONTEXT

MUSLIMS *in the* CAPE

Your history is one of obedience to the law and those in authority over you.

(Abdullah Abdurahman, *Cape Times*, 13 April 1937)

The Known Beginnings

The San, who were hunters and gatherers, were the first people to populate Southern Africa and are believed to have inhabited sub-Saharan Africa for most of the past 10,000 years. They were followed by the Khoikhoin, who were stock farmers, about 2,000 years ago. During the first few centuries of the Christian era, the Nguni peoples, who worked iron, practised subsistence agriculture and kept cattle, populated this part of the continent. Today this group forms the largest part of the area's population and has until recently been categorized as 'African'. The first encounter of the Khoikhoin with Europeans occurred soon after the arrival of Jan van Riebeeck on 6 April 1652. Sent by the Council of Seventeen, a Dutch shipping cartel, van Riebeeck arrived with some seventy other people. In 1795, when the Cape was captured by the British, the country saw the first influx of British. These two ethnic groups, the Dutch and the British, came to constitute the white community towards the end of the eighteenth century.

Adding to the demographical mixture of the Cape, the Dutch brought slaves from India, Ceylon, Mauritius, Malaya, Madagascar, Mozambique, the East Indies and elsewhere up to 1818. Despite considerable intermarriage across ethnic lines, separate communities developed for a number of sociological and political reasons. Remnants of the San fused with the slaves, some colonists and others to form the coloured community. Small communities of the Khoikhoin have survived up to this day in the north-western Cape and Namibia. In 1860, the Natal Colony introduced Indian indentured labour on its sugar plantations, thereby adding a fourth element to the region's existing racial pattern of Blacks, Coloureds and Whites.

The Muslims Arrive in South Africa

The history and demography of Muslims in Southern Africa is well documented.[1] Here I shall focus on the changing patterns within the Muslim community with regards to the questions of resistance to and collaboration with the various minority ruling groups.[2] Interwoven with these changing patterns is the question of solidarity between Muslims and Others, whether with the marginalized and oppressed Other or against the oppressing Other.

According to available documented evidence, Islam entered South Africa from two directions and during different periods. The first stream arrived either in the company of, or shortly after the coming of, the first colonists at the Cape in 1652. They hailed from various parts of the East and comprised labourers, political exiles or prisoners and slaves.[3] Together with local converts to Islam, they were usually referred to as 'Malays', despite the fact that less than one per cent of them came from today's Malaysia.[4] In the Cape, this community gradually formed a subgroup of what is commonly referred to as 'the coloured community'. A second stream of Muslims arrived in 1860 as indentured labourers from India, along with some Hindus. Their descendants are today concentrated in the northern provinces of Gauteng, Northwest, Mpumalanga, Northern and KwaZulu-Natal. A third and numerically insignificant stream arrived between 1873 and 1880, when about 500 liberated slaves were brought to Durban. Known as Zanzibaris, this group settled in and around Durban.

The Muslims of the Cape

It is the first stream, however, that concerns us here. Firstly, while there have been notable Muslim personalities from the northern provinces involved in the struggle against apartheid, the Muslims of the Cape have organized against it as a community on the basis of Islam. Secondly, it is in the Cape that a qur'anic hermeneutic of liberation has been forged.

The Muslim community of the Cape is a small one which has

survived against tremendous odds.[5] An important contributing factor in their survival as a distinct religious and cultural community was a strong sense of being different from, even superior to, the religious Other. This sense of religio-cultural superiority, together with economic considerations, often led to many of them identifying with the other 'superior group', the ruling class. The struggle for acceptance from the ruling class and the imperatives of survival as a distinct religious community made them amenable to frequent military co-option by the ruling military–political structures. Historical fears of the potential for Muslims to rebel were, however, always present in the ruling class and, indeed, continued up to the dying days of the apartheid regime.[6] These fears, the ruling class's rejection of all Blacks as equal partners in government and, for some at least, the ever-present Islamic appeal to egalitarianism and brotherhood, ensured that Muslims were never fully absorbed into the socio-political structures of the ruling class of apartheid.

Arrival and Survival

The early Muslim community comprised political exiles, slaves (many of whom were converts to Islam), ordinary criminals banished to the Cape and some free citizens, known as Mardyckers.[7] In the early days of the community's presence here, the Muslim slaves regularly met in secret in the homes of their 'free' co-religionists to observe some of their communal religious rituals. A key figure upon whom much of the religious leadership of the first Muslims depended was Shaikh Yusuf (Abidin Tadia Tjoesoep, d. 1699). Yusuf, a son-in-law of Sultan Ageng, the King of Bantam (now a part of Indonesia), was among the detained leaders of the Bantamese liberation struggle against the Dutch. Yusuf was banished to the Cape in 1694 along with a party of forty-nine followers. His arrival heralded the transformation of a mere Muslim presence in the Cape into a fledgling community of Muslims. Living on the farm of Petrus van Kalden, a Dutch Reformed minister, at Zandvliet, Yusuf became the primary source of religious guidance for Muslims and newly converted slaves. His arrival was followed in 1697 by that of the Rajah of Tamburah, another leader exiled to the Cape from the Indonesian Archipelago. From 1743 onwards the ranks of these Muslims, now widely dispersed throughout the colony, were strengthened with the arrival of some outstanding Muslim exiles.

The ability of the Muslims to formulate collective responses of resistance to the difficult conditions of marginalization and slavery imposed upon them, was severely restricted by a number of factors. These included their isolation and dispersion over a wide geographical area within the Cape, the diversity of their social origins and the lack of a developed common cultural identity.

Their socio-political standing as religious and political leaders prior to coming to the Cape meant that the Muslim exiles were also highly respected by the authorities there. These Muslims were, nevertheless, treated with considerable suspicion and located at a distance from the heart of the colony (Boeseken 1964, p. 4; Jeffreys 1939, p. 195). Historical evidence indicates that the Muslim slaves, exiles and free citizens related to each other in a spirit of fraternity. This situation may have been due to the bonds created by participation in a shared religion, on the one hand, and to an overall socio-political position of marginalization, on the other.

Early Muslim interaction with the religious Other cannot seemingly fit into a single category, nor is there any indication that this interaction was informed by the Qur'an, despite the availability of qur'anic knowledge. They interacted with the colonists as their benign overseers rather than as *ahl al-kitab* (People of the Book), a qur'anic category describing somewhat sympathetically Other religious communities in possession of a scripture.

The fact of a community's interaction being shaped by concrete socio-political conditions rather than by a sacred scripture is also seen in the Muslims dealing with those who did not belong to the ruling class. They interacted with the rest of the slave community, as fellows in a common yoke of marginalization, who might be won over to Islam. Furthermore, there is nothing to suggest that their perception of either the Nguni or the remaining sedentary Khoikhoin, differed in any way from that of the ruling class. In fact, one segment of the Muslims, the Mardyckers, shared responsibility for resisting the Khoikhoin attempts to regain some of their historical presence in the Cape.

Collaboration, Consolidation and Litigation

From the late eighteenth century, Islam in the Cape became an 'observable historical phenomenon' (De Blij 1969, p. 246). Despite the perpetuation of a wide array of repressive religious policies that continued well into the nineteenth century, this period 'witnessed a shift in emphasis towards more overt, unified forms of organization' (Bradlow 1987, p. 19). It was the beginning of Muslim resurgence and the spread of religious knowledge, a period of consolidation for the Muslims as a permanent and dynamic community with overt religious practices. Towards the end of the eighteenth century, with the British capture of the Cape in

1775, a clear shift became evident in the nature of colonial relationships with the colonized communities. In 1804 an ordinance allowing religious freedom was published, thus enabling Muslims to practise their religion without concealment from the authorities. The subsequent growing number of Muslims necessitated more overt forms of organization. This development was also facilitated by the loosening of the state's authority and the abolition of slavery in 1834.

It was in the socio-religious area that the most significant developments took place for the consolidation of the Muslim community. Foremost among these was the arrival in 1780 of another political exile, Tuan Guru (Imam 'Abd Allah Qadi Abd al-Salam, d. 1807). Guru, who hailed from Tidore in the Mollucan Straits, was detained for his role in conspiring against the Dutch and was imprisoned on Robben Island. Released in 1793, he led, in defiance of the law, the first open air *salah al-jumu'ah* (Friday congregational prayers) after his application for permission to do so was refused. This scholar also functioned as the community's first *imam* (religious leader) and its *qadi* (judge).

Several socio-religious structures were founded in this period. By 1795, when the occupation of the Cape by the British seemed imminent, Muslim support for the defence of the colony was procured in return for the 'toleration of their religion and the right to build a mosque' (Davids 1989). The British, upon taking control of the Cape, did not revoke the recently acquired rights gained from the Dutch. On the contrary, they even extended these. It is in this context that the Awwal Masjid (First Mosque) was built in 1798 with Tuan Guru as its *imam*.

The new benign and pragmatic attitude towards the Muslim community was directly related to the need of the British ruling power to secure maximum moral and military support from the inhabitants of the Colony. In return for such support, Muslims, at various times, received from the authorities permanent facilities to utilize in the fulfilment of their religious rituals.[8]

This was also a period when the community experienced intense religious disputes, such as conflicting claims of religious authority and legal rights to the property deeds of mosques. These disputes increased dramatically in the wake of the mosque and *slamseskool* (religious school) boom (Davids 1980). The ensuing Muslim leadership struggles, as well as the acrimony, time and energy devoted to them, seriously impaired the community's ability to deal with the tensions between collaboration and resistance; absorption into the structures of the ruling class or solidarity with the aspirations of the indigenous people.

By the end of the 1860s Muslims owning property showed some political awareness and the 'Malay vote' became a factor during municipal and government elections. This was particularly the case in the elections of 1875, when Abdol Burns, a taxi driver and ally of Saul Solomon, a Jewish member of the Empire League, emerged as a key figure to promote parliamentary political awareness among the Muslims.

Between Collaboration and Resistance

In South Africa as a whole, the Second Anglo-Boer War ended in 1902, with the Boers defeated. A Zulu rebellion against poll taxes in Natal in 1906 led to the killing of 3,000 Zulus and 30 Whites. In 1910 the Union of South Africa was formed as a self-governing British territory with the new constitution protecting the franchise rights enjoyed by the Coloureds under the British. The South African Native National Congress (established in 1912), later renamed the African National Congress (ANC), became the first national African political movement to oppose the increasing forced racial segregation and oppression. This was exemplified by the Native Land Act of 1913, which limited Blacks, seventy per cent of the population, to seven per cent of the land. In 1939, South Africa entered World War II on the side of the Allies and numerous Blacks contributed to the war effort, while some Afrikaners advocated neutrality or support for the Nazis. In 1948, the National Party (NP) came to power, determined to institutionalize racial discrimination in all walks of life. Packing the Senate, the Upper House of Parliament, with its supporters, the NP succeeded in 1956 in acquiring legal sanction for amendments to the country's constitution, thus ensuring that the Coloureds lost their franchise rights.

The 1886–1969 period witnessed an eightfold increase in the Muslim population of the Cape, from 15,099 to 120,000 (Kritzinger 1980, p. 34). While in the early days, especially, the vast majority of Muslims were poor and working as domestic servants, tailors and skilled artisans, a very distinct middle class also began to emerge. Professionals in this class, comprising mostly teachers, a few doctors and lawyers, played a significant role in the political life of the Cape during this period. This era saw a growth of Muslim political assertion which spearheaded a wider political awakening among Blacks in the Cape.

'Street Urchins and Hobbledehoys'

Two developments reflect the changing face of the Muslim community in the early part of this period: their response to the state's health initiatives during the outbreak of the smallpox epidemic of 1882 and their attempts to acquire direct representation in Parliament in the 1889 elections. Several measures taken by the colonial health authorities during the smallpox epidemics of 1807, 1812, 1840, 1858 and 1882 were rejected by Muslims as repugnant to their faith. They also resented what they regarded as intrusions into their lives by the colonial authorities. None of the measures then promulgated, however, resulted in the community response witnessed in 1886.[9] From 1882 onwards Muslims made it clear that their objections to the proposed Public Health Act (adopted in 1893) and the impending closure of the Tana Baru cemetery were religious and that 'their religion [was] superior to the law' (*Cape Times*, 2 September 1882). Abdol Burns, who had led a sustained campaign against the introduction of this Act, now led the defiance against its enactment. Two days after the official closure of the Tana Baru on 15 January 1886, about 3,000 Muslims, in defiance of the law, buried a Muslim child there. Subsequently the crowd attacked fifteen policemen who had followed the funeral procession, injuring several of them. Later that day a crowd of Muslims and Christians broke into the Dutch Reformed Church (DRC) cemetery, which had also been closed. Watched by the police, the group of 'street urchins and hobbledehoys' buried the remains of a 'young white boy' (Bickford-Smith 1989, p. 17). This uprising continued for several days and led to the imprisonment of Burns.

There are three significant elements in this uprising: the interfaith dimensions; the Muslim insistence on viewing politics and religion as two distinct forces and the Muslim willingness to defy the law when it appeared to be in opposition to Islam.

The Dutch Reformed Church resented what it perceived to be English interference in Church property rights and was by that period already part of the Afrikaner vanguard against British imperialism. They, however, specifically excluded Muslims from their organized opposition to the various health laws promulgated at the time. The records of the Muslim Cemetery Board of this period also do not give any indication that they discussed the idea of joint protest. However, when the uprising actually occurred, scant regard was given by ordinary Muslims and Christians to religious barriers and the newspapers referred to 'crowds of Malays and coloured people' (*Cape Times*, 19 January 1886). What appears to have happened was that a spontaneous solidarity of action among the marginalized took place without (perhaps despite) the religious leadership of these two communities.[10] This should not really be surprising, given that the Muslims have lived alongside the Christian Other throughout their presence in the Cape. 'Now we come to the great problem,' said a Christian missionary about this shared existence. 'Christians and Moslems live next door to each other and often rent rooms in the same house. They grow up from childhood together' (Hampson 1934, p. 273). Burns reflected the general local Muslim differentiation between religion and politics. It was state intervention in the ritual aspects of their religious lives that provoked their ire. Muslims in the nineteenth century were clearly prepared to fight for their faith, a faith interpreted in a narrow manner and one which accepted a dichotomy between God and Caesar. Despite the importance Muslims attached to the constitutional process and to being law-abiding citizens, when it appeared as if the law was undermining their faith, they were willing to defy it. Several reasons explain this new collective Muslim response to protect supposedly purely religious practices from encroaching political authority: their demographic increase, the growth in their socio-economic and concomitant political status and the concurrent decrease in state authority during this period.

Beyond Proxies to 'One of Our Own'

By the latter part of the nineteenth century, the Muslim elite, like other black elites, firmly believed in the legitimacy of the constitutional process and in justice through participation in it. The period from 1882 up to the Cemetery Uprising thus saw protracted legal struggles, which consisted of public meetings, petitions and meetings with the governor, parliamentary officials and local authorities. This process resumed soon after the Uprising with a major difference: Muslims now wanted to be represented by 'one of themselves' (*Cape Lantern*, 9 November 1889). Achmat Effendi's announcement in 1889 of his parliamentary candidature marked the beginning of Muslim and (Christian) coloured participation in parliamentary politics.[11] The Cape Parliament enacted measures specifically directed against the possibility of his election, thus putting paid to his attempt.[12] Despite Effendi's failure to win, 'the very fact that he stood', says Lewis, 'revealed a new political self-confidence amongst some blacks in the Cape' (1987, p. 11).

In August 1892, a large meeting mainly attended by Muslims under the leadership of Ozair Aly, denounced the Franchise and Ballot Act of 1892. The Act raised the franchise qualifications in order to exclude the large number of Blacks in the recently annexed Transkeian Territories. In the same year, the Coloured People's Association (CPA) was founded out of this opposition. Headed by Aly, this was the first national coloured political organization. The CPA's supporters were predominantly

Muslim, although it sought broad coloured support (Bickford-Smith 1989, p. 23). Both the Cemetery Uprising and the formation of the CPA reflect the fusion between Muslim and coloured political identities that, under Muslim leadership, was beginning by the turn of the twentieth century. For most Muslims this socio-political relationship precluded the need for them to organize separately.[13]

The Son of Slaves Mobilizes the Middle Classes

In 1902, the African Political (later People's) Organization (APO) was formed with the objective of defending and promoting coloured rights in South Africa. In 1905 Dr Abdullah Abdurahman became its president, a position he held until his death in 1940.[14] According to Lewis, the founding of the APO 'marked the start of successful black mobilization on a national scale in the country' (1987, p. 250). Preceding the ANC by a decade, it rapidly gathered more than 20,000 members distributed in over a hundred branches across the country.

Most of the energies of the APO were directed towards the goal of coloured and Muslim elite integration with white society. The moral–ideological path of solidarity with the rest of the black community and a broader black identity was, however, a permanent backdrop to the APO resolutions and its programme (Lewis 1987, p. 25). Under the unchallenged leadership of Abdurahman, the APO articulated coloured elite concerns and aspirations and overcame Muslim–Christian differences among this class. For the poorer classes, the sheer battle for survival amidst the ever-increasing hardships resulting from a deluge of discriminatory legislation called for co-operation across religious lines.

A Quickie with White Supremacy

The only organized example of Muslim collaboration with white supremacy is that of the Cape Malay Association (CMA, established in 1923). Already in 1923 its founder, Arshad Gamiet, supported General Albert Hertzog of the National Party and contested Abdurahman's seat in the municipal elections. Later that year, Gamiet and some associates, 'disillusioned with the APO which was not catering for the needs of the Muslim community' (Davids 1981, p. 199), formed the CMA. With their promises of concrete efforts to alleviate the social problems of the Muslim community and with the support of some of the local clerics, the CMA soon became quite popular with the Muslims.[15]

Davids attributes the CMA's collaborative role to the machinations of Hertzog and suggests that their initial objectives were purely socio-religious. 'Politics', Davids writes, 'was the last concern of the CMA' (1981, p. 208). Davids' assessment reflects an inadequate appreciation of the nature of politics. Any organization born in disillusionment with the APO had to be political. Within a context of conflicting ideologies, the decision to withdraw from a particular organization, knowing that such withdrawal would support an opposing ideology, is clearly a political option. More significantly, Davids ignores the fact that the basic ingredients of political ideology are pervasive in society and operate in a range of manifestations from the blatant to the more subtle. Although often unintended at a conscious level, the divestment of socio-religious concerns from their political ingredients usually has the effect of supporting an iniquitous status quo. In this regard the Muslim community of South Africa is no exception.

By 1925 the CMA had sixteen branches throughout the country. 'However', says Lewis, 'it was never as closely linked to the Nationalist Party as its Christian counterpart, the Afrikaner National Bond, was' (1987, p. 131). By 1926, it expressed its opposition to any legislation based on the principle of race, creed or class and by the time of its demise in 1945 it was back in the non-collaborationist camp.

From Appeals for Reform to Calls for Revolution

The APO's battles were all couched in moderate terms; they protested against iniquities within the system rather than challenging the system itself. With every successive government adding to the arsenal of discriminatory laws and every election producing an even more racist regime than its predecessor, challenge to the APO's commitment to protest-appeal politics was inevitable. By the late 1930s, dissatisfaction with the APO policies and a new wave of discriminatory legislation led to the formation of alternative organizations. These groups were committed to 'mobilizing the Coloureds to support the strategies of working class unity and direct action such as strikes, boycotts and demonstrations' (Lewis 1987, p. 181). The young coloured radicals were organized in two groups, both led by Muslims. Zainunnisa Gool, Abdurahman's daughter, led a pragmatic faction that blended class-struggle rhetoric with reformist–welfare activities. The 'more theoretically inclined and ideologically stringent faction' (ibid.) was led by Dr Goolam Gool, her brother-in-law, and his wife, Hawa Ahmad. Both these factions combined in 1935 to form the National Liberation League (NLL) with Dr Waradia Abdurahman, another of Abdurahman's daughters, being instrumental in setting up its Women's Bureau.[16]

The formation of the NLL, which partly contributed to the growing militancy within the ANC itself, heralded a new phase in black politics in South Africa; a phase which rejected white guardianship over Blacks. This period saw great stress on non-racial working-class unity and the use of mass direct action to oppose racial discrimination. The most lasting legacy of this group and of its more abiding successor, the Non-European Unity Movement (NEUM, established in 1943) was the formulation of the policy of non-collaboration. Until the unbanning of the ANC in 1990, this policy was to shape black politics and even the contours of a nascent Islamic theology of liberation in the 1980s.

In 1943, the government announced proposals for a Coloured Advisory Council. The NLL and all its allies rejected the proposals, denouncing them as a substitute for extended coloured franchise rights and the beginnings of a Coloured Affairs Department (CAD). Supporters of these proposals were denounced as 'Judases', 'yes men' and 'quislings' to be boycotted by the community, as an anti-CAD bulletin explained. 'Don't have any social or personal intercourse with them. Don't greet them. Don't have any conversations with them. Don't visit them, and don't invite them to your home. Don't meet them even if it's necessary to cross over to the other side of the street. Don't see them, even if you come face to face with them' (*Cape Standard,* 4 May 1943). This doctrine of militant and uncompromising mass protest action and non-collaboration, subsequently adopted by the ANC in 1948, was to shape the face of black resistance and would eventually be responsible for the political successes experienced in later years.

My interest here, which I will develop later in this chapter, is with the implications of this doctrine for Muslims and their sense of community in the Cape. The idea of a religious community connected by ties of faith was now being subtly challenged by the doctrine of non-collaboration. 'Community' began to imply participants in a common struggle for justice and the Other were those who collaborated in apartheid structures. As the struggle against apartheid progressed, the question 'Who is my brother or my sister?' acquired a decisive dimension.

Yes, But We're Muslims!

Several factors combined to result in the emergence of a politically aware tendency among young Muslims who, while they were determined to struggle alongside the rest of the oppressed, also wanted to do so from an Islamic perspective. Although the Abdurahmans and the Gools were prominent Muslim personalities, Islam as an ideology did not play a visible role in their political activity, nor did they appeal to the Muslim community to work for a just society from an avowedly Islamic perspective. With the clearer Marxist doctrinal accentuation of the National Liberation League and later the NEUM, the young Muslim intellectuals, on the whole, did not feel comfortable in these circles.[17] The NEUM did not have the appeal to Muslims of the APO, whose influence was now on the wane. Furthermore, for the working-class Muslims, the overwhelmingly middle-class base of the NEUM and its 'inability to cast oratory in popular symbolism' (Jeppie 1987, p. 84) made it largely irrelevant.

The emergence of a Muslim identity contributed to the search for an Islamic response to apartheid. This development accompanied the growth of a middle class and transcended the old Malay–Indian division. Fuelling the growth of this Muslim identity was the increase in missionary attacks on Islam and a number of specifically anti-Muslim measures by Christians.[18] The savagery of forced removals experienced by the black community from 1958 onwards resulted in Muslims being uprooted from their ancestral homes and disconnected from their mosques, the centres of Muslim community life. These hardships gave an impetus to the articulation of an organized and progressive Islam seen in the formation of the District Six-based Cape Muslim Youth Movement (CMYM, established in 1957) and the Claremont Muslim Youth Association (CMYA, established in 1958). Prominent in these attempts was a cleric, Imam Abdullah Haron (d. 1969) who later became one of the liberation struggle's most significant martyrs.

Like all their progressive predecessors, both of these organizations recognized and valued the unity of the oppressed. In September 1961, in response to a DRC attack on Islam, they issued a statement saying: 'We see in this attack on Islam a deliberate attempt to drive a wedge between us and other non-Islamic groups with whom we have hitherto lived in peace, harmony and friendship' (*Muslim News*, 29 September 1961). The unity of the oppressed was also a reason offered in the rejection of the 1961 invitation from the then Malaysian prime minister for the 'Malays' to 'return' to Malaysia. 'Their [the Cape Muslims'] life and future', replied one of the CYMA leaders, 'are inextricably tied up with the rest of the non-whites because they have suffered the same humiliation and oppression' (Fakhry 1961, p. 7).

Meanwhile, South African society was becoming more repressive and the government increasingly intransigent. On 21 March 1960 in Sharpeville, police killed sixty-nine unarmed Blacks and wounded another one hundred and eighty-six during demonstrations against the pass laws organized by the Pan-Africanist Congress (PAC). This was followed by the banning of the ANC and the PAC as well as the detention of thousands of activists.

In response to the repression and, perhaps mainly, to the hardships of the Group Areas Act, the CMYM and the CMYA organized a series of huge public meetings. At the first of these on 7 May 1961, the Call of Islam was launched and thousands of copies of a declaration against the injustices of apartheid were distributed.[19] The Call of Islam, a movement rather than an organization, however, did not survive for longer than a year. However, both the CMYA and the CMYM continued to play an important role in the development of a socially and politically relevant Islam. Their members later spearheaded the formation of the Cape Islamic Federation (CIF, established in 1962). When challenged by the CIF to adopt a firm stand against apartheid, the clerics, organized in the Muslim Judicial Council (MJC), denounced their challenge as 'youthful impetuosity' (*Muslim News*, 31 July 1964). The collaborationist position of the clerics is reflected in a *Muslim News* editorial:

> Has the government forbidden the worship of Allah? Has the government closed down or ordered the demolition of any mosque in a declared white area? If our government has ordered our Muslims to desert the faith of our forefathers, then our *ulema* would have been the first to urge us to resist, even to death. (ibid.)

A number of factors led to bitterness and demoralization on the part of the members of these progressive formations and resulted in their gradual demise by the mid-1960s. They might have succeeded in having a more lasting impact on the emergence of a progressive Islam if the objective socio-political conditions had been more favourable. The early 1960s, though, was a period when South Africa experienced its most ferocious period of repression and persecution. The Sabotage Act, introduced in 1962, provided for prolonged detention without trial while the '90-day' Act of 1963 virtually abrogated *habeas corpus*. With the capture of Nelson Mandela, Walter Sisulu and other ANC leaders on 11 July 1963, and their subsequent sentence to life imprisonment, the liberation movement was dealt a crippling blow. 'By the mid 1960s', noted Lodge and Nasson, 'the government had not only uprooted most of the underground but had also demoralized and routed the entire radical opposition' (1991, p. 6).

The Killing of the *Imam*

For the Muslim community the most direct and far reaching manifestation of this political repression was the murder of Imam Abdullah Haron by the security police in 1969, after four months in detention. The general demoralization of progressive forces throughout the country is also reflected in Muslim responses to Haron's martyrdom. Thirty thousand people attended his funeral. All the speakers at the funeral and *Muslim News*, the paper he had edited, eulogized his fine character. About the manner of his death, the cause that he died for or the crime of detention without trial, there was only silence; a silence which was to endure for another six years.

The silence of the clergy around the martyrdom of Haron led to a deep sense of betrayal and disillusionment on the part of young Muslims. It was left to an Anglican minister to stir the consciences of Muslims and all South Africans. Deeply concerned about the circumstances around Haron's death, Bernard Wrankmore 'wrestled with himself and with God' (De La Hunt 1984, p. 6). Seeking refuge in a Muslim shrine on top of Signal Hill overlooking Cape Town, Wrankmore undertook a forty-day fast, demanding a judicial inquiry into Haron's death. With the government unimpressed after forty days, he vowed to fast unto death unless it relented. On the sixty-seventh day, after the pleadings of numerous South Africans, and 'acting on his inner guidance' (ibid., p. 10), Wrankmore broke his fast. The regime remained unmoved and many a young Muslim was deeply touched by the witness for justice of a profoundly committed Christian.

Farewell to Collaboration

The period starting from 1970 may justifiably be described as the era which led to the demise of apartheid. The early 1970s saw the birth of a new generation of activists committed to the doctrine of Black Consciousness (BC). The BC movement, rejecting any role for Whites in the liberation struggle, gradually began to fill some of the void caused by the banning of the ANC and the PAC in 1962 and the virtual collapse of the NEUM. A wave of strikes in Durban in 1973 produced a new generation of trade union activists which led to the liberalization of the laws restricting black trade unions.

In an interesting example of theology following socio-political developments, this period witnessed a number of black theologians advocating Black Theology, a form of liberation theology.[20] Black Theology, according to its advocates, is intended to be both 'a theoretical weapon of struggle in the hands of the exploited black masses' (Mosala 1986, p. 175) and a theology of 'praxis which emerges in the heat of the historical struggles of Black Christian workers and peasants' (Mofokeng 1990, p. 38).

Despite the March 1973 crackdown on the BC movement, the banning of eight of its leaders and the killing in 1977 of Steve Biko, its most articulate advocate, the movement played a crucial role in advancing the struggle for self-respect and dignity among the oppressed. Its mobilization against the imposition of the Afrikaans language as the means of education in black schools and what was widely regarded as 'gutter education', culminated in the country-wide uprisings in June 1976. These uprisings permanently changed the course of South Africa's political future and, with it, the direction of the country's nascent Islamist movements.

Just as South African Christians committed to justice derived inspiration and guidance from liberation theology emerging in Latin America and elsewhere, Muslims were inspired by a theology of revolt against neo-colonialism and dictatorship.[21] At an international level, the 1970s saw the emergence of Islam as a global political force, its most visible manifestation being the Iranian revolution. Among young South African Muslims the works of the Iranian revolutionary, 'Ali Shari'ati (d. 1977) were widely read and discussed in *halaqat* (study circles), as were those of ideologues connected to the Islamist movements, such as Sayyid Qutb (d. 1966), the Egyptian scholar martyred by Nasser's regime, and the Pakistani founder of the Jama'at-I-Islami, Abul-A'la Mawdudi (d. 1979). In these *halaqat* young Muslims began to view Islam as an ideological option for a future South Africa.

The Islamic fundamentalism engendered by both the Iranian revolution in particular, and the Islamist movement in general, also implied a religious exclusivism which denied any virtue in those outside Islam. Coming at a time of heightening political awareness and activity, it was inevitable that tensions would arise between Muslim fundamentalists and other Muslims who were prepared to work with the religious Other. The impact of local political realities and international Islamist ideological trends led to the emergence of diverse tendencies within the local house of Islam. In the midst of this diversity though, it was clear that most Muslims were increasingly identifying with the broader liberation movements in the country. It was a time of deep searching for a South African expression of Islam.

During the 1970s, the movement for a socially relevant Islam was epitomized by both the Muslim Youth Movement (MYM, established in 1970 and unrelated to the earlier one based in District Six) and the Muslim Students Association (MSA, established in 1974). These organizations expressed their opposition to apartheid from time to time.[22] The local fortnightly, *Muslim News*, underwent a complete metamorphosis in 1975; it started to project a radical and dynamic Islam while vigorously promoting BC, often using qur'anic texts in its editorials for this purpose. The MYM, MSA and *Muslim News* were to play a significant role in spawning or supporting both Qibla (established in 1981) and the Call of Islam (established in 1984 and unrelated to the campaign launched in 1961). While the MYM and MSA also consistently articulated their opposition to apartheid, the sheer scale of the work of the Call of Islam and the militant rhetoric which accompanied Qibla's involvement ensured that these two organizations became synonymous with Muslim opposition to apartheid in the 1980s.

New Deal? No Deal!

Opposition to tricameralism needs to be located within the framework of the overall organization against apartheid during this period.[23] Lodge and Nasson (1991, pp. 35–40) cite several factors that ensured that the 1976 uprisings were to be merely the catalysts of the events that were to propel South Africa into an era of non-racialism and democracy within a period of less than twenty years: 1) the extraordinary political ascendancy of young black South Africans who lacked any 'direct memories of the polit- ical defeats or the social helplessness of black communities in an earlier era' (ibid., p. 38); 2) the economic recession of the late 1970s and early 1980s, which brought about a huge upswing in strike activity; 3) the aggressive police interventions in the strikes mentioned above, which 'added a bitter political dimension to industrial conflict and tended to politicize the workers' (ibid.); 4) union-inspired consumer boycotts which stimulated township politics; 5) the growth of trade unionism, which 'introduced a greater degree of leadership accountability, democratic participation and organizational structure' (ibid.) and 6) the proliferation of civic organizations which often began as small *ad hoc* groups to tackle high rents, the lack of electricity and high public transport fares.

Despite the fact that the above constituencies (i.e., youth, local com- munities and unions) have often been treated separately for organizing purposes and notwithstanding the tensions that often characterized the relationship between them, they were thoroughly interconnected. For example, the unionists were often the initiators of community civic organizations and youth activists enforced union-initiated consumer boycotts. This was also the nature of the interaction between these con- stituencies and various religious communities. Many of these activists were deeply religious people who influenced and were influenced by their own religious structures and organizations.

This period thus also saw a number of developments on the religious front which had a significant impact on the liberation struggle. Among these were the founding of Jews for Justice; the increasing involvement of the South African Council of Churches (SACC) in programmes to pro-mote political awareness and assist the victims of repression; the increas-ingly militant tenor of religious organizations' statements and their sup-port for economic sanctions; the rise to prominence of religious leaders such as the Reverend Allan Boesak, the Reverend Frank Chikane, Imam Hassan Solomon, Manibhen Sita and Sister Bernadette Ncube, who were deeply committed to the cause of political liberation and to the non-racial United Democratic Front (UDF, established in 1983). The establish-ment of the Institute of Contextual Theology, (ICT) also marked a new development in South African liberation theology. Contextual Theology, with its non-racial orientation, rather than Black Theology, the religious appendix of BC, became the dominant theme among most politically engaged Christian theologians. All of these factors ensured that the 1980s were to be the decade of freedom from white domination. Some observers have correctly remarked that, while 'the long struggle for black political rights in SA has been marked by several critical turning points . . . none was as crucial, or as dramatic as the events of the 1980s . . . It was the decade when the pillars of apartheid finally gave way under social, eco-nomic and political pressures from the black majority' (Lodge and Nasson 1991, p. 3).

While the political, demographic and economic strength of Blacks had been growing in the 1970s, it was only in the 1980s that 'a new determination and new tactics took hold' (ibid.). The year 1983 brought in the 'New Deal', a government 'reform' scheme to co-opt Coloureds and Indians as junior partners in apartheid while the Blacks were expected to exercise 'independence' in the most arid and barren thirteen per cent of the country. The majority of South Africans viewed this as an attempt to destroy any potential for political unity among the oppressed without conceding any real power to the state's newly co-opted partners.

The New Deal brought about the large-scale mobilization of people against apartheid, the like of which the country had never witnessed before. This was also the period when the ANC re-emerged as an impor-tant element in the internal struggle against apartheid. A host of commu-nity, student and religious organizations committed to the Freedom Charter, the ANC policy document, emerged and seized on various local issues to heighten opposition to apartheid. These organizations operated under the banner of the UDF.

One such Muslim organization was the Call of Islam, an offshoot from the MYM–MSA. Founded in June 1984 by a small group of dissi-dents who refused to sever their links with the UDF,[24] the Call soon became the most vociferous and organized Muslim group resisting apartheid. Mass rallies, public meetings, the Friday sermon, door-to-door campaigns, funerals for victims of police brutality, boycotts, street uprisings and a regular flood of religio-political pamphlets characterized their contribution. Several prominent religious leaders who belonged to the Call campaigned around the country against the New Deal and exhorted the Muslims to make common cause with the oppressed. Virtually all of their programmes were organized in concert with, or with the support of, their allies in the UDF.

Apartheid Divides! UDF Unites!

The introduction of tricameralism in 1984 and the ensuing nationwide revolt seemed to be the cue for Muslims to make their final break with apartheid and to identify with the oppressed. The UDF, with its appeal for all people to unite against the tricameral system, attracted Muslim leaders such as Imam Hassan Solomon, Shaikh Abdul Gamiet Gabier and Ebrahim Rasool and myself. The UDF created the conditions required for various sectors of the society to enter the struggle while retaining their own identities because it acted as a political front.[25] Rasool explained the relationship between political organization and religious awareness in the following manner: 'The UDF taught us that it takes a lot of grassroots organization to create the conditions whereby Muslims will take their rightful place in the struggle. It does not simply take an appeal from the Qur'an to create revolutionaries among Muslims. That [involvement] is the product of social conditions, theological reflection and organization' (1988b, p. 34). His statement is significant, for it encapsulates the basis of the emerging South African Islamic theology and qur'anic hermeneutic of liberation. The Qur'an, in order to be socially meaningful, is in need of moments within history. One such moment was now being forged within a context of oppression and struggle for liberation, a struggle shared by others outside the house of Islam.

Far from being a unified response of solidarity with the oppressed Other, this struggle also evoked considerable controversy within the Muslim community and 'unleashed a feverish flow of pamphlets and statements which flooded the mosques and homes of the Muslim community' (Tayob 1990, p. 31). None of the arguments articulated in public attempted to justify apartheid, though. The conservatives, instead, focused on a number of other issues in order to express their seemingly religious concerns. These included the intermingling of sexes during anti-apartheid rallies, the need to strengthen one's faith as a precondition for political change, the problem of the communist presence in the ranks of the anti-apartheid movement and the need to obey the lawful authority in order to avert *fitnah* (disorder). Above all, there was the argument of religious exclusivism. 'How can we stand together with the Christians, Hindus and Jews?'

The South African socio-political culture, with the all-pervasive ideology of apartheid had polarized its people to an unprecedented extent. The struggle against apartheid had a similar effect, albeit along entirely different lines. The social ostracism to punish collaborators, first espoused during the anti-CAD campaign in the 1940s was now being revived: 'collaborators' versus 'comrades'. People on both sides of the divide had 'Muslim', 'Hindu', 'Christian' or 'Jewish' names. The formidable presence of religious figures and organizations and, especially, the unprecedented Muslim–Christian religious solidarity that now formed an integral part of this struggle, ensured that questions of identity, affiliation and community assumed a stark and new dimension.

The formation of the UDF in 1983 and the subsequent visible participation of Muslims side by side with the religious Other, led to considerable debate and acrimony amongst some of the organized and activist Muslims who opposed this affinity with the religious Other. Fundamental theological issues, such as the nature of faith and the meaning of the fellowship of the *ummah* (community), arose and were regularly alluded to but were seldom examined in a systematic manner.

At both a theological and political level, the issues of faith and identity were vividly illustrated in August 1984 when nineteen religious leaders were arrested while defying a ban on entry into the black township of Gugulethu. What happened after we were taken to the cells at the Wynberg Magistrate's Court marks that day as particularly significant for the South African interreligious experience. Guarded by twelve uniformed policemen, nineteen of us, united in our quest for a just society, but belonging to different religious groups, discovered our common commitment to, and need of, God. Allan Boesak began by reading scripture, the Reverend Lionell Louw led the group in singing, Hassan Solomon prayed and I preached. We then rose and sang the anthem of the liberation movement, *Nkosi Sikelel' iAfrika* (God Bless Africa).

> We discovered each other: diverse in faiths but comrades in the struggle. Nineteen small people waiting in a cold cell on a magistrate . . . Here we experienced dialogue between religions on the highest plane. In eight hours, years of suspicion and mistrust were shattered. (Esack 1986, p. 54)

Within the Muslim community the march and subsequent arrests brought into focus the debate about the theological correctness of joint action with the religious Other against apartheid. Expressions of the commitment to work alongside the religious Other were seen in Muslim leaders addressing UDF rallies, joint mobilization against state structures, 'street action' and formal decisions by the Call to affiliate to the UDF. At a more overtly religious level, the presence of leading Christian leaders such as Boesak at Call meetings and of Muslim clerics in churches, as well as at the large number of interfaith services, accentuated the interreligious witness against oppression. The formation of the South African chapter of an international interfaith organization, the World Conference on Religion and Peace (WCRP) in 1984 served to provide a forum to deepen this solidarity and to explore the theological diversity that came along with it. Together with the Call, WCRP came to symbolize this commitment to interfaith involvement in the struggle against apartheid.

Side by Side on the Long Walk

The Call played the most significant role in persuading Muslims to accept the political necessity of, and theological legitimacy for, interfaith solidarity. It also broke new ground in South Africa with its unambiguous embracing of Christians and Jews as 'brothers and sisters' and 'believers'. The Call's first information brochure states that 'Non-Muslims have shed their blood to oppose the brutality of apartheid and to work for a just South Africa. We are then committed to work side by side with others for the destruction of apartheid society' (Call of Islam 1984, p. 4). This commitment to work with the Other went beyond a functional or utilitarian relationship, to the acceptance of the theological legitimacy of other faiths. Thus Solomon, then chair of the Call, said:

> All the messengers of Allah formed a single brotherhood. Their message is essentially one and their religion and teachings are one . . .
> Let us enter the future as brothers and sisters in the struggle. May Allah . . . strengthen all the believers in Him [emphasis mine] . . . until freedom and justice is concrete for all the oppressed in our country. (Solomon 1985, p. 5)

The South African chapter of the then Geneva-based WCRP was initiated by Bishop Desmond Tutu in 1983. This initiative was continued by three South Africans[26] who attended the Interfaith Colloquium on Apartheid convened in 1984 by Archbishop Trevor Huddlestone, regarded by many as the father of the international solidarity movement against apartheid. The organization's anti-triumphalism, commitment to dialogue within the framework of resistance to apartheid and opposition to religious syncretism were some of the factors that facilitated its acceptance among progressive Islamists. More important was its commitment to unite religious people in the struggle against apartheid.

The organization located itself among those 'conducting dialogue around practical matters' such as justice and peace, sharing the conviction that 'doctrines divide but humanity unites' (Lubbe 1988, p. 16). WCRP, furthermore, did not view itself as 'an exercise in abstract interfaith dialogue focusing merely on the analysis of religious concepts or customs . . . but proceeds from joint commitment to the struggle for justice and peace in South Africa.' (Kritzinger 1991a). WCRP soon emerged as the South African forum for interreligious dialogue between religious leaders who were also committed to the struggle for justice. Through its regular forums, it also supplied believers with a theological appreciation of the Other. It is significant that at the time of the formation of WCRP the Interfaith Forum was already in existence in Cape Town and the Call was aware of it. The Interfaith Forum, though, was essentially a dialogue group and the WCRP initiators in the Cape consciously decided on setting up an alternative structure that would focus on interfaith solidarity in the struggle against apartheid.

The Lone Rangers

Those who had previously quietly argued for collaboration with apartheid or against *fitnah* (disorder) now shifted the discourse to solidarity with the religious Other, a development which had by then become synonymous with resistance to apartheid. (In this respect Muslim discourse paralleled an earlier Christian one in the coloured community. During the first half of the twentieth century, anti-interfaith polemic was the standard fare of conservative Christian coloured politicians who supported apartheid, then known as the 'colour bar'.) Parallel to this politically and religiously conservative discourse ran another fundamentalist one, different in origin and orientation, but having the same outcome: a rejection of interfaith solidarity against apartheid.

Both of these discourses relied extensively on a number of qur'anic texts to support religious exclusivism in general and antipathy to Christians and Jews in particular. The Qur'an, as heavily contested text, once again had its role confirmed as the ultimate *hujjah* (argument) and *burhan* (proof) of truth, and, by implication, self-correctness.

The conservative response to interfaith solidarity against apartheid can best be described as obscurantist paranoia, which 'spawned its own form of political discourse, complete in itself and immune to rational argument' (Pipes 1989). The conservative attitude is reflected in the following quotation:

> Those Muslims who have been misled by the political leaders of the *Kuffar* and coaxed into anarchical movements of non-Muslims follow *kaafir* thought and *kaafir* methods . . . In joining the political organizations of the *kuffaar*, Muslims are following the path of *kufr* and *baatil* [falsehood] . . . Islam, therefore, does not permit its adherents to amalgamate with the organizations of *kufr* and anarchy. (*Majlis* n.d., 7 (2), p. 8)

The Majlis, an Eastern Cape-based tabloid, resorted to a combination of religious and political ideas to condemn the 'sinfulness of interfaith solidarity against apartheid' (Moosa 1989, p. 79). *Kufr* was linked with political destabilization which, in turn, fused with *fitnah*, the well-utilized charge of conservative traditionalism to invoke against any form of fundamental change (*Majlis* n.d., 8 (9), p. 7). This opposition to 'misled Muslims' who had been 'coaxed into the anarchical movements of the *Kuffaar*' (ibid.) was equally reflective of its own political position: one of sympathy towards the South African right-wing and collaborationist elements:

> While the group on the right of *kuffaar* politics collaborate primarily for pecuniary gain, the left collaborate with communists and Christian priests for *nafsani* [carnal] gains or *riya* [show] and *takabbur* [arrogance] . . . The real danger to the Islamic way of life [however,] is posed by collaborators with *kuffar* political organizations on the left. (Ibid.)

The Majlis evidently distinguished between different types of collaboration with *kufr*; it was not so much interfaith activity *per se* which earned the Call the wrath of *The Majlis* and its supporters, but interfaith solidarity against apartheid.

Coupled with the notion of Islam as an ideological option for a future South Africa was a religious exclusivism denying the potential for virtue in non-Islam. The radical fundamentalist discourse was based on a rejection of all the values of non-Islam, including that of the ruling class. This discourse was also confident that Islam could, and, indeed ought, to confront the world of *kufr*. Here one may note that the rejection of racialism and exploitation was incidental to this discourse. The essential radical fundamentalist critique was that these values did not belong to the realm of Islam. All forms of opposition to apartheid not rooted in Islam were, therefore, similarly to be eschewed and opposed.

The MYM–MSA and Qibla denounced the Call's commitment to interfaith solidarity and proposed an alternative Muslims-only front against apartheid (Muslim Youth Movement 1983, p. 17). The MYM–MSA argued that the Muslims' struggle involved both a specifically Islamic form of justice as well as a uniquely Islamic methodology. To co-operate with the religious Other in any ideological struggle, they argued, necessarily resulted in a dilution of one's Islam. In a widely circulated and, in MYM–MSA circles, commonly accepted, unpublished position paper, 'United Democratic Front: An Islamic Critique', Bradlow outlined the following objections to alliances with the religious Other in general and with the UDF in particular. First, political alliances have as their 'implicit strategy the maintenance of kafir [sic]' (Bradlow 1984, p. 9) and will prevent the 'presentation of Islam [to the oppressed] as the major liberating power' (ibid., p. 10). Second, in affiliating themselves to the UDF as religious organizations, Muslim groups have reduced Islam 'to the level of a religion in the western sense of the word [and have] submitted to the secularist ideology [and denied] the complete nature of Islam' (ibid.). Third, the concept of democracy is not only 'alien to the framework of Islamic government but acknowledging it is tantamount to an act of *shirk* [polytheism], associating others with Allah for He Alone is Sovereign' (ibid., p. 6).

There are several ideological assumptions characteristic of Muslim fundamentalism in these positions, the most significant being the notions that non-Islam is necessarily void of virtue and that freedom outside the parameters of Islam is of no consequence. Furthermore, they argued that the supposed representatives of God on earth can govern others without their consent. A brief look at some of the positions adopted by the MYM–MSA and Qibla with regard to their understanding of Islam gives a clearer idea of their response to the Call's relationship with the Other in general, and, more specifically, with the UDF. The MYM–MSA opposition to apartheid was based on a combination of ethico-religious indignation at racialism and sympathy for the oppressed. Furthermore, they had a passionate belief that only liberation along the path of Islam would be of any consequence.[27] As for Qibla, inspired by the 1979 events in Iran, it emerged as a militant and fundamentalist force which simultaneously supported BC and the notion of Islamic revolution. Qibla, although uniting with the MYM–MSA in their denunciation of the Call's commitment to interfaith solidarity, based their opposition on an entirely different premise. They argued that alliances are based on the burying of differences 'and that to plead for the burial of ideological differences is to plead for the burial of our methods of struggle . . . The *ummah* as an ideological community never buries its ideological differences but seeks to clarify them' (Riter 1983, p. 2). A perusal of their pamphlets and writings, however, reveals that Qibla's essential objection was directed at the Call–UDF alliance, whose political perspectives it opposed. Concomitantly, they defended all the positions of BC–PAC, presenting all its arguments in Islamic revolutionary terms.[28]

The Turning of the Tide

We may note that WCRP received a less acrimonious reception from most of the organized Muslims than its most prominent affiliate, the Call. WCRP's affinity for a Muslim community engaged in an anti-apartheid struggle was evident on a number of occasions, thus enhancing the organization's acceptability to the Muslim community.[29] While WCRP was making common cause with Muslims it was simultaneously pursuing a less often stated objective: that of drawing various religious communities closer into the anti-apartheid struggle.

From 1987 onwards, *al-Qalam* started giving WCRP positive coverage. The following year, the MYM also accepted an invitation to present an Islamic perspective at a three-day WCRP consultation on 'The Role of Believers in the Struggle'. This participation was in line with their newly developed position, which viewed 'interfaith links as vital in enhancing their common aspirations for a just South Africa where the dignity of all will be championed' (Muslim Youth Movement 1987). By 1989, with the exception of *The Majlis* and its allies, the groundswell acceptance of interfaith solidarity had eroded much of the initial resistance to it. The sheer force of a grassroots commonalty in the midst of an arduous struggle and the impending victory of the anti-apartheid forces seemed to have relegated the controversy to the drawing rooms of a few clerics, the classrooms of the few religious seminaries in South Africa and the portals of academia.

Conclusion: The Issues

In addition to this historical overview, by way of summary I want to highlight some of the pertinent issues for a qur'anic hermeneutic of religious pluralism for liberation.

Firstly, there is an intrinsic link between conservative theology and status quo ideology, however unjust or immoral the latter may be. In the

Cape, we observed how both Muslim and Christian religious conservatives tended to be politically conservative and supportive of the status
quo. This was evident in the 1940s when conservative Christian clerics
broke away from the APO to form right-wing support structures for the
NP. In 1961, the MJC also rejected active resistance to apartheid,
because among Muslims that resistance was being led by youth who were
also engaged in the task of finding a new and contextual expression of
Islam. The inverse of this is equally valid: the advocates of religious pluralism and of a contextual appreciation of the Qur'an, from the CMYM
and the CMYA to the Call and later also the MYM, were active in the
struggle against apartheid.

Secondly, the fact of peaceful interreligious coexistence, however
long it may have lasted, does not automatically translate into conscious
religious pluralism. From the earliest days of Islam in the Cape, the
Muslims lived side by side with people of other religions. While Islam
had the largest number of converts, there is no proof that Muslims actively opposed other faiths or engaged in organized proselytization until the
late 1950s. On the whole, Muslims valued their shared lives with the
Other and were resentful of any attempts to disrupt them. Yet, this has
been accompanied by a sense of religious superiority and a denial of salvation to anyone who did not share their religious affiliation. From this
brief historical overview, it would seem that the fact of social coexistence,
even over centuries, does not detract from very deeply ingrained religious
notions and memories that negate the full humanity of the Other. After
three hundred years of such coexistence, the advocates of religious chauvinism could still find a receptive audience among some Muslims. Both
the Calls of Islam had to work really hard to remind Muslims about their
shared history of suffering with the Other and their responsibility in recognizing the full humanity of the Other.

Thirdly, Goldziher was probably correct when he wrote that 'it could
be said about the Qur'an, what . . . Peter Werenfells said [about the
Gospels]: "Everyone searches for his view in the Holy Book" ' (cited by
al-Sawwaf 1979, p. 142). What cannot be claimed though, is that everyone finds, or even claims to find, everything that he or she searches for in
the Qur'an. South Africa has not seen a single statement justifying
apartheid on the basis of the Qur'an, nor has any Muslim scholar or cleric attempted to justify apartheid on Islamic theological grounds. The fee-
ble and largely undocumented attempts to support the status quo were
based on rejecting the nature of the struggle against apartheid, and arguments for obedience to the lawful authority and the need to avoid *fitnah*.

Fourthly, people's lives are not shaped by a text as much as it is shaped by the context. Being the victims of colonialism, or simply being Muslims, did not mean that the early Muslims necessarily identified with the indigenous people. The Khoikhoin were largely subdued after their first and unsuccessful uprisings against colonialism and the San were gradually decimated by the middle of the eighteenth century. Many Muslims, bearing the standard of the Union Jack and the Crescent, were prepared, even if at times with considerable reluctance, to assist the colonists in their subjugation of the indigenous people in return for short-term religious gains.

When it appeared as if the law was undermining their faith, Muslims were willing to defy it only from the late eighteenth century onwards. A willingness to defy the law for the sake of Islam thus only occurred under favourable objective conditions. Earlier Muslims living under a much more religiously repressive regime in the Cape may have secretly circumvented the law to practise their faith, but there is no record of any open defiance. Similarly, we observe that qur'anic exhortations to identify with the oppressed or to rise as God's witness-bearers for justice (4:137; 5:8) were mute in the absence of a facilitating context during the time of Haron's martyrdom in 1969. Instead, the memory of his death was reserved for another period when texts praising martyrdom were incessantly invoked as calls for Muslim resistance against apartheid.

The early Muslims, their understanding of Islam and their struggles for survival were shaped by their space and time. In as much as they were the first Muslims in South Africa, they were also the first local witnesses to the illusion of an essentialist ahistorical and monolithic Islam. Historically, the form in which Islam has manifested itself and has had its scripture interpreted has always varied greatly. The idea of a South African expression of the faith and, by extension, a South African qur'anic hermeneutic, is thus not only plausible, but has, in fact, always been operative.

Notes

1. The work of Achmat Davids (1980, 1984, 1985), although focusing on the Muslims of the Cape, is probably the most significant in this regard. Fatima Meer (1969) deals with the history of Muslims of Indo-Pak origin in the northern provinces. Da Costa (1990) has done important research on the origins of the first Muslims in South Africa. Naude (1985) and Dangor (1991) have supplied broad overviews of the demography of South African Muslims.

2. Throughout this study the word 'collaboration' is used in the pejorative sense of cooperation with something negative, in this case, the colonial powers or apartheid regime. This is generally the way the term is understood and used in South Africa.

3. F. R. Bradlow and M. Cairns' research into the origins of the early slave population

indicates that ethnically it was 'a very heterogeneous one . . . composed of negroes from West Africa, of Bantu speakers from Angola and Mozambique, of Negroid Polynesians from Madagascar, of Indians from India, and of varied groups of Polynesian type people from the Indonesian Archipelago and elsewhere in the Far East' (1978, p. 105). It is most likely that the majority of Muslims by birth came from this latter group.

4. In this context, the term 'Malay' is probably of linguistic rather than nationalistic derivation. Malayu was the common trading language of the Indonesian Archipelago from where many of the first Muslims in the Cape hailed (Davids 1981, p. 214). The attempts at the constitution of a 'Malay' ethnic subject and a critique of the 'Malay' identity have been discussed elsewhere (Lewis 1987; Jeppie 1987; 1988).

5. The Cape was governed by the Statutes of India, which prohibited any public expression or the propagation of any religion other than that of the Dutch Reformed tradition. A *placaat* (decree) to this effect was issued in 1642 by Jan van Diemen, the Governor General of Ambon, which was Dutch territory in present-day Indonesia. This *placaat*, which was reissued in 1657 by Johan Maetsuyker and was also applicable to the Cape, stated that offenders were to be punished with death (Shell n.d., pp. 2–3). Nearly two centuries later, in 1828, a local newspaper still had cause to lament the plight of the Muslims whose 'marriages were declared unlawful, and issues degraded. They were refused citizenship . . . could not hold landed property nor remain in the Colony, though born there, without special permission . . . They were compelled to perform public service gratuitously – punished at the discretion [of their masters] with stripes and imprisonment, unable to leave their homes without a pass, their houses entered and searched at the pleasure of the police' (*The South African Commercial Advertiser*, 26 July 1856, p. 12).

6. Adil Bradlow has shown how the personal 'assets' of Muslims as servants were 'forever contrasted with what was perceived to be the darker side of their character' (1985, p. 86). While concern tended to be voiced about individual acts of violence 'there is a subtle sense in which members of the ruling class remained aware of the possibility of such protest assuming a collective form' (ibid.). During the 1980s in South Africa, the state displayed particular fear at the ability of Muslims to galvanize fearlessly with community support. (See P. W. Botha 1987.)

7. The Mardyckers were brought to the Cape from Amboina in the Mollucan Straits as a 'labour force and to protect the newly established residency from the marauding indigenous people' (Davids 1989). Da Costa describes the Mardyckers as 'Malay' servants of the Dutch officials who journeyed from the East to the Netherlands' (1990, p. 48).

8. Another example of such co-option in lieu of support for religious facilities is that of the land offer to Frans van Bengalen in 1806. Described as a '*Mohamadaansche Veld Priester*' (Mohammedan field preacher), van Bengalen was granted land in 1805 on the lower slopes of Table Mountain as a burial ground for Muslims (Davids 1985, pp. 5–6) as a 'down payment' for his support to the Dutch. Subsequently, two Javanese (mainly Muslim) artilleries under his command were deployed at the Battle of Blaawberg in 1806. In 1847, Muslims, the vast majority of whom were conscripts, participated on the side of the Dutch in what the colonists named the Frontier Wars and the Nguni called Wars of Liberation. This participation was duly acknowledged by General Cloete who thanked the Muslims in 1846 'for services which they have rendered in arms for the protection of the country and the subjugation of our *kaffir* enemies' (cited in Kollisch 1867, p. 37). In this case, the 'thanks for services rendered' assumed the form of another mosque site upon which the Jami'ah Masjid, also known as the Queen Victoria Mosque, was erected in 1850 (Bradlow 1985, pp. 139–41).

9. This was the first urban uprising in the history of South Africa and both its underlying as well as immediate causes have been extensively dealt with by Davids (1984), Bradlow (1985) and Bickford-Smith (1989). In terms of underlying causes, Davids has argued that by the time of the 1882 epidemic the Muslims 'were more sure of their political power' (1984, p. 51); Bradlow has located Muslim resistance to the health regulations within a broader context of resistance to colonial medicine (1985, pp. 202ff.); Bickford-Smith has suggested that the

economic depression, 'when discontent born of poverty and hunger was intensified', may have been one of its causes (1989, p. 9). The more immediate reasons for the Cemetery Uprising may be summarized as follows: 1) the community's rejection of the various preventive health laws because disease was viewed as a divine affliction against which only God could provide protection; 2) hospital regulations prohibiting Muslim patients from having *halal* food; 3) Muslims who died from smallpox being denied Islamic burial rites and the accompanying ritual ablutions; 4) regulations demanding that the dead be buried in coffins which Muslims found unacceptable; 5) the Tana Baru, the only cemetery within walking distance of the predominantly Muslim residential area, being closed in January 1886. Muslims considered walking to the graveyard a religious obligation and rejected the alternative distant sites offered.

10. The Dutch or nascent Afrikaner community was by this time a part of the underclass in Cape Town and Afrikaans was the language of the poor. In all likelihood, the white family in this case belonged to an overwhelmingly Afrikaner class, later to be described as 'poor whites' (Davids 1989).

11. The Muslim community in the Cape by this time comprised both Coloureds, known as Malays, and Indians. When a further distinction among Coloureds in particular needs to be made, I refer to 'Muslims' and '(Christian) Coloureds'. During the period under discussion, though, the Indian Muslims, who were mainly traders, did not really identify with the 'Malay' Muslims. While the latter were politically organized through the African People's Organization (APO), the Indian Muslims founded the Cape British Indian Congress in 1919 to oppose the increasing discriminatory measures against Indians.

12. The Constitutional Ordinance Amendment Act was hurriedly passed through Parliament to reduce Effendi's chances. Effendi's candidature was widely supported throughout the country and signalled the beginning of (Christian) coloured support for Muslim political initiatives (Bickford-Smith 1989, pp. 22–5).

13. This also partly accounts for the collapse of the first Muslim political organization, the South African Moslem Association (established in 1903). Muslims, including Aly, were by then active in the Stone meetings, the forerunner of the African People's Organization (APO). When in 1910 some Muslims again sought to establish an organization catering exclusively for Muslim interests, leading clerics attacked the idea on the grounds that 'the existence of a separate political organization of Malays tended to weaken the political organization of the Coloured peoples on the whole, i.e., APO' (Lewis 1987, p. 85).

14. Dr Abdullah Abdurahman (1872–1940), the grandson of manumitted slaves, is one of the most remarkable figures in the history of resistance to oppression in South Africa. From the time that he first emerged on the public scene as the election agent of his brother-in-law, Achmat Effendi, in 1889 until his death in 1940, he was in the forefront of what was later cryptically referred to as 'the struggle'.

15. Davids cites oral evidence to the effect that Gamiet concluded a secret deal with Hertzog that the NP would be supported in the 1924 elections (1981, p. 199). On 17 June 1925 at the CMA's first ever conference, two cabinet ministers made their appearance, one of them D. F. Malan, subsequently prime minister. They heard Gamiet extolling the 'virtues of the white man and how the Malay people were aspiring to the highest form of civilization' (*Cape Times*, 18 June 1925). 'Together with the white man', said Gamiet, 'they form the bulwark against retrogression and the lowering of standards' (ibid.).

16. This radicalization of black politics is also reflected in developments within the ANC, which saw a younger and more militant generation rising to prominence. They were encouraged by the wartime idealism, the growing militancy of black trade unions and left-wing activists in the NEUM to found the ANC Youth League in 1944. It was in the Youth League that Nelson Mandela and Oliver Tambo first came to national prominence.

17. Despite the discomfort of many Muslims in these organizations, their campaigns (particularly the anti-CAD campaign) and, more importantly, the harshness of the Group Areas Act promulgated in 1952, ensured that, for the majority of Muslims, ideas of collaboration were

finally abandoned. In 1953 a number of relatively, in some cases completely, unknown Muslim organizations issued a statement in support of a key piece of apartheid legislation: the Separate Representation of Voters Act Validation and Amended Bill of 1953. Other than the Cape Malay Choir Board, none of them were of any significance.

18. Some examples of these are the accusation in 1933 that Muslims were adopting white children in order to 'lighten' their race with the purpose of 'taking the country over', the banning of the training of Muslim nurses in St Monica's Home by Bishop Lavis in 1948 and the vigorous work of the Anglican Mission to Muslims during this period. Particularly controversial was the redistribution of a booklet, *The Story of Haji Abdullah* (1870) in the early 1960s. This was supposedly the story of a Muslim who was disgruntled with his faith and found greater spiritual satisfaction in Christianity.

19. The declaration of the Call of Islam, published in *Muslim News*, 31 March 1961, read in part: 'For too long a time now have we been, together with our fellow-sufferers, subjugated, suffered humiliation of being regarded as inferior beings, deprived of our basic rights to Earn, to Learn and to Worship. We therefore, call upon our Muslim Brethren and all brothers in our sufferings to unite under the banner of Truth, Justice and Equality to rid our beloved land of the forces of evil and tyranny' (p. 4).

20. 'The situation of crisis', wrote a prominent black theologian, 'has brought black politicians, economists, social scientists, religious leaders and theologians who are in prison as well as those who are still outside to a tactical stop. They have had to stop and . . . search for new and more meaningful answers to pertinent questions which are posed by it and devise new strategies of advancing the cause of liberation' (Mofokeng 1990, p. 37)

21. The expression 'theology of revolt' is used here in the sense of a set of theological ideas which informs and inspires Muslims to oppose colonialism and political oppression. My reluctance to describe this as liberation theology stems from the fact that such theology is seldom applied to theological precepts based on narrow ruling-class or male chauvinist ideological interests.

22. From 1979 onwards, *al-Qalam*, the MYM mouthpiece, consistently opposed participation in apartheid structures, arguing that this 'would amount to being party to oppression of the majority of "Blacks"' (February 1984) and that all government initiated reforms were meant 'solely for cosmetic purposes' (March 1985) to effect political adjustments within the existing socio-political framework. The movement itself became more vocal in its opposition to apartheid in the early 1980s as it commenced 'its courtship with reality' (Omar 1987, p. 2).

23. The President's Council, a group of people nominated by the state president, proposed a new constitution whereby two new parliaments, one for Coloureds and the other for Indians, were to be created in addition to the existing one for Whites. This constitutional arrangement came to be known as tricameralism. The three chambers governed their 'own affairs' and the white chamber had the added responsibility of 'general affairs' as well as of 'black affairs'. Any conflict between the three chambers was resolved by the President's Council where the ratio of White, Coloured and Indian was 4:2:1.

24. This group comprised three students at the University of Cape Town, 'Adli Jacobs, Ebrahim Rasool, and Shamiel Manie and the author, a theologian, Mawlana Farid Esack. The group was first named Muslims Against Oppression. This name was hurriedly adopted to comply with legal requirements for the publishing of pamphlets, and *The Call of Islam* was the title of its newsletter. Sometime later that year, completely ignorant of the fact that a similar group with an identical name had existed in the Cape a mere twenty years before, the group began to refer to itself as the Call of Islam.

25. The Call made much of the front nature of the UDF to legitimize its participation therein and argued that every component was able to retain its own ideology (Rasool 1988a, p. 109). Earlier on, Bradlow had cogently argued that, while the UDF had not emerged as a single cohesive political party with a clear ideological platform, 'the claim that it lacks any ideological cohesion or force is unfounded, if not ridiculous' (Bradlow 1984, p. 3). He argued that the 'national democratic struggle' which was to culminate in a unitary democratic state, a stated

objective of the UDF, was by itself ideological.

26. These were Cassiem Saloogie, a Muslim in the leadership of the Transvaal Indian Congress, Yasmin Sooka, a Hindu barrister, and the Reverend Gerrie Lubbe, a Protestant pastor.

27. The MYM's views are reflected in *al-Qalam*, a Muslim monthly. The following statements are taken from its editorials: 'Ours is a heritage of leadership to liberate man from the bondage of man' (August 1986); 'We [Muslims] have the right to lead' (January 1986); 'the people of this country will have to be made aware that within Islam lies a solution to their problems and to the problems of the rest of the world' (January 1980).

28. Most of those who were identified with Qibla or who belonged to it in the 1980s have since connected with the PAC or the BC movement, thus giving credence to the allegation that their opposition to the Call of Islam's commitment to interfaith solidarity was never principled; rather, they rejected the Call's choice of the religious Other, i.e., the ANC and the UDF and their supporters. Ironically, on the day before Qibla's protest inside the Primrose Park Mosque against the Call of Islam's collaboration with the religious Other, a local daily, *The Argus* (16 June 1983), carried a notice of a joint Qibla–Azapo meeting in Paarl for the following day (Azapo being a prominent BC grouping).

29. The most publicized of these was the support afforded to Muslims in 1986 when the Dutch Reformed Church synod adopted a motion denouncing Islam as a 'false religion' and as a 'threat to Christianity in South Africa, Africa and in the world' (DRC 1986, Para. 50.3.2.4; Muslim Youth Movement 1986, p. 6).

0 65 42 - 5 30 7 48 3

Qta street;

1;

Minjin Indian

5208
1137 239

n Jobe cabano

Mway-od
847 402 5847
Deacon Joseph
Mbyb
Minerva Anis

Graduate Student, Travel Room

Waiting 31a1b 1a2

Polished Sewn 5x6

Home economics

54D15 — CDUMA
31GBB ~ 34X2M

15 2. 2122

279

2

BETWEEN TEXT &
CONTEXT
In SEARCH of MEANING

The religious act is . . . always both a faithfulness to a tradition, a re-statement and a rupture, a novelty in relation to a personal history. The act of believing is a decision that finds real meaning based on a tradition and a drawing away from it with a view to re-creation.

(Muslim–Christian Research Group 1989, p. 43)

Interpreters are People

Belief in the eternal relevance of the Qur'an is not the same as belief in a text which is timeless and spaceless. In order to relate qur'anic meaning *to* the South African crucible, the progressive Islamists were compelled to relate it *from* some historical moment. The Qur'an, as Cragg says, 'could not have been revelatory had it not been also "eventful"' (1971, p. 17). There is a theological and historical basis for justifying a contextual approach to the Qur'an itself and the role of people in elaborating its meaning. This approach has enabled many a progressive Islamist in South Africa to engage the apartheid regime meaningfully and in solidarity with the religious Other. They have done so despite the qur'anic warning to those of faith against 'taking the Christians and Jews as their *awliya'* (friends/allies/supporters)' (5:51).

Even the earliest Muslims acknowledged the importance and reality of people being interpreters of the Qur'an and the inevitable lack of certainty which accompanies such a task. During the Battle of Siffin (657),[1] the supporters of Mu'awiyah (d. 680) demanded that hostilities cease and that their dispute with 'Ali ibn Abi Talib (d. 661) be resolved by

49

resorting to the Qur'an as an arbitrator. 'Ali's dilemma reflected that facing many a Muslim committed to the Qur'an:

> When Mu'awiyah invited me to the Qur'an for a decision, I could not turn my face away from the Book of Allah. The Mighty and Glorious Allah declared that 'if you dispute about anything, refer it to Allah and His Apostle'. [However,] this is the Qur'an, written in straight lines, between two boards [of its binding]; it does not speak with a tongue; it needs interpreters and interpreters are people. (Cited in al-Razi 1979, p. 248.)

'Interpreters are people' who carry the inescapable baggage and conviviality of the human condition. Indeed, each and every generation of Muslims since the time of Muhammad, carrying its peculiar synthesis of the human condition, has produced its own commentaries on the Qur'an (and various kinds of interpretations with every generation). The present generation of Muslims, like the many preceding ones, faces the option of reproducing meaning intended for earlier generations or of critically and selectively appropriating traditional understandings to reinterpret the Qur'an as a part of the task of reconstructing society.

More than fourteen centuries after the revelation of the Qur'an, in a far southern corner of Africa, believers in the Qur'an have opened their lives and struggles to the meaning of its message. They have asked the text to enter their context of oppression and struggle for freedom. The hermeneutical issues arising from this encounter between text and context, their implications for the emergence of qur'anic hermeneutics as a contemporary discipline and their relation to (or rupture with) tradition are the subject of this chapter.

What is Hermeneutics?

The distinction between interpreting something on the one hand, and the rules and problems of interpretation on the other, is something which has been known from the earliest days of both biblical and qur'anic studies. Thus, 'while the term "hermeneutics" itself dates back only to the seventeenth century, the operations of textual exegesis and theories of interpretation – religious, literary and legal – date back to antiquity' (Palmer 1969, p. 35). According to Palmer, (ibid., pp. 44ff.) two broad streams may be discerned in the search for a definition of hermeneutics. The first stream regards hermeneutics as a general body of methodological principles which underlie interpretation, while the second stream views it as the philosophical exploration of the character and necessary conditions for all understanding. Carl Braaten covers both approaches when he defines hermeneutics as 'the science of reflecting on how a word or an event in a past time and culture may be understood and become existentially meaningful in our present situation' (Braaten 1966, p. 131). 'It involves', he says, 'both the methodological rules to be applied in exegesis as well as the epistemological assumptions of understanding' (ibid.). Since Rudolf Bultmann, though, the term hermeneutics is 'generally used to describe the attempt to span the gap between past and present' (Ferguson 1986, p. 5). How do people make sense of a text? And different people different sense of the same text? And the same people under a different set of circumstances? What is a text? These are some of the questions which hermeneutics addresses.

Hermeneutics assumes that every person comes to a text carrying his or her own questions and expectations and that it would be 'absurd to demand from any interpreter the setting aside of his/her subjectivity and interpret a text without preunderstanding and the questions initiated by it [because without these] the text is mute' (Bultmann 1955, p. 251). In the singular form, 'hermeneutic', the conscious acknowledgement of these assumptions is brought to the fore. 'A given hermeneutic is essentially a self-consciously chosen starting point containing ideological, attitudinal and methodological components designed to aid the work of interpretation and facilitate maximum understanding' (Robinson 1964, p. 5.) As I shall indicate later in this chapter, questions of meaning and authority of the text are irrevocably linked to questions regarding the nature of the text. Within conflicting rationalities and conceptions of justice, South African Muslims, however, have not experienced the historical tale of the Qur'an primarily as a set of arguments about the text. The South African experience is about the Qur'an's diverse uses and receptions in particular socio-political circumstances. In other words, Muslims did not argue about the nature of the Qur'an; instead they differed on its role and ways of understanding it. This bring us to a specific discipline within hermeneutics.

Reception Hermeneutics

Reception hermeneutics is usually discussed as one of the categories of functionalism in textual studies (Buckley 1990, p. 330). As with much else in the social sciences, one finds various typologies rather inadequate when attempting to relate them to Islamic traditional scholarship. Functionalism, normally contrasted with revelationism, focuses on the use of a text and claims that certain texts are scripture only in so far as they pass 'certain pragmatic and functional tests' (ibid.). While Muslim scholars and organizations involved in the search for a contextual appreciation of the Qur'an do see its essential value in terms of its function today, none would see themselves in opposition to 'revelationists'. Such a category, arguably, does not exist among Muslims. This is not to deny that there are clear differences in focus. Indeed, with some shift in meaning, one can actually speak of 'functionalism' in the Islamic tradition.

Reception hermeneutics focuses on the process of interpretation and how different individuals or groups have appropriated it. According to Francis Schussler-Fiorenza, such interpretation 'needs to take into account, not only the text or its original audience, but also the transformation between past and present horizons' (1990, p. 23). Reception hermeneutics would thus change the analysis of the different ways in which a text was or is received 'into a task of the study of the meaning of that text' (ibid.). In contrast to historical positivism, which would incline towards a fixed meaning, reception hermeneutics asks that diverse receptions of the texts, 'including present popular understanding of the text as concretization of its meaning, be included in the problem of the interpretation of the text' (ibid.). In so doing, Schussler-Fiorenza says, reception hermeneutics 'would include within the task of interpretation the problem of the shift in horizons of diverse audiences and the transformation between past and present horizons of expectations toward the text' (ibid.).

The significance of reception hermeneutics and its potential for incorporation into Muslim approaches to the text becomes evident when one understands how the Qur'an is viewed by Muslims.

What is the Qur'an?

The Qur'an as scripture had been dealt with very extensively in Muslim and Other scholarship, both critical and confessional.[2] Here I shall confine myself to a brief explanation of what the term *qur'an* means to Muslims. The majority of Arabic scholars hold the view that the word *qur'an* is a past participle derived[3] from the Arabic root *qara'a*, which means 'he read', or an adjective from *qarana*, 'he gathered or collected' (Lane 1980, 7, p. 2504). In the Qur'an itself, *qur'an* is employed in the sense of 'reading' (17:93), 'recital' (75:18) and 'a collection' (75:17). Literally *'al-qur'an'* thus means 'the reading', 'the recitation' or 'the collection'. From the literal meaning, especially the idea of a 'collection', it

52

is evident that *qur'an* is not always employed by the Qur'an in the concrete sense of a particular scripture as it is commonly understood. The Qur'an more regularly refers to itself as a revealed discourse unfolding in response to the requirements of society over a period of twenty-three years (17:82; 17:106).

For Muslims the Qur'an as the compilation of the 'Speech of God' does not refer to a book inspired or influenced by Him or written under the guidance of His spirit. Rather, it is viewed as His direct speech. Ibn Manzur (d. 1312), the author of *Lisan al-'Arab*, reflects the view of the overwhelming majority of Muslim scholars when he defines the Qur'an as 'the inimitable revelation, the Speech of God revealed to the Prophet Muhammad through the Angel Gabriel [existing today] literally and orally in the exact wording of the purest Arabic' (n.d., 5, p. 3563).

No Text is an Island unto Itself

The socio-historical and linguistic milieu of the qur'anic revelation is reflected in the contents, style, objectives and language of the Qur'an. This contextuality is also evident from the distinction made between the Meccan and Medinan verses[4] and from the way its supposedly miraculous nature is located in the 'purity of its Arabic', its 'eloquence' and its 'unique rhetorical style'. In the relationship between the revelatory process, language and contents, on the one hand, and the community which received it, on the other, the Qur'an is not unique; revelation is always a commentary on a particular society. Muslims, like others, believe that a reality which transcends history has communicated with them. This communication, supposed or real, took place within history and was conditioned by it. Even a casual perusal of the Qur'an will indicate that, notwithstanding its claim to be 'a guide for humankind' (2:175) revealed by 'the sustainer of the universe' (1:1), it is generally addressed to the people of the Hijaz who lived during the period of its revelation.

Muslim scholarship generally has been reluctant to explore this relationship and its implications for the genesis of the Qur'an as well as for its interpretation. The reluctance to pursue the question of temporal causality that might be present in the background is a direct consequence of the passionate commitment to the preservation of the Otherness of the Qur'an as God's speech. The reasoning seems to be that if this-worldly events 'caused' revelation then somehow revelation is not entirely 'otherworldly'. Instead, 'they [the traditional scholars of the Qur'an] have set arbitrary limits to investigations of the myriad historical strands that, from a naturalistic perspective, coalesced in the prophetic–revelatory event that brought forth Islamic tradition and faith' (Graham 1980b, p. 21).

Despite this unwillingness to examine the implications of the situational character of the Qur'an, the principle of contextuality itself is generally accepted by all traditional scholars of the Qur'an, including those of fundamentalist persuasion. 'Although the Qur'an addresses itself to all of humankind', acknowledges Abul- A'la Mawdudi (d. 1979), 'its contents are, on the whole, vitally related to the taste and temperament, the environment and history and customs and usages of Arabia' (1988, pp. 26–7). Mawdudi goes further to suggest that without such particularity doctrine would consist of 'mere abstractions' whose impact would be destined to 'remain confined to the scraps of paper on which it was written' (ibid.). Along similar lines, although more restrained, is Sayyid Qutb's (d. 1966) emphasis on the Qur'an's dynamism in the Arabian context. 'We see', he says, how the Qur'an took it [society] by the hand step by step, as it stumbled and got up again, strayed and was righted, faltered and resisted, suffered and endured' (1954, p. 91).

These attempts to remove the Qur'an from its historical and linguistic place of birth both reflected and contributed to a greater rigidity than had been common among the earliest interpreters of the Qur'an. It was, however, rooted in the Muslim's own commitment to the Qur'an and 'a legitimate religious anxiety in its abiding relevance' (Cragg 1971, p. 17). I agree with Cragg that this anxiety was 'groundless' and that the 'significance of the Qur'an is sure enough and abides beyond such nervous and mistaken defence' (ibid.).

Progressive Revelation

The picture which the Qur'an portrays of the Transcendent is one of God actively engaged in the affairs of this world and of humankind. One of the ways in which this constant concern for all of creation is shown is in the sending of prophets as instruments of His progressive revelation. Translating this divine concern and intervention into concrete moral and legal guidelines requires understanding the contexts of these interventions. The principle of *tadrij*, whereby injunctions are understood to have been revealed gradually, best reflects the creative interaction between the will of God, realities on the ground and needs of the community being spoken to. The Qur'an, despite its inner coherence, was never formulated as a connected whole, but was revealed in response to the demands of concrete situations. The Qur'an itself is explicit about the reasons for the progressive nature of its revelation. Firstly, the fact that it came as day-to-day guidance necessitated this manner of revelation. It is 'a Qur'an which

We only gradually unfolded so that you may recite it to the people step-by-step and (therefore) We have revealed it only in pieces'. (17:106) Secondly, Islam unfolded in the midst of a struggle and Muhammad needed the ongoing support and solace from his encounters with revelation. In response to the question from his detractors as to 'why it was not revealed to him all at once' (25:32), the Qur'an says, 'Thus that we may strengthen your heart thereby. We have arranged it well' (ibid.).

The most cogent traditional scholar of the progressive model of revelation is undoubtedly Shah Wali Allah Dehlawi (d. 1762) who developed an elaborate theory of the relationship between revelation and its context. Following on his notion of Unity of Being, where everything is closely integrated, he emphasises the interrelation of the cosmic, divine, terrestrial and human powers and effects in the universe. God would thus not speak into a vacuum nor would He convey a message formed in a vacuum. According to Dehlawi the ideal form of *din*, which he interprets to mean primordial ideal religion, corresponds to the ideal form of nature. 'Actualized manifestations of the ideal form descend in successive revelations depending on the particular material and historical circumstances' of the recipient community (Hermansen 1985, p. 147). Every succeeding revelation reshapes the elements 'previously found into a new gestalt which embodies *din*, in an altered form suitable to the recipient community' (ibid.). It thus follows that, according to Dehlawi, with every succeeding context, *din* has adapted 'its form, beliefs, spiritual practices to the customs, previous faiths and temperaments of the nations to which it has been revealed' (Dehlawi 1952, 1, p. 187). In this schema of revelation, God's way of dealing with humankind is compared to a physician who prescribes different medication to his or her patients in the various stages of their illness; to hold on to a pre-Muhammadan community would, in Dehlawi's view, be tantamount to an adult using medicine prescribed for a child or using yesterday's medicine for today's ailment.

The 'arbitrary limits' set by traditional scholars of the Qur'an in investigating the historical strands in revelation, referred to by Graham (1980b, p. 21), did not exclude the principle of progressive revelation. This principle, which characterized the entire revelatory process, is best manifested in the disciplines of *asbab al-nuzul* (events occasioning revelation, sing. *sabab al-nuzul*) and that of *naskh* (abrogation). In the case of events occasioning revelation, however, traditional qur'anic studies reduced the 'event-ness' of the text to story telling while in the case of abrogation, its significance was confined to the legal sphere.

Events Occasioning Revelation (*Asbab al-Nuzul*)

At a first glance, a bit of a clumsy translation; one rather walks a tightrope here. *Asbab al-nuzul* 'deals with the transmission of the *sabab* of the revelation of a chapter or verse and the time, place and circumstances of its revelation. It is verified by the well-known principles of transmission from the pious predecessors' (Khalifah 1835, p. 269). To render *sabab* as 'cause' would suggest that the event created the text and I am not sure whether I want to fly into the face of orthodoxy as directly as this; 'events occasioning revelation' is simultaneously a clear and ambiguous rendition.

Andrew Rippin's survey of classical works on *asbab al-nuzul* (1988a) shows that, unlike most of the works on the subject of abrogation which contain a detailed exposition and defence of the discipline, as well as listing its supposed occurrence in the Qur'an, the works dealing with *asbab al-nuzul* essentially confine themselves to its occurrence. This lack of discussion of *asbab* as a discipline shows the relative absence of any serious consideration in traditional qur'anic scholarship of the question of the historicity and contextuality of the text.

Asbab al-nuzul have been transmitted by Muhammad's Companions and scrutinized for reliability in the same way as the general *hadith* literature (Azami 1978, pp. 189–99). It is thus not uncommon to find some reports regarded as 'unsound' or differing reports from Muhammad's Companions relating to a single revelation. In such cases, the more 'reliable' account is preferred or attempts are made to synchronize the apparent contradiction in different accounts. In traditional Islamic studies, *asbab al-nuzul* forms an important element in the studies dealing with the campaigns and the biography of Muhammad, interpretation and with legal matters. Despite the neglect that it has suffered as a discipline, its significance is evident from the 'frequency of the claim that no assistance is greater in understanding the Qur'an than a knowledge of when and in what circumstances its verses were revealed' (Burton 1977, p. 16). Describing the function of *asbab* in exegesis, Rippin says that 'its function is to provide a narrative account in which basic exegesis of the verse may be embodied. The standard interpretational techniques of incorporating glosses, masoretic clarification (e.g., with variants), narrative expansion and, most importantly, contextual definition predominate within the structure of the *sabab*' (1988b, pp. 2–3). Rippin concludes that on many occasions it seems that *asbab* reports are cited by commentators for no apparent purpose of interpretation: 'They are cited and then ignored' (ibid.). From the context of these citations, though, he opines that 'they are adduced out of a general desire to historicize the text of the Qur'an in order to be able to prove constantly that God really did reveal His book to humanity on earth; the material thereby acts as a witness to God's concern for His creation' (1988b, p. 2).

Given the general impression in the Qur'an of a God who is constantly involved in the affairs of humankind, this is certainly a credible reason for the adduction of a *sabab*. Jalal al-Din al-Suyuti (d. 1505), in fact, says that the constant reminder of the presence of God in the universe is one the functions of the *sabab* (al-Suyuti 1987, 1, p. 29). 'The *sabab*' as Rippin says, 'is a constant reminder of God and is the rope, that being one of the meanings of *sabab* in the Qur'an, by which human contemplation ascends to the highest levels even while dealing with the mundane aspects of the text' (1988b, p. 1).

The regular reference to the occasion of revelation in the interpretation of the Qur'an, the dates and the circumstances of the individual revelations and its significance for the question of abrogation or *naskh* are all indications that there is more to the Qur'an than a text. In fact, because every chapter 'is so vitally linked with its situational background . . . knowledge of the occasions of revelation is of extreme importance and numerous verses will remain incomprehensible without it' (Mawdudi 1988, p. 3). The significance of this becomes apparent when we read texts which at superficial reading convey an idea of a tribal God bent on holding together a small community at the expense of a broader humanity. In later chapters, I shall show how an appreciation of the occasions of revelation of these texts actually opens them to a pluralist and liberatory reading.

Naskh (Abrogation, Clarification or Particularization?)

Literally *naskh* means 'the removal of something by something else [and] annulment' (Ibn Manzur n.d., 6, p. 4407). In traditional qur'anic studies and Islamic jurisprudence, however, it means the verification and elaboration of different modes of abrogation. The proof text for the notion of *naskh* is Qur'an 2:106: 'Any message (*ayat*) we abrogate or consign to oblivion We replace with a better for a similar one. Do you not know that God has the power to will anything?' The modes of *naskh* may be classified as follows: 1) the qur'anic abrogation of divine scriptures that preceded it; 2) the repeal of some qur'anic texts that are said to have been blotted out of existence; 3) the abrogation of some earlier commandment of the Qur'an by the later revelations, while the text containing those commandments remained in the Qur'an; 4) the abrogation of a prophetic practice by a qur'anic injunction and 5) the abrogation of a qur'anic injunction by the prophetic practice.

The significance attached to *naskh* may be gauged from the fact that a large number of independent works were produced on the subject. Besides the literature on the theory of *naskh*, one finds a number of reports attributed to the Companions of Muhammad emphasizing the need to acquire knowledge of the abrogating and abrogated verses of the Qur'an.[5] Despite this emphasis, there is probably no other discipline in traditional qur'anic studies to rival it in confusion regarding its validity, meaning and applicability. This confusion accounts for the fact that many have doubted its validity beyond the first of the modes listed, i.e., that of the Qur'an abrogating previous divine scriptures (Al-Razi 1990, 3, pp. 245–52).

A number of latter-day reformists such as Sir Sayed Ahmad Khan (d. 1898) and contemporary scholars such as Isma'il al-Faruqi (d. 1986) rejected *naskh*. They argued that the revelations that came earlier in certain circumstances and which were modified or improved later, were not actually abrogated. Instead of viewing previous rulings as abrogated by subsequent ones, it was more appropriate to continue regarding them as valid to be implemented in conditions similar to those in which they were revealed. Much of the concern of these scholars centred around the question of the authority of the text. When almost every passage or practice which is held as abrogated by one scholar is questioned by another, then there is little doubt that the question of scriptural authority itself is involved.

The various transformations in the meaning of the term *naskh* are responsible for much of this confusion, as Dehlawi has pointed out (1966, p. 40). Some Companions, as Ibn Qayyim al-Jawziyyah (d. 1350) illustrates, used the word in the sense of 'either', 'exception', particularizing the meaning or clarification of a previous verse (1895, 1, p. 12). Its early usage thus did not necessarily include 'abrogation', with which it subsequently came to be synonymous. These different meanings of the word were later confused and little or no distinction was drawn between them. According to Dehlawi, the Companions and Followers (i.e., the generation of those early Muslims who did not meet Muhammad but knew one or more of the Companions) took *naskh* in the literal sense of 'removal' and not in the more technical sense used by the scholars of the theoretical bases of Islamic law (Dehlawi 1966, p. 40). The use of the term *naskh* in its general sense thus enhanced the number of abrogated verses which, according to Dehlawi, had reached five hundred (ibid.).

It has been the trend among scholars of the Qur'an to reduce the number of abrogated verses (al-Faruqi 1962, pp. 40ff.; Hassan 1965, p. 187). The repeal of the individual verses in the Qur'an was not generally favoured and various ways were used to either reduce their number or to deny their actual occurrence while accepting such a possibility.[6] Abu Muslim al-Isfahani (d. 1527), for example, denied the theory of *naskh* entirely. Muhammad ibn Idris al-Shafi'i (d. 820) and Fakhr al-Din al-Razi (d. 1209) argued that the possibility of abrogation does not actually mean that it occurred (Al-Shafi'i 1973, 2, p. 285; al-Razi 1990, 3, p. 246). Al-Suyuti reduced the number of repealed verses to twenty-one while Dehlawi, arguing that most of them could be reconciled, reduced them to five (1966, pp. 41–6).

Whatever the various opinions surrounding *naskh*, there is unanimity about what Fazlur Rahman describes as 'the situational character of the Qur'an' (1966, p. 10). Both the entire revelation as well as specific verses were generally revealed within the context of particular social conditions. As Muslim society was taking shape, the qur'anic revelation kept up with the changing conditions and environment.

The principle of progressive revelation is best illustrated in the issue of the prohibition on the consumption of alcohol. In the Meccan period the Qur'an mentions alcohol among the blessings of God, along with milk and honey (16:66–9). In Medina a number of Muslims desired an expressed prohibition of alcohol. In response to this, we have a verse where the Qur'an says: 'They ask you about alcohol and games of chance; tell them that there is a great deal of harm in them but there are also certain benefits for people in them; but their harm is greater than their benefits' (2:219). After a party at the home of one of the Medinan host community a number of people actually became drunk and when one of them led the evening prayers he mispronounced certain words from the Qur'an. When this was reported to Muhammad, the following verse was revealed: 'Do not approach prayers when you are under the influence of alcohol so that you should know what you are saying' (4:43). Much later, according to another report, there was another party where drunkenness led to a brawl when some people quoted pre-Islamic poetry against rival tribes. In response to this incident the following text of the Qur'an was revealed: 'Alcohol, games of chance, divining by arrows and idol-altars are an abomination and work of the devil. The devil wants to sow discord and rancour among you and that you should become oblivious of your duty of praying to God. Therefore desist from alcohol. Are you then going to desist?' (5: 90–1).[7]

Progressive Revelation as a Tool for Progressive Islam

The principle of progressive revelation, as is evident from the disciplines of *asbab al-nuzul* and *naskh*, reflects the notion of the presence of a Divine Entity who manifests His will in terms of the circumstances of His people, who speaks to them in terms of their reality and whose word is shaped by those realities. For Muslims committed to discovering the will of God for society today, the message of the Qur'an, as Rahman says, 'despite it being clothed in the flesh and blood of a particular situation, outflows through and beyond that given context of history' (Rahman 1966, p. 11). This word of God thus remains alive because its universality is recognized in the middle of an ongoing struggle to rediscover meaning in it. The challenge for every generation of believers is to discover their own moment of revelation, their own intermission in revelation, their own frustrations with God, joy with His consoling grace, and their own guidance by the principle of progressive revelation. For the numerous Muslims who experience existence as marginalized and oppressed communities or individuals, this discovery clearly has to take place amidst their own Meccan crucibles of the engagement between oppressor and oppressed, the Abyssinian sojourn amidst the gracious and warm hospitality of 'the Other' and the liberating praxis in Medina.

The disciplines of *naskh* and *asbab al-nuzul* have both come to form significant elements in contemporary attempts to contextualize the message of the Qur'an, to recapture territory from the ever-expanding unthinkable in Islamic thought. They are being embraced as key elements in a broader tapestry of historical relevance, contextuality and social justice.[8] Reformist scholars all agree that the task of interpretation today must consider the time, location and an understanding of how tenets and directives respond to the contemporary context. They also share a commitment to the inner unity of the Qur'an and a rejection of random and selective citation (Rahman 1982a, pp. 3, 20; Asad 1980, p. 7; Ansari 1977, 1, p. 161). The objective is not to search for accounts of isolated historical incidents] which occurred in the prophetic era and then attempt to construct a 'politically correct' view on the basis of these. The Qur'an is, after all, not merely a collection of individual and disjointed injunctions. It is also an integrated whole with a definite ethos; 'an exposition of an ethical doctrine where every verse and sentence has an intimate bearing on other verses and sentences, all of them clarifying and amplifying one another' (Asad 1980, p.vii). An understanding of that interaction and context is a condition for reapplying it. To understand the Qur'an in its historical context is not to confine its message to that context; rather, it is to understand its revealed meaning in a specific past context and then to be able to contextualize it in terms of contemporary reality.

Traditional Qur'anic Scholarship and Hermeneutics

Two terms are usually employed in qur'anic studies to refer to interpretative activity: *tafsir* and *ta'wil*. From the root *'fassara'* (literally, 'to explain' or 'elucidate') or *asfara* (literally, 'to break'), the verbal noun *tafsir*, although only occurring once in the Qur'an, in 25:33 ('Abd al-Baqi 1945, p. 519), came to be used technically for exegesis around the fifth century AH/eleventh century CE.[9] The other term frequently employed in regard to exegesis is *ta'wil*. Some scholars use both words in the sense of 'elaboration', while others make a distinction between them using *tafsir* to denote external philological exegesis, the exoteric/external, or a reference to both secular and divine books. *Ta'wil*, from *'-ww-l*, (literally, 'to interpret' or 'to elaborate') is then taken to refer to the exposition of the subject matter, the esoteric/ inner or exegesis dealing purely with a divine scripture. Later, *ta'wil* became a technical term to denote the rejection of the obvious meaning of a verse and adoption of an inner interpretation (Ahmad (Jullandri) 1968, p. 73).[10]

The term 'hermeneutics' is rather new in Muslim discourse on the Qur'an and is not used at all in traditional or confessional scholarship. The absence of a definitive term for hermeneutics in the classical Islamic disciplines, and its non-employment on a significant scale in contemporary qur'anic literature, however, does not mean that definite hermeneutical notions or operations in traditional qur'anic studies or the other classic disciplines are absent. Firstly, the hermeneutical problem was always experienced and actively pursued, rather than thematically posed. This is evident from early discussions on *asbab al-nuzul* and *naskh*. Secondly, as I indicated earlier, the distinction between actual commentary and the rules, methods or theory of interpretation governing it, dates from the earliest exegetical literature. This was systematized in the discipline of principles of *tafsir*. Thirdly, traditional *tafsir* has always been categorized. These categories, 'Shi'ite', 'Mu'tazilite', 'Ash'arite', 'juristic', etc. are acknowledged to say something about the affiliations, ideology, period and social horizons of the exegete. To date though, little has been written by Muslims in a historico-critical manner about the relationship between the social horizons of the exegete and his or her exegesis or about the explicit or implicit socio-political or philosophical assumptions underlying their theological predilections, all of which are key concerns of contemporary hermeneutics.

The meaning assigned to a text by any exegete cannot exist independently of his or her personality and environment. There is therefore no plausible reason why any particular generation should be the intellectual hostages of another, for even the classical exegetes did not consider themselves irrevocably tied to the work of the previous generation. The emergence of *tafsir* as a science in Islam is itself proof of the creativity of exegetes who still continue to be inspired by, assimilate, elaborate upon and even reject the work of their predecessors.[11] Qur'anic scholarship today does not require appeals to the intellectual genius or the spiritual heights of pious predecessors. What is required of the interpreter today is a clear understanding of where he or she comes from, a statement of his or her baggage as the word of God is being approached.

The question of the relationship of the birth of the text to its authority and meaning is one left largely unexplored. Unlike early biblical scholarship, which generally agreed that the Bible was a 'production', of God or men, in Islam the traditionalist perspective goes beyond this: the Qur'an as 'production' is itself disputed, as was the question of its (historical) 'event-ness'. Anything seen as remotely conceding any aspect of qur'anic revelation is summarily dismissed as making 'conceptual room for posing a potentially dangerous question about the authority of scripture' (Akhtar 1991, p. 102). For Muslims, God is the author of the Qur'an. From this perspective one cannot even begin to consider the prospect of an 'objective' attempt to get into the mind of the author in order to understand what is intended by the text.

As the progressive South African Islamists discovered in the 1980s, the task of relating the text to the present context in a concrete manner invariably brings one face to face with all the contemporary ideas of hermeneutics and plurality of meanings. While this is a challenge which was, and is being, confronted, there are no illusions that, for the believer, the engagement with hermeneutics is painless. While hermeneutics may deal essentially with the problem of the recovery of meaning, it goes beyond the search for the ultimate in interpretative methodology. Hermeneutics therefore poses three considerable difficulties for confessional Islamic scholarship. Firstly, the insistence of hermeneutics on contexts and human contingency in the recovery of meaning implies that the Qur'an does not 'mean' something outside socio-historical contexts but 'is always possessed of *Deutungsbedurftigheit* . . . a text in need of interpretation' (Martin 1982, p. 367). In other words, without a context a text is worthless. While this may conveniently bypass the question of the Qur'an's existence outside history, it does not adequately address the traditional idea that the true meaning of the Qur'an is what God means by it. Secondly, the stress on human agency in producing meaning is really opposed to the idea that God can supply people with watertight 'correct' understandings, what Arkoun describes as 'essentialist and unchangeable concepts of rationality which divine intellect protects and guarantees' (Arkoun 1987b, p. 3). The idea that human constructions and contexts make God's presence in the world 'possible' is no less profound for traditionalism than a direct challenge to notions of revelation, infallibility and authenticity. As Aitken has argued, 'to write large the significance of human agency is to see that meaning is itself a contest within power relations; divinity lies within the working of that contest and cannot be predicated transcendentally outside the contest as the guarantor of a finally achievable meaning' (1991, p. 4).

Thirdly, traditional Islamic scholarship has made a neat and seemingly unbridgeable distinction between the production of scripture, on the one hand, and its interpretation and reception, on the other. This distinction is the crucial factor in the shaping of qur'anic hermeneutics, for it implies that the only hermeneutics Islam can presently cope with is that pertaining to interpretation and reception.

In contrast to the impersonalism of the modern scientistic worldview that considers language as autonomous, reception hermeneutics argues that the locus of meaning for people is persons. Reception hermeneutics does not try to recover an author's elusive intention. Instead, it studies the contributions to the ongoing and ever-changing understandings of a text. Basing itself on exegetical literature in the widest sense, which may include a radical Islamist's pamphlet or a traditional cleric's sermon, reception hermeneutics would examine the many different ways a text was received, made concrete and interpreted.

Two Contemporary Approaches

Fazlur Rahman (d. 1988) is arguably the foremost reformist scholar in contemporary Islam who remains rooted in notions of an essentialist faith, while Mohammed Arkoun represents a radical break with traditional epistemology. Along with Nasr Hamid Abu Zaid, the exiled Egyptian scholar, Arkoun is an example of Muslim scholarship embracing contemporary hermeneutical insights and literary criticism. His thinking is arguably the most radical in contemporary Islam and, along with Abu Zaid, he displays a deep insight into the contemporary discourses on language, semiotics and hermeneutics. Both Rahman and Arkoun have made an enormous contribution to the methodology of interpretation and to qur'anic hermeneutics respectively, despite the lack of depth in Rahman's work in this field and the repetitive nature of Arkoun's over the last few years.

Fazlur Rahman: A Modernist Rooted in God-Consciousness

My interest in Fazlur Rahman, a Pakistani scholar and graduate from the universities of Oxford and the Punjab was first awakened while at the *madrassah* in Karachi. Our rector, the late Mawlana Yusuf Binnuri, extolling the achievements of our institute, mentioned the important contribution which it had played in forcing Rahman into exile. Rahman had taught in the United Kingdom and Canada before working as the Director of the Institute of Islamic Research in Pakistan. While he was in this post, he was forced into exile for his views on the nature of the Qur'an. He passed away in 1988 in the United States, where he was a professor in Islamic Studies at the University of Chicago.

Among contemporary Muslim scholars the concern for the contextuality and programmatic nature of the Qur'an is best represented by Rahman. His views on the Qur'an and revelation are covered in a chapter in his books *Prophecy in Islam: Philosophy and Orthodoxy* (1958) and *Islam* (1966) while his ideas on hermeneutics and interpretation are dealt with extensively in *Islam and Modernity: Transformation of an Intellectual Tradition* (1982a) and in an article, 'Interpreting the Qur'an' (1986b).

Rahman, a passionate believer, regards the Qur'an as 'a unique repository of true answers to virtually all situations' (1982a, p. 5), and believes that, in returning to it, 'modern man [will] be saved through religion' (ibid. p. 40). He insists that revelation intends obedience rather than information and believes that 'the Qur'an is the divine response, through the Prophet's mind to the moral and social situation of the Prophet's Arabia, particularly the problems of the commercial Meccan society of his day' (ibid, p. 5). He believes that the Qur'an really originated outside this world. This ontological otherness of the Qur'an is seen in the fact that it was '*verbally revealed* [italics in original] and not merely in its meaning and ideas' (1966, pp. 30–1). According to him, this 'divine message broke through the consciousness of the Prophet from an agency whose source was God' (1988, p. 24). In this sense it also became a part of Muhammad's speech. It is this area of overlap that earned Rahman the wrath of traditional Muslim scholars.

but orthodoxy lacked the necessary intellectual tools to combine, in its formulation of the dogma, the otherness and verbal character of the revelation, on the one hand, and its intimate connection with the work and religious personality of the Prophet, on the other; i.e., it lacked the intellectual capacity to say both that the Qur'an is entirely the Word of God and, in an ordinary sense, also entirely the word of Muhammad. (1966, p. 31)

Rahman here refers to the events prior and subsequent to the *mihnah,* a Muslim version of the Inquisition[12] which resulted in traditionalists emphasizing the externality of the Qur'an (1966, p. 31). He insists that while the Qur'an 'itself certainly maintained its otherness . . . objectivity and the verbal character of the revelation, [it had] equally certainly rejected its externality vis-a-vis the Prophet' (ibid.). Rahman is arguably the first modern reformist Muslim scholar to link the question of the origin of the Qur'an to both its context and interpretation. It is also a connection with which contemporary hermeneutics is also concerned and which is crucial for the question of meaning. Rahman's writings, however, display little insight into hermeneutics as a contemporary discipline. Beyond what has been said, he regrettably leaves unexplored the crucial question of the relationship between the origin of the text and its interpretation. By contemporary Muslim standards his views are fairly radical, but he concentrated on methods of interpretation, rather than on the implications of his views on the nature of revelation for interpretation and meaning.

There are two key concepts in Rahman's approach to qur'anic interpretation: understanding the Qur'an within 'its proper context which is the struggle of the Prophet and the background of that struggle' (1986b, p. 46); and ensuring that the underlying unity of the Qur'an flows through all interpretation (ibid., p. 45). Rahman laments the 'general failure to understand the underlying unity of the Qur'an' (1982a, p. 2) which has led to a 'piecemeal, *ad hoc* and extrinsic treatment of it' (ibid, p. 4). His criticism of the 'extrinsic treatment' of the Qur'an reveals the inadequacy of his hermeneutical methodology and his insistence on an 'objective' appreciation of the Qur'an's meaning. His criticism of the two groups of Muslims, the philosophers and Sufis, who, he believes, often understood the underlying unity of the Qur'an, is a case in point (ibid., p. 3). Rahman argues that this unity was imposed from without rather than derived from 'a study of the Qur'an itself' (ibid.). While their ideas were 'adapted somewhat to the Islamic milieu and expressed in Islamic terminology', 'this thin veneer could not hide the fact that their basic structure of ideas was not drawn from within the Qur'an itself' (ibid.). He there-fore concludes that their intellectual constructs had an 'artificial Islamic character' (ibid.).

Rahman argues strongly that there are intellectual constructs which can be 'objectively' arrived at and 'objectively' defined as 'Islamic' (1982a, pp. 8–11). Arguing that a subject-interpreter can break free from the shackles of his or her 'effective history' (Gadamer's term; Gadamer 1992, p. 267), Rahman believes that it is possible to go beyond one's self and to arrive at absolute/objective meaning (Rahman 1982a, pp. 8–11).

In *Islam and Modernity*, Rahman argues the case for an 'adequate hermeneutical method' 'exclusively concerned with the cognitive aspects of revelation' (1982a, p. 4). The *a priori* hermeneutical keys for the 'pure-ly cognitive effort' (ibid.) are faith and the willingness to be guided. 'While faith may be born from this effort', he says, 'more patently, faith may and ought to lead to such cognitive effort' (ibid.). Rahman argues that the process of drawing meaning or, more appropriately, guidance, from the Qur'an, can be compared to the process of dynamic revelation. Contemporary exegesis must, therefore, focus on the historical circum-stances of revelation as the most valuable means of understanding (ibid., pp. 1–11). He proposes a process of interpretation involving a double movement: from the present to the qur'anic period and then back to the present (ibid., p. 20). His methodology is diagrammatically illustrated below:

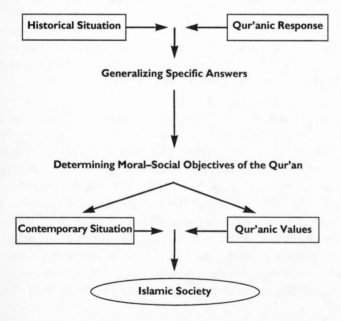

The first movement consists of understanding the Qur'an as a whole and in terms of specific injunctions revealed in responses to specific situations. This proceeds in two steps. The first step, studying the historical situation and its ethico-moral requirements, precedes the study of the qur'anic texts in the light of specific situations (Rahman 1982a, p. 6). The second step is to generalize those specific answers and frame them as statements of general moral–social objectives that can be drawn from the specific texts in the light of their socio-historical background and the often stated rationale behind the law (ibid.).

The second movement involves applying the general objectives achieved under the first in the present concrete socio-historical context. This application requires a study of the present situation in order to change it and to determine priorities to implement qur'anic values afresh.

Rahman: A Critique

In much of his approach, Rahman shows a lack of appreciation for the complexity of the hermeneutical task and the intellectual pluralism intrinsic to it. This absence of grey areas is the most serious inadequacy in his approach. Faith leads to understanding, he insists, without seeing that these can be intrinsically linked to each other. Similarly, he deplores what he calls 'Islam's pitiable subjugation of religion to politics . . . rather than genuine Islamic values controlling politics' (1982a, pp. 139–40) without acknowledging the dialectical relationship between the two. His criteria of knowledge are based on the primacy of cognition and he ignores the relationship between cognition and praxis. Lastly, as Moosa points out, 'he does not attempt to capture the aesthetic whole, but is pre-eminently preoccupied with the historical cognition which would focus on moral values.' (Moosa 1987b, p. 19).

Rahman's work displays an overriding concern for the 'basic moral élan' (1966, p. 32) of the Qur'an. The twin pillars of this morality, he tirelessly proclaims, are God-consciousness and social justice (1982a, p. 155). While he insists that his commitment to these is derived from the Qur'an and not read into it, they do effectively become significant hermeneutical keys in his methodology. He thus reads into the Qur'an whatever conforms to the requirements of God-consciousness and social justice and, invoking *ijtihad* (scholarly creative endeavour), applies the principle of progressive revelation to conform with it.

Rahman, however, displays a regrettable ignorance of the structural causes of injustice and refers to the need for social justice in somewhat condescending terms. Those who are engaged in political struggles employing an Islamic perspective are dismissed as 'using Islam' (1982a, pp. 139–40). By so doing, he ignores the fact that the study or articulation of the Qur'an within a particular socio-political framework is not confined to those intent on challenging an unjust status quo.

The idea that those committed to the removal of injustice are 'political' or 'ideological' beings and those committed to its preservation are 'apolitical' or 'spiritual' is long since discredited. The South African engagement with the Qur'an and the visible manner in which religion itself became contested territory testify to the fact that apparently apolitical readings of the Qur'an were as much influenced by the power arrangements as any decidedly ethico-political reading. As Tracy says, 'There is no historyless, discourseless human being' (1987, p. 107).

The objectivist approach and belief in gaining access to 'the real truth', as I have shown, flow through Rahman's work. Yet his own ideas are not entirely free from ambiguity. On at least one occasion he affirms 'tentativeness' as a value intrinsic to modern thought. Addressing the task before the Muslim intellectual, he says that 'modern thinking, on principle, must reject authoritarianism of all kinds . . . Openness to correction and, in this sense, a certain amount of doubt, or rather tentativeness lie in the very nature of modern thought which is an ever-unfolding process and always experimental (1970, p. 651). Elsewhere he has acknowledged that although 'the meaning of a proposition may be universally true; this does not imply that understanding of that meaning is also universal' (1982b, p. 191). He has regrettably not interwoven this 'tentativeness', which may accommodate pluralism, into his overall methodological approach. He has also not seen how the objectivism that underpins his entire approach to the Qur'an must effectively work against any ideas of heurism and pluralism. Rahman's approach to the Qur'an from the perspective of its all-pervading insistence on *taqwa* and commitment to social justice is, nonetheless, a welcome departure from Arkoun's idea that the ideal search for knowledge is motivated by seemingly neutral reason.

Mohammed Arkoun: Deconstructing Revelation

This Algerian Muslim scholar has written a number of books on Arab and Islamic thought. He received his Ph.D. from the Sorbonne, where he currently teaches the history of Islamic thought. Arkoun's writings show considerable affinity with recent trends in French academic thought, especially structural linguistics, the post-structuralist writings of Paul Ricoeur and Michel Foucault and the deconstructionism of Jacques Derrida.

The discourse on revelation and historicity led by Arkoun is decidedly more radical and critical than that of any other contemporary Muslim scholar. A critic of orthodoxy, he rejects any links between his 'modern perspective of radical thought applied to any subject . . . and *islahi* (reformist) thinking' (1987b, p. 2). Arkoun argues that the present crisis of legitimacy for religion compels scholars to 'only speak of heuristic ways of thinking' (ibid., p. 10). While he insists on a historical-sociological-anthropological approach, he does not deny the importance of the theological and the philosophical. Instead, he says that he wishes 'to enrich them by the inclusion of the concrete historical and social conditions in which Islam always has been practised' (ibid., p. 3). Arkoun presents a number of 'fundamental heuristic lines of thinking . . . to recapitulate Islamic knowledge and to confront it with contemporary knowledge in the process of elaboration' (ibid.).

1. Human beings emerge in societies through various changing 'uses' (activity, experience, sensation, observation etc.). Each use in society, he says, 'is converted into a sign of this use [and] realities are expressed through languages as systems of signs' (1987b, p. 8). This development occurs prior to any interpretation of revelation. Furthermore, scripture, 'is itself communicated through natural languages [which are] used as systems of signs' (ibid, p. 9) and each sign is 'a locus of convergent operations [i.e., perception, expression, interpretation, translation, communication] which engages all of the relations between language and thought' (ibid.). Two serious consequences for traditional thinking on revelation and language follow: the notion of the sacredness of Arabic is no longer tenable and, more significantly, 'the core of Islamic thought is represented as a linguistic and semantic issue' (ibid.).

2. All the signs and symbols produced by a human being (i.e., semiotic productions) in the process of his or her social and cultural emergence are inextricably bound to historicity. *As a semiotic articulation of meaning for social and cultural uses* [emphasis mine], the Qur'an is subject to historicity.[13] Arkoun raises the fundamental hermeneutical question thus: 'How can we deal with the sacred, the spiritual, the transcendent, the ontology, when we are obliged to recognize that all this vocabulary which is supposed to refer to stable, immaterial values, is submitted to the impact of history?' (1988, p. 70).

3. Faith does not exist on its own independent of human beings, nor does it come from a divine will or grace; rather it is 'shaped, expressed and actualized in and through discourse' (1987b, p. 10).[14]

4. The traditional system of legitimization represented by classical Islamic theology and Islamic jurisprudence and their vocabulary does not have any epistemological relevance. In other words, they are useless for the elaboration of knowledge today. These disciplines and their vocabulary, he argues, are too compromised by the ideological biases imposed on them by 'the ruling class and its intellectual servants . . . [and] are authoritative only because they refuse to be engaged by the changing scientific environment' (1988, pp. 64–5).

The application of Arkoun's ideas is best understood in the way he analyses the processes of revelation and the way the written text became a canon, i.e., sacred and authoritative. Following Ricoeur (1981a, p. 15; 1981b, pp. 15–16), Arkoun distinguishes between three levels of the word of God.

The first is the word of God as transcendent, infinite and unknown to humankind as a whole with only fragments of it having been revealed through the prophets.[15] Second are the historical manifestations of the word of God through the Israelite prophets (in Hebrew), Jesus of Nazareth (in Aramaic) and Muhammad (in Arabic). (It was memorized and transmitted orally during a long period before it was written down (1987b, p. 16)).[16] Third, textual objectification of the word of God takes place (the Qur'an becomes a *mushaf*, i.e., written text) and the scripture is available to the believers only through the written version of the book preserved in the officially closed canons.[17] Arkoun's analysis of revelation, its objectification and interpretation as well as the believers' interaction with these on the one hand, and its relationship to the history of salvation on the other, is diagrammatically illustrated on the following page.[18]

Here we see what Arkoun describes as the descending movement of the word of God and the ascending movement of the interpreting community towards salvation according to the vertical perspective on all creation as it is imposed by the qur'anic discourse. 'The interpreting community is the subject–actant of the whole terrestrial history represented, interpreted and used as a precarious stage to prepare the salvation according to the History of Salvation narrated by God as an educative part of revelation' (Arkoun 1987a, p. 16). Arkoun argues that the individual relationship to the book as the word of God is equally a socio-political relation to the community: 'The psychological function of the revelation as a message to the heart is inseparable from its social efficacy to transcend divisions and competitions, its legitimizing value for the political order' (ibid., p. 17).

Arkoun's historico-anthropological perspective on the phenomenon of revelation in history and the relationship of the believing community to

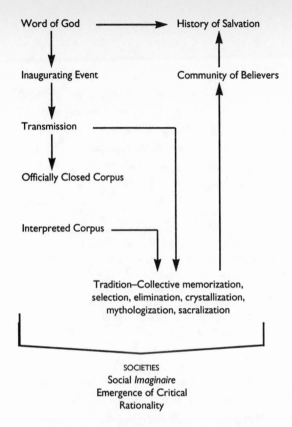

Word of God ──────────▶ History of Salvation

Inaugurating Event   Community of Believers

Transmission

Officially Closed Corpus

Interpreted Corpus

Tradition—Collective memorization,
selection, elimination, crystallization,
mythologization, sacralization

SOCIETIES
Social *Imaginaire*
Emergence of Critical
Rationality

it can easily be interpreted as a scientific reduction of something essentially transcendental. He denies this on two grounds. First, his perspective, he argues, includes the transcendental and does not put it beyond the parameters of 'the true rationality' (ibid., p. 27).[19] Second, the rationality used at the theological stage of reason, Arkoun says, is more 'related to the collective *imaginaire* than to the critical reason' (ibid., p. 28). Since theological reason is 'unable to recognize that it produces *imaginaire* rather than rationality' (ibid., p. 27), this task belongs to those who operate beyond the confines of theological reason but, who nonetheless, embrace it.[20]

Arkoun: A Critique

My critique of Arkoun's ideas must be viewed in the light of the inescapable links that exist between the formulation of ideas and our histories, a notion seemingly endorsed by Arkoun, as well as my own objective of locating the hermeneutical task within a specific context of a struggle for justice.

Scholars, their critiques of the theories of knowledge and the way it is produced, as well as the intellectualist solutions which they offer, also operate within history. One cannot view revelation and tradition historically and ideologically and then take an ahistorical or ideology-free view of oneself and of one's own critique. For the contemporary scholar, Arkoun argues that 'the problem of authority does not today depend on any religious or secular institutions, in so far as reason has established its authority *vis-à-vis* outside authorities (revelation, church, *shari'ah*, state,)' (1988, p. 68). Writing in another context, but with relevance to our subject here, Gutierrez describes this appeal to ideological neutrality in the following terms:

> The last systematic obstacle for any theology committed to human liberation is a certain type of academicism which posits ideological neutrality as the ultimate criterion; which levels down and relativizes all claims to absoluteness and all evaluations of some ideas over others. This is the theological equivalent of another great ideological adversary of liberation: the so-called quest for the death of ideologies or their suicide at the altars of scientific and scholarly impartiality. (1973, p. 25)

What Arkoun's critique of the authority structures fails to recognize, is that authority does not only derive from formal institutions, but also from other systems of meaning such as academicism. Furthermore, modernity itself functions as an appendage to liberal ideology, which is not without its hegemonic interests. Leonard Binder has raised the pertinent question of whether the critique of Muslim liberals has not been a 'form of false consciousness, an abject submission to the hegemonic discourse of the dominant secular Western capitalist and imperialist societies, an oriental orientalism, or whether it was and is practical, rational and emancipatory' (1988, p. 5).

The call for 'knowledge as a sphere of authority to be accepted and respected unanimously, a knowledge independent of ideologies, able to explain their formation and master their impact' (Arkoun 1988, p. 69), does little other than further the ideological interest within which such knowledge is located and formulated. Knowledge, like any other social tool, while it can be critical, is never neutral. As Segundo has argued, 'every hermeneutic entails conscious or unconscious partisanship. It is partisan in its viewpoint even when it believes itself to be neutral and tries to act that way' (1991, p. 25).

The notion of any sphere of authority being 'respected unanimously', as advocated by Arkoun is surprising coming from a scholar whose ideas are able to find an audience precisely because of the absence of unanimity. Any form of unanimity, including intellectual unanimity, inevitably implies the formation of another orthodoxy with its implicit denial of the validity of dissent.

Arkoun's ideas imply that there can be a class of 'super readers', expert historians or linguists who will be able to access the true meaning of a text. Schussler-Fiorenza has outlined how such an approach 'falsely presupposes that the later horizon [of the reader] exists within the earlier horizon [of the author]' (1990, p. 23). Besides underplaying the temporal distance between text and interpreter, it also 'minimizes the fact that no text has been written so that philologists could read and interpret it philologically or so that historians may read it historically' (ibid.).

When one pursues 'independent knowledge' with 'exact methods' and ignores the meaning of the text for the contemporary situation and for people of faith, then one effectively places oneself and a small group of other 'objective' intellectuals outside and above the vast majority of believers for whom the text is a living document. This may be the choice which a scholar living in Antarctica can make. For those living in South Africa during the apartheid years one could not do so and retain one's integrity as a human being.

For me, a fundamental question remains: for whom and in whose interests does one pursue the hermeneutical task? That this is a political question is beyond doubt and may suggest a desire to use the text as 'pretext'. Arkoun has cogently argued that the history of qur'anic interpretative activity is precisely this. I am unconvinced that it can be otherwise or that this is intrinsically objectionable.

Understanding a Text

By way of drawing this chapter to a close and laying the basis for the next one, I want to look at the three elements intrinsic to any process of understanding a text: the text itself and the author, the interpreter and the act of interpretation.

Getting into the Mind of the Author

As I mentioned earlier, in the case of the Qur'an where God is regarded as the 'author', the question of identifying with the author in order to get to the real meaning behind the text is problematic. While it is inconceivable that Muslims would claim to get into the mind of God, it is not so far-fetched for some to claim that God has taken control of their minds. This alternative path to understanding through inspiration–intuition is not without precedent in Muslim approaches to the scripture and it enjoys considerable popularity in traditional and mystical Islamic scholarship. In this methodology piety is combined with scholarship to produce meaning. Piety is also supposed to serve as a barrier between personal opinions and the truth. Muhyi al-Din ibn 'Arabi (d. 1240), for example, suggests that God played a direct role in his understanding of the text (n.d., 1, pp. 3–4).

For others, Muhammad becomes the key agent present in producing meaning. Muhammad, it is claimed, appears to the interpreter in a vision, to clarify a difficult point or to indicate the correct interpretation. In effect, the notions of God or Muhammad getting into the mind of the interpreter or vice versa are really the same. To get to the 'true meaning' of the text, as intended by God, many Muslims would, in effect, ask: 'What did Muhammad understand by this text?' Traditional exegetical scholarship, while rejecting any ideas that an interpreter can get into the 'mind' of God, nevertheless, implicitly bases many of its arguments on the assumption that its interpretation is the meaning intended by God. (The dutiful proclamation of 'God knows better' at the conclusion of most of such works, notwithstanding.) Traditional Islamic scholarship, in dealing with qur'anic texts, effectively works along the lines of a pious form of historical positivism. Meaning, for Rahman and the traditionalist, is located within the text and can be retrieved by 'pure minds'.

We have no right to exclude the possibility of the personal usefulness of this approach, nor can one ignore the fact that mystical movements of interpretation had as much impact on popular Islamic practices in certain contexts as the *shari'ah* – if not more. However, the problems involved in consciously applying this approach to the socio-political arena or the domain of public morality in a definitive manner are far too serious for any significant consideration here. Firstly, identification with the author, the first recipient of the text or the primary audience, in whatever form (cognitive, spiritual, psychological, etc.), does not take into account the differences in the historical situations of the recipient of the text and the interpreter. The relatively common experiences of people may minimize their divergent outlooks in different historical periods, but do not in any way negate them. Secondly, the essentialist and absolutist religio-political claims – 'God has inspired me or us with the correct interpretation' – which must follow any understanding so acquired are not consistent with the quest for pluralism. The problem of conflicting claims of 'purified minds' – one person's saint is invariably another's charlatan – and consequently conflicting monopolies over absolute truths, is a serious one with little or no space in any discourse on pluralism. These problems are, of course, not peculiar to the intuition–scholarship approach. Here I only wish to underline some of the problems with any approach which cannot be subjected to rational, ethical and sociological scrutiny.

The Interpreter: A Beast of Many Burdens

I have argued that the inevitable active participation of the interpreter in producing meaning actually implies that receiving a text and extracting meaning from it do not exist on their own. Reception and interpretation, and therefore meaning, are thus always partial. Every interpreter enters the process of interpretation with some preunderstanding of the questions addressed by the text – even of its silences – and brings with him or her certain conceptions as presuppositions of his or her exegesis. Meaning, wherever else it may be located, is also in the remarkable structure of understanding itself. 'There is no innocent interpretation, no innocent interpreter, no innocent text' (Tracy 1987, p. 79).[21]

The urgent need of contemporary qur'anic scholarship is to remove preunderstanding from the much-maligned *tafsir bi'l-ra'y* (interpretation based on considered reasoning) which, in conservative discourse, has come to mean baseless and devious theological or political concoctions superimposed on the Qur'an (Shafiq 1984, pp. 22–3). Once this task is accomplished, one can proceed to examine and discuss the legitimacy, usefulness and justice of particular preunderstandings above or in contrast to others. Preunderstanding is a condition of living in history. By itself, preunderstanding has no ethical value; the ethics or absence of them, are located in an acknowledgement or denial of its presence.

The absolute and undisputed reference point for Muslims is the Qur'an and, for Sunni Muslims, the Prophet's conduct, and these remain the criteria to determine normative Islam. The unavoidable point of departure for approaching these criteria, however, is one's self and the conditions wherein that self is located. In ignoring the ambiguities of language and history and their impact on interpretation, there is no effective distinction between normative Islam and what the believer 'thinks' it to be. Both traditionalism and fundamentalism deny any personal or historical frame of reference in the first instance. While they will insist that normative Islam is 'to be judged solely by the Qur'an and the prophetic practice', they will throughout their discourse simultaneously imply 'and we have correctly understood these'.

Interpretation: No Escape from Language, History and Tradition

The past is not past, it is present. Any person who uses a language 'bears the preunderstandings, partly conscious, more often preconscious, of the history and traditions of that language' (Tracy 1987, p. 16). There is no escape from this. The meaning of words is always in process. I remember my mother telling about a friend, who in her teens, offered to take her to the cinema in his *kar,* which is old Afrikaans for both 'car' and 'cart'. With much anticipation she awaited a drive in a car and was brought back to earth by the clatter of the hooves belonging to a pair of horses. Today *kar* only means 'car'. To use any word, as Cantwell-Smith has illustrated, 'is to participate at a given point – or more strictly, at least two points – in the ongoing historical process of its meaning' (1980, p. 501). The literal meaning of any form of speech is problematic and never value free. This is especially the case with symbolic and sacred speech. Cantwell-Smith has illustrated how the 'magnificent' and always 'impressive device of language' is inescapably imprisoned within imperfection.

> What is communicated to the hearer or reader is sufficiently close to what is intended by the speaker or writer, that we do well to be awed and grateful; and yet it is in principle never exactly the same – and especially not in important or subtle or deep matters. Since the meaning for any person of any term or concept, let alone of any phrase or sentence is integrated into that person's experience and worldview, is or becomes a part of it . . . Therefore, meaning can never be exactly the same for any two persons . . . nor for any two centuries . . . nor for any two regions. (Cantwell-Smith 1980, p. 502)

'The radical plurality of our differential languages and the ambiguity of all our histories' (Tracy 1987, p. 82) are unavoidables in any attempt at understanding. The problem of language is thus not confined to the interpreter but also extends to the tradition or text being interpreted. Any act of interpretation is a participation in the linguistic–historical process, the shaping of tradition and this participation occurs within a particular time and place. Our engagement with the Qur'an also takes place within the confines of this prison; we cannot extricate ourselves from and place ourselves above language, culture and tradition. I agree with Tracy that 'every interpreter comes to the text bearing those complex histories of effects we call tradition. There is no more a possibility of escape from tradition than there is the possibility of an escape from history or language. (1987, p. 16).

Reformist thinking argues that the crisis in the world of Islam and the inability of Muslims to make a meaningful contribution to contemporary issues is due to tradition. The answer for many of these Muslim reformist scholars is to bypass tradition and 'to go back to the Qur'an'. This argument does not take into the account the fact that exegesis is not entirely independent from the text but actually belongs to its historical productivity. Exegesis is not just an interpretation but 'rather an extension of the symbol and must itself be interpreted' (Martin 1982, p. 369). How is it possible to bypass tradition and argue that historical interpretations, an intrinsic part of tradition, must be judged by the understanding gained from the Qur'an itself? Can one emerge at the one end of a vacuum without ever having entered it, with the Qur'an as a disembodied soul floating at the other end? No scripture, least of all a text simultaneously abounding with symbolism and an all-pervasive contextuality as the Qur'an evidently is, emerges from a vacuum and comes to us unencumbered by 'the plural and ambiguous history of the effects of its own production and all its former receptions' (Tracy 1987, p. 69).

Conclusion: Whose Morality? Which Justice?

In chapter 1 I detailed the unfolding of the hermeneutical crisis in South Africa. I also explained how the experience of studying the historical situation and its ethico-moral requirements occurred under specific socio-political conditions. Such study has impacted upon the way progressive Islamists in South Africa understood the ethico-moral requirements of Meccan–Medinan society and of the Qur'an's response to it.

By whose standards would 'the moral–social objectives' of the Qur'an and 'moral–social requirements of society' (Rahman's terms) be defined? The South African experience and, more specifically, the struggle, confronted many a progressive Islamist with the problem of religious pluralism and how God might address Himself to South Africa's people. I showed that the conservative pro-apartheid cleric in South Africa saw a rather different moral–social objective in the qur'anic message than the anti-apartheid Islamist; the eighteenth-century Muslim in the Cape saw a different moral–social objective in the Qur'an than that seen by the twentieth-century Muslim. The struggle for justice in South Africa that resulted in this hermeneutical crisis came about because its people were suffering under rulers with absolutist claims to 'know'. The oppression of the people of South Africa was based on this 'knowing'. It is thus not surprising that the hermeneutical responses to that situation of oppression–liberation should also involve the quest for pluralism.

How does a theology of pluralism that emerges from a liberation struggle view the traditionalist notions of absolute or universal meaning and the historical positivist's belief that access to 'true meaning' is possible? How does a hermeneutic of liberation respond to the argument that it is possible to ascertain the meaning intended by the author of a text? I have already indicated how a denial of the link between preunderstanding and interpretation is to reject the other's interpretation as eisegetical flights of imagination and accept one's own as the 'uncovering of truth'. This attitude, I have said, invariably leads to the fundamentalist assumption that there is not only a singular truth, but also a singular understanding of it, inevitably that of the speaker or writer.

Arkoun's heuristic methodology, in contrast to that of Rahman, is rooted in pluralism. He argues with impressive effect that the remarkable similarities in the theological and intellectual developments among the Abrahamic religions should be the new basis of dialogue (1987a). However, in the search for meaning, the hermeneutical quest, when we do not address the question 'For whom and in whose interest?', then pluralism simply becomes 'a passive response to more and more possibilities, none of which shall ever be practised' (Tracy 1987, p. 90). 'This is the perfect ideology for the modern bourgeois mind. Such a pluralism makes a genial confusion in which one tries to enjoy the pleasures of difference without ever committing oneself to any particular vision of resistance, liberation and hope' (ibid.).

For those who eke out an existence on the margins of society, living under the yoke of oppression and struggling with the equally oppressed Other in the hope of liberation, a pluralism of splendid and joyous intellectual neutrality is not an option. On this basis, I argue for the freedom to rethink the meanings and use of scripture in a racially divided, economically exploitative and patriarchal society and to forge hermeneutical keys that will enable us to read the text in such a way as to advance the liberation of all people.

Notes

1. Upon the assassination of 'Uthman in 656, 'Ali became the Caliph. His accession to the caliphate, though, was opposed by a number of Companions who insinuated that he was a party to his predecessor's assassination or that he was unwilling to pursue the assassins. Soon after becoming the Caliph, he marched against those who refused to pledge allegiance to him. During this expedition 'Ali moved to the plains of Siffin where 'Uthman's nephew, Mu'awiyah, had camped. Intermittent battles and skirmishes raged until June–July 657 when Mu'awiyah's forces, with copies of the Qur'an tied to their lances, demanded that the dispute be submitted to the Qur'an for arbitration.

2. Basic works for the general critical study of the Qur'an include Nöldecke (1909–38), Bell (1970), Watt (1969), al-Said (1975), Abu Zaid (1993) and Goldziher (1970). Jeffreys has done important work regarding the use of non-Arabic words in the Qur'an (1938) as well as the process of compilation and transcription (1937). Critical studies on the process of compilation and transcription have also been done by Wansbrough (1977) and Burton (1977).

3. A minority of scholars, prominent among whom is al-Shafi'i (d. 820), holds that *qur'an* is not derived but is a proper noun, 'in the same manner of the *tawrat* and the *injil*' (al-Nimr 1983, p. 6). This opinion, traced back to 'Abd Allah ibn Mas'ud, would read the word as *quran*, i.e., without a *hamzah* (Ibn Manzur n.d., 5, p. 3563).

4. Islamic scholarship has divided qur'anic revelation into two distinct chronological periods; the Meccan and Medinan. The Meccan texts focus on the three essential elements of Islamic doctrines: the unqualified and absolute unicity of God, the prophethood of Muhammad and the final accountability of people in the presence of their Sustainer. The Medinan revelations deal with issues of community-building and the resulting problems. Laws regarding socio-political relations, based on the ethico-moral injunctions revealed in the Meccan phase, were elaborated. The intellectual and political challenges presented by the new neighbours of a governing Islam, the Jews and the Christians, were dealt with, as were the problems posed by those who feigned allegiance to Islam, the hypocrites.

5. 'Ali ibn Abi Talib is reported to have seen a man in the mosque of Kufa replying to religious questions put to him by the people around him. He asked the man whether he could distinguish between the abrogating verses and the abrogated ones. When he replied in the negative, 'Ali accused the man of deceiving himself as well as others and prohibited him from speaking in the mosque again (al-Suyuti 1987, 2, pp. 20ff.).

6. The *Mu'tazilah* justified the doctrine of the createdness of the Qur'an on the basis of Qur'an 2:106. They contended that if the Qur'an could be subjected to abrogation then it could not be eternal. However, a group of them, according to al-Razi (1990, 3, p. 248), denied the theory of *naskh*.

7. Rahman explains the motivation behind this gradual prohibition as follows: 'When the Prophet was in Mecca, Muslims were a very small informal community; it was not yet a society. It appears that most of them did not drink at that time. Later, when the prominent Meccans converted to Islam around the year 614, like Hamza, the uncle of the Prophet, and 'Umar Ibn al Khattab, there were some among them who did drink. But this phenomenon did not cause any problems for the Muslims because they were not a society as yet, but only an informal community. When, however, the Muslims moved to Medina they not only became a society but a sort of informal state. Drinking at that time did develop into a problem.' (Rahman 1986b, pp. 47–8)

8. Using *naskh* as the cornerstone of their reformist methodology are Taha Mahmud (d. 1985), the executed Sudanese scholar, and the Republican Brothers. The deployment of *naskh* as the most significant element in the methodology of reinterpreting Islam has been detailed in the writings of the group's most prominent legal scholar, Abdullahi an-Na'im, in his work on civil liberties, human rights and international law (1990).

9. The earliest term employed for works of interpretation seems to have been *ma'ani* (literally, 'meanings') (ER, '*tafsir*') This is itself significant in its implicit pluralist assumptions. This term, as well as *tafsir*, was also applied to Arabic and Greek commentaries on Aristotle, as well to the explanations of lines in pre-Islamic poetry. Goldfield has demonstrated how the basic nomenclature for concepts in interpretation in Islam indicates a much longer familiarity with these terms than the few decades since Muhammad's demise in 632 (1993, p. 15).

10. Early exegetes such as al-Tabari and al-Maturidi used the terms interchangeably, as is evident from the titles of their commentaries, *Jami' al-Bayan an Ta'wil Ay al-Qur'an* and *Ta'wilat al-Qur'an*, respectively. In later editions, al-Tabari's exegesis subsequently came to be renamed *Jami' al-Bayan fi Tafsir al-Qur'an*, itself an indication of the pejorative connotations applied to the word *ta'wil*.

11. Specialist exegetes appeared after the development of various Islamic sciences and each undertook the study of the qur'anic commentary according to his specialization. Examples of these are al-Zujjaj who did exegesis from a syntactical perspective; al-Wahidi and Abu Hayyan from that of morphology; al-Zamakhshari from the angle of rhetoric and eloquence; al-Razi from a theological perspective. Scholars such as Ibn al-Arabi and Kashshani based their exegetical works on gnosis while others like Qurtubi concentrated on aspects of jurisprudence. In addition to these, a number of exegetes adopted interdisciplinary approaches. They include Isma'il al-Haqqi, Shihab al-Din Mahmud al-Baghdadi and Nizam al-Din al-Nisaburi.

12. The controversy on the createdness of the Qur'an reached feverish heights during the reign of Abu'l-'Abbas al-Ma'mun (813–833) who instituted the *mihnah*, a kind of public inquisition, in 833 (Watt 1950). Most leading officials and other prominent personalities were forced to publicly profess that the Qur'an was created and failure to do so led to persecution and even to death. With a few exceptions, most theologians submitted publicly. The most prominent among the exceptions was Ahmad ibn Hanbal (d. 855) who was flogged and imprisoned for his beliefs (Patton 1897; Madelung 1985).

13. The implication of this is that '*there is no access to the absolute* (emphasis in original) outside the phenomenal world of our historical terrestrial existence' (Arkoun 1987b, p. 8). He thus insists on 'historicity as a dimension of the truth' (ibid., p. 9); truth which is shaped by 'changing tools, concepts, definitions and postulates' (ibid.). Here he challenges all 'medieval thinking based on essences and substances' (ibid.), presumably including the notion of a 'stable scripture'. His emphasis that there is no access to the absolute seemingly, leaves the possibility of a stable and essential truth.

14. 'Discourse as an ideological articulation of realities as they are perceived and used by different competing groups' (Arkoun 1987b, p. 10), he explains, 'occurs prior to the faith' (ibid.). 'Conversely faith, after it has taken shape and roots through religious political and scientific discourse, imposes its own direction and postulates on to subsequent discourses and behaviours' (ibid.).

15. This level is expressed in the Qur'an by such expressions as *al-Lawh al-Mahfuz*' (the well-preserved tablet) (85:22) or the *Umm al-Kitab* (archetypal book) (43:4).

16. He emphasizes that defining scriptures as speech worded by God Himself does not change the linguistic and historical fact that the messages of Jesus and Muhammad are transmitted in human language and collected in an orthodox closed corpus in concrete historical conditions (Arkoun 1987b, p. 16).

17. This textual objectification, according to Arkoun, was contingent on many historical facts depending on social and political agents, not on God. Some of the 'imperfect human procedures' which determined the shape of the written word to which he refers are 'oral transmission', the use of 'imperfect graphic form . . . conflicts between clans and parties . . . and unreported readings' (1987a, p. 5).

18. Reproduced from Arkoun 1987a, p. 28.

19. 'The transcendence claimed in the traditional theological interpretation of the Book is the projection of the religious *imaginaire* back to the inaugurating age of revelation. It becomes a psychological, cultural process of transcendentalization, mythologization, sacralization and ideologization in various changing conditions. This process is included in the anthropological problematic' (Arkoun 1987a, p. 27).

20. Arkoun argues that 'critical reason engaged in the study of the societies of the Book knows the distinction between *imaginaire* and rationality; it integrates both in the same project of intelligibility without reducing one to the other on an illusionary basis. From this exercise emerges a new rationality which avoids the prejudices of the secularized positivists or the polemical model, as well as the so-called spiritual, divine or transcendental model' (1987a, p. 28).

21. Cantwell-Smith summarizes this point so eloquently that a lengthy quote bears reproduction here: 'If you yourself are a Muslim writing a commentary; or a Sufi *pir* instructing your

murid [disciple]; or are a conscientious jurisconsult deciding a tricky point of law; or are a modern Oxford-educated Muslim reflecting on contemporary life; or a twelfth-century Shirazi housewife . . . or are a left-wing leader of the slave revolt of the Zanji protesting against what seem to you the exploitation and hypocrisy of the establishment – in all such cases the correct interpretation of a particular Qur'an verse is the best possible interpretation that comes to you or that you can think up' (1980, p. 492). He goes on to say that he does not mean a cunning concoction or that the interpretation is irresponsibly contrived; on the contrary, the interpreter is constrained by the very fact of his or her esteeming this as the word of God, 'to recognize as the most cogent among all possible alternatives that interpretation' is in his or her opinion 'the closest to universal truth and to universal goodness'. 'You choose not what is the best for you', he says 'but what in your judgement is the best absolutely, cosmically' (ibid., p. 492).

3

HERMENEUTICAL KEYS

The ENGAGED INTERPRETER & the
SEARCH for LIBERATING MEANING

I am the Prophet of mercy, I am the Prophet of battle.

(*Hadith*, cited in Ibn Taymiyyah 1924, p. 8)

You cannot separate Muhammad, the prayer leader, from Muhammad, the *jihad* leader; the hand that held the *miswaak*[1] also held the sword.

(Call of Islam 1985, *Unite for Justice*, p. 1)

A Hermeneutic of Liberation

In the first chapter we saw how qur'anic texts pertaining to justice, oppression, resistance, the armed struggle and interfaith solidarity against oppression were frequently invoked by the progressive Islamists during the uprisings of the early 1980s. Standing within the struggle for justice was itself a good point from which to get a better view of the text. In other words, the location of the interpreter itself became a consciously chosen hermeneutical key.

The criteria which these engaged interpreters employed in their approaches to the Qur'an and their choice of one particular meaning over another were diffused in numerous tracts, discussion-cum-reflection circles and public speeches. These criteria and the methods used to get to them, however, were never systematically defined and justified, nor were they carefully examined in the light of Islamic theology. I now want to move on to weave the qur'anic rhetoric of liberation used during the 1980s into a more coherent theological theory and hermeneutic of religious pluralism for liberation. In doing so, I shall be focusing on the theological and political nature and implications of each of the following hermeneutical keys within the context of a society characterized by injustice, division and exploitation: *taqwa* (integrity and awareness in relation to the presence of God); *tawhid* (divine unity); *al-nas* (the people); *al-mustad'afun fi'l-ard* (the oppressed on the earth); *'adl* and *qist* (balance and justice) and *jihad* (struggle and praxis).

A Qur'anic Theology of Liberation

Speaking about liberation during the apartheid years in South Africa has made the meaning of liberation obvious enough: liberation from all forms of racism and economic exploitation. A deeper awareness of the nature of injustice, the role of socio-political structures and the importance of a truly participatory process of liberation has led to a clearer definition of a theology of liberation. A theology of liberation, for me, is one that works towards freeing religion from social, political and religious structures and ideas based on uncritical obedience and the freedom of all people from all forms of injustice and exploitation including those of race, gender, class and religion. Liberation theology tries to achieve its objectives through a process that is participatory and liberatory. By this I mean that it is formulated by, and in solidarity with, those whose socio-political liberation it seeks and whose personal liberation becomes real through their participation in this process. Furthermore, an Islamic liberation theology derives its inspiration from the Qur'an and the struggles of all the prophets. It does so by engaging the Qur'an and the examples of the prophets in a process of shared and ongoing theological reflection for ever-increasing liberative praxis.

While the idea of the Qur'an as a revolutionary text was very much in vogue in Iran as well as among those South African Muslims in sympathy with that revolution (the MYM, al-Jihad and Qibla) during this period, there is little to suggest that the specifics of the hermeneutical perspectives emerging there were studied in any depth in the Cape. Several theological revolutionary notions, such as the socio-political implications of divine unity (*tawhid*) and the option for the oppressed (*mustad'afun fi'l-ard*) widely propagated in Iran, particularly by the Mujahidin-I-Khalq, did, however, find their way into the local Islamic liberation discourse. Here they were fleshed out and painted in South African colours. The notions of an Islamic theology of liberation and its hermeneutical keys emerged from the qur'anic reflections engaged in by Islamists in the many groups where young Muslims gathered to reflect on the relevance of the Qur'an and *sunnah* (practice of the Prophet) to their lives and to the struggle against apartheid. The affinity of these Islamists to Islam was thus expressed through seeking support from the earliest forms of theological legitimation, the Qur'an and *sunnah*, rather than to post-Muhammadan legal or theological tradition. 'The Review of Faith', a manual for Call of Islam activists, states this as follows:

> Our reflections must at all times lead to a deepening of our under-standing of faith. [These reflections] are one dimension of our jour-neying to Allah. We . . . need to develop the closest possible relation-ship with His message. He speaks to us through the Qur'an and the *Sunnah* of all the Prophets . . . If we are going to test our actions in the light of the Qur'an and *Sunnah*, then we must also have the determination to approach these two sources directly. (Call of Islam 1985, The Review of Faith, p. 53)

One of the consequences of resorting to the text while bypassing the cler-ics was that most of the qur'anic concepts used during this period were free from the legal or 'orthodox' meanings which tradition had accorded them. Within the South African context, these concepts were never employed systematically. One needs to consider whether they were prior-itized in any particular order, whether they come from the text or the context, and how authentic they are as hermeneutical concepts.

Any discussion of the theological and legal validity of these concepts would have meant taking on the traditional clerics in debates in areas with which the Islamists were largely unfamiliar. The clerics had, further-more, generally been on the sidelines during this period. The Islamists did not perceive any need to resort to traditional theology and it was widely felt that the categories developed by traditional scholarship, such as the abode of enmity (*dar al-harb*), the abode of Islam (*dar al-Islam*), etc., were irrelevant to, or insufficiently developed for, the context of both modernity and liberation. Furthermore, those most active in the struggle were simply not interested in scholarly analysis of the categories they invoked. Often this was because of the intensity and immediacy of the demands of the struggle. A more significant reason, however, was the notion that praxis was a legitimate basis for theory. Addressing the lead-ership of the MYM, Mawlana Ebrahim Moosa, their then national direc-tor, emphasized the relationship between liberating praxis and theory as follows:

> Liberating praxis, as opposed to practice, should be our major watchword. By praxis we mean doing and reflecting. The *halaqat* should be active circles of knowledge and practice (praxis) which

integrate organic intellectuals (*'alim/ 'ulama'*) with activists (*mujahids*) to fulfil the description of the early Muslim community: Gallant warriors by day and monks by night. (Moosa 1987a, p. 4)

The question of the order or priorities of these hermeneutical concepts or keys is a significant one. For the Islamist, while they may be prioritized theoretically, all of them are equally significant practically. An unwillingness to prioritize them is based on the idea that the theological cannot be separated from the ideological, the spiritual from the mundane, nor the text from its context. The way these keys are intertwined, i.e., their dialectical nature, is also seen in the question of the origins of these hermeneutical keys. During the 1980s, they were certainly presented as coming from the text. Indeed, the Islamists who used liberation rhetoric from a fundamentalist perspective will probably insist that their theological insights have been worked out prior to and outside the historical process. In fact, they may even deny that they have been 'worked out' and insist that they are an eternal given for anyone who looks into the text. The reality, though, is more complex. These keys emerged from an ongoing engagement between the South African struggle and theological reflections in which the text undoubtedly played a significant role. It is more appropriate to say that truths experienced in the struggle were affirmed and challenged by these theological reflections and the text.

Dogma may precede praxis, but not in the case of a theology that is committed to liberation. Theology, for the marginalized, is the product of reflection which follows on praxis for liberation. The qur'anic statement 'and to those who struggle in Our way, to them We shall show Our ways' (29:29) affirms this view of 'doing' theology. The history of all forms of theological thought in Islam, as elsewhere, confirms what Friedrich Hegel (d. 1831) said about philosophy: 'it rises only at sundown' (cited in Gutierrez 1973, p. 11).

How Genuine is this Product?

Questions pertaining to authenticity are probably the most significant ones here. How authentic was this idea of Islam now being advertised on the market? What is authenticity? Who determines it? What should be authentic for whom? All theological categories, no matter how authentic an air has been afforded them by the passing of time, are always the product of ideology, history and seemingly apolitical reflections. Studies in the emergence and development of supposedly pure theological concepts such as the eternity of the Qur'an, *bila kayf*,[2] *qada* and *qadr*,[3] all conclusively prove that, while the text was the weapon with which the battles to affirm or deny them were fought, they were inevitably shaped by history (Madelung 1985; Watt 1991; Bell 1970). To the extent that history is the story of the victors, these concepts are equally those of the victors. This is not to comment on their correctness or incorrectness. I rather wish to emphasize that the process that led to the elaboration of doctrines and that fixed their final status and form was as human as that which gave rise to concepts such as the preferential option for the marginalized.

Looking at life from the underside of history, liberation theology is in some ways an attempt to retrieve authenticity from the victors, to free it from the notion that it is irrevocably tied to the powerful. It also questions the notion of a final authenticity that can be wrapped up neatly in a creed, but argues that liberating praxis leads to greater authenticity. To the marginalized – the essential subjects of the kind of theology that emerged in South Africa during the 1980s – the question of authenticity was never a crisis or even a focal point. Given that the focus of liberation theology is the 'non-subjects' of history, the marginalized, they were the determiners of authenticity based on their interests.

The Keys to Understanding

In reflecting on the hermeneutical keys that have emerged from the South African engagement with the struggle for liberation and with the Qur'an, I shall try to show how a qur'anic hermeneutic of liberation would work, with its continuous shift between text and context and the ongoing reflections on their implications for each other. I shall also underline the significance of these keys as indispensable tools for understanding the Qur'an in a society characterized by oppression and an interreligious struggle for justice and freedom.

The first two keys, *taqwa* (an awareness of the presence of God) and *tawhid* (the unity of God), are aimed at developing the moral and 'doctrinal' criteria with which to examine the other keys and the 'theological glasses' with which to read the Qur'an in general and, more specifically, the texts dealing with the religious Other. Despite the seemingly theological nature of these two keys, they, like all theological precepts, are also formulated and understood within a specific historico-political context, and are presented as such. The second two keys, *al-nas* (the people) and the marginalized (*al-mustad'afun fi'l-ard*) define the location of our interpretative activity. While all contexts wherein the interpreter is located must necessarily bear upon the outcome of her or his interpretation, interpreters also have the freedom to position themselves differently in relation to any situation in order to arrive at a specific kind of interpretation. The last two, justice (*'adl* and *qist*) and struggle (*jihad*), reflect the method and the ethos that produce and shape a contextual understanding of the word of God in an unjust society.

Taqwa: Protecting the Interpreter from Him or Herself

Taqwa, from the Arabic root *w-q-y*, literally means 'to ward off', 'to guard against', 'to heed' or 'to preserve' (Lane 1980, *'t-q-y'*)[4] and has been used in all these senses in the Qur'an (e.g., 3:25, 120).[5] In the qur'anic sense it may be defined as 'heeding the voice of one's conscience in the awareness that one is accountable to God'. Jafri has shown how, among all the ethical terms adopted by the Qur'an, 'the most widely applicable and most inclusive of all is the term *taqwa*' (1980, p. 127). Its comprehensive sense of embracing both responsibility to God and to humankind is evident from the following texts:

> Thus as for him [or her] who gives to others and is conscious of God [*ittaqa*] and believes in the ultimate good, We shall facilitate his [or her] path towards ease; as for him [or her] who is stingy and thinks himself [or herself] self-sufficient and calls ultimate good a lie, we facilitate for him [or her] the way to distress. (Qur'an 92:4–10)

> O humankind! We have created you all out of a male and a female, and have made you into nations and tribes so that you might come to know one another. Verily the noblest of you in the sight of God is the one who is most deeply conscious of God [*atqakum*]. (Qur'an 49:13)

The Qur'an links *taqwa* to belief in God (10:63; 27:53; 41:18) and regards its attainment as one of the objectives of serving God (2:21). Those who prefer the short-term advantages of this world are often contrasted with those who have *taqwa* (4:77; 6:32; 12:57). What is significant, though, is the way the Qur'an links *taqwa* to social interaction and concern for others, such as sharing (92:5; 7:152–3), fulfilling covenants (3:76; 7:52) and, especially, kindness (3:172; 4:126; 5:93; 16:127).

The Qur'an emphasizes the need for a community and individuals deeply imbued with *taqwa* who will carry on the prophets' task of transformation and liberation (3:102–5, 125; 8:29). According to the Qur'an, a commitment to God's people is an inseparable part of a commitment to God. However, this does not imply that the two dimensions of this commitment are identical; a *muslim* is, in the first instance, someone who has submitted to God in both a social and personal sense. *Taqwa*, as the South African Islamists have argued, is the struggle to remain true to this commitment in all its dimensions.

In a message on the occasion of the Festival of Charity (*'Id al-Fitr*) at the end of *Ramadan*, the Call said:

> Our involvement [in the liberation struggle] after Ramadan will show whether we have learnt *taqwa*, whether we really became aware of the plight of the oppressed. The hallmark of a Muslim who has truly fasted is his preparedness to throw in his lot with the rest of the oppressed in the struggle for the liberation of all the people in this country. (Call of Islam 1985, *Eid Mubarak*, p. 1)

The progressive Islamists, however, also saw the need to protect themselves, to exercise *taqwa*, with regard to the many challenges thrown up by a struggle where the main concerns were often the immediate and the mundane. How to remain true to one's self and one's commitment to God was an ongoing and deep concern. The notion of *taqwa*, arguably, represented the most formidable challenge to the progressive Islamist who sought to actualize his or her Islam in contemporary terms. Several internal documents of the Call and the MYM testify to the serious grappling with the question of *taqwa* in the midst of a socio-economic struggle (MYM 1978, 1983; Call of Islam 1987). *Taqwa* was also seen as the key to understanding the Qur'an: '*Taqwa*', said Ebrahim Rasool, then national secretary of the Call, 'is the basic pre-requisite for understanding and reading the Qur'an and is the protective measurement against the use of the Qur'an and the random appropriation of texts for legitimating ideology which is alien to the Islamic world view' (Rasool 1987).

In its first self-description, the Qur'an refers to itself as 'a guidance for those who are on the path of *taqwa*' (2:2). Not only is *taqwa* presented here as the first hermeneutical key, but also as a quality towards which believers have to aspire, outside and beyond the immediate task of interpretation. There is an insistence too on a relationship between discovering truth and living it. The acceptance of *taqwa* as a hermeneutical key has significant implications for both the engaged interpreter and the act of interpretation.

The Qur'an often presents conjecture and personal whim as the two elements which distort its meaning. These are frequently contrasted with revelation (10:36; 53:3); guidance (2:120; 6:56, 116; 26:50; 50:3); understanding and knowledge (2:78, 145; 4:157; 45:17, 23, 53:27); and truth (5:47; 10:36), all of which are central elements in the hermeneutical task. (Traditional theology has regularly accused theological or ideological adversaries of *zann* and *hawa* [baseless speculation and personal fancy] in order to dismiss their exegetical opinions. These accusations are invariably arbitrary and usually mask the ideological predilections of traditional theology.) A qur'anic hermeneutic of liberation, with *taqwa* as a key, ensures that interpretation remains free from both theological obscurantism and political reaction, as well as from the purely subjective speculation of individuals, even though they may be from the ranks of the oppressed and the marginalized.

The second significant consequence of *taqwa* as a hermeneutical key is that it facilitates an aesthetic and spiritual balance in the life of the engaged interpreter. A hermeneutic of liberation is forged in the midst of a socio-political struggle, a struggle which often confines its perspective to the immediate and the politically expedient. *Taqwa* forces the engaged interpreter to embark on a process of introspection, a process for which there is often neither the time nor the inclination. In South Africa, as elsewhere, activists stumbled from crisis to crisis, and the obvious way of responding was with the immediate and the concrete in mind. The logical consequence of this was that immediate political exigencies dominated qur'anic interpretation entirely and the struggle was deprived of the more profound and universal sense of history and broader vision that a comprehensive reading of a scripture such as the Qur'an offers.

A third consequence is that it commits the engaged interpreter to a dialectical process of personal and socio-political transformation. The guidance the Qur'an claims to offer is an active guidance to those who are not mere observers or 'objective' students but who have entrusted themselves to it for such guidance. This 'engaging the Qur'an' in the process of revolutionary struggle also means an engagement of the self with it. This, in turn, ensures a balance between active participation in social and self-transformation. 'Change, according to the Qur'an', says a Call document, 'is a dialectical process of simultaneous conversion of hearts and [socio-economic] structures' (Call of Islam 1988, p. 13).

The search for a hermeneutic of liberation assumes that there is a group of people who are serious about the reconstruction of society alongside principles of justice, freedom, honesty and integrity. Only those struggling to concretize these qualities in their own lives during a liberation struggle aimed at constructing a new society, can be entrusted with the moral and ethical responsibility of managing such a society. In addition to the significance of *taqwa* for the activist as interpreter, *taqwa* has implications for him or her as an activist and may prevent the activist from becoming a mirror image of the very tyrant being fought. There is some truth in the perception of many people that 'politics is a dirty game'. Some of the finest individuals participating in the struggle against apartheid have been motivated by an intense and noble hatred for the suffering resulting from it. It is, however, not infrequently that one observes the same individuals being transformed into cold and calculating Machiavellian political entities who, as a matter of course, violate democracy and common human decency.

While *taqwa* is also an essential source of support for the engaged interpreter struggling to understand the Qur'an, there is still no guarantee of absolute meaning. However, *taqwa* ensures that the Muslim walks in the grace of God, a grace that allows him or her to remain on the path even while struggling to find it. 'And whosoever observes *taqwa* in respect of God, for him [or her] He will create an opening' (Qur'an 15:2). Furthermore, in the face of a discredited and quietist clergy on the one hand, and a morally bankrupt tyranny on the other, *taqwa* serves as a shield against revolutionary deception and activist arrogance. We have witnessed the way in which revolutionary regimes in Eastern Europe, China, Zimbabwe, Iran and elsewhere have come to power on the basis of a commitment to freedom, equality and justice, and how these rights were subsequently only available to the ruling clique and their supporters. *Taqwa* is the antithesis of the self-deception that leads individuals, movements and governments to believe that they are still for people when the reverse has, in fact, become the case. From my reading of the Qur'an, it would seem as if *taqwa*, rather than 'objective scholarship', is the most significant hermeneutical key to minimize the extent to which the text can be manipulated for narrow personal or ideological advantage.

Tawhid: An Undivided God for an Undivided Humanity

From the root *w-h-d*, *tawhid* means 'to be alone', 'one', 'an integrated unity'. Although this form of the word does not appear in the Qur'an, *tawhid* has come to be synonymous with the unity of God. Belief in *tawhid*, 'faith in God, the Solitary without a partner, the Embodiment of Unity, the One whose Unity is unceasing and with whom there is none' (Ibn Manzur, 6, p. 4761), is the basis of the qur'anic worldview: 'Say: He is the One God. God, the Eternal, The Uncaused Cause of all Being. He Begets not, and neither is He begotten. And there is nothing that could be compared with Him' (112:1–4).

There are numerous other verses in the Qur'an which directly or indirectly deal with the unity of God and *tawhid* has correctly been described as 'the foundation, the centre and the end of the entire [Islamic] tradition' (Royster 1987, p. 28). Islam's comprehensiveness or holism is rooted in the principle of *tawhid*. The conviction that *tawhid* is at the heart of a comprehensive socio-political worldview, although not entirely novel, has grown enormously in the last few decades, particularly in some of the ideological currents in Iran that led to the 1979 revolution.[6] Foremost among those who advocated *tawhid* as a worldview aimed at realizing the unity of God in human relations and socio-economic systems was 'Ali Shari'ati (1933–77) and the Mujahidin-I-Khalq of Iran. The following quote from Shari'ati gives an idea of the revolutionary appreciation of *tawhid*:

> In our Islam, *tawhid* is a world view, living and meaningful, opposed to the avaricious tendency for hoarding and aims for eradicating the disease of money worship. It aims to efface the stigma of exploitation, consumerism, and aristocracy . . . Whenever the spirit of *tawhid* revives and its historical role is comprehended by a people, it re-embarks on its [uncompleted] mission for consciousness, justice, people's liberation and their development and growth. (Cited in Irfani 1983, pp. 36–7)

The notion of *tawhid* as a way of looking at life was widely used by the engaged interpreters in South Africa, both against the traditional separation between religion and politics and against apartheid as an ideology. During this period, *tawhid* was increasingly viewed as both an ideological source and a sacred frame of reference. Concepts such a '*tawhidi* society' and 'the sociological implications of *tawhid*' were often referred to. The following are a few examples of the way in which the term was used in South Africa'. A Qibla pamphlet declared the aim of the Islamic movement to be the establishment of a system in South Africa which 'is compatible with the logic of *tawhid*' (Qibla n.d., *Neither Oppressed, Nor Oppressor Be!*, p. 1). 'Muslims are Muslims', stated *Worldview*, the newsletter of the MSA, 'because of their belief in the *tawhid* of God – a *tawhid* which goes beyond mere verbal acknowledgements and which necessarily demands that Muslims act in the face of injustice . . . This *tawhid*, which exhorts us to fight in Allah's way, must fully consume our consciousness on this road of toil and struggle [for liberation]'. (*Worldview* 1984, p. 6).

Muhammad Amra, then leader of the MYM, spelt out his understanding of the 'process of *tawhid*' in a message on the occasion of the *'Id al-Fitr* celebrations:

He [Muhammad] spent 13 years in Makkah teaching . . . *tawhid* [to]
the early Muslims. He organized individual Muslims into a group
and after the *hijrah* . . . he organized them into . . . an *ummah*. He
then extended the *tawhid* from the individual and the group to the
state. This is the most important mission of our beloved *Nabi*
Muhammad (SAW); to destroy all false gods, [and] establish a
tawhidi society on the earth. (1986, p. 14)

Linking orthodoxy to a peculiarly South African orthopraxis, the Call, in
an appeal to boycott the sanction-busting New Zealand rugby tour in
1988, declared that. '*Tawhid* implies that . . . he is not a Muslim who
goes to mosque on a Friday and to racial sport[7] on a Saturday . . . He is
not a Muslim who buys his plane ticket for *Hajj* and his season ticket for
racial sport' (Call of Islam 1985, *All Blacks Out!!!*, p. 1).

There were diverse opinions about the nature and vision of a *tawhidi*
society and little attempt was made to spell out its detailed implications
for South Africa or how it related to *tawhid* as belief. What is clear,
though, is that in addition to its affirmation as theological dogma, *tawhid*
was, and still is, widely seen as having two specific applications in the
South African context. At an existential level, it means the rejection of
the dualistic conception of human existence whereby a distinction is
made between the secular and the spiritual, the sacred and the profane.
Religion thus becomes a legitimate, even necessary, means with which to
alleviate political injustice. At a socio-political level, *tawhid* is opposed to a
society which sets up race as an alternative object of veneration and
divides people along the lines of ethnicity. Such division is regarded as
tantamount to *shirk* (associating others with God), the antithesis of *tawhid*.

Apartheid was denounced as 'openly reject[ing] the *tawhid* nature of
mankind as told to us in the Qur'an: "mankind is a single nation" (Call
of Islam 1985, *Interfering with the Sanctity of Islam*, p. 2). It was viewed as
a form of *shirk* because, in terms of social outlook and practice, it consciously divided people along ethnic lines, thereby denying the unity of
humankind, which is a reflection of *tawhid*. It furthermore set up race as
an alternative to divinity and as a form of *shirk*; apartheid was described
as 'the path of division, the path of *shirk*' (Call of Islam 1985, *Muslims
Against the Emergency*, p. 1).

In contrast to the divisive nature and *herenvolkism* of apartheid,
'apartheid as associationism (*shirk*)', Islamists offered the view of *tawhid*
as divine holism with socio-economic implications. The qur'anic text
'God's nature upon which He created humankind' (30:30) thus became
an exhortation to create a non-racial and unitary society in opposition to

the racial divisions of apartheid. In relating *tawhid*, the most important principle of Islamic belief, to the quest for an undivided society, Islamists touched deep chords in the aspirations of the South African masses.[8]

A statement made by three ANC cadres just prior to their being sentenced to death expands on this dream of a unitary South Africa built on the ashes of apartheid: 'The new South Africa must reflect our oneness, breaking down the destructive idea and practices of defining our people by race, colour or ethnic group' (*Upfront* 1989, p. 21) Another ANC cadre, Ashraf Karriem, explaining in court why he had embarked on the path of armed struggle, said 'Islam sees South Africa as oppressive and exploitative and believes in the oneness of God and the oneness of people' (*The Argus*, 10 November 1988, p. 1).

Tawhid, like *taqwa*, is for the engaged interpreter both a necessary component of preunderstanding as well as a principle of interpretation. In an unpublished speech, Rasool exemplified its first role as follows:

> Belief in *tawhid* with all its implications must have absolute hegemony in our consciousness and, until this has happened, we cannot convincingly say that we fully realize the meaning of 'Say indeed, God's guidance is the true guidance' [Qur'an 2:120]. Once belief in the *tawhid* of God, with its implications, is embedded in our consciousness, and we accept Allah's guidance as the true guidance, we have [acquired] Islamic subjectivity. (1983)

The Qur'an deals with all dimensions of existence as an extension of an interconnected reality. God's word, reflecting His personality, contains the highest degree of holism and comprehensiveness. Consequently, the qur'anic moral philosophy covers all dimensions of human activity. Even the idea that the Qur'an deals with spirituality and politics or morality and economics does not adequately reflect the comprehensiveness of the Qur'an, for this implies that these are distinct from each other. It rather views all of these as integrated aspects of existence.

Viewing *tawhid* as a hermeneutical principle means that the different approaches to the Qur'an – philosophical, spiritual, juristic or political – must be regarded as components of a single tapestry. All of these are required to express the fullness of its message, for no single approach can adequately express it. A number of Call and MYM internal documents insist that each of these approaches, particularly the political one, be mindful of the principle of *tawhid* lest the Qur'an becomes a mere tool to argue for a specific view entirely divorced from its basic ethos (MYM 1978, pp. 2–4; 1987, pp. 3–4; Call of Islam 1988, p. 4).

An approach to the Qur'an based on *tawhid* does not imply that all its dimensions ought to receive equal public or private attention or expression all the time. The Qur'an is, after all, not understood in a vacuum. 'The comprehensive nature of Islam', says the MYM, 'begs total leadership, but necessitates heightened political leadership especially in South Africa' (MYM 1983, p. 6). The emphasis on the horizontal or so-called this-worldly dimensions of the Qur'an as a 'spiritual requirement of a community steeped in ritualism' (Rasool 1987, p. 3) was drawn from texts such as Qur'an 107.

> Have you observed the one who belies *al-din*?
>
> That is the one who is unkind to the orphan,
> and urges not the feeding of the needy.
>
> So, woe to the praying ones,
> who are unmindful of their prayer,
>
> They do good to be seen,
> and refrain from acts of kindnesses.

Engaged interpreters, such as Rasool, argued that 'a narrow view of formal worship deprives a community of spiritual life and an emphasis on the struggle of the oppressed is thus needed to restore life to its worship' (ibid., p. 3).

In constructing a qur'anic hermeneutic of liberation, *tawhid* would demand rejecting a discourse based on *shirk*, i.e., one of dualism whereby theology is pursued separately from social analysis. To discover the theological element in a particular socio-economic or historical situation is to imply an understanding of the latter. Such understanding will not come from avoiding the so-called this-worldly, nor will that assist in bringing to light the theological element in every human endeavour. The Islamic ideal is integrated entities committed to one God and to holism.

The People('s Understanding) Shall Govern!

Nas, from the root *n-w-s* or *'-n-s*, refers to 'the people' as a social collective and is usually employed as such in the Qur'an (e.g., 114:5–6; 72:6). The Qur'an places humankind in a 'world of *tawhid* where God, people and nature display a meaningful and purposeful harmony' (Shari'ati 1980, p. 86). The divine trust was placed exclusively in humankind's hands (33:72), thereby lifting humankind beyond matter to the status of guardians of earthly life. The centrality of humankind is reflected in

God's choice of them as His vicegerent on the earth, and by the blowing of God's spirit into them at the time of their creation (15:29; 32:9; 38:72).

The Qur'an says that God chose humankind for His vicegerency on the earth and designated humankind as the earthly carrier of His responsibilities: 'Lo I am to create a vicegerent on the earth', God announced (2:30). To the protests of the angels that humankind would 'wreak corruption and shed blood therein while we offer Thy limitless glory, and praise Thee, and hallow Thy name.' (ibid.), God responded that He knew what they did not know (2:31). Thus distinguished, humankind becomes the carrier of 'a great trust' (33:72) and the 'recipient of enormous power' (4:32–3; 16:12–15). All the angels were commanded to bow down in front of Adam as the personification of humankind (2:34), despite the fact that they were created from light with no leanings towards evil while humankind was created from 'darkened mud' (55:14).[9]

According to the Qur'an, the spirit of God covers all of humankind and gives them a permanent sanctity (e.g., 15:29; 17:22, 70, 21:91). Despite the regular reminders of the inevitable return to God, the spiritualizing of human existence, which regards earthly life as incidental, is unfounded in the qur'anic view of humankind. The human body, being a carrier of a person's inner core and of the spirit of God, is viewed as sacred, and physical concerns are, therefore, not incidental to the Qur'an.

Throughout the Qur'an, God's gentle sustainership over humankind is evident on the one hand (2:243; 10:60; 12:38; 13:6) and an intense identification with His servants on the other. God refers to humankind as His who are always in a state of journeying to Him (23:60), and describes Himself as 'Lord of the people' (114:1). On several occasions, the Qur'an identifies the interests of humankind with those of God[10] and financial assistance to people is regarded as a loan to, or an investment, with God.[11] Humankind, all of them, are described in a *hadith* as 'the family of God' (al-Albani 1979, 1, p. 189).[12]

The 1980s saw the emergence of the notion of 'the people' as a significant concept of resistance in the popular imagination. 'The people' as a socio-political category was presented as the revolutionary alternative to the apartheid state, its institutions and its values. The emergence of the University of the Western Cape as a 'people's university', the growth of 'people's courts', the search for 'people's history', and the development of 'people's theatre', all during the 1980s, were but some of the manifestations of this concept. All of these were aimed at bringing about a greater awareness of, and involvement in, the struggle against apartheid. They were, furthermore, intended to build viable alternatives to the structures and institutions of apartheid and to infuse people with the sense of self-esteem that comes from assuming personal and political responsibility for one's own life. These were all elaborations of the growing call that 'the people shall govern', a phrase from the Freedom Charter, the principal document of the ANC.

As I showed in chapter 1, the idea of the elevation of 'the people' as sovereign and a standard of legitimacy met with considerable Muslim ideological resistance.[13] An inability to recognize various and distinct kinds of sovereignty has confused many committed Muslims who believe in an elusive sovereignty that resides in a solitary proprietor, God. Yet, God clearly does not exercise sovereignty in a political sense. The logical outcome of confusing the sovereignty of God with that of temporal political sovereignty has been that people assume sovereignty in God's name. This simply has to lead to tyranny in His name.[14] The call of the people of South Africa, that power and sovereignty belonged to them, was an affirmation of a basic political right which had been denied to them. It was a call to free the rulers of temporal coercive political power and to enable the people to determine their own political destiny. The notion of popular sovereignty was located in the unjust control of political sovereignty and was entirely unrelated to the sovereignty of God. The vast majority of South Africans had been walked over since the arrival of the colonists in 1652. Nothing of the dignity and honour promised by God, or the manifestations of His spirit blown into humankind, had been allowed to surface during more than three centuries of relentless and ruthless oppression and economic exploitation. In opposition to a history of subjugation, the cry that emerged from the oppressed was that 'the people shall govern'.

Given the stewardship of humankind on the earth and God's overwhelming concern for them, two hermeneutical implications follow. First, it becomes essential that the Qur'an be interpreted in a manner which gives particular support to the interest of people as a whole or which favours the interests of the majority among them, rather than that of a small minority.[15] Second, interpretation must be shaped by the experience and aspirations of humankind as distinct from, and often opposed to, that of a privileged minority among them.

The notion of humankind as a hermeneutical key poses two theological problems which require a considered response; the first problem relates to the value of people as a measurement of truth and the second relates to the question of authenticity.

First, if one accepts the understanding and role of humankind as outlined above, then does it follow that the interest of God is identical with that of humankind? If so, is this not a way of elevating the *humanum,* the truly human, as criteria of truth, even the criterion of truth, a criterion whereby Islam itself is to be judged? Humankind as a hermeneutical key is located and affirmed within the framework of *tawhid* and grounded in the absolute. Without people using language, there is no concept of God to speak of, no divine intervention in history, and for the Muslim, without revelation there is no real meaning of humankind as *humanum.* Thus, one may argue that while the *humanum* is a criterion of truth, it is not an autonomous *humanum* as an absolute criterion that is being advocated, but one drawing its sustenance from *tawhid.* Furthermore, humankind is one hermeneutical principle among others and this serves to balance its role in the overall interpretative process.

Second, a legitimate concern of all those committed to the sacredness of the text is what may be described as 'hermeneutical promiscuity', where anyone is allowed to get into bed with the text. When a particular group whose legitimacy has been traditionally established and upheld is no longer in control of interpretation, what guarantees does one have that the sacredness of the text will not give way to an exegetical free-for-all where every text is stripped entirely of its religious legitimacy?

From the outset, it is important to acknowledge that the very idea of qur'anic hermeneutics challenges traditional concepts of the sacredness of the text. Irrespective of the piety, awe and reverence with which the text has been approached by traditional scholarship, the text has always been something about which scholars have differed. Furthermore, in a context of injustice, if concepts such as the sacredness or theological legitimacy of a text are not related to the struggle for justice, then these concepts are themselves little more than additional weapons in the ideological arsenal of injustice. As for the problem of 'hermeneutical promiscuity', one can argue that this task is embarked upon by Muslims who have chosen to be committed to the text. Their interpretation is not the wild speculation of individuals but a goal-oriented communal search for meaning. The goals of this interpreting community come from the depths of their humanity and are affirmed in the text beyond any doubt.

I have outlined the importance of humankind and the significance of their interests and experiences as factors in shaping a qur'anic hermeneutic. The Qur'an, however, singles out a particular section of humankind, the marginalized, and makes a conscious and deliberate option for them against neutrality and objectivity, on the one hand, and the powerful and oppressors, on the other.

From the Vantage Point of the Disempowered and Marginalized

From the root *d-'-f*, *mustad'af* refers to someone who is oppressed or deemed weak and of no consequence and is treated in an arrogant fashion. The *mustad'afun* are thus those people of 'inferior' social status who are vulnerable, marginalized or oppressed in the socio-economic sense. The Qur'an also uses other terms to describe the lower and impoverished classes of society, such as *aradhil* (marginalized) (11:27; 26:70: 22:5), the *fuqara'* (poor) (2:271; 9:60) and the *masakin* (indigent) (2:83, 177; 4:8). The major difference in the term *mustad'afun* is that someone else is responsible for that condition. One can only be *mustad'af* as a consequence of the behaviour or policies of the arrogant and powerful.

The Qur'an deals with the *mustad'afun* in three categories: Muslim, *kafir* and those comprising both groups. Qur'an 4:75 exhorts the Meccan community of Muslims to 'fight in the way of God and of those *mustad'afun* men, women, and children, whose cry is "Our Lord! Rescue us from this town whose people are oppressors"'. Qur'an 7:150 uses the term with reference to Aaron, the brother of Moses, who complained that the Israelites had weakened or marginalized him. Qur'an 34:31-3 deals with the *mustad'afun* as the rejecting and ingrate Other and distinguishes between the 'wrongdoers' who were oppressed on the one hand, and the arrogant and powerful (*mustakbirun*), on the other.

> Those who had been marginalized will say unto those who had gloried in their arrogance 'Had it not been for you we would certainly have been believers!'
>
> [And] those who were wont to glory in their arrogance will say unto those who had been marginalized: 'Why – did we keep you [forcibly] from following the right path after it had become obvious to you? Nay it was but you [yourselves] who were guilty!'
>
> But those who had been marginalized will say unto those who gloried in their arrogance: 'Nay, [what kept us away was your] devising of false arguments night and day against God's messages – as you did when you persuaded us to blaspheme against God and to claim that there are powers that could rival Him! (34: 31-3)

The contrast between the *mustad'afun* and the *mustakbirun* in this text occurs in other parts of the Qur'an as well. Unlike this text, which describes them as hurling accusations at each other, elsewhere the Qur'an makes a clear choice for the *mustad'afun* against the *mustakbirun* even though the former may not be Muslim (7:136-7; 28:5).

And so We inflicted Our retribution on them, and caused them to drown in the sea, because they had given a lie to Our messages and had been heedless of them.

Whereas unto the people who had been deemed utterly low, we gave as their heritage the eastern and western parts of the land We had blessed (7:136–7)

In the chapter of the Qur'an called *al-Qasas* (The Story) a preferential option for the *mustad'afun* is made in unambiguous terms, despite their rejection of God. This preferential option for the oppressed is reflected in the particularized identification of God Himself with the oppressed, the lifestyles and methodology of all the Abrahamic prophets, the qur'anic denunciation of the powerful and the accumulation of wealth, and the Qur'an's message of liberation to women and slaves. Furthermore, a number of verses link faith and religion with a humanism and a sense of socio-economic justice. A denial of these is linked with a rejection of justice, compassion and sharing (107:1–3, 104; 22:45).

According to the Qur'an, virtually all the prophets, including Muhammad, came from peasant or working-class backgrounds and the option for the marginalized seems to be implicit in their very origins. All the Abrahamic prophets mentioned in the Qur'an had their origins among the peasants and were generally shepherds in their formative years. The singular exception, Moses, was destined to sojourn in the desert of Madyan where he was employed as a shepherd for eight or ten years (28:27). One may describe this as a process of 'deschooling' in the ways of the powerful, in anticipation of his mission as a prophet of God and a liberator of his people.

Opposition invariably came from the ruling and dominant classes, whom the Qur'an describes as the *mala'* (rulers or aristocracy) (11:27, 38; 23:24, 33; 26:34), *mutrafun* (ostentatious) (34:34; 43:23), and the *mustakbirun* (arrogant) (16:22; 23:67; 31:7). Support for the prophets was usually forthcoming from the *aradhil* (lower classes), the *fuqara* (poor) and the *masakin* (indigent). Al-Tabari describes Muhammad's followers as 'the weak, the destitute, young men and women. However, of the elderly and socially distinguished none [initially] followed him' (1879, 3, p. 1563). In fact, the disdain of the aristocracy for social intercourse with slaves, serfs and workers was a significant factor blocking their own entry into Islam. In Muhammad's latter years in Mecca, the aristocracy indicated their willingness to enter Islam if he got rid of the 'riff-raff' surrounding him. The Qur'an condemned such offers and warned Muhammad against considering them (8:28, cf. 6:52–4).

There are other qur'anic examples of this tension between the powerless and the powerful. Moses entering the court of Pharaoh in his shepherd's garb; Jesus emerges as a powerful advocate of the poor struggling against the entrenched Jewish priesthood and the merchants who had allied themselves to the Roman conquerors and Hud remonstrates with those 'who build a landmark on every elevated place to amuse themselves and fine buildings in the hope of living therein forever' (Qur'an 26:128). Salih shatters the hopes of the rich and the corrupt by his refusal to be co-opted into their value system (1:62); Joseph resists the sexual harassment of the powerful and wealthy Zulaikhah and suffers the consequences of it (12:23–30) and Shu'aib struggles against the merchants for economic justice (11:89). The choice of prophets from particular social origins and the appeal which their message had, and continues to have, for the marginalized and the oppressed shows the revolutionary content of their messages, which threaten to destroy socio-economic systems based on exploitation or belief systems based on *shirk* and superstition.

The insurrectionary and preferential option for the *mustad'afun* is particularly evident from the way of life of Muhammad and his early followers in Mecca. He was instructed by the Qur'an to remain committed to the marginalized despite the short-term financial and economic advantages for Islam which would have followed the subsequent entry into Islam of the wealthy and the powerful had he abandoned them (80:5–10). This would have meant a reversion to pre-Muhammadan monotheism, which did not challenge the socio-economic practices of Quraysh in any way. This identification with the marginalized was also a personal choice of the Prophet, as is evident from his prayer to 'continue living among the poor, to die among the poor and to be raised among the poor' (Ibn Maja 1979, p. 84). His wife, 'A'ishah, described his character as a 'living reflection of the Qur'an' (Ibn Hanbal 1978, 2, p. 188). This is significant and is equally applicable to the option that he exercised for the *mustad'afun.* Muhammad's personal way of life and path also reflects the qur'anic bias. It was the result of a particular choice that he had made for himself when wealth was available. He washed his own clothing, patched it, repaired his sandals, served himself, gave fodder to his camel, ate with his servant, kneaded dough with him, and carried his own goods to the market (Ibn Fudi 1978, p. 152). Anas ibn Malik says: 'Dates were presented to the messenger of God and I saw him eating them. Due to hunger he was sitting on the support of something.' (Al-Tirmidhi 1990, p. 138).

Muhammad's way of life, however, was not merely a choice based on personal asceticism but was part of the qur'anic objective of an egalitarian social order. The existing socio-economic order was denounced for its inequalities and this denunciation went along with active measures to empower the *mustad'afun*. Muhammad abolished ground rent, usury and all speculative and exploitative economic practices. Usurious transactions were prohibited with a warning of 'war from God and His Prophet' against those who continued such practices (Qur'an 2:279). Creditors were exhorted to recover only their capital sums, 'but if you dispense even of that then it would be more virtuous for you' (2:280). The abolition of the leasing of lands negated landlordism and these ordinances or legal injunctions were backed up by qur'anic exhortations to the wealthy to spend whatever was beyond necessity (2:219). To facilitate the empowerment of the poor and dispossessed, the Qur'an announces that in the wealth of the rich there is an intrinsic share for them (70:25; 51:19). The principle of distributive justice was unambiguously affirmed so 'that the wealth should not only circulate amongst the rich' (59:7). Elaborating on this principle, Muhammad mentioned various forms of wealth and power that had to be shared with those who did not have them 'until we thought that none among us had the right to any of our superfluities' (Ibn Hazm n.d., 6, p. 157).

The social and economic implications of the doctrine of *tawhid*, the idea that one Creator means a single humanity, were evident from the beginning of the prophetic mission. At the heart of Muhammad's opponents' contempt was his lowly origin and his option for others from a similar background. The aristocracy of Mecca, with their commercially vested interests, were threatened both by his challenge to their traditional religion based on *shirk* and his emphasis on justice for the oppressed and marginalized.

The most significant text of the South African qur'anic discourse on liberation is undoubtedly Qur'an 28:4–8. This particular text was quoted with unceasing regularity at the rallies of virtually every Islamist organization – both fundamentalist and progressive – during the uprisings of the 1980s, as well as in their magazines, newspapers and pamphlets. The text reads as follows:

> And it is Our will to bestow Our grace upon the *mustad'afun* on the earth, to make them the leaders), and to make them the heirs, and to establish them firmly on the earth, and to let Pharaoh and Haman and their hosts experience through those [the Israelites] the very thing against which they sought to protect themselves. (28:5)

The use of *mustad'afun* in this text was applied to all the oppressed people of South Africa, irrespective of their religious background, as is evident from the following two quotations:

> O *Mustad'afeen* of our land, the system that we have fought against for so long and paid for so dearly in life, blood, and property is evil and rotten to the core. (Qibla n.d., *One Solution, Islamic Revolution*, p. 2)

> [The task of the Muslim community is] to join forces with the progressive streams among the *mustad'afun* . . . to contribute towards the unity of the *mustad'afun*, . . . to declare clearly to the oppressors: 'If you rise against the oppressed or stand in the path of the oppressed, we are commanded by God to defend ourselves against injustice and oppression.' (Solomon 1985, p. 6)

The text referring to the *mustad'afun fi'l-ard*, cited above, occurs in the beginning of the chapter of the Qur'an called *al-Qasas* (The Story) (28), a chapter which deals essentially with the flight of the Israelites from Egypt. The significance of this example of liberation and of God's commitment to the political freedom of people, irrespective of their faith commitment, is more closely examined when we consider the question of solidarity with the religious or rejecting Other in chapter 6. Here I only wish to point out that the case of the *mustad'afun* in these verses, a reference to the Israelites who were oppressed by Pharaoh and the Egyptian ruling class, reflects God's preferential option for the oppressed. Furthermore, the promise of liberation is held out despite the absence of any commitment to faith in God and belief in His prophets. As for Pharaoh, the signs rejected by him seem to have been more than just the prophethood of Moses or the divinity of God, because in that rejection most of the Israelites shared. The signs rejected by Pharaoh evidently included the oppressed and marginalized.

In the discussion of *tawhid* and *al-nas* we have seen how apartheid divided the people of South Africa. 'The people' in South Africa were transformed into a mass of *mustad'afun* under a vicious system which not only meant separation, but an existence of discrimination and the criminalization of any attempt to escape from it. The engaged interpreter in South Africa may certainly ask, 'If God regards the Israelites as His people and demands that His prophets become of them, destroy their oppressors and lead them into freedom, then why would He treat the people of South Africa any differently?'

The need for the interpreter both to place himself or herself among the marginalized and within their struggles, as well as to interpret the text from the underside of history, is based on the notion of the divine and prophetic preferential option for the oppressed. Those committed to liberation in South Africa have thus argued that a similar bias must be exercised by anyone who approaches the Qur'an and who wants to bring its basic spirit to life. This is a conscious denial of 'objectivity'. In its place is offered a subjectivity which enables one to walk in the path of the prophets.

The engaged interpreter approaches the text with a conscious decision to search for meaning, which responds creatively to the suffering of the *mustad'afun* and holds out the most promise for liberation and justice. It is within a context of oppression that the interpreter is called upon to bear witness to God. A commitment to humankind and active solidarity with the *mustad'afun* results in a re-reading of both social reality and the text from their perspective. This re-reading and the engagement in social analysis from that point of departure shapes the search for a qur'anic hermeneutic of pluralism for liberation. The objective of this search is an effective qur'anic contribution to the ongoing struggles for justice on the part of the country's people; a struggle whose participants are mainly the religious Other, for they are the overwhelming majority of the *mustad'afun*.

Through the Eyes of Justice

The Qur'an uses two terms to refer to justice: *qist* and *'adl*. *Qist* means 'equity', 'justice', 'to give someone his or her full portion' (Lane 1980, 'q-s-t'), and the agent noun *muqsit* is one of the names of God. *'Adl* means 'to act equitably, justly, or rightly' (ibid., *'adl'*). These two terms are used interchangeably in the Qur'an (49:9; 2:282) and, according to it, justice forms the basis of the natural order: 'And God has created the heavens and the earth in truth; and so that every person may be justly compensated for what he [she] had earned and none be wronged' (45:22). This verse, as well as Qur'an 39:69, equates justice with truth. 'God (Himself) bears witness that He is the Upholder of justice' (4:18). In two verses, the Qur'an exhorts the faithful to uphold justice as an act of witness unto Him (4:135; 5:6) and those who sacrifice their lives in the path of establishing justice are equated with those who achieved martyrdom in 'the path of God' (3:20).

An understanding of *'adl* and *qist* based on *tawhid* is well illustrated in the first verses of the chapter of the Qur'an titled 'The Gracious':

The Most Gracious has imparted this Qur'an. He has created humankind; He has imparted unto him [her] speech. The sun and the moon follow courses computed; the stars and the trees submit; and the skies He has raised high; and He has set up the balance of justice in order that you may not transgress the measure. So, establish weight with justice and fall not short in the balance. It is He who has spread out the earth for [all] His creatures. (55:1–10)

These verses place humankind and the task of doing justice within the context of their responsibility to the Creator, on the one hand, and the order which runs through the cosmos, on the other.[16] It is within this overall context that humankind are being warned against 'transgressing the measure' and exhorted to 'weigh [your dealings] with justice'. The enforcement of justice is given as one of the objectives of revelation (56:25) and it is seen as a stepping stone to *taqwa* (5:6). Some scholars, such as Ibn Qayyim al-Jawziyyah, are, in fact, of the opinion that justice is the *raison d'être* for the establishment of religion: 'God has sent His Messengers and revealed His Books so that people may establish *qist*, upon which the heavens and the earth stand. And when the signs of justice appear in any manner, then that is a reflection of the *shari'ah* and the religion of God' (1953, pp. 14–16).

Islamic society is expected to uphold justice as the basis of socio-economic life. The Qur'an is often specific about those areas of social affairs wherein lapses are most likely to occur, such as the trust of orphans and adopted children (4:3; 33:5), matrimonial relations (4:3; 49:9), contractual dealings (2:282), judicial matters (5:42; 4:56), interfaith relations (60:8), business (11:65), and dealings with one's opponents (5:8). The Qur'an postulates the idea of a universe created with justice as its basis. The natural order, according to the Qur'an, is one rooted in justice and deviation from it is disorder (*fitnah*). The status quo in a particular social order, irrespective of how long it has survived or how stable it has become, does not enjoy an intrinsic legitimacy in Islam. Injustice is a deviation from the natural order and, like *shirk*, though it may stabilize over centuries as did *shirk* in pre-Islamic Mecca, it is, nonetheless, regarded as a disturbance in 'the balance'. In the qur'anic paradigm, justice and the natural order based on it are values to be upheld, while socio-political stability *per se* is not.[17] When confronted with this disturbance in the natural order through the systematic erosion of human rights (or threats to the ecosystem), the Qur'an imposes an obligation on the faithful to challenge such a system until it is eliminated and the order is once again restored to its natural state of justice. In another text that was very significant in South African Islamic liberatory discourse, the Qur'an presents revelation itself as the ideological weapon whereby disorder (*fitnah*) must be countered: 'Indeed we have sent our Apostles with clear proof; And through them we have bestowed revelation and the balance so that humankind may behave with *qist*; And we have provided you with iron, in which there is awesome power as well as (other) benefits for humankind' (57:25). The Qur'an establishes itself as a dynamic force for justice, legitimates the use of iron with 'its awesome power' as a means of achieving it and encourages an active struggle for it. The Qur'an, as indicated here, repeatedly contrasts justice with oppression and transgression (3:25; 6:160; 10:47; 16:111) and imposes on its followers the obligation to destroy the latter and establish the former.

Virtually every publication, speech or sermon by the progressive and fundamentalist Islamists during the 1980s appealed to the qur'anic demand for the faithful to rise as 'God's witnesses for justice'. If a single concept could be said to have been the axis around which Muslim resistance to apartheid rotated, then it was that of justice for the oppressed and marginalized. Texts denouncing injustice and demanding justice were tirelessly invoked and when the text did not specify it, then justice was read into the translation as an implication. For example, the verse 'And fight them on until there is no more *fitnah* and the *din* is for God' (2:193) was regularly presented as 'Fight them on until there is no more tumult and oppression and there prevail justice and faith in God.'

Besides being potent anti-apartheid weapons, for which abundant references could easily be found in the Qur'an, for most progressive Islamists justice and equity were also key socio-economic concepts which had to lead to an egalitarian and just society. The qur'anic understanding of justice may be said to embrace the socio-economic dimensions but, as is evident from the qur'anic texts cited, the term it employs, *qist*, is wider in scope than these. The crying need of the South African people for socio-economic justice has often resulted in a rather myopic view of the qur'anic meaning of justice. Consequently terms such as *'adl* and *qist* and their qur'anic antonyms, *zulm* and *'udwan* (evil/oppression and transgression) were invoked primarily to refer to political justice or injustice within the context of racial domination. Justice employed in such a context thus seldom embraced, for example, the socio-religious liberation of women. Similarly, the idea of *zulm al-nafs* (to wrong oneself), an important dimension of the qur'anic understanding of injustice, was never invoked in Muslim liberation rhetoric, nor did it receive any coverage in the speeches or written works that emanated in the period under discussion. At an internal organizational level, both the Call and the MYM acknowledged the need to redress the unbalanced appreciation of *'adl* and *qist* although they failed to do much in practical terms. Internal MYM papers appealed to its membership to become rounded personalities with a commitment to comprehensive justice. Towards the end of the 1980s the MYM increasingly took up the more radical issue of gender discrimination in the *shari'ah*. The Call has, since its inception, dealt with various other dimensions of injustice such as the oppression of women and religious minorities in Muslim countries and humankind's injustice toward the physical environment. This attention, though, was invariably drowned under the more vociferously proclaimed and vigorously pursued political dimensions of injustice.

The present work is an argument for the legitimacy of hermeneutical ideas emerging out of the interaction between Islam and the South African struggle for liberation. However, the uncritical imposition of the requirements of the struggle and the ideas coming therefrom on to the text is to deprive the struggle of the visionary insights that a scripture such as the Qur'an is capable of supplying. The context of a liberation struggle not only has something to say to the text; the text also has something to say to that context.

The Qur'an offers itself as an inspiration and guide for comprehensive insurrection against an unjust status quo. It, furthermore, asks to be read through the eyes of a commitment to the destruction of oppression and aggression and the establishment of justice. In a situation of injustice, the Qur'an, by its own admission, is compelled to be the ideological tool for comprehensive insurrection against oppression in all its manifestations. This has two implications. Firstly, one cannot justify adopting an objective approach to the Qur'an while one is surrounded by oppression, institutionalized or not, without searching for ways in which the Qur'an can be used against it. Neutrality or objectivity in such a context is, in fact, a sin which excludes one from the ranks of those imbued with *taqwa*, those to whom the Qur'an pledges guidance. Secondly, the approach to the Qur'an as a tool for insurrection presupposes all the ideological and theological commitments as well as an affinity to the values discussed earlier on in this chapter. These values are concretized in a struggle with humankind and the oppressed to create an order based on *tawhid* and justice. This struggle continues during the process of understanding the Qur'an.

Jihad as Praxis and a Path to Understanding

Jihad literally means 'to struggle', to 'exert oneself' or 'to spend energy or wealth' (Ibn Manzur, n.d., 1, p. 709). In the Qur'an, it is frequently followed by the expressions 'in the path of God' and 'with your wealth and your selves'. For Muslims, the term *jihad* has also come to mean the 'sacralization of combat' (Schleifer 1982, p. 122). Despite its popular meaning as a sacred armed struggle or war, the term *jihad* was always understood by Muslims to embrace a broader struggle to transform both oneself and society. The Qur'an itself uses the word in its various meanings ranging from warfare (4:90; 25:52; 9:41) to contemplative spiritual struggle (22:78; 29:6) and even exhortation (29:8; 31:15).

I have rendered *jihad* as 'struggle and praxis'. Praxis may be defined as 'conscious action undertaken by a human community that has the responsibility for its own political determination . . . based on the realization that humans make history' (Chopp 1989, p. 137). Given the qur'anic comprehensive use of the term and the way *jihad* is intended to transform both oneself and society, one may say that *jihad* is simultaneously a struggle and a praxis.

The commonly assumed definition of *jihad* in South African liberatory rhetoric reflects a break with traditional juristic understandings of it. 'Jihad', said a Qibla pamphlet, 'is the Islamic paradigm of the liberation struggle . . . an effort, an exertion to the utmost, a striving for truth and justice' (Qibla n.d., *Arise and Bear Witness*, p. 2). Similarly, the Call argued that, for Muslims 'the struggle for freedom and justice in South Africa is a sacred one. Any Muslim who abandons the struggle in South Africa, abandons Islam. *Jihad* in the path of God is part of the *iman* of a Muslim' (Call of Islam 1985, *We Fight On*, p. 1). The centrality of justice as the objective of *jihad*, rather than the establishment of Islam as a religious system, was common in virtually all the public pronouncements of the Islamists. 'The purpose of *jihad* is to . . . destroy and eradicate injustice and not to replace one unjust system with another, or to replace one dominant group with another. *Jihad* is, therefore, a ceaseless, continuous, super conscious and effective struggle for justice' (Qibla n.d., *Arise and Bear Witness*, p. 2). Numerous anecdotes of resistance in the lives of the first generation of Muslims as well as the abundant qur'anic texts dealing with *jihad* were regularly invoked in support both of the essentially nonviolent uprisings and the armed struggle.

Praxis as a source of knowledge has always been widely recognized in Islamic scholarship and the Qur'an itself is explicit in its view that theory can be based on praxis: 'And to those who strive in us [our path] to them we shall show our ways' (29:69). The Qur'an lays great emphasis on orthopraxis and strongly suggests that virtuous deeds and *jihad* are also ways of understanding and knowing. The Qur'an establishes *jihad* as the path to establishing justice and praxis as the way of experiencing and comprehending truth. *Jihad*, as praxis serving as a hermeneutical key, assumes that human life is essentially practical; theology follows. As for the presence of the divine in the process of transformation, the verse stating that 'God does not change the conditions of a people until they change what is in themselves' (13:11), was regularly invoked to insist that history and society is the terrain where, for people, transformation effectively takes place.

In South Africa a continual assessment of the meaning and contemporary relevance of the Qur'an occurred through this foundation of praxis: 'This involvement [in the struggle], the conflict that this involvement is going to lead to, our solidarity in the *halqah* [study circles] and our [qur'anic] reflections are going to teach us . . . This is the meaning of "and to those who strive in Our path, to them We shall show Our ways"' (Call of Islam 1988). Along with liberation theologians elsewhere, these activists turned to praxis as 'a way of making theology less a false theology, less an academic illusion and less an incoherent abstraction' (Chopp 1989, p. 37). 'The Review of Faith', a Call manual for activists, talks about 'a dialectical process whereby our jihad will be informed by the Qur'an and our faith as much as our understanding of these will be informed by our jihad' (Call of Islam 1985, The Review of Faith, p. 41).

In the midst of an ongoing experience of suffering and resistance, on the one hand, and a commitment to praxis as an expression of faith, on the other, a clear implication is made that both faith and understanding take shape in the concrete programmes of resistance against suffering and dehumanization. While all the progressive Islamists agreed on actual participation in the day-to-day struggles of the oppressed, the specific organizational and ideological framework within which '*jihad*-as-praxis' occurred was the subject of intense debate. In chapter 1 we saw that, while there was considerable discussion about 'a purely Muslim involvement' in the struggle, this did not actually materialize. As soon as those Muslims desirous of working in isolation started organizing, they were inexorably drawn into the work of others. On the other hand, groups like the Call and al-Jihad had from an early stage already been committed to a particular movement's liberative praxis, that of the ANC–UDF.

The major issue for an organization like the Call was thus not whether its understandings and approaches to qur'anic concepts should be shaped by the liberation struggle, but whether they could be shaped entirely by a particular political tendency within it. The way this question was dealt with is also reflective of a hermeneutical method which is simultaneously liberative and heuristic (working through trial and error).

Some people say that they do want to join this group or that group because they are not hundred percent sure where it is going to end; and that they cannot afford to make errors with the future of the *ummah*. Excessive fear of making mistakes can often be a mask behind which we hide our cowardice and our unwillingness to drop our partnership with unjust systems, because it benefits us financially. It is also convenient for them to attack others for tactical errors in the struggle because they do not understand that errors come from action. Because they are not doing anything, it is hardly surprising that they do not commit any errors. (Call of Islam 1988, p. 37)

At an internal level, these issues were dealt with in a less polemical, more considered manner. Within their own ranks they also raised the following questions:

a) To what extent should we allow our praxis, which is increasingly limited to UDF programmes and takes place within the ideological framework of National Democracy, to be the exclusive foundation whereby our qur'anic reflections take place?

b) Can an Islamic movement afford to link itself to purely secular movements in the way that we have? To what extent has this secularized us as individuals and as a group? Has it blocked the growth of a truly comprehensive attitude to the Qur'an? (Call of Islam 1987, p. 5)

The organization attempted to respond to these concerns by greater emphasis on qur'anic reflection, internal moral exhortations and prayer. This was wholly inadequate against the underlying ideological messages, imbibed from a deep commitment to solidarity, within the 'organizations of the people'. The significant point in this theological method, though, is a rejection of the traditional ideas of theology and interpretation as happening before and outside of a historical process, a notion that presupposes that a reading and understanding of the text provide one with absolute certainties. In its place heuristic 'reflections' were offered. Those who claimed to have access to certainties were the ones paralysed into inaction despite the desire of some among them to engage injustice. Those who were committed to tentativeness were actually fully engaged in the struggle. The attitude of the progressive Islamists finds a resonance in Christian liberation theology in Latin America:

One must make a philosophical judgement among the existing philosophical methodologies in order to get an authentic and liberative understanding of human existence. In like manner, one must make a political judgement on the political processes and movements around, choosing the one that lends itself best to ensuring the liberative authenticity on the part of the one who makes that commitment. But there are no magical, eternal guarantees in the revolutionary process as such (Boff 1985, p. 99).

Conclusion: The Qur'an Speaks

I have explained the way God identifies with *al-nas* and the relationship between God's path and that of *al-nas*, His preferential option for the oppressed and marginalized and the importance of establishing justice. The Qur'an undertakes to teach the believing activist in the midst of his or her struggle to establish *tawhid*, *taqwa*, and to give concrete effect to the preferential option for the oppressed through *jihad*. As Ayatullah Mahmud Taleghani (d. 1979) put it, 'the way of God is that way which leads to the well-being of human society as a whole, the way of justice, of human freedom so that a few cannot gain dominance . . . appropriating for themselves the natural resources which God has placed at the disposal of all' (Taleghani 1982, p. 79). To engage in qur'anic hermeneutics in a situation of injustice is to do theology and to experience faith as solidarity with the oppressed and marginalized in a struggle for liberation. This represents a break from both traditional and modern theology. It is different in at least three aspects.

Firstly, the most significant difference is in the location of the interpreter. When *jihad* is invoked on the streets in concert with the religious Other rising against injustice; when the Qur'an is invoked in a court of law as legitimation for the armed struggle; and when God is fervently petitioned before a raid on a government building or on the eve of the outcome of a trial on charges of terrorism, then the break with more 'religious' or 'academic' ways of approaching theology is very significant. In fact, it stands in opposition to both.

Liberation theology insists that, in conditions of oppression and marginalization, Islam can only truly be experienced as the liberative praxis of solidarity. This is in contrast to both traditional and modern theology. The former struggles to retain its hold over the believers with its reduction of Islam to the formal rituals, themselves stripped of spiritual depth by the preponderance of legalities. Modern theology, on the other hand, as Rebecca Chopp has pointed out, is located in and addresses itself to the secularity of the privileged world and the serious thinkers therein, while liberation theology is located in and addresses the marginalized world.

Secondly, theology living in a world of 'violence and hope, reflection and action, spirituality and politics means that theology is always, to use Gutierrez's expression, "[consciously] a second act" ' (cited in Chopp 1989, p. 59). While faith may come before liberative praxis as a form of preunderstanding, theology does not. What others may thus denounce as *post hoc* theological justification is regarded by liberation theology as both inevitable and a privileged option.

Thirdly, truth, for the engaged interpreter, can never be absolute. As one's hermeneutic continuously moves on, one is pushed towards ever-increasing and authentic truth; truth which, in turn, leads to greater liberative praxis. There is no point at which God has disclosed the truth to the interpreter, but it continues to be disclosed, for there is no end to *jihad* and thus no end to His promise to disclose. The Qur'an is explicit that there is a 'Truth' to be known and it is possible to have deep convictions about it. That only dimensions or layers of this truth are knowable, however, is acknowledged in traditional and modern scholarship. The difference in liberation theology is that

> it does not aim to prove eternal truths that are to be applied subsequently to history; it does not merely reflect on existential truth that is poetically disclosed through history. Rather liberation theology helps create truth . . . for theological reasoning is uttered upon a truth that is a way, upon a Word who has pitched . . . tent in the midst of history. (Chopp 1989, p. 61)

It was and remains inevitable that this word of God that has pitched its tent in the midst of history would be affected by the storms, rain, wind and, yes, the sunshine, surrounding it. The word has regularly become contested terrain as various entities staked claims to its ownership. For Muslims in South Africa during the 1980s, much of the controversy of these claims revolved around the question of space for the religious Other. The progressive Islamists argued fervently that faith and *taqwa* enabled them to access the text. They ignored the clerics, and insisted that the word also had space for all the marginalized. The word of God also excludes; but the excluded were now seen to be those who, despite possessing the correct formulae of faith, had made themselves unworthy of the description *muslim* by their participation in the structures of oppression.

Notes

1. The *miswak* (here *miswaak*) was a twig used by the early Arabs, including Muhammad, for cleaning teeth. Its use is still in vogue among a number of Muslims who adhere to a literalist interpretation of the *sunnah*. The reference to it in this quotation is thus also a backhanded criticism of the selective interpretation of the meaning of *sunnah* by Muslim traditionalists.

2. Literally, 'without how', i.e., to accept certain qur'anic doctrinal statements without further enquiry. With the notion of *bila kayf*, the Ash'arites attempted to resolve the conflict between reason and revelation. This notion was particularly employed to respond to the apparently anthropomorphic expressions regarding God in the Qur'an.

3. Literally, 'to measure, estimate', later meaning 'to assign specifically by measure' as though God measured out His decrees. It deals with the doctrine of predetermination, i.e., God, by His *qada* (decree) and *qadr* (power), determines all events and acts.

4. Al-Zamakhshari, an exegete who frequently supplies the pre-qur'anic meaning of words, explains that the word *waqin* was used in pre-Islamic days for a horse which exercised caution in protecting its hoofs against injury due to uneven or stony surfaces (n.d., I, p. 36) The root *w-q-y* thus came to denote protecting something or oneself from whatever is harmful. Jafri has demonstrated how the term in pre-Islam was void of any religious, moral or ethical connotations and how the Qur'an transformed its usage into a term of 'great moral significance of the most comprehensive . . . ethical quality in a man's life' (Jafri 1980, p. 117).

5. In its various forms the term occurs 242 times in the Qur'an, of which 102 times are in Meccan verses and the rest in Medinan ones. In common Muslim discourse, and in several English translations of the Qur'an, its meaning has been confined to 'the fear of God'. The Qur'an does use it in a manner which embraces this connotation (2:24, 46, 103, 206, 273; etc.), but this is an inadequate description of the term. The Qur'an uses *khawf* far more frequently to convey the meaning 'fear'.

6. The idea was certainly not alien to the classical scholars of Islam as is evident from the following comment on levels of *zakah* (social tax) by Abu Hamid al-Ghazzali (d. 1111): 'The first level [of *zakah*] is that of those who have grasped the true meaning of *tawhid*, fulfilled their agreement and surrendered all their wealth. They neither keep a gold coin nor a silver one and never reach the level on which *zakah* has to be paid' (cited in Ahmad 1979, p. 94).

7. In apartheid South Africa there were two parallel sport systems which were administered separately and frequented by different sets of spectators. Racial sport was supported by the government, organized along racial lines and played by people who argued that politics should not be allowed to interfere with sports. Non-racial sport was premised on the slogan 'No normal sport in an abnormal society'. All those connected to non-racial sport disciplines avoided any association, as players or spectators, with any event organized by the government-supported groups.

8. This does not imply a denial of differences between people. On the contrary, the qur'anic view of humankind accepts the diversity of tribes and culture. It, however, rejects the notion that these can be a legitimate criteria for superiority of any kind. This diversity is, in fact, a challenge to draw closer to each other (9:13) and to appreciate the Other as another manifestation of God's presence and His grace (30:22).

9. The qur'anic expressions are '*min salsal ka'l-fakhkhar*' (55:14) and '*min salsal min hama'in masnun*' (15:26) which translate as 'sounding clay, like pottery' (Asad 1980, p. 825) and 'sounding clay, out of dark slime, transmuted' (ibid., p. 385), respectively.

10. See Qur'an 2:277–81; 9:71; 31:4–5. Even the formal rituals of worship which are normally regarded as entirely 'vertically' oriented are permeated with the factor of *al-nas* and thus assume a 'horizontal' dimension. Examples of these are the emphasis on the performance of prayers in congregation (2:43), the social dimensions inherent in *hajj* (the pilgrimage to Mecca) (2:197–200), the prophetic warning that there are many people who fast but derive

nothing from it except hunger (i.e., it does not teach them compassion) (Ibn Maja 1979, I, p. 549) and the linking of zakah (social tax) with the obligations to God (2:277; 9:60, 18; 23:1–4).

11. See Qur'an 2:245; 5:12; 6:17; 56:11; 57:16; 64:17; 73:20. The close relationship between obligations to God and those to al-nas is vividly illustrated in the response to allegations of injustice against 'Umar al-Khattab (d. 644), the second Caliph, in the case of a piece of sequestered land at Rabdhah (Nait-Belkacem 1978, p. 145). 'Umar sequestered the land and set it aside to serve as general pasture land to be shared by all the citizens. The owners of this land came to him complaining that it belonged to them: 'We have fought for it during jahiliyyah [pre-Islamic ignorance]. It belonged to us even when we entered Islam. Why then have you sequestered it?' 'Umar replied, 'All goods belong to God; al-nas are the creation of God. If I were not obliged to do certain things to remain in the path of God, I would not have sequestered a single span of land' (ibid.).

12. Although appearing in a work by Albani of supposedly weak hadith, this hadith is nonetheless frequently invoked by Muslims and has thus acquired a value in reception which I feel free to appeal to.

13. The period 1986–7, in fact, saw an abortive attempt to introduce a Muslim fundamentalist version of the popular political slogan, Amandla ngawethu (Power is Ours). The short-lived alternative was Amandla lillah (Power for God). The idea that popular sovereignty is a heretical alternative to divine sovereignty has been a consistent theme in fundamentalist writings which enjoyed considerable popularity in South Africa in the late 1970s and early 1980s.

14. The inevitable link between making political claims on behalf of God and tyranny was recognized during the early days of Islam by Abu Dharr (d. 653), a Companion, in an encounter with Mu'awiyah. The latter insisted on expropriating community property in the name of God. ('All property belongs to God', was Mu'awiyah's argument.) Abu Dharr responded saying: 'You say this in order to draw the conclusion that since you are the representative of God, all property belongs to you. You ought to say that all property belongs to the people' (Nait-Belkacem 1978, p. 145).

15. The notion of al-maslahah al-'ammah (the common good) or al-masalih al-mursalah (public interest) as a juristic principle, even a source of law, although not undisputed, has for long been operative in Islamic jurisprudence. However, its determination has essentially been confined to the jurists and clerics.

16. Verse 10 of this passage ('And the earth He has spread out for all living things') is more specific in focusing on the ecosystem and on social justice. The earth thus belongs to all who inhabit it, not only humankind, and humankind, as the vicegerent of God upon it, have a responsibility to be just in their dealings with all its co-inhabitants.

17. The post-Mawardi–Sunni theory of state saw stability elevated to a religious principle. Any disruption to that stability, irrespective of its underlying values, was regarded as fitnah, which was invariably equated with mischief. This post-Mawardian negative attitude towards rebellion though, as Ayalon points out was itself a departure from a still earlier concept, commending the removal of an impious ruler by force. 'No obedience to a creature in disobeying the Creator', ran an oft-quoted hadith (n.d., p. 146).

REDEFINING SELF
& OTHER
IMAN, ISLAM & KUFR

The munafiks [hypocrites] in our town who just make all the trouble . . . want to change our deen [religion] and say Muslims must go to the townships and help the black koeffaar and to tell our children to fight and make trouble agenst [sic] the government . . . What have we Muslims to do with all these things. Let us leave this politics and other business to the koeffar . . . Let them take the dunja [this world] and let us not forget our iebaadaat [rituals] works and we will take the aagira [hereafter].

(Letter to Editor, Muslim Views, October 1991)

The Ever-Decreasing Chosen and the
Ever-Increasing Frozen

Terms of exclusion and inclusion seem to be intrinsic to all religions and are usually ethically loaded. The two most frequently invoked ethical terms in the Qur'an are undoubtedly *iman* and *kufr* (usually loosely translated as 'faith' and 'disbelief'). In Muslim discourse though, *iman* has largely been substituted by *islam* as the key term for self-identification. The word *islam*, for example, occurs only eight times in the Qur'an whereas *iman* is found forty-five times. Similarly, the correlative of *iman*, *mu'min*, in its various forms, appears more than five times as frequently as *muslim*. This development is itself significant for any discussion of the Other in Islam.

One of the manifestations (and consequences) of the process of Islamic theology becoming more and more rigid was the reification of terms such as *islam, iman* and *kufr*. In other words, these words are no longer seen as qualities that individuals may have; qualities that are dynamic and vary in intensity in different stages of an individual's life. Instead, these terms are now regarded as the entrenched qualities of groups, bordering on ethnic characteristics. The way these terms are employed in the Qur'an and, to a lesser extent, in exegetical literature, shows that the relationship between the earliest meanings of these terms and their present-day usage is rather frayed. While some aspects of their contemporary usage are obviously rooted in their early meanings, there are other aspects that have been ignored entirely. Any notion of 'actual' or 'true' meaning is of course problematic, because we can only approach the question from our horizons. There is, nevertheless, a case for reflecting upon the way words were used by the first authors or speakers and by those who read, listened to or interpreted a text.

In looking at the way these terms were used in the Qur'an, one should not avoid qur'anic texts that appear to encourage religious exclusivism. Some texts that have been selected for reflections on the key terms in this chapter and on selected themes in the next thus represent the 'difficult texts' in Muslim pluralist discourse, texts that are often bypassed by Muslim apologists and those engaged in interfaith dialogue. A simultaneous commitment to both the text and to interreligious solidarity necessarily requires a transcendence of what Riffat Hassan has described as an 'inauthentic dialogue based on abbreviations' (1986, p. 132). These texts are, in fact, very significant for a qur'anic discourse of pluralism that also seeks to advance people's liberation from racial discrimination and other forms of oppression. Many of the advocates of religious pluralism for liberation and justice desire to live alongside the Qur'an with integrity and simultaneously participate in authentic relationships with those of other faiths. Rediscovering and reappropriating the subsumed meanings of these terms, rather than avoiding them, are prerequisites for this authenticity.

Underpinning my examination of these terms is the belief that the Qur'an is concerned, and presents God as being 'concerned with something that persons do, and with the persons who do it, rather than with an abstract entity [called belief]' (Cantwell-Smith 1991, p. 111). Those who have suffered the consequences of the *herrenvolkism* of another people have no alternative but to search for more inclusive categories. Where these theological categories are also seen as divinely ordained, one has to find alternative ways of reading them. Thus, *muslim,* and all its positive connotations, for both this world and the hereafter, cannot merely refer to the biological accident of being born in a Muslim family. Similarly, *kafir* cannot refer to the accident of being born outside such a family.

In view of the significance of the exegetical tradition outlined in chapter 2, I shall regularly refer to the work of selected exegetes who represent some of the broad streams in qur'anic exegesis and Islamic theology. These include the traditional (Ibn Jarir al-Tabari, d. 923); scholastic, both Mu'tazilite and Ash'arite (Mahmud ibn 'Umar al-Zamakhshari, d. 1144, and Fakhr al-Din al-Razi, d. 1209); the esoteric tradition (Muhyi al-Din ibn al-'Arabi, d. 1240), as well as some more contemporary exegetes, both Sunni (Rashid Rida, d. 1935) and Shi'ite (Muhammad Hussain al-Tabataba'i, d. 1981). A perusal of their views has the value of connecting my own insights with those of tradition. Furthermore, I shall show that their interpretations can often serve as a basis for developing notions of particular relevance to those who live in divided and unjust societies.

The idea that the qur'anic *islam* is not the sole possession of Muslims who identify with the historical *ummah* (community) of Islam has found an echo in numerous works by Muslim scholars. This acknowledgement of the potential of others outside the house of reified Islam to respond to God, and the challenge of submitting to Him (i.e., *islam*) in their own ways, is more widespread than is commonly supposed.[1] In various ways, numerous Muslim scholars have acknowledged that

> primordial and universal *islam*, i.e., the attitude of surrender to the Absolute in co-fraternity, can be discerningly discovered and acknowledged in the most varied symbols and patterns of belief and action, in the religions and ideologies of the past and present . . . Any sincere response to the call from the hidden Mystery, the source of existence, realizes existential and personal *islam*. (Troll 1987, p. 15)

A careful study of *iman, islam* and *kufr*, and their usage in both the Qur'an and its exegesis, bears out this position. There is, however, a need to transcend the liberal discourse advocating some form of religious pluralism in most of the works by Muslim modernists. This discourse often ignores the position of the Qur'an on *kufr* because the Qur'an denounces, rejects and asks Muslims to oppose the Other or aspects of Otherness; all notions that liberalism has difficulty dealing with. A hermeneutic of pluralism for liberation does not seek to ignore this denunciation but to redefine it. Therefore, an attempt is made to deal with the ideological connotations acquired by these terms and to present a conscious preference for a new meaning, which seeks the liberation of all people.

Rethinking *Iman*

This following text seems to be useful for examining the way in which the Qur'an uses the term *iman* and its noun, *mu'minun*.

> Indeed, the *mu'minun* are those whose hearts tremble with awe whenever God is mentioned; and whose *iman* is strengthened whenever His *ayat* [signs] are conveyed unto them; and who place their trust in their Sustainer. Those who are constant in prayer and spend on others out of what We provide for them as sustenance. It is they who are truly the *mu'minun* . . . (Qur'an 8:2–4)

This text is the most explicit in defining a *mu'min*. While the word *mu'min* here is widely interpreted to mean 'a complete *mu'min*', the very idea of completeness or incompleteness in *iman* highlights the dynamism in the concept, a dynamism further underlined in the idea of *iman* being increased or strengthened. The text also lends itself to reflections on the nature of the relationship between *iman* and righteous deeds, a relationship which is central to this study. Lastly, this text succinctly embraces the various requirements of *iman* dealt with in greater detail elsewhere in the Qur'an. As for the background of this text, it features in the beginning of a Medinan chapter titled 'The Spoils of War' (Qur'an 8) which deals largely with the events surrounding the Battle of Badr (623) and the sanctity of treaties. Appearing at the beginning of the chapter, this text is widely regarded as a rebuke to some of Muhammad's Companions who displayed an exaggerated interest in the spoils accrued from that battle. This unseemly interest resulted in considerable acrimony. After being told that such spoils rightfully belonged to the community as a whole, and that eagerness for material wealth should not be allowed to impair their social relations, the Companions were now reminded about the nature of faith, faith which was being injured by their greed.[2]

As is the case with most key religio-ethical terms in the Qur'an, *iman* is seldom discussed, even by lexicographers, solely with regard to its etymological roots. Instead, there is frequent reference to its use in the Qur'an and in Islamic theology. *Iman* is the verbal noun of the fourth form from the root *a-m-n*. The root suggests 'being secure', 'trusting in', 'turning to', from which follows its meanings of 'good faith', 'sincerity', and 'fidelity' or 'loyalty'. The fourth form (*amana*) has the double meaning of 'to believe' and 'to give one's faith'. Its primary meaning is 'becoming true to the trust with respect to which God has confided in one by a firm believing with the heart; not by profession of belief with the tongue only' (Lane 1980, 1, p. 7). When *a-m-n* is followed by the particle *bi*, it means 'to acknowledge' or 'to recognize'. It is also used in the meaning of 'trust' in the sense that one feels secure upon trusting something (al-Baidawi n.d., 1, p. 43).

The term, or variations thereof, appears approximately 244 times in the Qur'an. Most frequently recurring is the expression 'O those who have *iman*' of which there are 55 instances. While the term is used essentially with reference to the followers of Muhammad, in 11 instances it refers to Moses and his followers and in 22 instances to other prophets and their followers. It is used in the Qur'an in the sense of being at peace with oneself and in the sense of contentment (16:112). In 4:83 and 2:125 it means 'security from external threats', while 2:283 employs the term in the sense of 'depositing something with someone for safekeeping'. Qur'an 33:72 employs it in the sense of 'a trust'. In its fourth form (*amana*), the verb is usually followed by the particle *bi* and then means 'to have faith in', 'to recognize', 'to trust'. The object of this 'having faith' or 'recognition' can be God, (2:177; 4:38); the Qur'an specifically, or revelation in general (2:4; 2:177; 4:136); Muhammad or prophets in general (2:177) and, particularly, the Last Day (2:4; 4:38; 6:93). Occasionally the verb is used in its fourth form without any preposition or object (3:110; 6:48). Given the context of these verses, one may assume that the object was understood. Its use in this form connects the meaning of both security and faith with the implicit idea that those who have faith will attain peace and security. One can say that, according to the Qur'an, '*iman* is an act of the heart, a decisive giving oneself up to God and His message and gaining peace and security and fortification against tribulation' (Rahman 1983, p. 171).

Three interconnected themes may be discerned from Qur'an 8:2–4, the text selected for discussion here (see p. 117): the dynamic nature of *iman*, the interrelatedness of *iman* and righteous deeds and *iman* as a personal response to God.

There are very many definitions of *iman* in Islamic theology. Depending on their definition various theologians have either rejected (in most known cases) or accepted the idea of *iman* as dynamic and able to increase or decrease. *Iman* has variously been defined as one or more of the following: affirmation, verbal testimony, belief or righteous conduct. Those who defined *iman* as the collective of belief, affirmation and righteous conduct have, on the basis of the text under discussion, argued that, given that *iman* can increase, it must mean something more than recognition (*ma'rifah*) and verbal testimony (*iqrar*). They have, furthermore, argued that the expression in the above text 'these are truly the *mu'min-un*' means that qualities required are inherent in what is called *iman* (al-Razi 1990, 15, p. 124).

Most of the interpreters argue that in the statement 'it increases their *iman*', it is the affirmation and contentment aspects of *iman* that increase, rather than *iman* itself. Al-Tabari says: 'To their affirmation attained hitherto is added more affirmation' (1954, 9, p. 179), while al-Zamakhshari says that the increase is 'in conviction and satisfaction in the soul' (n.d., 2, p. 196). In a more detailed elaboration of this text, al-Razi (1990, 15, p. 124) offers three explanations for interpreting the increase as one in certitude, affirmation and awareness (rather than in *iman* itself): 1) more and stronger proof leads to further removal of doubt and, at the same time, increase in certainty; 2) the greater amount known, the more the affirmation and 3) an increase in *iman* means an increase in the awareness of 'the greatness of God's power and wisdom' (ibid.). The reasoning followed by al-Razi and others in all three explanations ignores the idea of *iman*, a vibrant faith in the presence of God, being increased either as a direct consequence of righteous conduct or as coming from the grace of God subsequent to it; an idea explicit in the other texts dealing with increase in *iman* (Qur'an 3:173; 8:2; 9:124; 33:22; 48:04; 74:31).

Ibn 'Arabi, al-Tabataba'i and Rida, in different ways, accept the idea of *iman* itself increasing. Ibn 'Arabi speaks of this increase as 'a progression from the stage of knowledge to that of certainty' (n.d., 1, p. 252). While Rida interprets the increase in *iman* as '(greater) certainty in obedience, strength in contentment, abundance in recognition' (1980, 9, p. 591), he is, nevertheless, categorical that these qualities belong to *iman*: 'The truth is that the *iman* of the heart itself increases and decreases' (ibid.). Al-Tabataba'i echoes this in his explanation of this phrase: 'The light of *iman* radiates gradually upon the heart and this continues in intensity until it reaches perfection . . . *Iman* then continues to increase, and grows firm until it reaches the stage of certitude' (1973, 9, p. 11).

The distinction made by some interpreters, between *iman* and its supposed accompaniments such as certitude, affirmation, fear/awe and contentment, is more suited to the debates of scholasticism than to the personal quest for God. However, despite the reluctance of some to acknowledge that *iman* itself is dynamic, all agree that the various components of, or adjuncts to, *iman* increase or decrease. (The unusual logic employed to avoid the inevitable conclusion, from a qur'anic perspective, that *iman* itself is subject to increase or decrease is seen in the second article of the *Wasiyyat Abi Hanifah*, the last admonition of

Abu Hanifah (d.767) to his followers, containing a synopsis of his theology: '*Iman* cannot grow or decrease. In fact, its weakening can be conceived only in connection with an increase of *kufr* and its progress in connection with a weakening of *kufr*' (EI, '*iman*'). This position actually implies the possibility of one simultaneously being both a believer and a 'non-believer'.)

The most significant issue is that *iman* is a personal recognition of, and active response to, the presence of God in the universe and in history. The personal and active nature of *iman* must imply that it fluctuates and that it is dynamic. Several of the exegetes mention two *hadiths* narrated by al-Bukhari and Muslim: 'The least of *iman* will save one in the hereafter' and '*Iman* is of [various] kinds and has seventy branches. The highest is the testimony that there is no deity except God and the lowest is the removal of an obstacle from the road. And [even] modesty is a branch of faith' (al-Zamakhshari n.d., 2, p. 196; al-Razi 1990, 15, p. 124). Even if, as some theologians have argued, the original source of *iman* may be divine grace, it still relates to the deepest senses of human beings, human beings who are in different degrees being transformed with every social or personal encounter.

The Qur'an recognizes various levels of *iman*. This text speaks of the '*mu'minuna haqqan*', which most of the interpreters have interpreted as 'perfect *mu'minun*'. The vast majority of Muslims do not fulfil the criteria outlined in the Qur'an 8:2–4, and yet are not excluded from the ranks of *mu'minun*. An account which deals specifically with this text and which is explicit about two levels of *iman* is that involving Hassan al-Basri (d. 728). Asked if he was a *mu'min*, he responded by saying: '*Iman* is of two kinds: if you asked me about *iman* in God, the Angels, His Books, His Prophets, the Last Day, Paradise and the Fire, the Resurrection and the Judgement, then I am a *mu'min*. If, however, you were to ask me about the word of God "*innama'l-mu'minuna*" Then, by God! I do not know' (al-Razi 1990, 15, p. 126; al-Zamakhshari n.d., 2, p. 196). This is itself proof that the reality of levels of *iman* is more widely accepted than the notion of a stable and immutable *iman* would suggest. Increase in faith is established by the text of this verse and by several other qur'anic texts, explicitly 3:173; 9:124; 33:22; 48:4; 74:31 and implicitly 47:17; 17:13; 19:76.

We may summarize the three major reasons for arguing that *iman* is dynamic and mutable. Firstly, however *iman* is defined, we observe that *iman* is also acknowledged by the Qur'an and the early Muslims to be of more than one kind and existing at various levels. Secondly, whenever the Qur'an addresses the early followers of Islam as 'O you who have attained unto *iman*', it urges them to remould themselves in a particular direction, to orient themselves away from the various wrongs in society and towards God. They were required to act in a certain manner rather than to claim ownership of a particular substance termed *iman*. Thirdly, the understanding that *iman*, too, is an active attribute of character is also supported by the fact of its opposite, which is *kufr*. As I shall indicate, 'the context of the term "they rejected" (*kufr*) show that according to the Qur'an, to "disbelieve" is an active attitude to life as a whole . . . the opposite of *iman* is an active attribute of character, the attitude of heedlessness and scorn and pride' (Izutsu 1966, p. 119–20).

After defining a *mu'min* in terms of 1) the essentially spiritual/personal, (their 'hearts tremble with awe when God is mentioned'); 2) the religious ('they are constant in prayer') and 3) the socio-economic ('spend on others out of what [God] provide[s] for them as sustenance'), Qur'an 8:2–4 goes on to describe the possessors of these characteristics as 'the truly faithful' or 'the true believers'. If these are 'the truly faithful', then the question arises as to whether there is another category of 'merely faithful'? Are these characteristics part and parcel of what is called *iman* or are they outside it? If the latter, then what is the relationship between these characteristics and *iman*?

These questions assumed tremendous importance in the discipline of scholastic theology (*kalam*) and were debated with much acrimony. The views of the various interpreters also differ and, in the case of al-Zamakhshari and al-Razi, they closely correspond to that of the schools with which they identified. Al-Tabari does not express himself explicitly on this issue. However, he does suggest that there is a binding connection between *iman* and righteous deeds. 'A *mu'min* is one', he says, 'whose heart trembles at the mention of God, obeys His orders, submits to His remembrance in fear of Him and His punishment' (1954, 9, p. 178). While al-Zamakhshari says that these characteristics are required for 'perfect *iman*', he links the increase in *iman* to possessing greater truths and an increase in righteous deeds (n.d. 2, p. 196). Al-Razi is even more explicit about the relationship between *iman* and the characteristics mentioned in this text. Referring to the preceding verse ('Obey God and His Prophet if you are a *mu'min*'), he says that '*iman* has to result in obedience' (1990, 15, p. 121) and that the verse under discussion is a commentary of the verse preceding it. '*Iman*', he says, 'is not attained until this obedience is attained and this is only accomplished when the five characteristics are fulfilled' (ibid.).

Ibn 'Arabi avoids the scholastic discourse on the relationship between *iman* and righteous deeds. Yet one gets a clear sense that, for him, *iman* is intrinsically connected to the pursuit of ever-deepening faith. We have seen how he has interpreted increase in *iman* as progressing from mere rational acknowledgement of the presence of God, to the stage of certainty. Furthermore, the care to be devoted to the quality and presence of heart which must characterize one's worship as an extension of *iman* is also clear in his interpretation of this text (n.d., 1, p. 252). After defining *iman* as 'all the knowledge, belief and required action', Rida (1980, 9, p. 590) repeats a *hadith* in al-Bukhari and Muslim that 'the least of faith will save one in the hereafter' and another stating that *iman* has seventy branches as 'clear testimony' of this definition (ibid.).

The insistence on viewing righteous deeds as an intrinsic part of *iman* is well founded in the Qur'an, where the phrase 'those who have *iman* and who do righteous deeds' occurs no less than thirty-six times. What is evident is that *iman* is intrinsically connected to righteous deeds whether they are part and parcel of *iman* or as a necessary consequence of it. 'The separation of faith from action', as Rahman says. 'is, for the Qur'an, a totally untenable and absurd situation' (Rahman 1983, p. 171). Perhaps the best elaboration of this relationship is offered by Izutsu. 'The strongest tie of semantic relationship binds *salih* [righteousness] and *iman* together into an almost inseparable unit. Just as the shadow follows the form, wherever there is *iman* there is *salihat* [righteous deeds] . . . so much so that we may feel justified in defining the former in terms of the latter and the latter expressed in terms of the former' (1966, p. 204).

It is important to note that, whatever the differences in the relationship between *iman* and righteous deeds, traditional scholarship has usually interpreted these in a very narrow sense, i.e., as the rituals of reified Islam. While *iman* is often connected to the rituals, as in Qur'an 8: 2–4, this is not always the case. There are numerous other examples where the reference is to *iman* and righteous conduct in a general and unspecified sense.[3] Furthermore, the Qur'an is quite categorical about the smallest act of righteousness being rewarded, without insisting on *iman* as a condition.[4]

This discussion of the relationship between *iman* and righteous deeds brings us to several significant issues: 1) the status of those who have *iman* in the sense of affirmation but whose lives are bereft of 'righteous conduct', even if the latter is interpreted as the rituals of reified Islam; 2) the worth of righteous conduct unaccompanied by *iman* in the sense of affirmation or assent as elaborated in Islamic theology and 3) the possibility of *iman* unaccompanied by assent, as elaborated in Islamic theology.

These questions were of particular relevance to Muslims in South

Africa during the 1980s. Among the engaged Muslims there was utter disdain for the members of the community who identified with the apartheid regime and a deep sense of shame that they continued to regard themselves as members of the 'believing community'. While a *hadith* 'whosoever walks with the oppressor has gone forth from Islam' was widely invoked, these activists stopped short of denying that the collaborators were 'believers'. Instead, the more ambiguous expression of 'politically apostate' was used and the word 'Muslim' was placed in inverted commas when referring to them.

In stark contrast to the behaviour of the collaborationist Muslims, the country saw young Jews and Christians going to jail because of their refusal to serve in the apartheid army. Similarly, numerous deeply committed Christians, both clergy and laity, preferred torture and incarceration as the price of a deeply held conviction that faith in God implied an undying commitment to the dignity and freedom of His people. How could the faith of the former be affirmed and that of the latter denied if one earnestly believed that one's God was a just God who was 'the Lord and Sustainer of the people'? The question of the faith and the righteousness of the Other thus assumed an urgency and intimacy that escaped all of those uninvolved in the struggle. Such an urgency and intimacy was, in all probability, alien to medieval theologians who lived in Muslim majority lands and who often functioned under the benign patronage of the ruler.

Having sketched something of the background to these seemingly theological questions, one can now discuss them. While the first question, the *iman* status of the unrighteous, is not the most pertinent in terms of the overall subject of this study, it is useful for throwing light on the second and third.

In the Qur'an, in exegetical literature and in general Muslim discourse, the word *iman* is used in several different ways: 1) as the act of assenting to the existence of God, the ultimate accountability to Him and to the prophethood of Muhammad; 2) for belonging to the religious community of Islam irrespective of the actual faith commitment or the lack of any such commitment and 3) as an ongoing struggle to concretize faith in God in one's personal and social conduct. As for the first sense, al-Razi has argued succinctly that *iman* is affirmation because this is what it means in the Arabic language (1990, 1, p. 29). After such affirmation one becomes a member of the community of believers, i.e., the second sense. That there were various levels of actualizing that affirmation among different parts of the community and individuals is clear from the Qur'an, which at times refers to the believers as an established socio-religious community. For example, Qur'an 6:82 speaks about 'those who have *iman* and do not mix their *iman* with injustice' while 49:9 refers to a group among the *mu'minun* acting wrongfully.

'Abd al-Ra'uf (1967) has focused on the meaning of *mu'min* as derived from *amn* ('to become secure' or 'to render security'), and has argued the case for a sociological appreciation of *iman*. 'Fear of insecurity', he argues, 'was the major stumbling block against the faith in the early days'. He suggests that 'an obvious substitute [for tribal security] was the formation of a social organization in the framework of the tribe, in which the members of the group were to be as closely knit together in a common bond other than the blood tie (1967, p. 98). While *mu'minun* undoubtedly referred to a sociological group, it is, nevertheless, doubtful if the mere naming of a group as 'the secured', as 'Abd al-Ra'uf suggests, would have had sufficient effect to allay the insecurity of potential converts. Secondly, the term 'those who have *iman*' was already used in Mecca, albeit infrequently, at a period when the Muslims were socially at their most vulnerable and insecure. Whatever the weakness in 'Abd al-Ra'uf's arguments, it is clear that, as a group, some people were described as *mu'minun* even when the actions of all the individuals therein did not accord with their faith commitments.

In Muslim society, being born in a Muslim household has always, in practice, been sufficient cause for inclusion among the *mu'minun* on condition that one never verbally rejects that heritage. This means that even the act of 'affirmation with the tongue' is, in practice, dispensed with, for there is no formal mechanism for testing the faith commitment of an individual when he or she reaches the age of moral responsibility. It is clear that *mu'min* also meant, and continues to mean, someone with an essentially socio-religious, rather than personal, faith commitment (expressed in the rituals of Islam or in one's general demeanour). It would, therefore, be an extraordinary, unjust act of chauvinism to deny the legitimacy of *iman* as faith in a God who is utterly beyond human conceptions and a faith which is expressed in a life totally in conformity with the ethos of the Qur'an and its emphasis on righteousness.

That there were *mu'minun* in the non-sociological sense of the word, i.e., outside the Muhammadan community, is clear and generally acknowledged. This acknowledgement, though, is confined by conservative Islam to the prophets and their followers who preceded Muhammad. As will be indicated in the following chapter, the Qur'an itself is explicit about the *iman* of the People of the Book. On several occasions it employs the term for those who coexist with the community of

Muhammad, but are not a part of it. It furthermore affirms the validity of all righteousness as acts or behaviour which result in God's grace.

In addition to Qur'an 8:2–4, a number of other texts that relate *iman* to the heart support the view that, in addition to the socio-religious understanding of *iman*, it is also, perhaps even primarily, a matter of deep inner and personal conviction (e.g., 16:106; 49:7–8; 58:22). In at least one case the Qur'an is explicit about withholding the description *mu'min* from those who have formally joined the community of Muslims (49:14–15). Here some Bedouin were told that the act of formally entering into the community of Islam was distinct from *iman*. Islam, in the sense of formally submitting to the new order brought about by Muhammad, was merely the beginning of a faith that still had to acquire roots in their hearts.[5] The implication of this passage might have been that joining the community of Muslims did not necessarily reflect a personal faith. In this sense 'faith' and 'conviction', rather than 'belief', are more accurate renderings of *iman*. Cantwell-Smith has pointed out that ' "belief" is a derivative and can be an exceedingly watered down and inoperative matter, compared with the richness and warmth and the engagement of "faith" ' (1991, p. 111). We have seen that the Qur'an acknowledges a diluted form of *iman*. When a whole tribe converted to Islam by way of a treaty with Muhammad, we must understand this treaty in terms of Arab–Bedouin cultural practices. Therefore, this practice may not have meant the same thing for all members of the tribe and the name 'Muslim' could well have been a new identity of treaty rather than of faith. This could also help to explain the seemingly opposite use of *iman* in the following qur'anic passage: 'O those who have *iman*, have *iman*' (4:126). In the Qur'an, the most significant sense is the second one, i.e., 'an active quality, one that commits the person and by which he [or she] is caught up into a dynamic relationship with his [or her] Maker and his [or her] fellows. It is the ability to see the transcendent, and to respond to it; to hear God's voice and to act accordingly' (Cantwell-Smith 1991, p. 112).

Given that *iman* is also a deeply personal response to God, it cannot be confined to a particular socio-religious community. Such attempts would be a denial of the universality of God Himself. This is why the Qur'an is explicit about the *iman* of those outside the socio-religious community of *mu'minun*. If *iman* can embrace the removal of a banana peel from the road, how can it not embrace the lifelong response of an individual to the voice of God as he or she perceives it and manifests it in an abiding life of service to those with whom God himself has chosen to identify, the oppressed and marginalized?

Redefining *Islam*: From a Noun to a Verb

The following text, particularly the first sentence, is an important one in Muslim claims that the only expression of religiosity acceptable to God since the prophethood of Muhammad is Islam, the religion institutionalized by Muhammad. Furthermore, most interpreters have used this opportunity to define and elaborate on the meaning of *islam*.

> Behold, the *din* with God is *islam*; and those who were vouchsafed the scripture aforetime, out of mutual jealousy, differed only after knowledge had come unto them. But as for the one who rejects/is ungrateful (*yakfur*) for the signs of God, behold God is swift in reckoning. (Qur'an 3:19)

The entire third chapter of the Qur'an, 'The Family of Imran', wherein this text appears, is Medinan. It follows on from 'The Cow' and, similarly, deals at length with the People of the Book. In 'The Family of Imran' though, far more attention is devoted to the Christians and to attempts by the opponents of Islam to wipe it out from its stronghold, Medina.

The selected text is preceded by one whereby God, the angels and 'people of knowledge' bear testimony to God's unity and thereby uphold justice. While the text's use of the word *islam*, based on the root *s-l-m*, may be interpreted here to refer to a reified conception of Islam, the preceding verse uses it in an unambiguously personalist manner. The text is followed by an instruction to Muhammad to tell his opponents that his path is simply one of submitting his being/attention to God and that this is also the path required of them.

This is one of several verses in the Qur'an which refers to *islam* as the only *din* acceptable to God. In other verses *islam* is described as God's choice for the community of Muhammad and the completion of His favour upon it (5:3). Those whose 'breasts had been opened to *islam*' are described as 'following a light from his [her] Lord' (39:22). The intensifying particle '*inna*' in the text under discussion is usually seen as affirming the singularity of *islam* as the acceptable *din* to God. This view is seemingly corroborated by another text in the same chapter: 'Do they seek, perchance a *din* other than God? [Although] it is unto Him that whatsoever is in the heavens and on earth surrenders (*aslama*) willingly or unwillingly, since unto Him all must return . . . And unto Him/for Him we are *muslimun*. For whoever goes in search of a *din* other than *islam*, it will never be accepted from him [or her], and in the life to come he [or she] shall be among the lost' (3:83–5).

An examination of the terms *din* and, more especially, *islam,* is obviously central to an understanding of these verses and of the question of Islam and religious exclusivism or pluralism. I shall briefly mention the views of some of the interpreters regarding these terms in this text, before discussing these within the context of a process of reification. This process has eroded the more pluralist understanding of the term *islam* and supplanted it with a rigid and formal religious system.

Al-Tabari   'Verily the *din* with God is *al-islam,* which is simultaneously the way of viewing as well as responding to "reality". Today the *islam* which is acceptable to God is that embodied in the Qur'an' (1954, 3, p. 212). As Smith has pointed out, *islam* for al-Tabari, on 'one level implies both the act of joining the group of Muslims/muslims and the name of that group, and, on another level . . . personal surrender of the heart' (Smith 1975, p. 219).

Ibn 'Arabi   'Verily the true *din* with God is this *tawhid* which He has prescribed for Himself. His *din* is, therefore, the *din* of the submission of one's entire being . . . [to be a Muslim means that I have] severed myself from my ego and achieved annihilation in Him' (n.d., 1, p. 105).

Al-Zamakhshari   'The [preceding] statement "there is no deity save Him" is *tawhid* while "upholding justice" is equity if this is followed by "verily the *din* by God is *islam*" then it implies that the meaning of *islam* is equity and *tawhid.* This is the religion according to God; all else is not *din*' (n.d. 1, p. 245).

Al-Razi   'From the linguistic origin of *din* as "recompense" *din* has the meaning of obedience which is the cause of recompense.' . . . 'Islam has three meanings: entry into Islam i.e., into submission and obedience, entry into peace and purifying all service for God' (1990, 7, p. 220).

Rida   According to God, *al-din,* the injunctions of God and the response which the servants impose upon themselves, the authentic *islam,* is the intensely personal submission of the individual to God and the universal spirit in which all religious communities partake . . . This submission bears no relationship to conventional Islam which is trapped in imitation and in ethno-sociological communities' (1980, 3, p. 267).

Al-Tabataba'i   *Islam* is absolute submission to the truth of belief and of action . . . This verse refers to *din* in the meaning of a single *shari'ah* which does not differ from the previous *shari'ahs* except in the natural capacities of the various recipient communities' (1973, 3, p. 121).

There are a number of studies dealing with the meaning of the word *din* and its use in the Qur'an.[6] Most Muslim works, and all of the exegetical works under discussion, deal with its meaning in a theological manner while the task of a more linguistic analysis has essentially fallen to non-Muslim critical scholarship. Both from traditional dictionaries (Ibn Manzur, n.d., 2, p. 1467–70) and from the textual studies of scholars such as Cantwell-Smith (1991, pp. 102 ff.), one may conclude that the word *din* in seventh-century Arabia had several different meanings which may be classed in three principal groups: 1) the concept of systematic religion;[7] 2) the verbal noun, 'judging', 'passing judgement', 'passing sentence'; and, along with this, 'judgement', 'verdict'; 3) the verbal noun 'to conduct oneself', 'to behave', 'to observe certain practices', 'to follow traditional usage' and, subsequently, abstract noun, 'conformity', 'propriety', 'obedience', 'customs' and 'standard behaviour'.

Muslim scholarship has elaborated the meaning of *din* within the context of interpreting *islam* as *din*. Significantly, while most of the explanations, in varying degrees, carry the implicit acceptance of *din* as form, i.e., that it is and, indeed, ought to be, expressed within systematic and institutionalized religious life, these explanations focus essentially on process, on *din* as personal submission to God. None of the meanings of the word given by the interpreters correspond to that of 'institutional religion', although some meanings may have such implications. While they all recognize that, at one level, the *din* of *islam* was one among several reified religious systems, and, for all of them, the superior one, it is evident that 'this was not the primary reference for their understanding of *islam* as *din*' (Smith 1975, p. 229). Rida, however, defines *din* in a universal manner which excludes mere formal identification with a socio-historical Islam, while openly acknowledging the legitimacy of religious paths other than reified Islam. According to Rida, this intensely personal submission of the individual to God and the universal spirit, in which all religious communities partake, bears no relationship to conventional Islam.

In a concise, but lucid study, Yvonne Haddad has elaborated on the conception of the term as it appears in the various periods of the Qur'an's revelation (1974). According to Haddad, there were four distinct periods

when the term was employed and, while the various periods saw changes
in the usage of the term, 'the essence of the meaning . . . appears to have
remained constant' (1974, p. 122). In the first and second Meccan periods, the term appears as a verbal noun and mostly with the word *yawm*
(day), as *yawm al-din*, (i.e., the Day of Requital). In the earliest chapters
of the Qur'an the emphasis is on humankind's response to God, of either
denial or agreement. The manner in which denial or agreement is used in
the Qur'an though, makes it apparent that it bears little relation to a verbal rejection or affirmation of *din* or *yawm al-din*. It is rather a denial of a
lifestyle of response or non-response to God and the idea of ultimate
accountability with which the Qur'an is concerned. In the third Meccan
period *din* seems to emphasize a personal commitment of the individual
to God. However, Haddad has shown that in the last part of the Meccan
period, there is an identification of the unchanging *din* with the 'community of Abraham' and 'the straight path'. From then onwards the emphasis seems to be on a community of believers (1974, p. 119). This leads on
to the Medinan period when the emphasis on *din* as personal commitment is switched to the use of the term for commitment in the collective
sense. For the first time the term 'the true *din*' is now used. The one 'true
response', it was being promised, would be established above other
responses (cf. Qur'an 61:9).

Before proceeding to examine the concept of *islam* and *islam* as *din*,
one needs to highlight the following underlying issues. Firstly, the term
din was employed with various meanings within the Arabian peninsula
during the seventh century. It was inevitable that the Qur'an would use it
within the confines of those understandings. The absence of the plural
form, *adyan*, is perhaps reflective of this, because religious life was not as
fully reified then. Secondly, the Qur'an is engaged in a dynamic relationship with its hearers; it speaks and uses expressions in terms of the understanding of a community or individuals at a particular stage of their
development. Thus, *din* is not employed in the communal sense in the
early Meccan context. Thirdly, to deny or to affirm *din* or *yawm al-din*
had little or nothing to do with verbal or theoretical affirmation or rejection. Affirmation or rejection related to a personal lifestyle of response to
God and a higher moral imperative or one of actively displaying contempt for these. Fourthly, the present near universal understanding of *din*
as 'religion' and the corresponding virtual elimination of *din* as a personal
response to God is unfounded in the text of the Qur'an, as well as in traditional exegesis.

Let us now consider the meaning of the word *islam*[8] and the concept of *islam* as *din*. The infinitive of *aslama*, *islam* means 'to submit', 'to surrender', 'to fulfil or execute'. In the context of the expression 'he entered into *al-silm*', *islam* is interpreted as the name of a religion. The term also means 'reconciliation', 'peace' or 'wholeness', as Rida has demonstrated (1980, 3, p. 257) and as a number of Muslim liberals and apologists for Islam have stressed (Ameer Ali 1974, p. 137; Muhammad Ali 1990, p. 4).

'Naming the *din* of truth "*islam*"', Rida says, 'corresponds to all the linguistic meanings of the word, particularly "submission"' (1980, 3, p. 257). Asad's rendition of *islam* as '(humankind's) self-surrender unto God' (1980, p. 69) seemingly gathers within it the various interpretations of *islam*. As a verbal noun, the term appears only eight times in the Qur'an whereas its foundation verb, *aslama*, appears twenty-four times. I agree with 'Abd al-Ra'uf who suggests that the relative infrequency of the use of *islam* 'is characteristic of the Qur'an which is less concerned with words related to metaphysical and static thinking, than with words intrinsically related to active and dynamic conceptions' (1967, p. 94).

The term *islam*, despite the infrequency with which it appears in the Qur'an, is central to Muslim self-definition. That this term, rather than *iman* which appears much more frequently, should be so pivotal, is itself pregnant with questions about the transformation that the self-definition of the community of Muhammad has undergone. It is with this in mind that the meaning of *islam* is now considered.

Cantwell-Smith has traced the 'reificationist conceptualization of *islam*' (1991, p. 108) and shown how the original meaning of words such as *islam* and *kufr* in traditional peninsular Arabic and their early acceptance in Muslim conviction was 'something much more vibrant searching and transporting' (ibid., p. 110). He has argued that, while it is clear that the words *islam* and *din* 'could conjure up the idea of Islam as a reified entity, one religion among others, this was by no means the only, and, indeed, not even the primary, interpretation' (ibid., p. 109). His arguments have been adequately supported by the more systematic exegetical research undertaken by Jane Smith (1975) into the definitive qur'anic texts wherein the term appears.

Among the interpreters whose works are presently being reflected upon, Rida stands alone in his explicit distinction between reified and non-reified *islam*. He argues that the usage of *al-islam* to mean the doctrines, traditions and practices of those people who are known as Muslims, is new, based on the phenomenological principle of 'religion being what its followers have'. This is *al-din* in the sense of an ethno-sociological community (*jinsiyy*) or custom (*'urf*) (1980, 3, p. 361).[9] He argues that social and customary Islam, 'which varies according to the differences which have occurred to its adherents in the way of uncritical acceptance, has no relationship with true *islam*'. 'On the contrary', he writes, 'it is subversive of true faith' (ibid.).

At a superficial glance, many of Rida's arguments may be viewed as modernist. The works of Cantwell-Smith and Smith, however, prove that he is closer to the earliest interpretation of this text and of *islam* than contemporary Muslim conservatism may want to concede. A more detailed look at the conclusions reached by them bears this out. Firstly, the Qur'an employs the term *islam* much less frequently than other related terms. However, where it is employed, it is in a manner where it can be, 'and on many grounds almost must be, interpreted, not as the name of a religious system, but as the designation of a decisive personal act' (Cantwell-Smith 1991, p. 110). The Qur'an refers three times to *islam* in the context of *din* (3:19; 3:85; 5:3). At a further two places the reference is implicitly personal (6:125; 39:22) and at two others explicitly so (49:17; 9:74). It is thus hardly surprising that, particularly in early exegetical scholarship, the verbal noun form was primarily interpreted as such. Secondly, the personalist interpretation is 'in fact, closer to the straightforward and simple meanings of the Arabic words' and 'historically, this was the interpretation given to these passages by many, if not most, of the Muslim religious thought in the early centuries' (Cantwell-Smith 1991, p. 113).

The systematic study of this subtle transformation was taken up by Smith who has shown that there has been a 'historical flow, involving both movement and continuity, that takes us from what *islam* meant to what it "has meant" and what it "means"' (1975, p. 222–3). We are dealing with a term the interpretation of which is 'dynamic, both within the understanding of individual writers and as expressed by the historical development of the concept from one age to another' (ibid.). Furthermore, she shows that the interpretations of the term have developed along the following two axes of investigation. The first concerns the relation between the external and the internal aspects of surrender, i.e., between *islam* as affirmation and *islam* as external conformity: there is general agreement that, in the light of verses such as 3:83; 49:14 and others, that while *islam* can be applied to an act that is purely external, it is really only when that act is performed with the full inner acceptance and affirmation of the one who submits, that it can be considered *islam* in the full sense of the word (Smith 1975, p. 66).

The second interpretation concerns the individual and the group aspects of *islam*. The 'original meaning' of *islam* is located in a 'fusion of the individual and group interpretations' (ibid., p. 228). Smith also notes that 'while it (*islam*) was once inclusive on the level of the relationship of individual and group, there have been significant changes in the way "*islam*" has been used, which are specifically related to time'. In the traditional commentaries *islam* is both individual submission and the name of the group, but with the primary emphasis on the former, and with the dual usage generally by implication. When interpreters failed to make a distinction between the personal act of submission and the community of Muhammad, then the reference was 'always to the historical group of *Muslimun* at the time of Muhammad rather than to the particular group existing and fully organized at the time of the writing of each *tafsir* [commentary]' (Smith 1975, p. 228).

In any study of the use of a single term it is easy to ignore the fact that that term is actually lived out and understood within a set of explicit, albeit unstated, 'givens'. In this case, *islam*, in even the most personalist interpretations offered by Rida, was also lived out as a set of injunctions within the parameters of formalized *shari'ah*. In the Qur'an itself, however it is employed, it is within the context of numerous other texts dealing with a developing religious community with its own laws and institutions. More specifically, both from the context of numerous injunctions relating to the socio-religious life of the community such as those relating to marriage, divorce, diet, inheritance etc. and from the actual statement in Qur'an 5:3, 'This day have I perfected for you your *din* and completed my favour unto you and chosen for you *islam* as a *din*', the group and reified sense is inescapable. *Islam* was also the designation given by God to the path of *islam* that a particular community of Muslims were to follow.

The problem with the dominant contemporary Muslim discourse is that it is based on the idea that *islam* is only reified Islam. Clearly, both the personalist sense as well as the group sense are contained in the word and in the texts wherein it occurs. Both senses must, therefore, be acknowledged in any attempt to make space for the one within the other: the importance of personal submission within the framework of group identification as well as the possibility of personal submission outside the parameters of the historical community of Islam.

The fact of a non-reified *islam* is clear from the Qur'an and from the interpreters whose views I have examined here. The Qur'an is explicit about two such forms: the *islam* of the prophets who preceded Muhammad and their communities, and submission to the will of God by the various non-human elements in nature (3:73). Of significance for the present study is a third form: *islam* in individuals and communities who

132

share common space, geography or time with the adherents of reified Islam: in other words, those known today as Muslims.

Even in a traditional exegetical work such as al-Tabari's, it is evident that *din* is viewed as an active response to the will of God rather than ethno-social membership of a particular group. This, of course, does not mean that al-Tabari, or even al-Zamakhshari, is open to accepting as *muslims* those who dissociate themselves from such a group. Al-Tabari, for example, states that the Prophet came with both the 'exposition of truth' (*bayan al-haq*) and the way to serve truth (*din al-haq*) (1954, 12, p. 58) which, as Smith has pointed out, is significantly different from 'the true *din*' (*al-din al-haq*). '*Din al-haq* thus means not "the true *din*" which would have to be *al-din al-haq*, but obedience, submission, service to truth in terms of what God has made known in His *huda* [guidance] and *bayan* [discourse]. This then is the *din Allah* (not the religion of God but the service of God) the total response to God Himself' (Smith 1975, p. 74).

Traditional exegesis is thus not entirely without the germs for religious pluralism. Despite the insights that a study of these works may provide and the crutches these may afford to any attempt at rethinking difficult texts, we need to remember the context wherein traditional scholars wrote; it simply did not produce the kinds of questions that modernity or South African apartheid have raised. It would thus be untenable, as I argued in the beginning of this chapter, to base the search for a theology of religious pluralism and for liberation purely on the ideas produced in their works.

Notwithstanding the present-day use of texts such as Qur'an 3:19 and 39:22 to affirm the superiority of Islam over other faiths, the universal underpinnings in the term *islam*, lead one to the understanding that the text embraces all of those who submit to the will of God. This embrace includes the religious Other along with 'the diversity of some of the obligations and the forms of practices in them, and with which they have been enjoined' (Rida 1980, 3, p. 257). In the words of Rida, 'the true *muslim* is one who is unblemished by the errors of *shirk*, sincere in his [or her] actions and having faith, from whatsoever, community, in whatever period or place . . . This is the meaning of "Whosoever desires a *din* other than *islam* will never have it [his or her choice] accepted" [Qur'an 3:85]' (Rida 1980, 3, p. 257).

From a careful study of *islam* in the Qur'an and in the various contexts already mentioned, it is evident that it has the potential to be freed from the gloss of medieval theology and the historically bound context of intra-community polemics that characterized the Prophet's Hijaz. The inclusivist meaning of *islam* is, at times, also apparent from the context of a particular text. An example of this is the context of the text cited by Rida above, where the statement 'Do they pursue a *din* other than that of God' can only render an inclusivist meaning if the context is also considered.

The South African reality of people with 'Muslim' labels actively participating in the oppression of millions of black people, on the one hand, and people wearing an array of religious Other labels – and some refusing to wear any religious label – sacrificing their lives for the cause of justice and freedom, on the other, easily convinces one of the necessity to go beyond labels. Where these labels are formulated by God, we are left with no option but to find meanings truer to the image of a God obsessed with justice. The Qur'an portrays a *muslim* as someone who submits to a divinity beyond, and more abiding, than that *muslim* and beyond reified religion. God is *akbar* (greater than) any conception of Him or any form of institutionalized or non-institutionalized service to Him. It is to God that the Qur'an persistently requires *islam*.

Rethinking *Kufr*

I have selected the following verses to underpin my reflection on the qur'anic use of the word *kufr*:

> Verily, as for those who reject/are ungrateful [*yakfur*] for the signs of God, and slay the Prophets against all right, and slay people who enjoin justice, announce unto them a grievous chastisement. It is they whose works shall come to nought, both in this world and in the life to come; and they shall have none to succour them. (Qur'an 3:21–2)

This text combines the apparently doctrinal (*kufr*) with the apparently socio-political (justice) in a manner that goes beyond liberal discourse. It does not only denounce *kufr* and those who obstruct justice, but promises them a 'grievous chastisement' and the loss of any support. The second verse (3:22) is also an example of a text used to deny the significance of all forms of religiosity, however sincere, if they are not rooted in reified Islam. Furthermore, the various exegeses on this text offer interesting insights into the interpretation of *kufr* and its application, or otherwise, to Jews and Christians. Finally, these interpretations are illustrative of the failure of classical exegesis to distinguish between *kufr* as an active attitude of individuals (or a collection of individuals) and the socio-religious (and often ethnic) identity of a group.

This text follows the one discussed on page 126 (3:19) wherein the 'true *din* according to God' is stated to be *al-islam* and where

Muhammad is instructed to declare to those who dispute with him that they have an obligation to submit (to God). However, if they turn back, then he, Muhammad, will be freed from any responsibility towards them because his task is only to proclaim the message. This text is followed by a reference to those who have been given 'a portion of the Scripture' but refuse to have their affairs judged by the Book of God. This refusal, the Qur'an says, is rooted in religious arrogance and a denial that the fire will touch them beyond a few days (3:23–4).

The expression 'those who reject the signs of God' in Qur'an 3:21–2 is one of several ways of describing the (rejected) Other in the Qur'an using some form of the word *kufr*. Other forms are the participial noun *kafir*, and its plural, *kuffar* or *kafirun*.[10] *Kufr* in the Qur'an and in Muslim discourse has become the term most pregnant with all that is despised in the rejected Other. It is a word that has entered several other languages, from Turkish to French, as a term of abuse. More pertinently, in a slightly altered form, *kaffir*, it has entered South African racist discourse as the most potent abusive expression for the black majority. Leonard Thompson, a South African historian, asserts that they were called *Cafres* because it was believed that 'there are no signs of belief or religion to be found among them' (1985, p. 73). In the South African example, we find the perfect fusion between religious and ethno-ideological chauvinism: *kafir* as a 'violent symbol of religious exclusion' (Omar 1991, p. 9) and *kaffir* as racist demonizing of the Other. In this context, the task of rethinking *kufr*, is thus deeply human and firmly connected to the search for justice.

Lexicographers such as Ibn Manzur (n.d., 5, pp. 3897–902) and Lane (1980, 7, pp. 2620–2) give several meanings of *kufr*, most of these illustrated by a qur'anic text. It is agreed that it means 'to conceal', the sense in which its earliest usage is known. Later it came to be used for concealing something with the intention of destroying it. However, its most common earlier usage was 'concealing an act of grace or kindness' i.e., 'ingratitude' (al-Baidawi n.d., 1, p. 50). Much later, when *islam* came to represent an act of God's grace, the word came to be synonymous with denying it. A *kafir* came to mean someone who, having 'received God's benevolence, shows no sign of gratitude in his [or her] conduct, or even acts rebelliously against his [or her] benefactor' (Izutsu 1966, p. 120). Izutsu has shown that while the word *kafir* itself contains an important element of disbelief, 'it must be remembered, this is not the only basic semantic constituent of the word, nor is it the original one' (ibid., p. 26). From an examination of pre-Islamic literature he has shown that the 'real core . . . of its semantic structure was not "un-belief", but rather "ingratitude" or "unthankfulness"' (ibid.).

Looking at the way these texts have been approached in the selected exegetical works provides a useful background for further reflections on the word *kufr*. Al-Zamakhshari and Ibn 'Arabi do not make any specific application of the term here, with Ibn 'Arabi interpreting 'those who reject the signs of God' as 'those who are veiled from the *din*' (n.d., 1, p. 105). Both al-Tabari (1954, 3, p. 216) and al-Razi (1990, 7, p. 231) say that this refers to the People of the Book while al-Tabataba'i (1973, 3, p. 123) and Rida (1980, 3, p. 262) are more specific and suggest that it refers to the Jews of Mecca and Medina especially.

In the Qur'an the word is used with all these meanings. Qur'an 57:20 uses it in the sense of 'tiller of the soil' while 2:153; 14:7, 15; 26:57, 85; 26:18; 27:40; 29:66; 30:33 and 39:7 are examples of where it is used to mean 'ungrateful'. Most frequently, though, is it used as the opposite of *iman*. Izutsu has argued that, in the Qur'an, the word *kafir* came to acquire the secondary meaning of 'one who does not believe in God', 'because it occurs very frequently in contrast to the word *mu'min*' (1966, p. 26). He is, furthermore, correct in arguing that if 'the nature of a word is such that it comes to be used with remarkable frequency in specific contexts alongside its antonym, it must of necessity acquire a noticeable semantic value from this frequent combination' (ibid.). It is, however, crucial to bear in mind that *kufr* even as an antonym of *islam* or *iman*, is as much a conscious attitude and a set of concrete actions as I have shown *islam* and *iman* to be. Therefore, even if it has come to mean disbelief, it remains something conscious, deliberate and active rather than a casual ignoring or disregard of the existence of God.

Despite the frequency with which the Qur'an moves into the area of identifying *kufr* with disbelief, its earliest meaning should never be abandoned, because its most significant semantic element is lost when we view it in supposedly purely doctrinal terms. Muhammad Asad (d. 1992), a contemporary interpreter, has also argued that, given the pre-Muhammadan meaning of the word in Arabic,

> the term *kafir* cannot be simply equated, as many Muslim theologians of post-classical times and practically all Western translators of the Qur'an have done, with 'unbeliever' or 'infidel' in the specific, restricted sense of one who rejects the system of doctrine and law promulgated in the Qur'an and amplified by the teachings of the Prophet – but must have a wider, more general meaning. (1980, p. 907)

In the more widely used sense of 'rejecter of faith', *kafir* was first applied
to some Meccans who insulted Muhammad and, later, in Medina, to various elements among the People of the Book as well. Subsequent to
Muhammad's demise at Medina (d. 652) its usage was liberally extended
by various groups to exclude the internal Other with whom one differed.
From a study of the Qur'an in the light of the hermeneutical keys elaborated in chapter 3, one is led to agree with Asad that, from its usage in
the Qur'an, a *kafir* is 'one who denies (or refuses to acknowledge) the
truth in the widest, spiritual sense' (Asad 1980, p. 907). The Qur'an portrays *kufr* as an actively and dynamic attitude of ingratitude leading to
wilful rejection of known truths, God's gifts, and, flowing from this as
well as intrinsically connected to it, a pattern of actively arrogant and
oppressive behaviour.

From the linguistic roots of *kufr* discussed above, it is evident that
kufr really indicates an attitude of wilful disavowal or rejection of a gift.
The chapter of the Qur'an *Al-Rahman* (55), with its refrain about denying the grace of God, conveys a similar meaning. This denial is the most
significant operative element in *kufr*. In the same way that gratitude, if it
is to be meaningful, must go beyond verbal declarations, ingratitude is
also an active attitude and a pattern of behaviour that emerges from the
acknowledgement of debt.

As the text under discussion indicates, *kufr* was connected to the
active and violent opposition to the prophets of God and a determination
to destroy their mission. Thus, the Qur'an, on several occasions, links
kufr to those who worked 'to sway people away from the path of God'
(6:26; 7:45; 8:36). From the text under discussion, we see that this opposition even included the actual or attempted assassinations of the
prophets of God and those who fought for justice (4:155; 5:70; 8:30).
Rather than *kufr* denoting a mere abstract or passive choice of non-belief,
the Qur'an portrays *kufr* as a characteristic that one actually strives for
(16:106; 22:51; 34:5). The *kuffar*, according to the Qur'an, struggle in
the way of evil (4:76) and violently resist God's will for humankind
(25:55). The Qur'an does not only link *kufr* with a refusal to spend one's
wealth on the poor (2:254; 3:179; 9:34, 35; 41:7) but also with spending
it to prevent people from drawing nearer to God and to righteousness
(8:36). Instead, the typical *kafir* oppresses the weak (4:168; 14:13) or
maintains silence in the face of evil and oppression (5:79).

The idea of the *kafir* in violent opposition to God should not be confused with theological, rational or philosophical problems with the notion
of a supreme deity, for the *kafir* freely acknowledged the existence of such

an entity (2:61–3; 31:25; 33:9, 78). However, the monotheism which existed in pre-Islamic Arabia was one without any threatening socio-economic implications for the powerful. For Muhammad though, 'monotheism was, from the beginning, linked up with a humanism and a sense of social and economic justice whose intensity is no less than the intensity of the monotheistic idea' (Rahman 1966, p. 12). The God the Meccans rejected was one who demanded the concrete transformation of society, from exploitation to justice, from selfishness to selflessness, from arrogance to humility and from a narrow tribalism to the unity of all those committed to this new vision of society.

The Qur'an portrays *kufr* as an important factor that both shaped a bloated image of the Self and manifested itself in it and in the accompanying contempt for the weak Other. As Izutsu points out, *kufr*, in the Qur'an, as the denial of God and His unity actually 'manifests itself most characteristically in various acts of insolence, haughtiness presumptuousness and arrogance' (1966, p. 120) and the idea that wealth makes one entirely independent from others and God (9:34, 35; 13:18). The *kuffar* were contemptuous of those who chose the path of *islam* and regularly mocked them (10:79; 15:11; 18:106). This contempt for the *muslim* Other was not purely because of the faith choices they had made, but because they were weak and vulnerable (34:32). When they were not among the weak themselves, they were mocked because they chose to identify with the weak and spend their wealth in supporting them (9:79). More frequently than not, *kufr* had its roots in a displaced sense of tribal superiority and class arrogance. The *kuffar* mocked the lowly origins of the early followers of Islam and, the Qur'an suggests, they felt that their hoarded wealth freed them from any moral obligations to others or accountability to God. (7:48; 9:79; 19:77.)

Am I saying that *kufr* has nothing to do with dogma? Not quite, for there is no doubt that *kufr* also relates to a denial of dogma. The object of *kufr* in the Qur'an is at various times the unity of God, scripture, the signs of God, the resurrection and the prophets. More specifically, the Qur'an denounces as *kufr* notions of the divinity of Christ (4:171; 5:17) and any attempt to ascribe paternity to God (19:91–2; 9:30). In looking at the seemingly doctrinal nature of *kufr* in the Qur'an, several significant issues have to be borne in mind if one is determined to avoid injustice to those who do not carry the 'Muslim' label.

Firstly, whenever the Qur'an links *kufr* to doctrine it does so within a real socio-historical context and is convinced that sincere belief in the unity of God and ultimate accountability to Him would lead to a righteous and just society. Denying God is, for example, connected to breaking promises and spreading corruption (2:28) and denying the resurrection to the refusal to spend a part of their wealth on the poor (41:7). In the light of the argument that beliefs and the consequences of holding them are always intrinsically connected, one cannot refer to *kufr*, or any other notion, as 'purely doctrinal'. This would be affording doctrine an ahistorical sense which is not borne out by the very dynamic interplay of revelation and society.

Secondly, the Qur'an portrays the *kafir* as someone who has actually recognized the unity of God and Muhammad as His Prophet, but who, nevertheless, wilfully refuses to acknowledge it. The linguistic meaning of *kufr* as (consciously) 'covering something' is consistent throughout the Qur'an when matters of the seemingly doctrinal are raised and the Qur'an repeatedly accuses the *kafir* of concealing the truth, despite clear knowledge of it. 'They recognized [the integrity of] Muhammad', the Qur'an says, 'as much as they recognized their own kith and kin' (2:146; 6:20).[11] The deliberate nature of *kufr* is, furthermore, seen in the fact that the Qur'an often uses different forms of the verbs *k-dh-b*, (to lie) and *k-t-m* (to conceal) as synonyms of *kufr* (2:42, 159, 174).

Thirdly, it is an antagonistic attitude to *islam* and to *muslims*, in the sense of submission to God and to a people who wanted to organize their collective existence on the basis of such submission, that the Qur'an denounces as *kufr*. This is rather different from disagreeing with reified, particularly contemporary, Islam or opposing the socio-religious community known as Muslims.

Finally, the Qur'an is also specific about the motives of the *kuffar*'s decision to refrain from professing belief. They understood that belief implied more than a mental shift to another idea or set of ideas, but that it required a radical change in personal life, in values and in socio-economic relations. They opted for *kufr*, the Qur'an says, because of narrow material gains (21:53; 26:74; 31:21), tribal bonds (43:22) and because *islam* would disturb the unjust social order (3:21).

It is impossible to separate the *kufr* denounced in the Qur'an from the personal and social attitudes of Muhammad's opponents as individuals or a group in Mecca or Medina. We have to try to find exactly where we see such attitudes to *islam* and such patterns of socio-political behaviour in order to develop a contemporary application of the term *kufr* and not the mere transference of labels.

I now want to turn my attention to the commentaries dealing with the second characteristic of the *kuffar* dealt with in the verse 'They slay the Prophets against all right, and slay people who enjoin justice and they slaughter those among the people who enjoin justice.' The commentaries particularly show how these labels become transferred and, as a result, the religious Other imprisoned in collective guilt. A common thread of issues connected to justice runs through the exegesis of the phrase: collective guilt and punishment, facing the consequences of one's deeds and the relationship between those sent as prophets of God and those struggling for justice.

Much attention is devoted to the verb *q-t-l* and its various renditions. For most of the interpreters, the problem is the use of the perfect tense, *yaqtulun*, which refers to the present act of killing, whereas the commonly accepted idea among them is that this refers to the past when the Jews supposedly slew prophets who were sent to them.[12] Most of the interpreters opt for *yaqtulun*. With a rather transparent and heavy dose of racism, they apply the text to all Jews, including those who coexisted with Muhammad in Medina. The guilt also applies to the Jewish contemporaries of Muhammad, they argue, because they 'approved of their predecessors' actions' (al-Zamakhshari n.d., 1, p. 346). Furthermore, 'they [the *mushrikun* of Mecca] attempted the assassination of the Prophet and of the *mu'minun*, and would have succeeded if it were not for the protection of God' (ibid.). Rida offers an equally racist explanation of the corporate guilt. 'The killing of Prophets who had preceded them [the Jews of Medina]', Rida wrote, 'is ascribed to them as a community in its burdens since the vestiges of the past are visited upon those in the present' (1980, 3, p. 261). Al-Tabataba'i follows suit, although in a more strident vein: 'The unjustified slaughter of prophets and those who enjoined justice and equity and who prohibited from oppression and aggression was an ingrained habit and characteristic running in them as confirmed by the history of the Jews' (1973, 3, p. 123).

The notion that evil runs through the blood of some groups, particularly the Jews, is also carried through in interpretations of the second accusation; 'and they slaughter those among the people who enjoin justice'. Both al-Tabari (1954, 3, p. 216) and al-Zamakhshari (n.d., 1, p. 347) suggest that this is a specific reference to individuals among the Jews who opposed the killings of prophets and they limit its application to those who oppose sin in the moralistic sense. While al-Tabataba'i does not have anything noteworthy to say at this juncture, al-Razi, Ibn 'Arabi and, especially, Rida, make some very significant statements about the status of those who struggle for justice; they compare their status to just one level below that of the prophets. None of the interpreters, however, use this opportunity to draw attention to the important fact that, within these religiously Other communities, there had always existed elements in the midst of injustice who stood firm against severe odds, a fact born out by all the accounts of the event that was supposed to have occasioned the revelation of this verse.[13] To tar these individuals with the same brush as those whom they opposed is itself manifest injustice.

After arguing that this verse is proof that those who enjoin the good and forbid evil in conditions of fear are just below the elevated stages of the prophets, al-Razi cites a *hadith* that 'the preferred *jihad* is a truth spoken in the presence of a tyrant' (1990, 7, p. 232). Ibn 'Arabi talks about justice being the shadow of *tawhid* and says that 'whosoever denies the shadow has denied the essence' (n.d., 1, p. 51). Rida believes that this is a reference to the wise and to sages 'who guide people to general justice in everything and made it the spirit and support of virtue' (1980, 3, p. 262). He also agrees that 'their status in guidance and righteousness follows that of the Prophets' (ibid., p. 263). He is quite categorical that they include those 'convinced by religion and the areligious who, despite this, [their areligiousness], enjoined justice from an intellectual and rational basis' (ibid.). Rida then notes a very interesting point which his mentor, Muhammad 'Abduh, made about this text: 'By the use of the expression *min al-nas* [among people] rather than *min al-mu'minin* [among the *mu'minun*], the comprehensiveness of this text is illustrated' (ibid., p. 263).

All the classical scholars refrain from making any substantial comment about the last part of this text, i.e., 'announce unto them a grievous chastisement' other than saying that this punishment is to be meted out in the hereafter. Rida is decidedly specific about the people to whom this text applies: 'This punishment', Rida wrote, 'afflicts those among them [the Jews] during the era of prophethood in this world; afterwards they join those who preceded them in the hereafter' (ibid., p. 263). He thus implicitly excludes Jews who come after the prophetic era. In stark contrast to this, al-Tabataba'i suggests that all Jews will be punished up to the Day of Requital:

> They are warned of chastisement in this world as well as in the hereafter . . . [where] punishment is the fire of hell. As for this world, it is what they have suffered of massacres, dispersion and expulsion, loss of life and property, and what God has imposed upon them of enmity and hatred among them. These are to continue up to the Day of Judgement, as has been clarified in the Qur'an. (1973, 3, pp. 123–4)

The assumptions of collective guilt arising from 'collective *kufr*' are significant for any discourse on faith and justice. It is to these assumptions, which are not entirely without foundations within the Qur'an itself, that I now turn.

Regarding the last part of the text under discussion, 'it is they whose works shall come to nought, both in this world and in the life to come; and they shall have none to succour them', al-Tabari simply states that 'their attempts to harm Muhammad will come to nought, that they will be humiliated by people and that God will withhold His grace from them' (1954, 3, p. 217). Al-Razi, al-Tabataba'i and even Ibn 'Arabi leave little doubt to whom this reference is made; all Jews 'up to the Day of Judgement'. 'Their lot in this world', says al-Razi, 'includes the substitution of acclamation with blame, of praise with damnation . . . the slaughter of children, the expropriation of their wealth, their enslavement and other forms of obvious disgrace' (1990, 7, p. 233). Ibn 'Arabi's commentary, while free from this kind of bitterness, nevertheless, also implies a sense of uninterrupted corporate (Jewish) culpability in *kufr* and rejection of the prophets.

In dealing with the Other, most of the interpreters display a confusion, identifying a particular part of a specific community, living in a confined geographical area, with all those who, by choice or accident of birth, belong to or identify with that community irrespective of the differences that may separate its diverse components. It is only when the application of a particular description is too starkly specific that such a distinction is made. This kind of confusion is also implicit in the qur'anic text. The text often insists, explicitly and implicitly, that there are exceptions for virtually every negative statement about the Other. There are several illustrations of this in the Qur'an: the denunciation of the *a'rab* (Bedouin) as 'severest in *kufr* and *nifaq*' (9:97, 101) is followed by an exception that there are others 'who believe in God and the Last Day, consider what they spend' (9:99, 102). In another example, we see that Abraham is allowed to pray for his progeny (2:128) but, when he suggests that his leadership should be extended to his offspring, the Qur'an firmly states that the promise of God is unrelated to blood relations and that it excludes the oppressors (2:124). Similarly, after a long discourse on the promise that Abraham made on behalf of his offspring and the subsequent commitments of the Israelite prophets to abide by them (2:128–33), the Qur'an concludes: 'That is a people who have passed; for them is what they earned and for you is what you earn' (2:134). This text is repeated in several other instances (2:134, 136, 141). However, the Qur'an also ignores this distinction at times (e.g., 29:13; 27:83) and here the reader actually requires the will to see these distinctions, in order to avoid blanket judgements. This is an issue intrinsically related to justice. The qur'anic commitment to justice and the linking of the prophets to those who enjoin justice, on the one hand, and *kufr* to those who support injustice, on the other, require a determination to make such distinctions, and to search for the hermeneutical means to make this possible. Other than its emphasis on *kufr* as active and dynamic, the Qur'an also refers to the *kuffar* as a group, without necessarily alluding to their activities, i.e., it acknowledges their existence as a distinct group which it names *kuffar* or *kafirun*. It is noteworthy that such references occur most frequently within the context of armed conflict between them and the Muslims (e.g., 3:140, 150, 155; 4:84; 33:22). Furthermore, it also addresses groups in corporate terms and this raises significant questions about group identity, personal responsibility and corporate guilt.

The qur'anic position on these questions appears to be contradictory and should be viewed in the context of tribal society and the Qur'an's own ethical objectives. 'The ideal of the tribe', says Izutsu

> was the Alpha and Omega of human existence. The bond of kinship by blood, the burning sense of honour based on the all-importance of blood relations, which required that a man should take the side of his tribal brothers regardless of whether they were right or wrong, love of one's own tribe, bitter scorn of the outsiders; these furnished the final yardsticks by which the people of *Jahiliyyah* measured personal values. (1966, p. 58)

While the Qur'an had to assume and 'speak' within a given context of such unbridled tribalism, it also wanted to impose on every individual the responsibility for his or her deeds. The ascribing of the murder of prophets to the Jews is a case in point. While the Qur'an asks the Medinan Jews 'Why, then, did you slay the Prophets of God aforetime?' (2:91), it appears to put the blame for the crimes on to them. In the sense that, as a part of the group they may have owned the deed, as some of the interpreters have suggested, this may be an appropriate question. However, it does not follow that they ought to be held accountable for it, for to do so would be to align oneself with manifest injustice. The Qur'an, we may say, used the existing institutions and turned them on their heads in order to give a new sense of values to society in place of the blind commitment to the group. Abu Jahl, a leading figure among the *mushrikun*, is reported to have described Muhammad as 'one who, more than anyone else, has cut the bond of kinship by blood and wrought that which is scandalous' (Izutsu 1966, p. 58). While the Qur'an sometimes appears to speaks in terms of those loyalties and identities, it consciously and determinedly moves away from them.

The Day of Judgement and the ultimate accountability of individuals in front of God is particularly illustrative of the Qur'an's determination to break from notions of collective responsibility. On that day, the Qur'an says, all their much-valued ties of blood relations will be rendered utterly meaningless (80:34–37; 58:22; 9:113–114). 'On [the] day when everyone will [want to] flee from his [or her] brother [or sister], and from his [or her] mother and father, and from his [or her] spouse and children' (80:34–36) it will be every individual, with his or her actions, who will be put in the balance.

Conclusion: From Counting Labels to Judging Content

To affirm the dynamic nature of *iman*, *islam* and *kufr* and their nuances is to affirm the basic ethos of justice in the Qur'an. According to the Qur'an, it is not labels that are counted by God, but actions that are weighed (2:177; 99:7–8). One cannot hold hostage to the ethos of *kufr* which characterized their forebears, those who, by accident of birth, are a part of any group, nor others who subsequently emerge from it; nor can we do this to individuals who existed within that group, but were non-participants in *kufr*. Similarly, one cannot attribute the faith commitment and faith of preceding generations of *muslims* to contemporary Muslims.

The objective towards which the Qur'an moves is more significant than the premise from which it starts. The fact of group identity should not be allowed to subvert a principle of personal accountability that the Qur'an explicitly and repeatedly affirms. If individuals are held accountable for deeds that are going to be weighed, then one is left with no alternative but to affirm the dynamic nature of *islam*, *iman* and *kufr*. Individuals are ever-changing entities. Every new encounter with ourselves and others, every deed that we do or refuse to do, is a step in our perpetual transformation.

Notes

1. Sayyidain (1972), Talbi (1981; 1985), Engineer (1982), Vahiduddin (1983), Rahman (1983; 1988), Faruqi (1983), Hanafi (1988), Ayoub (1989; 1991) and al-Badawi (1991) are but some of the contemporary Muslim scholars who have argued the case for an appreciation of *islam* beyond its institutional and historical forms.
2. It may be justifiably inferred from the context of this verse that *iman* is contrasted with

greed for material wealth.

3. E.g., 3:56; 4:57, 122; 5:9; 6:48; 7:42; 10:9; 11:23; 13:29; 14:23; 18:30, 107; 19:60; 22:50; 24:55; 25:70; 27:58; 31:8; 32:19.

4. E.g., 2:281; 3:24; 4:40, 85; 12:56; 16:111; 28:84.

5. The *islam* referred to in this text is the formula *aslamtu* which was used as the formal declaration of submission to the Prophet's authority.

6. The word *din*, in various forms, occurs 94 times in the Qur'an; 65 times as a verbal noun, 26 times in the possessive case (i.e., 'my *din*', 'your *din*') and only three times in its verbal form. It occurs about as frequently in both the Meccan and Medinan texts. Significantly, nowhere is it used in its plural form, *adyan*.

7. Cantwell-Smith demonstrates how this was a relatively 'new concept . . . as part of the impingement on Arabia at the time of new ideas, movements, and sophistication from the surrounding cultures' (1991, p. 101). 'Arab life', he writes, 'had facets that modern scholars may . . . have dubbed 'the religion of' the pre-Islamic Arabs. But the customs and orientations to which the modern student gives that name had not been organized or systematized or reified either sociologically or conceptually in the area itself by their new participants' (ibid., p. 102).

8. As with the studies on the origins of *din*, those on *islam* broadly follow the pattern of an unambiguously confessional approach, which examines the term through the 'faith eyes' of the scholar and putatively objective studies by non-Muslim scholars. In the course of research for this present study, no Muslim work specifically dealing with the term was encountered. In addition to the works of Izutsu and Cantwell-Smith, who devote considerable attention to the term, Lidzbarsky (1922), Ringgren (1949) and Robson (1954) have produced some general studies on the term, while Kunstlinger (1935), 'Abd al-Ra'uf (1967), McDonough (1971) and Smith (1975) have dealt with the term as it appears in the Qur'an or, in the case of the latter, as it has been understood in works of exegesis.

9. 'The compelling factor in the lives of a particular ethno-sociological community (*millah jinsiyyah*)', wrote Rida, is 'the contemporary situation of its members and not its known or unknown origins [as a religious community]' (1980, 3, p. 361). 'And the *din* of the People of the Book was transformed into an ethnic phenomenon in this sense: it is that which prevented the People of the Book from following the Prophet in what he brought of the explanation of the spirit of the *din* of God. Islam is that which all the Prophets had, along with the diversity of their laws' (ibid.).

10. The Qur'an does, however, use several other participial nouns to describe those who oppose or reject its message, albeit none of them as frequently as those based on *k-f-r*. These words themselves function as some kind of interpretation of what *kufr* means. They include 'mischief makers' (*mufsidun*) (3:63; 10:40; 29:36); 'deniers' (*mukadhdhibun*) (56:51; 52:11; 56:92); 'liars' (*kadhibun*) (16:105; 23:90; 16:39; 29:3); 'wrongdoers'/'oppressors' (*zalimun*) (2:258; 6:33; 29:31; 29:49; 61:7).

11. See also 2:89; 3:69, 70; 3:85; 3:98; 4:115; 16:83; 27:14; 31:25.

12. Al-Tabari says that 'most of the people from Medina, Hijaz, Basrah and Kufa as well as all the other major centres recited it as "*yaqtuluna*" (they slay). Some of the later readers from Kufa, based their reading on that of 'Abd Allah ibn Mas'ud, who recited it as "*yuqatiluna*" (they fight)'. (1954, 3, p. 216). In addition to the weight of majority opinion, the supposed incident about which this verse was revealed was another reason why the reading *yaqtulun* was adopted in preference to *yuqatilun*.

13. The account of this incident is given as follows: 'It is narrated that Abu 'Ubaydah ibn Jarrah said: "I asked the Messenger of God which person will suffer the severest punishment on the Day of Resurrection." He said: "Someone who killed a Prophet or [who killed] a person who enjoined good and forbade evil." Then the Prophet read this verse and said: "O Abu 'Ubaydah, the Israelites killed forty three Prophets in the morning in a single hour. A hundred men from among the slaves of the Israelites enjoined the murderers with good and forbade them from evil. All of these men were killed by the end of the day"' (al-Tabari 1954, 3, p. 216; al-Razi 1990, 7, p. 231; al-Zamakhshari n.d., 1, p. 348).

5

THE QUR'AN &
THE OTHER

PLURALISM & JUSTICE

Dignity lies in the reality, not in the appearance.

(Al-Tabataba'i 1973, 1, p. 193)

An All-Seeing God Who Does Not
Turn a Blind Eye

The Qur'an presents a universal, inclusivist perspective of a divine being who responds to the sincerity and commitment of all His servants. From this, two questions arise. Firstly, how does traditional qur'anic interpretation present a parochial image of a deity that does not differ from that postulated by the Medinan Jews and Christians which is denounced in the Qur'an? This is an image of a deity who belongs to a small group of people and who, having chosen His favourites, turns a blind eye to the sincere spiritual and social commitments of all others outside this circle. Secondly, how does the universality of the Qur'an's message relate to the exclusivism and virulent denunciation of the Other, indeed, even its exhortation to wage an armed struggle against the Other?

While the context of individual verses dealing with the religious Other is often carefully recorded by the earlier interpreters, they do not show any understanding of the overall historical context of a particular revelation.[1] The task of shedding historical light on various texts, has until recently, been primarily the domain of non-Muslim scholars. Muslim reluctance to deal with the question of contextualization beyond the search for an isolated occasion of revelation, has led to a generalized

146

denunciation of the Other, irrespective of the socio-historical context of the texts used in support of such rejection and damnation.

The qur'anic position towards the Other unfolded gradually in terms of the Other's varied responses to the message of Islam and to the prophetic presence. Any view to the contrary would invariably lead to the conclusion that the Qur'an presents a confused and contradictory view of the Other. For those unable or unwilling to see the gradualist and contextual nature of qur'anic revelation, there have been two ways of dealing with the problem of 'contradictory texts' regarding the Other: liberal scholars have often just ignored the verses denouncing the Other, while traditionalist and conservative scholars have resorted to what can only be described as forced linguistic and exegetical exercises to compel inclusivist texts to produce exclusivist meanings.

The idea of the gradual and contextual development of the qur'anic position towards the religious Other has significant implications. Firstly, one cannot speak of a 'final qur'anic position' towards the Other and, secondly, it is wrong to apply texts of opprobrium in a universal manner to all those whom one chooses to define as 'People of the Book' or 'disbelievers', in an ahistorical fashion. It is not that the traditional exegetes are incapable of examining the context of a particular verse and thereby limiting its application. The problem is that this contextualization is only done when the Qur'an refers to the Other in positive terms. In such cases every attempt is made to limit its meaning and application. Most traditional scholars, for instance, insist on limiting the generosity of the more inclusivist texts to a particular individual such as the King of Abyssinia, who gave refuge to an early group of Muslims, or 'Abd Allah ibn Salam, a Jewish convert to Islam.

Beliefs and behaviour are not genetic elements, like the colour of one's eyes, in supposedly homogeneous and unchanging communities. It is to guard against the injustices of such generalizations that texts of opprobrium referring to other religious communities or the associationists are usually followed or preceded by exceptions (e.g., Qur'an 3:75). Furthermore, qualifying or exceptive expressions such as 'from among them' (3:75), 'many among them' (2:109; 5:66; 22:17; 57:26), 'most of them' (2:105; 7:102; 10:36;), 'some of them' (2:145) and 'a group among them' (3:78), are routinely used throughout the qur'anic discourse on the Other.

The Qur'an provides only the basis for the attitude of Muslims towards the Other at any given time. The qur'anic position, in turn, was largely shaped by the varying responses of the different components of the Other, to the struggle for the establishment of an order based on *tawhid*, justice and *islam*. More often than not, these responses assumed concrete political forms in decisions to side with or against the Muslim community. Much of the qur'anic opprobrium is directed at the way doctrine was used to justify exploitative practices and tribal chauvinism. It is not as if the Qur'an avoided the discourse on power or denounced the exercise of political power; it was concerned about whom political power served and who suffered as a consequence of it.

How Does the Qur'an Describe the Other?

The following are the most frequent of the expressions used in the Qur'an to refer to various types of people in general religious terms: *mu'minun*, 'righteous'; *muslimun*, 'People of the Book', 'Jews', 'Christians', 'associationists'; *kafirun/kuffar* and *munafiqun*. I shall make some brief observations about the qur'anic use of these terms before I examine the context of its attitude towards the Other.

1. The terms usually used in translation are often, at best, approximations of their Arabic meanings. The Qur'an, for example, does not use the equivalent of the words 'non-Muslim' or 'unbeliever'; yet these are the most common English renderings of *kafirun/kuffar* both in the process of translation and internal usage within the Arabic language.

2. Some of these terms, such as *mu'minun* (literally, 'the convinced ones') and *muslimun* (literally, 'submitters') or 'People of the Book' and 'Christians' or 'Jews' are frequently used interchangeably in the Qur'an. It is essential to maintain the qur'anic distinction in their various uses in order to avoid a generalized and unjust condemnation of the Other.

3. In addition to these nouns, the Qur'an also employs descriptive phrases such as *alladhina amanu* (literally, 'those who are convinced') instead of *mu'minun* and *alladhina kaffaru* (literally, 'those who deny/reject/are ungrateful') instead of *kafirun* (literally, 'deniers'/'rejecters'/'ingrates'). These descriptive phrases express specific nuances in the text and indicate a particular level of faith conviction or of denial/rejection/ingratitude in much the same way as 'one who writes poetry' has a different nuance from 'poet'.

4. References to these groups are occasionally to a specific community within a historical setting and, at other times, to a community in a wider sense, transcending one specific situation.

5. Besides the terms of opprobrium such as *kafir*, *munafiq* (hypocrite),[2] and *mushrik*, the other terms are rarely used in a negative or positive

manner without exceptions. While praise or reproach are usually inherent in some of these terms, this is not without exception. Indeed, the Qur'an, at times, describes the reprehensible acts committed by some of those from among the Muslim or believing community as *kufr* or *shirk* (39:7).

6. These terms are often, but not always, used in the sense of a historico-religio-social group. The hypocrites and righteous were invariably referred to as individuals and the term *muslim* and its various forms, for example, is also frequently invoked to refer to the characteristic of submission in an individual, group or even an inanimate object.

The People of the Book

Given the situation of seventh-century Arabia and the Qur'an's own internal objectives of affirming *tawhid* as part of the legacy of pre-Muhammadan revelation, the Qur'an devotes considerable attention to the *mushrikun* and the People of the Book as two distinct categories. When Muhammad and his group of followers, the 'Emigrants' or 'Exiles', arrived in Medina in 622, they found its inhabitants comprised mainly Arabs and Jews.[3] Aws and Khazraj, the two major Arab tribes, lived in the desert areas of Yathrib, later renamed Medina. Aws lived in the area of al-'Awali (the high places) alongside the Jewish tribes of Qurayzah and al-Nadir. The Khazraj lived in the lower and less fertile areas of Yathrib, where they were the neighbours of another prominent Jewish tribe, Banu Qaynuqa'. The vast majority of Aws and Khazraj entered Islam and key figures among them had, in fact, invited the Prophet to come to Medina to assume the leadership role over them after their intermittent tribal wars.

In Medina, where Muhammad became the ruler of a cosmopolitan society, the Jewish communities played a significant economic, political and intellectual role. The Jews, not infrequently the power brokers of Arabian tribes from whose regular intertribal wars many political gains were made, comprised twenty-odd tribes. The most prominent of these were Banu Qurayzah, al-Nadir and Qaynuqa'. Together with Banu 'Awf and Banu al-Najjar, both Jewish tribes, they owned some of the richest agricultural lands in the south of Medina. Khaybar, however, was the largest centre of Jewish concentration in the north of Hijaz, between Yathrib and Taymah. The strategic distribution of Jewish power centres ensured their control of large areas of fertile land for development. These centres were thus fortified and amply provided with weapons. Prior to the

149

coming of Muhammad, as Ahmad notes, the Jews enjoyed complete liberty, 'concluded offensive and defensive alliances and carried on feuds' (Ahmad 1979, p. 27). Narrow tribalism characterized intra-Jewish relations 'so much so that they could not live as one religious group [nor] close ranks even at the time of the Prophet when they faced banishment' (al-'Umari 1991, 1, p. 44). On the whole, the Jewish tribes denied the veracity of Muhammad's mission and his claims to prophethood.

Soon after he entered Medina, Muhammad twinned all the Exiles with their hosts, known as the 'Helpers', in a formal relationship of fraternity. This reflected the basis of the new society: faith rather than tribe. The relationships between the Exiles and the Helpers and between the Muslims and the Jews were formally outlined in a document 'forming all of them into single community of believers but allowing for differences between the two religions' (Lings 1983, p. 125). Also known as the Treaty of Medina, the authenticity of this document is widely acknowledged, although there is disagreement as to whether it is a single agreement or a combination of two or more agreements reached over a long period (Rodinson 1980, p. 152; al-'Umari 1991, 1, pp. 99–102). It is evident that at the initial stages of his stay in Mecca, Muhammad had no prejudices against the Jews. On the contrary, as Maxine Rodinson remarks 'he regarded the contents of the message he brought as substantially the same as that received years ago by the Jews on the Sinai' (1980, p. 158). The following extract from the treaty indicates how questions of freedom of belief, sanctity of religious and personal property and obligations of mutual defence and solidarity were dealt with: 'The Jews of *Banu 'Awf* will be a community with the *mu'minun*; the Jews shall have their religion and the Muslims theirs, their allies and their persons shall be safe except for those who behave unjustly, for they hurt but themselves and their families' (cited in al-'Umari, 1991, 1, p. 107).

The fraternal relationship between Aws and Khazraj had made the old alliances between them and their erstwhile Jewish allies redundant. Despite the treaty they had entered into with Muhammad, the Jews, nevertheless, longed for a return to their erstwhile position of influence and authority. Muslim accounts suggest that this resentment was sufficient to lead many Jews, initially secretly and later openly, to identify with the Quraysh in their desire to annihilate Muhammad and his followers. Subsequent Jewish breaches of the treaty, usually on the eve of, or during a war with, the Quraysh, or alleged attempts on the life of Muhammad, led to the expulsion of Banu Qaynuqa', Banu al-Nadir and Banu Qurayzah from Medina.[4]

Another religious community who were, in the main, physically absent from Medina but were, nevertheless, a significant part of the Muslim–Other qur'anic discourse, were the Christians. Muhammad had encountered Christians as religious ascetics on his travels as a business-man,[5] as slaves and visiting traders in Mecca and even as neighbours in Medina. Prior to their presence in Medina, Muslims encountered and enjoyed the protection and hospitality of an established Christian state and found among them 'the best of neighbours' (Ibn Sa'd 1967, 1, pp. 235–40) during the first and second flights to exile in Abyssinia. All of these early Muslim encounters with the Christian Other were character-ized by warmth towards and affirmation of the Muslims by the Christians. Much later, Christians were included in the qur'anic injunc-tion to 'fight against those who believe not in Allah, nor in the Last Day, nor forbid that which has been forbidden by Allah and His messenger and who do not acknowledge the *din* of truth among the People of the Book until they pay the tax with willing submission and feel themselves subdued' (9:29).

Theologically though, much of the early Muslim understanding of Christianity and Christology seems to have filtered through to the Muslims in an indirect manner from the Jewish community, until much later, when a delegation of religious leaders from the Christians of Najran in southern Arabia, north-east of Yemen, came to Medina in 632. According to Muslim accounts, most of the discussion centred around seemingly theological matters. These accounts also suggest that the major factor that prevented the Najran delegation from recognizing Muhammad's prophethood was their indebtedness to their political mas-ters, who opposed Muhammad. Explaining his refusal to acknowledge the Prophet, the bishop is reported to have told his companions: 'The way these people have treated us! They have given us titles, paid us stipends and honoured us. But they are absolutely opposed to him [Muhammad], and if we were to accept him, they would take away from us all that you see' (Ibn Hisham n.d., 3, p. 271). The delegation prayed in Muhammad's mosque and entered into an agreement with him where-by he would send a capable Muslim to them to assist in the arbitration of some internal disputes. Furthermore, taxes would be exacted from them in return for receiving protection from the Muslim state.[6]

The tension in the religious–ideological relationship between the Muslims and the People of the Book was inevitable. The Qur'an claimed an affinity with scriptural tradition, and furthermore, claimed to be its guardian. An unwelcome response was inevitable on the part of those who claimed their scripture to be legitimate and final, in and by themselves. Much of the Qur'an's attention to the Other in Medina is, therefore, devoted to this tension. The frequency of the qur'anic references to the People of the Book and their shared scriptural history are among the reasons why most Muslim literature dealing with the Other focuses on the People of the Book. There are several other reasons for the preoccupation with this category. Since most of the *mushrikun* converted to Islam after the liberation of Mecca (630), at the earliest stages of its history, Jews and Christians were essentially the communities that Muslims and their jurisprudence had to deal with. The historical encounter over territory (both ideological and geographical) was also largely between Muslims and Christians. In the modern period, as Muslims are struggling to overcome the divisions of the past and to find avenues of coexisting and cooperating with those of other faiths, they find it theologically easier to focus on a category with which the Qur'an seems to have some sympathy. Finally, the present pre-eminence of the Western world – itself a product of a predominantly Christian and, to a lesser extent, Jewish heritage – in the fields of technology, science and politics, requires some Muslim focus on relations with the People of the Book, even if only as one way of coming to terms with the fact of this pre-eminence or domination.

There are however, several problems in focusing on the People of the Book as a distinct contemporary religious group in the belief that this is the same referent as that in the Qur'an. The qur'anic position towards the People of the Book and even its understanding as to who constitutes the People of the Book went through several phases. There is, however, agreement that the term has always applied to the Jews and Christians whom Muhammad encountered during his mission. The Qur'an naturally dealt only with the behaviour and beliefs of those of the People of the Book with whom the early Muslim community were in actual social contact.[7] To employ the qur'anic category of People of the Book in a generalized manner of simplistic identification of all Jews and Christians in contemporary society is to avoid the historical realities of Medinan society, as well as the theological diversity among both earlier and contemporary Christians and Jews.[8] To avoid this unjust generalization, therefore, requires a clear idea from their sources of their beliefs, as well as their many nuances, that characterized the various communities encountered by the early Muslims. Given the paucity of such extra-qur'anic knowledge, one would either have to abandon the search for a group with corresponding dogma today or shift one's focus to an area of practice and attitudes rather than dogma.

In practice, the latter option had always been exercised. In none of the disciplines of exegesis, Islamic history or legal scholarship have Muslims known anything approximating consensus about the identity of the People of the Book. There was even disagreement as to which specific groups of Christians and Jews comprised the People of the Book. At various times, Hindus, Buddhists, Zoroastrians, Magians and Sabeans were included among or excluded from the People of the Book, depending on the theological predilections of Muslim scholars and, perhaps more importantly, the geo-political context wherein they lived.[9] In all of these attempts to extend the boundaries of the qur'anic People of the Book, Muslim scholars implicitly acknowledged the situation-bound nature of the qur'anic categories.

A recognition of the need for solidarity between all oppressed people in an unjust and exploitative society requires going beyond the situation-bound categories of the Qur'an. This is not as radical an idea as it may appear at first glance. The Qur'an, for example, makes frequent and lengthy references to the *munafiqun*. This category, admittedly not a definite socio-religious grouping in the prophetic era, was, however, subsequently adopted by various protagonists in intra-Muslim polemics against their opponents (al-Tabari 1879–1890, 2, p. 467). It remains, however, a qur'anic category which has been dropped in Muslim scholarly discourse because it was so clearly situation bound. I do not wish to suggest that there are no Christians who believe in the concept of a triune deity. Justice, however, requires that no one be held captive to categories which applied to a community or individuals fourteen centuries ago, merely because they share a common descriptive term, a term that may even have been imposed on them by Muslims and rejected by them. 'These are a people who have passed on. They have what they earned and you shall have what you have earned' (Qur'an 2:141).

There is another significant reason why the category of People of the Book should be regarded as of dubious relevance in our world today. In the context of the political and technological power exercised by the Judaeo-Christian world, on the one hand, and Arab monetary wealth on the other, Muslim *rapprochement* with that world, based on the simplistic analogy that Jews and Christians are the contemporary People of the Book, could easily, and probably correctly, be construed as an alliance of the powerful. A qur'anic hermeneutic concerned with interreligious solidarity against injustice would seek to avoid such alliances and would rather opt for more inclusive categories which would, for example, embrace the dispossessed of the Fourth World.[10]

The *Mushrikun*

Initially referring to the Meccans who revered physical objects such as sculptures or heavenly bodies as religiously sacred entities, the term *mushrikun* was also employed to refer to the People of the Book by some Muslim jurists. Two factors led to an early recognition that all *mushrikun* are not the same and were not to be treated equally: 1) the qur'anic accusation of *shirk* against the People of the Book (e.g., 9:31), while simultaneously regarding them as distinct from the *mushrikun* and, 2) the subsequent wider Muslim contact with the world of non-Islam. Later, as the *Shorter Encyclopaedia of Islam* observes,

> in the course of the dogmatic development of Islam, the conception of *shirk* received a considerable extension . . . [because] the adherents of many sects had no compunction about reproaching their Muslim opponents with *shirk*, as soon as they saw in them any obscuring of monotheism, although only in some particular respect emphasised by themselves . . . *Shirk* has thus become, no longer simply a term for unbelief prevailing outside of Islam, but a reproach hurled by one Muslim against another inside of Islam. (SEI, '*shirk*')

As with the category of the People of the Book, here, too, one finds that the actual application of the neat divisions has been far more problematic than most traditional scholars are wont to admit. There is evidently a need to rethink these categories and their contemporary applicability or otherwise. It is now more apparent than ever that the religious situation of humankind and the socio-political ramifications thereof are far more complex than previously understood. The following are but a few indications of this complexity: 1) the emergence of the new religious movements in Japan and India for example, where, in some cases, people claim to be both Christians and pagans or Buddhist and Hindu Catholics respectively; 2) the situation in large parts of Asia, Australia, Latin America and Africa, where people combine a commitment to Islam, Christianity and even Judaism, with other traditional 'pagan' practices such as the veneration of graves, sacred relics and invoking deceased ancestors for spiritual blessings or material gain and 3) the systematic use of formal and institutional religion in the aforementioned areas to oppress, exploit and even eliminate entire nations among the indigenous people. In these situations, the marginalized and oppressed have often resorted to their ancient religions as a means of asserting their human dignity. Like *tawhid*, *shirk* had its implications in Meccan society and one needs to retain a sense of this in a contemporary consideration of the believers in *tawhid* as well as the *mushrikun*. Referring to the early qur'anic texts, Rahman argues that they can only be understood against their

Meccan background, 'as a reaction against Meccan pagan idol-worship and the great socio-economic disparity between the mercantile aristocracy of Mecca and a large body of its distressed and disenfranchised population' (1982c, p. 1). 'Both of these aspects', he says 'are so heavily emphasised in the Qur'an that they must have been organically connected with each other' (ibid.).

The Religious Other in the Qur'an

What is the Qur'an's general attitude towards the religious Other, underpinning the more specific injunctions and doctrinal issues that it raises from time to time?

Firstly, the Qur'an relates dogma to socio-economic exploitation. In chapter 4 I argued that the Qur'an insists on connecting orthodoxy with orthopraxis. This is equally applicable to the communities and individuals, in Mecca as well as Medina, who rejected the Prophet's message of *tawhid* and social justice. The Qur'an makes it clear that it was the rejection and ignorance of *tawhid* that had led to social and economic oppression in Meccan society. The shorter Meccan chapters are particularly poignant in the way this point is made.

> Woe to those who defraud others; who, when they take measure from people, take it fully.
>
> And when they measure out to others or weigh out for them, they give less than is due.
>
> Do they not think that they will be raised again?
>
> To a mighty day. The day when people will stand before the Lord of the worlds . . .
>
> Woe on that day unto the rejecters who give a lie to the Day of Requital (83:1–11).

Similarly, chapter 102 insists that it is abundance of wealth which diverts people from belief in God and the Day of Requital:

> You are obsessed by greed for more and more until you go to your graves
>
> Nay, in time you will come to understand . . .
>
> You would most surely behold the blazing fire [of hell] . . .
>
> And on that Day you will most surely be called to account for what you did with the boon of life!

Chapter 104 links the illusionary power of amassed wealth with the attempts to defame and slander the early Muslims in Mecca.

> Woe unto every slanderer, fault finder!
>
> Who amasses wealth and counts it a safeguard, thinking that his [or her] wealth will make him [or her] live forever!
>
> Nay, but [in the life to come such as] he [or she] shall indeed be abandoned to crushing torment!

Chapter 90 asserts that a denial of the presence of an all-powerful God causes people to squander their wealth: 'Does he think that no one has power over him? He will say: I have spent abundant wealth' (90:5–6). Furthermore, this chapter links faith to an active social conscience: 'to free a slave', 'to feed on a day of hunger' and 'to exhort one another to perseverance and to compassion' (90:13–15). By implication, it also links *kufr* to the refusal to display mercy towards others. In this text those who reject 'the signs of Allah' are those whose actions do not correspond with the actions of ones who have chosen to 'ascend the steep path'. The rejecters of 'the signs of Allah' are, therefore, those who deny mercy and compassion. This linking of the rejection of God and *din* to the denial of mercy and compassion is even more explicit in chapter 107.

> Have you observed the one who belies *al-din*?
>
> That is the one who is unkind to the orphan,
> and urges not the feeding of the needy.
>
> So, woe to the praying ones,
> who are unmindful of their prayer,
>
> They do good to be seen,
> and refrain from acts of kindnesses.

The texts of opprobrium revealed in Medina, which relate to the various Jewish and Christian communities and individuals encountered there by the Prophet and the early Muslims, reveal a similar relationship between 'erroneous' beliefs and the socio-economic exploitation of others. Equally significant is the fact that, although the Jews were closer to Muslims in creed, the Qur'an often reserves the severest denunciation for some of them. Similarly, the Sabeans were widely believed to have worshipped stars, even angels, yet they were included among the People of the Book (al-Razi 1990, 3, p. 112–13). According to the Qur'an, the Jews and

Christians justified their exploitation of their own people by claiming that their scriptures permitted such practices. The Qur'an denounced this exploitation of the ignorance of ordinary illiterate people who had no 'real knowledge of the Scriptures' (2:78) by the priests of the People of the Book. The contempt for, and exploitation of, the marginalized by some of the People of the Book is further seen in their justification, that they had no moral obligation to be just towards the illiterate.

> And among the People of the Book there is many a person who if you entrust him [or her] with something of value, will faithfully restore it to you; and there is among them many a person who, if you entrust him [or her] with a tiny gold coin, will not restore it to you unless you keep standing over him [or her]. This is because of their assertion, 'No blame can attach to us [for anything that we may do] with regard to these unlettered folk and [so they lie about God], being well aware. (3:75)

This text is immediately followed by a denunciation of those who 'barter away their bond with God and their pledges for a trifling gain' (3:77) and of 'a section among them who distort their Scripture with their tongues, so as to make you think that it is from the Scripture while it is not' (3:79). Thus, we see that while their bond and their pledges were with a transcendent God, their crimes were very much about the exploitation of the people of God. The Qur'an's insistence on the links between erroneous teaching of the People of the Book and their exploitative practices is also evident in the way these two accusations are fused in an interesting text from the chapter titled 'Repentance' (9:31–5):

> They have taken their rabbis and their monks – as well as Christ, son of Mary – for their lords beside God, although they have been bidden to worship none but the One God, save whom there is no deity: the one who is utterly remote, in His limitless glory, from anything to which they may ascribe a share in His divinity!

> They want to extinguish God's guiding light with their utterances: but God will not allow this [to pass] for He has willed to spread His light in all its fullness . . .

> O you who have attained unto faith! Behold, many of the rabbis and monks do indeed wrongfully devour the possessions of others and turn away from the path of God. But as for all who lay up treasures of gold and silver and do not spend them for the sake of God – give unto them the tiding of grievous suffering: on the day when that [hoarded wealth] shall be heated in the fire of hell and the foreheads and their sides and their backs branded therewith, 'These are the

treasures which you have laid up for yourselves! Taste, then [the evil] of your hoarded treasures!'

Secondly, the Qur'an explicitly and unequivocally denounces the narrow religious exclusivism which appears to have characterized the Jewish and Christian communities encountered by Muhammad in Hijaz. The Qur'an is relentless in its denunciation of the arrogance of Jewish religious figures and scathing of the tribal exclusivism that enabled them to treat people outside their community, especially the weak and vulnerable, with contempt. This contempt for other people, the Qur'an suggests, was very much rooted in notions of being the chosen of God. According to the Qur'an, many among the Jews and the Christians believed that they were not like any other people whom God had created, that their covenant with God had elevated their status with Him and that they were now the 'friends of Allah to the exclusion of other people' (62:6). The Qur'an alleges that they claimed a privileged position with God merely by calling themselves Jewish or Christian. In other words, it was a claim based on history, birth and tribe rather than on praxis and morality. Thus, they claimed to be 'the children of Allah and His beloved' (5:18) and 'considered themselves pure' (4:48). In response to these notions of inherent 'purity', the Qur'an argues, 'Nay, but it is Allah who causes whomsoever He wills to grow in purity; and none shall be wronged by even a hair's breadth' (5:49). The same text links these notions of being God's favourites to their socio-economic implications and suggests that this sense of having an exclusive share in God's dominion leads to greater unwillingness to share wealth with others: 'Have they perchance, a share in Allah's dominion?' the Qur'an asks, and then asserts: 'But [if they had] lo, they would not give to other people as much as (would fill) the groove of a date stone!' (4:53). 'Do they perchance, envy other people for what Allah has granted them out of His bounty? And *among* them are such as believe in Him and *among* them are such as have turned away' [emphasis mine] (4:55).

The Qur'an denounces the claims of some of the People of the Book that the afterlife was only for them and 'not for any other people' (2:94, 111), that the fire (of hell) would only touch them 'for a limited numbered days' (3:24) and that 'clutching at the fleeting good of this world will be forgiven for us' (7:169). The Qur'an, furthermore, takes a rather dim view of the boasts of the Jews and Christians that their creeds were the only ones of consequence. While the Qur'an does not accuse the Christians of claiming to be free of any moral accountability in their behaviour towards the non-Christians, they too, according to the Qur'an, held that they were the beloved of God.

> And they say: 'None shall enter paradise unless he [or she] be a Jew or a Christian'. Those are their vain desires. Say: 'Produce your proof if you are truthful.' Nay, whoever submits his [or her] whole self to Allah and is a doer of good, will get his [or her] reward with his [or her] Lord; On such shall be no fear nor shall they grieve. (5:18)

> And the Jews say the Christians have nothing [credible] to stand on and the Christians say the Jews have nothing to stand on while both recite the Book. Even thus say those who have no knowledge. So Allah will judge between them on the Day of Resurrection in that wherein they differ. (2:111–13)

Attempts to appropriate the heritage of Abraham and make it the property of a particular socio-religious group are also denounced: (3:69) 'It is not belonging to the community of Jews or Christians which leads to guidance, but the straight path of Abraham' (2:135). Abraham 'was neither a Jew nor a Christian, but an upright person who submitted to Allah' (3:67).

Thirdly, the Qur'an is explicit in its acceptance of religious pluralism. Having derided the petty attempts to appropriate God, it is inconceivable that the Qur'an should itself engage in this. The notion that Abraham was not a Jew or a Christian, but 'one of us' (i.e., a Muslim) is at variance with the rejection of all exclusivist claims in these texts. For the qur'anic message to be an alternative one, it had to offer the vision of a God who responds to all humankind and who acknowledges the sincerity and righteousness of all believers. The Qur'an, thus, makes it a condition of faith to believe in the genuineness of all revealed religion (2:136; 2:285; 3:84).

The Qur'an acknowledges the *de jure* legitimacy of all revealed religion in two respects: it takes into account the religious life of separate communities coexisting with Muslims, respecting their laws, social norms and religious practices and it accepts that the faithful adherents of these religions will also attain salvation and that 'no fear shall come upon them neither will they grieve' (2:62). These two aspects of the Qur'an's attitude towards the Other may be described as the cornerstones of its acceptance of religious pluralism. Given the widespread acceptance, among the most conservative Muslims, of respect for the laws of the religious Other, even if only in theory, and the equally widespread rejection of their salvation, I want to focus on the latter.

The Qur'an specifically recognizes the People of the Book as legitimate socio-religious communities. This recognition was later extended by

Muslim scholars to various other religious communities living within the borders of the expanding Islamic domain. The explicit details, restrictions and application of this recognition throughout the various stages of the prophetic era, and subsequently in Islamic history, point to a significant issue in dealing with the Other. The socio-religious requirements of the Muslim community, such as community building and security, rather than the faith convictions, or lack thereof in these other communities, shaped the Qur'an's attitude towards them.

There are a number of indications in the Qur'an of the essential legitimacy of the religious Other. Firstly, the People of the Book, as recipients of divine revelation, were recognized as part of the community. Addressing all the prophets, the Qur'an says, 'And surely this, your community (ummah), is a single community' (23:52).[11] The establishment of a single community with diverse religious expressions was explicit in the Charter of Medina. Secondly, in two of the most significant social areas, food and marriage, the generosity of the qur'anic spirit is evident: the food of 'those who were given the Book' was declared lawful for the Muslims and the food of the Muslims lawful for them (5:5). Likewise, Muslim men were permitted to marry 'the chaste women of the People of the Book' (5:5). If Muslims were to be allowed to coexist with others in a relationship as intimate as that of marriage, then this seems to indicate quite explicitly that enmity is not to be regarded as the norm in Muslim–Other relations. Interestingly, this text mentions believing women in the same manner as the women of the People of the Book: '[permissible in marriage] are the virtuous women of the believers and the virtuous women of those who received the Scripture before you' (5:5). The restriction of the permission to the women of the People of the Book indicates that this ruling related to the social dynamics of early Muslim society and the need for community cohesion. The fact that most jurists, while agreeing on marriage to women of the People of the Book, who are also the people of Dhimmah, differ as to whether it is permissible if they are from states hostile to Islam, also reflects this point (al-Tabari 1954, 5, pp. 212–14). Thirdly, in the area of religious law, the norms and regulations of the Jews and of the Christians were upheld (5:47) and even enforced by the Prophet when he was called upon to settle disputes among them (5:42–3). Fourthly, the sanctity of the religious life of the adherents of other revealed religions is underlined by the fact that the first time permission for the armed struggle was given, was to ensure the preservation of this sanctity; 'But for the fact that God continues to repel some people by means of others, cloisters, churches, synagogues and mosques, [all places] wherein the name of God is mentioned, would be razed to the ground' (22:40).

The qur'anic recognition of religious pluralism is evident not only from the acceptance of the Other as legitimate socio-religious communities but also from an acceptance of the spirituality of the Other and salvation through that Otherness. The preservation of the sanctity of places of worship was thus not merely in order to preserve the integrity of a multi-religious society, as contemporary states may want to protect places of worship because of the role they play in the culture of a particular people. Rather, it was because God, who represented the ultimate for many of these religions, and who is acknowledged to be above the diverse outward expressions of that service, was being worshipped in them. That there were people in other faiths who sincerely recognized and served God is made even more explicit in Qur'an 4:113: 'Not all of them are alike; among them is a group who stand for the right and keep nights reciting the words of Allah and prostrate themselves in adoration before Him. They have faith in Allah and in the Last Day; they enjoin what is good and forbid what is wrong, and vie one with another in good deeds. And those are among the righteous'. If the Qur'an is to be the word of a just God, as Muslims sincerely believe, then there is no alternative to the recognition of the sincerity and righteous deeds of others, and their recompense on the Day of Requital. Thus, the Qur'an says:

> And of the People of the Book there are those who have faith in Allah and in that which has been revealed to you and in that which has been revealed to them, humbling themselves before Allah, they take not a small price for the messages of Allah. They have their reward with their Lord. Surely Allah is swift to take account. (3:198)

> And whatever good they do, they will not be denied it. And Allah knows those who keep their duty. (3:112–14)

From Where Then the Image of Religious Arrogance?

Why did this inclusivism and, indeed, justice, not become the predominant trait of the Islamic theological appraisal of the Other and Otherness? The ideal answer to this question would require an examination of the historical development of Islamic theology and the history of Islam's encounter with the Other as a whole. I shall, however, confine myself to looking at the arguments that traditional exegesis employed to circumvent the obvious meaning of inclusiveness in qur'anic texts, and to reflecting on the alternative opinions provided by some more contemporary exegetes. The following is one of the two texts that are most explicit about the legitimacy of religious diversity:[12]

> Surely those who have faith and those who are Jews and the Christians and the Sabeans, whoever has faith in Allah and the Last Day and does good, they have their reward with their Lord, there is no fear for them, nor shall they grieve. (2:62)

Most of the exegetes exercise themselves to no avail to avoid the explicit meaning of these texts, i.e., that anyone who has faith in God and the Last Day and who acts in a righteous manner will attain salvation. This refusal to recognize the efficacy of all religious paths to salvation after the coming of Muhammad is argued on the basis of the doctrine of supercessionism. According to this doctrine 'any given religious dispensation remains valid until the coming of the one to succeed it; then the new dispensation abrogates the previous one' (Ayoub 1989, p. 27). Those who heard of the message of Moses were thus obliged to believe in it and to follow the Torah until the coming of Jesus, whose message superseded that of Moses until the coming of Muhammad, when the final form of faith was irrevocably determined.[13]

There are two ways in which the majority of scholars have approached this text to circumvent the more apparent meaning. It was argued that 2:62 had subsequently been abrogated by 3:85, 'Whosoever desires a *din* other than *islam* shall not have it accepted from him [or her].' This is a very significant opinion attributed to Ibn 'Abbas and 'a group among the exegetes' by al-Tabari (1954, 1, p. 323).[14] Some of the exegetes whose works are under consideration here either rejected this opinion or ignored it. Those who rejected it argued that the idea of God abrogating a promise militates against His justice and that, being God, He will not fail to uphold a promise. The abrogation theory would have been the easiest avenue to obtain the much desired exclusivist interpretation. However, with the case against it rather apparent, the exegetes had little option but to resort to some creative and often contradictory exegetical devices to secure damnation for the Christians, Jews and Sabeans.

Given their assumption that salvation is confined to those who have faith in and followed Muhammad as a prophet, the text presented two significant problems to these exegetes. The first problem was the inclusion of 'those who have faith' alongside the Other and the second one was the qualifying phrase 'whosoever have faith among them,' which seemed to imply that 'faith' is used in a different sense from that employed in the first descriptive phrase, 'those who have faith'.

Al-Zamakhshari, along with several others,[15] dealt with the first problem by redefining 'those who have faith' in a manner that equalizes the four categories in 'falsehood'. 'They are the ones', Al-Zamakhshari wrote, 'who believe with their tongues without their hearts agreeing', i.e., the hypocrites (n.d., 1, p. 146). 'Whosoever among these rejecters/ deniers acquires a pure faith and genuinely enters into the community of Islam will have no fear come upon them, neither will they grieve' (ibid.). Al-Tabari defines 'those who have faith' in this text as 'the ones who accept what the Messenger of Allah brought them of Allah's truth' (1954, 1, p. 317) and then proceeds to distinguish between the application of the phrase 'whoever among them who has faith' to this category, and the following three. According to him, when the phrase 'whoever among them has faith' is applied to 'those who have faith' then it means 'remaining committed to that faith and not changing'. In the case of the Christians, Jews and Sabeans, however, he argues that it means 'coming to belief, i.e. entering Islam' (ibid. pp. 320–1). The view that the acceptable Other refers to converts from other religions, the most common view in qur'anic exegesis, is regularly applied to virtually all of those texts that distinguish between the Others who remained rejected by God and those who were acceptable and to whom salvation was promised.[16]

Exegetical Difficulties

Criticism of the abrogation theory, regarding God reneging on a promise or causing a past generation to suffer for the intransigence or disbelief of a present generation, is clear. Furthermore, the following text (Qur'an 3:85), the supposedly abrogating text, is no less inclusive than Qur'an 2:62, discussed on page 162, which is supposed to have been abrogated. 'If one goes in search of a religion other than self-surrender unto God [Asad's rendition of *islam*], it will never be accepted from him [or her] and in the life to come he [or she] shall be among the lost' (3:95). What is significant about this opinion is that Ibn 'Abbas and 'a group among the exegetes' actually held the opinion that this verse, at an earlier stage, did offer salvation to groups outside the community of Muslims. Ibn 'Abbas is one of the earliest commentators of the Qur'an. It was only much later, when the exegetes had recourse to more sophisticated exegetical devices, that alternatives to this theory became possible in order to secure exclusion from salvation for the Other.

The interpretation offered by al-Zamakhshari that 'those who have faith' is actually a reference to the hypocrites, arbitrarily imputes an antithetical meaning to the phrase, without any theological or linguistic support. This is hardly conducive to understanding any text. The chaos in interpretation that must inevitably come from this kind of device, no matter how illustrious the exegete, has serious implications for any attempt to understand the Speech of God. Whenever the Qur'an uses the word *iman* with reference to the hypocrites, it does so with the word *q-w-l* or variants thereof, meaning that they only say or claim that they believe (2:8, 14, 86; 3:119; 5:41, 61). Finally, throughout the Qur'an the expression 'those who have attained to faith/conviction' is used 239 times explicitly in the sense of 'those who have faith'. The case for a single exception to all of these with the effect of rendering an opposite meaning, requires a more significant explanation than has been provided.

Then there is the theory that the Jews, Christians and Sabeans mentioned in this verse are those who actually converted to Islam. In a sense, the entire early Muslim community were 'converts' to Islam, although the term seems to be uncommon in early Islamic literature. It is, however, possible that, as the community acquired a settled character, new entrants were known or even referred to as 'new Muslims'. Such a term was indeed in use, *maslamah,* and is employed by al-Tabari (1954, 7, p. 498) and al-Zamakhshari (n.d., 1, p. 459) in this context (*maslamah ahl al-kitab*). There is, however, no indication that these converts existed as a socio-religious category apart from the earlier Muslims, which would have warranted their exclusion from the category of 'those who have faith,' or that the terms 'new Muslims' or 'converts' were widely used. On the contrary, the serious attempts to cement the Exile–Helper link as well as various other tribal links, would indicate that Muhammad would not have brooked the formation of yet another intra-Muslim category. In the very unlikely event that these new Muslims were regarded, even if only occasionally, as a sub-category of the 'believers', then it would have been far more plausible to refer to them as such in a text promising salvation.

More significant though, is the fact that the converts are already included in the first category and there is no convincing need to single them out as Jews, Christians and Sabeans. Nor could there have been any doubt regarding the salvation of these new Muslims who, as Christians or Jews before embracing Islam, were certainly closer in faith to 'those who have faith' than a *mushrik.* If the erstwhile *mushrikun* were eligible for salvation upon embracing Islam, then there could have been no doubt about the salvation of the Jews or Christians who did so.

All is Not Lost!

Rashid Rida pays considerable attention to the inclusivist meaning of these texts, cites supportive texts, deals at length with the question of salvation for those who did not encounter a prophet, or receive his or her message, and even reflects on the necessity or otherwise of believing in the prophethood of Muhammad as a condition of salvation. Rida interprets 'those who have faith' as 'those Muslims who followed Muhammad during his lifetime and all those who follow him until the Day of Resurrection'. He says that 'whosoever among them who has faith' is a specification of the other three groups mentioned, i.e., those among the Jews, Christians and Sabeans who believe with a 'correct faith' (1980, 1, p. 336).

Al-Tabataba'i recognizes the idea of 'those who have faith' as a description of a socio-historico-religious group, like the other three, and not only of a group of people for whom faith is always a vibrant and growing personal quest. 'The context of the phrase "whosoever believes in Allah"', he says, 'shows that it refers to genuine faith and that the phrase "those who have faith", refers to those who call themselves Muslims' (1973, 1, p. 193).

Both conclude on a similar note: all those who have faith in God and act righteously, regardless of formal religious affiliation, will be saved 'for Allah does not favour one group while mistreating another' (Rida 1980, 1, p. 336). 'No name, no adjective', says al-Tabataba'i, 'can do any good unless it is backed by faith and righteous deeds. This rule is applicable to all human beings' (1973, 1, p. 193). Both Rida and al-Tabataba'i view these texts as a response to the exclusivism invoked by those, including Muslims, steeped in sectarianism and narrow religious chauvinism. 'Salvation', Rida wrote, 'is not to be found in religious sectarianism but in true belief and righteous conduct. Muslim, Jewish or Christian aspirations to religious importance are of no consequence to Allah, nor are they the basis upon which judgements are made' (1980, 1, p. 336).

In an interesting contextualizing of Qur'an 2:62, Rida seems to acknowledge Jews, Christians and Sabeans as 'believers'. He views the message of this verse as a repetition of an earlier promise in this chapter ('those who follow My guidance will have no fear neither shall they grieve', 2:38) and an anticipation of a similar promise that follows in 4:123–4, which clearly refers to being a *mu'min* as a condition of salvation. 'It will not be accordance with your vain desires nor the vain desires of the People of the Book. Whoever does evil, will be requited for it and he [or she] will not find for him[self or herself] besides Allah a friend or a helper. And whoever does good deeds whether male or female and he [or she] is a *mu'min* will enter the Garden and they shall not be dealt with unjustly' (4:123–4).

Al-Tabataba'i refers to Qur'an 2:111, saying that 'the only criterion, the only standard, of honour, happiness is the real belief in Allah and the Day of Resurrection, accompanied by righteous conduct' (1973, 1, p. 193). The position taken by Rida and al-Tabataba'i regarding the validity of other religious paths is consistent with the universal ethos of the Qur'an and the meaning of the texts under discussion. This interpretation is borne out by reflections on the Qur'an's attitude towards the fact of religious diversity.

The Qur'anic Response to Religious Diversity

In chapter 4 the meaning of *din* in the context of *islam* was discussed. Some brief comments regarding the unity of *din* are appropriate here, before reflecting on a text that opens up the discussion of the relationship between *din* and *shari'ah*, incorporating the idea of 'competing in righteousness' as a reason for both religious diversity and for referring to God the ultimate questions regarding this diversity.

The Qur'an regards Muhammad as one of a galaxy of prophets, some of whom are mentioned specifically in the Qur'an while 'others you do not know' (40:78). The same *din*, the Qur'an declares, 'was enjoined on Noah, Abraham, Moses and Jesus' (42:13) 'You are but a warner', the Qur'an tells Muhammad, 'and every people has had its guide' (13:08, see also 16:36 and 35:24). The fact that the Qur'an incorporates accounts of the lives of these predecessors of Muhammad and makes it part of its own history is perhaps the most significant reflection of its emphasis on the unity of *din*. These prophets came with identical messages which they preached within the context of the various and differing situations of their people. Basically, they came to reawaken the commitment of people to *tawhid*, to remind them about the ultimate accountability to God and to establish justice. 'And for every *ummah* there is a messenger. So when their messenger comes the matter is decided between them with justice, and they will not be wronged' (10:47).

The Qur'an declares that 'unto every one of you have We appointed a [different] *shir'ah* (path) and *minhaj* (way)' (5:48).[17] In a similar vein, it says: 'To every community, We appointed acts of devotion, which they observe; so let them not dispute with you in the matter, and call to your Lord. Surely you are on a right guidance' (22:67). Since the views of the

respective exegetes on 22:67 are likely to agree with their views on 5:48
on the principal issue of the validity of various religious forms in the
Muhammadan and post-Muhammadan eras, this discussion will be confined to 5:48. The interpretations of this text also contain fairly lengthy
discussions on the differences between *din* and *shari'ah*.

> We have revealed to you the Book with the truth, verifying that
> which is before it of the Book and a guardian over it. So judge
> between them by what Allah has revealed and follow not their
> desires, [turning away] from the truth that has come unto you. For
> every one of you we have appointed a *shir'ah* and a *minhaj*. And if
> Allah had pleased, He would have made you a single *ummah*, but
> that He might try you in what He gave you. So vie with one another
> in virtuous deeds. To Allah you will all return, so that He will inform
> you of that wherein you differed. (5:48)

Most of the exegetes have interpreted *shir'ah* as *shari'ah* and *minhaj* as a
'clear path' . Both al-Razi and Rida have elaborated on the etymological
meaning of *shir'ah* and *shari'ah*: 'In the literal sense it is a path to the
water or the source of water for the river or its like'. From the Qur'an
itself and the various interpretations of *shari'ah*, *din* and the differences
between them, it is evident that the former is exclusive while the latter
pertains to particular communities, as al-Tabataba'i's commentary on
this verse makes clear: '*Shari'ah* is a path for a community among communities or a Prophet among Prophets who was sent with it . . . *Din* is a
pattern, a divine and general path for all communities. Thus, *shari'ah* is
amenable to abrogation while this is not the case with *din* in its broad
sense' (1973, 5, p. 350).

Rida compares the various *shari'ahs* 'which can abrogate' one another
to *din*, 'which is one' (1980, 5, p. 351). He then compares this relationship to that of the specific injunctions in the *shari'ah* of reified Islam,
'where one finds the abrogating verse and abrogated ones, to reified
Islam itself' (ibid., 5, p. 351). This, he suggests, is 'because Allah does
not wish to impose on His servants anything other than a single *din* which
is [non-reified] *islam*' (ibid.). 'In order for them to attain this [diversity in
a single *din*]', Rida says, God 'has charted different paths and ways
depending on their differing capacities . . . Thus, He says "If Allah had so
willed, He would have made you a single community"' [5:351] (ibid.).
This comparison of the intra-religious abrogation to interreligious supercessionism seemingly supports the view that the appearance of Islam
nullifies the religious paths that preceded it, and now live alongside it.

Yet this is not Rida's opinion in his views on the question of whom this text addresses. This question is obviously significant in interpreting the text's meaning: addressing a vague historical humankind, rather than a contemporary community sharing the same geographical space and time with the Muslims in Medina, would put an entirely different complexion on to it. Unsurprisingly, and despite the immense exegetical difficulties involved, most of the exegetes suggest that this verse addresses the communities of earlier prophets (al-Tabari 1954, 6, p. 272; al-Razi 1990, 12, p. 14). 'The reference here' (i.e., 5:48), al-Tabari says, is 'to every Prophet who had actually passed away and their communities which preceded our Prophet, whereas he is the only person being addressed. Although the addressee is the Prophet, the intention is to convey an account of the Prophets who preceded him and their communities' (1954, 6, p. 272).

Aware that this contradicts the apparent meaning of the text, al-Tabari explains that 'it was customary among the Arabs that when a person with an absentee attached to him was addressed with the intention of saying something about the absentee, then the addressee would be focused on. In this manner information about both is conveyed' (ibid). Rida prefers the obvious meaning, i.e., that it refers to the Muslims, the People of the Book and to humankind in general (1980, 1, p. 413). This inclusivism is reflected in his interpretation of the text: 'We have made for everyone a *shari'ah* . . . and a path for guidance. We have imposed upon them its paths for the purification of their souls and their reformation, because the paths based on knowledge and the paths of spiritual cultivation vary with the differences in society and the human potential' (ibid., 6, p. 413). Viewing the deceased adherents of supposedly abrogated *shari'ahs* as the addressees of this text dispensed with the need for any detailed discussion of the text itself or its implications for religious pluralism. The traditional interpretations of the text present several difficulties and are evidently inconsistent with both its context and apparent meaning. These difficulties compel me to choose an alternative, inclusivist, interpretation.

1. The entire qur'anic discussion, including the preceding sentences of 5:48 and the subsequent verse, refers to the relationship between the Prophet as arbitrator in an actual community. The context of this text makes it plain that other religious communities coexisting with the Muslims in Medina are addressed, not an ahistorical community existing in a non-physical world or in a different historical context.

2. The text under discussion, 5:48, says that, upon returning to God, 'He will inform you of that wherein you differed'. If one supposes that this text refers to the pre-Muhammadan communities whose paths are acknowledged as valid, pure and divinely ordained for a specified period, as the doctrine of supercessionism holds, then there is no question of the Muhammadan community differing with them, nor a need for information regarding the differences.

3. The text asks that the response to this diversity be to compete with each other in righteous deeds. Given that any kind of meaningful competition can only be engaged in by contemporaneous communities who share similar advantages or disadvantages, one can only assume that the partners of these Muslims were to be those Others who lived alongside them.

In the light of these points, the text can best be understood as follows. One observes that it comes towards the end of a fairly lengthy discourse on the significance of specific scriptures for specific communities. Qur'an 5:44–5 deals with the Torah, which has 'guidance and light', 'should not be sold for a trivial price', and those Jews who do not judge by its injunctions are denounced as 'ingrates' and 'wrongdoers/oppressors'.[18] This is followed by 5:46–7 which describes the revelations to Jesus Christ in similar terms ('a light and guidance and an admonition for those who keep their duty') and a denunciation of the followers of Christ who do not judge by their standards as 'transgressors' (see also 7:170). It is at the end of this chronological discourse on the significance and importance of adhering to revealed scripture that the text 'To each of you we have given a "path and and a way"' appears. Given this context of recognizing the authenticity of the scriptures of the Other, it follows that the text refers to the paths of the religious Other in a similar vein.

As for its meaning, the essence of this text is located in the words *shir'ah* and *minhaj*; both relating to 'a path'. While paths must be clear, comfortable, scenic and even, at times, a part of one's goal, they are never synonymous with it. The word *shari'ah* and its variants appear only three times in the Qur'an; the word *Allah* approximately three thousand times. Hassan Askari, referring to the question of religious pluralism, asks 'How may it be that the One and Transcendent, the Creator and Almighty is equated with the form of one religious belief or practice? And if we equate thus, we make a God out of that religion, whereas we are all called upon to say: "There is no deity except God"' (1986, p. 322). The text thus means that God has determined a path for all people, both as individuals and as religious communities; that one should be true to the path determined for one. Furthermore, should it be so covered by cobwebs that it is no longer possible for one to move along it, then one is free to choose another of the paths determined by God. The purpose is to vie with one another in righteousness towards God.

The text discussed here (5:48) is one of two that specifically employ the metaphor of competition. Both appear in a Medinan context of the Prophet engaging the People of the Book. The second reads as follows:

> And each one has a goal towards which he [or she] strives/direction to which he [or she] turns) [*li kulli wijhah huwa muwalliha*]; so compete with one another in righteous deeds. Wherever you are, Allah will bring you all together. Surely Allah is able to do all things. (2:148)

While the phrase *likulli wijhah huwa muwalliha* is open to both the senses given in this translation, the context of this text would suggest that its focus is narrower than the advocates of religious pluralism may want to believe, i.e. the second translation 'direction to which he turns' is more appropriate. Commenting on this verse, al-Razi quotes Hassan al-Basri as saying that *wijhah* refers to *shir'ah* and *minhaj*. He adds that the verse would then mean that the phenomenon of a variety of *shari'ahs* has its virtues. 'Undoubtedly *shari'ahs* differ in terms of the varieties of people as they vary with the different personalities. It is thus not far-fetched that they should differ with the passing of time with reference to one person. This is why the idea of *naskh* (abrogation) and change is correct' (al-Razi 1990, 4, p. 145).

Al-Zamakhshari says that the phrase refers to the different directions a person faces to pray in the other religions and that the challenge to the Muslims is to compete with the Other (n.d., 1, p. 205). Al-Tabataba'i says that since there is 'nothing inherently reverential about directions of prayer . . . one should not waste one's time and energy in disputation and argumentation about it' (1973, 1, p. 327).

Given that Qur'an 5:48 is explicit in its reference to various *shari'ahs* and *minhaj*, I briefly return to some exegetical comments on this verse. The idea of competing in righteousness that it expresses is also evident in the verse presently under discussion (2:148). Al-Tabari interprets this text to mean; 'Hasten, O people, to righteous deeds, and attachment to your Lord by fulfilling the duties in the Book revealed by Him unto your Prophet. He has revealed it in order to test you so that the virtuous may become obvious from the sinner' (1954, 6, p. 272).

Both al-Razi and al-Zamakhshari offer some brief comments, saying that the testing refers to the diverse *shari'ahs*, i.e. 'whether we acted upon it obeying Allah or pursued doubts and half-hearted righteousness' (al-Razi 1990, 14, p. 15; al-Zamakhshari n.d., 1, p. 640). Seemingly to counterbalance his ideas on the validity of religious pluralism, Rida introduces his views on competing in goodness with a lengthy discussion on the supposed unsuitability of both the 'stagnant legal severity of Judaism . . . [and] the legal leniency . . . spiritual excesses . . . and acquiescence to worldly power' (1980, 6, p. 418) of Christianity. He then contrasts this with the supposed supremacy of a moderate and dynamic Islam. Finally, he says:

> What is wrong with you . . . that you look at *din* in terms of what divides and disperses, ignoring the wisdom of diversity and the objectives of *din* and *shari'ah*. Isn't this a departure from guidance and pursuing your own fancy . . . You have to make the *shari'ahs* a cause of competition in goodness not a cause for enmity and competing in prejudice. (Ibid.)

While al-Tabataba'i suggests that the challenge to compete in righteousness is directed to the Muslims, he nevertheless concludes that they should not occupy themselves with these differences (1973, 5, p. 353).

What is evident from these examples is that the metaphor of competition in righteousness is not regarded seriously in exegesis.[19] While none of the exegetes whose works are under perusal explicitly excludes the Other, it is only Rida and al-Tabataba'i, the latter by implication, who include the Other. The inclusion of the Other, from the context of the text, however, is inescapable. The challenge to competition is immediately preceded by a statement on the diversity of religious paths: 'And if God had pleased He would have made you a single *ummah*. However He desires to try you in what He gave you. So vie with one another in righteous deeds.'

Given that this competing in righteousness is between diverse communities, several implications follow. Firstly, righteous deeds that are recognized and rewarded, are not the monopoly of any single competitor, as the Qur'an says: 'O humankind, We have created you from one male and female. We have made of you tribes and nations so that you may know one another. In the eyes of God, the noblest among you is the one who is most virtuous' (49:13). Secondly, the judge, God, has to be above the narrow interests of the participants. Thirdly, claims of familiarity with the judge or mere identification with any particular team will not avail the participants. Fourthly, the results of any just competition are never foregone conclusions.

The Qur'an makes several references to the theological difficulties of religious pluralism and of *kufr*. If God is One and if *din* originates with Him, why is it that humankind is not truly united in belief? Why do some people persist in rejection when 'the truth is clearly distinguished from falsehood' (2:256; 23:90)? Why does God not 'will' faith for everyone? These were some of the questions that appear to have vexed Muhammad and the early Muslims. In response to these, several texts urge an attitude of patience and humility; these questions are to be left to God who will inform humankind about them on the Day of Requital. In addition to the text under discussion (5:48), which addresses the people who have a *shir'ah* and *minhaj*, saying 'unto God you will return, so that He will inform you of that wherein you differed', the following text also conveys the call to patience and humility:

> Will you dispute with us about God, while He is our Lord and your Lord? And we are to be rewarded for our deeds and you for your deeds? (2:139)

> God is your Lord and our Lord: Unto us our works and unto you your works; let there be no dispute between you and us. God will bring us together and to Him we shall return. (42:15; 2:139)

As for those who persist in *kufr*, the Qur'an says;

> If your Lord had willed, all those on earth would have believed together. Would you then compel people to become believers? (10:99)

> If God had so wanted, He could have made them a single people. But He admits whom He wills to His grace and, for the wrongdoers there will be no protector nor helper. (42:8)

> Revile not those unto whom they pray besides God, lest they wrongfully revile God through ignorance. Thus, unto every *ummah* have we made their deeds seem fair. Then unto their Lord is their return, and He will tell them what they used to do. (6:108)

The Prophetic Responsibility

If, as I have argued above, the Qur'an acknowledges the fact of religious diversity as the will of God, then a significant question that arises is that of Muhammad's responsibility to the adherents of other faiths. Rahman has correctly described the qur'anic position regarding this relationship as 'somewhat ambiguous' (1982c, p. 5). From the Qur'an it would appear as if the fundamental prophetic responsibility was twofold. Firstly, with regard to those who viewed themselves as communities adhering to a divine scripture, it was to challenge them about their commitment to their own traditions and their deviation from them. Secondly, with regard to all of humankind, it was to present the Qur'an's own guidance for consideration and acceptance. There are two ways of approaching this ambiguity. One way is to relate the first responsibility to the second one, for they are not entirely divorced from each other, and the other is to understand the context of different responsibilities and their applicability to specific components of the Other, at specific junctures in the relationship with the Other.

The qur'anic challenge to the exclusivist claims of the People of the Book has been discussed earlier in this chapter. At other times, various groups and individuals, among the People of the Book in particular, were challenged by Muhammad regarding their rejection of the signs of God (3:70–1; 3:98), their discouraging of others to walk the path of God, (3:98–9) and their knowingly covering the truth with falsehood (3:70; 3:98–9). Muhammad, as indicated earlier, was expected to challenge them regarding their commitment to their own scriptures (5:68), their deviation from these, and their distortion thereof. Muslim scholarship has largely argued that, given this distortion, nothing in the scriptures has remained valid. In dealing with the qur'anic references to the truth contained in these scriptures and exhortations to the People of the Book to uphold it, Muslim scholars have limited this obedience to the scripture to those texts which putatively predict Muhammad's prophethood. Notwithstanding this recognition of the legitimacy of the Other revealed scriptures, Muhammad is still asked to proclaim: 'O humankind! I am a Messenger of God unto all of you' (7:158). Muhammad thus had a task of proclaiming and calling in addition to that of challenging (16:125; 22:67).

On the face of it, these seem to be a set of contradictory responsibilities for, if a text is distorted, how can one ask for adherence to it? In the second responsibility, that of inviting, the question arises regarding the purpose of inviting to one's own path if that of the Other is also authentic. Firstly, the problem of the authenticity of texts as against their being distorted and, therefore, invalid, only arises if one thinks in terms of a singularly homogeneous and unchanging entity called 'the People of the Book' and all qur'anic references to it divested of contextuality. It has been shown above that this is not the case. The Qur'an itself is silent about the extent and nature of this distortion and castigates 'a section of the People of the Book'. As indicated on pages 158–61, the uniformity of praise or blame for a particular religious group is contrary to the pattern of the Qur'an. It is thus possible that the references to the authenticity of their scriptures refer to those held by the rest. Indeed, even the qur'anic denunciation of particular doctrinal 'errors' is not uniform in tone, indicating thereby either a particular moment in the Muslim encounter with the Other, or different components of the Other with specific nuances to those 'errors'. Secondly, Muhammad's basic responsibility in inviting was to call to God. For some components of the Other, the response to this call was best fulfilled by a commitment to Islam. Thus they were also invited to become Muslims. For others, the call was limited to *islam*. The invitation to the delegation of Najran is one such example when, after they declined to enter into Islam they were invited to 'come to a word equal between us and you that we worship none but God, nor will we take from our ranks anyone as deities' (3:64). The Qur'an, thus, is explicit only about inviting to God and to the 'path of God'. In the following text, for example, the instruction to invite people to God comes after an affirmation of the diversity of religious paths. Here again one sees the imperative of inviting to God, who is above the diverse paths emanating from Him.

> Unto every community have we appointed [different] ways of worship, which they ought to observe. Hence, do not let those [who follow ways other than yours] draw you into disputes on this score, but summon [them all] unto your Sustainer: for, behold, you are indeed on the right way. And if they try to argue with you, say [only]: God knows best what you are doing.

> [For, indeed,] God will judge between you [all] on Resurrection Day with regard to all on which you were wont to differ. (22:67)

Conclusion: The Pre-Eminence of Pluralism

The basis for the recognition of the religious Other was clearly not the acceptance of reified Islam and Muhammad's prophethood with all its implications; nor was it the absence of any principles. The fact that it was Muhammad and the Muslims who defined the basis of coexistence, and who determined which form of submission was appropriate for which community, clearly implies a qur'anic insistence on an ideological leadership role for itself. It was explicit in the qur'anic approach to relationships with other religious groups. It is a significant departure from the liberal position, which equates coexistence, and freedom with absolute equality for all. A fundamental question arises here: how is this qur'anic position compatible with pluralism and justice?

It has already been indicated in chapter 4 that the pre-eminence of the righteous does not mean a position of permanent socio-religious superiority for the Muslim community. The Muslims as a social entity were not superior to the Other, for such a position would have placed them and their parochial God in the same category as others who were denounced in the Qur'an for the crimes of arrogance and desiring to appropriate God for a narrow community. The qur'anic reprimand to other communities is that they cannot base their claims to superiority on the achievements of their forebears: 'That is a community that is bygone; to them belongs what they earned and to you belong what you earn, and you will not be asked about what they had done' (2:134). There is no reason to suppose that this should not be applied to the post-Muhammadan Muslim community.

Furthermore, the Qur'an does not regard all people and their ideas as equal, but proceeds from the premise that the idea of inclusiveness is superior to that of exclusiveness. In this sense, the advocates of pluralism had to be 'above' those who insisted that the religious expressions of others counted for nothing and that theirs was the only way to attain salvation. The relationship between the inclusivist form of religion and the exclusivist form can be compared to that of a democratic state and fascist political parties, as Askari has cogently argued.[20]

Inclusivity was not merely a willingness to let every idea and practice exist. Instead it was geared towards specific objectives, such as freeing humankind from injustice and servitude to other human beings so that they might be free to worship God. As has been explained, according to the Qur'an, the belief that one is not accountable to God and *shirk* were intrinsically connected to the socio-economic practices of the Arabs. In order to ensure justice for all, it was important for Muhammad and his community to work actively against those beliefs and not accord them a position of equality.

The responsibility of calling humankind to God and to the path of God will thus remain. The task of the present-day Muslim is to discern what this means in every age and every society. Who is to be invited? Who is to be taken as allies in this calling? How does one define the path of God? These are particularly pertinent questions in a society where definitions of Self and Other are determined by justice and injustice, oppression and liberation and where the test of one's integrity as a human being dignified by God is determined by the extent of one's commitment to defend that dignity.

Religion, it is evident, has not only been a participant in the struggle to both retain the apartheid status quo and to destroy it; religion itself has been a battlefield. It is within the context of this contest that our discussion in the following chapter, on *wilayah* as solidarity or collaboration, is located.

Notes

1. In a study of al-Tabari's treatment of Christianity and Christians, Charfi, for example, laments the 'little sense that there is of any development or gradation in the qur'anic position towards the Christians from the earliest Meccan verses to the final Medinan ones' (1980, p. 145). Nor, indeed, is there any sense of the context or social location of the exegete. 'Aside from the mention of the intellectual lineage to which an individual author pays respect', observed McAuliffe, 'it is frequently difficult to determine from internal evidence alone whether a commentary was written in Anatolia or Andalusia, whether its *mufassir* [commentator] had ever seen a Mongol or a Crusader or had ever conversed with a Christian or ever conducted business with one' (1991, p. 35).

2. This term is mostly used in the Qur'an to describe those inhabitants of Medina who had outwardly accepted Islam, but were suspect for various reasons. They were unreliable during times of crises (33:12–14), avoided participation, financial or physical, in *jihad* (47:20–31) and even looked forward to the time when the Prophet would be expelled from Medina (63:8).

3. The question of whether the Jewish communities were arabized Jews or judaized Arabs has not been resolved. These communities were possibly founded by refugees who fled from Palestine after Jerusalem was destroyed by Nebuchadnezzar in 586 BCE (Saunders 1982, p. 11). 'They were Arabic in language, in many customs and in aspects of their social organization, and were clearly not subject to Talmudic discipline. And yet, if they were originally Arabs, any consciousness of such relationship had evaporated in consequence of their having absorbed a Jewish exclusivist outlook. They felt themselves quite different from the Arabs among whom they lived and had erected a self-sufficient barrier around themselves' (Spencer-Trimingham 1979, p. 249).

4. Although tensions between the Jews and the Muslims were evident for some time before the Battle of Badr (624), the first time that Muhammad acted against the Jews was immediately after this battle when Banu Qaynuqa' was expelled for allegedly plotting the assassination of Muhammad. Banu al-Nadir and Banu Qurayzah were expelled subsequent to their alleged collaboration with the enemy at the Battle of Uhud (625) and the Trench (627) respectively. The last Jewish stronghold, Khaybar, fell to the Muslims in 628 after a long siege in response to their alleged incitement of the Meccans to restart hostilities against the Muslims. For two very different perspectives on the fate of Banu Qurayzah subsequent to the Battle of the Trench, see al-'Umari 1991, I, pp. 134–8 and Ahmad 1979, pp. 67–94.

5. The most widely known of these encounters is with a Syrian monk whom Muslims have come to know as Bahira. He was supposed to have predicted that Muhammad was destined to become a Messenger of God (Ibn Sa'd 1967, I, p. 146).

6. The agreement, *inter alia*, stated that 'no bishop will be displaced from his bishopric, no monk from his monastery and no testator from the property of his endowment' (Ibn Sa'd 1967, I, p. 419). This community survived for at least two hundred years after the death of Muhammad (Spencer-Trimingham 1979, p. 307).

7. The history, stages and nature of this encounter have been dealt with extensively by both traditional and contemporary scholarship, Muslim as well as non-Muslim. Barakat Ahmad (1979), Watt (1953), Rahman (1982c) and Newby (1988) are among the host of scholars who have dealt with the early Muslim–Jewish encounter. For the encounter between Muslims and Christians, see Ibn Taymiyyah (1905), Bell (1970), Wijoyo (1982), Cragg (1985) and McAuliffe

(1991). The heresiographer, al-Shahrastani (d. 1153) devotes much attention to the category of People of the Book (1961). For Muslim relations with Jews and Christians as *dhimmis*, see Ye'or (1985).

8. The qur'anic accusation of *shirk* against the Christians because of their alleged worshipping of three deities (4: 171–3; 5: 72–3,) is a case in point; most Christians insist that the doctrine of the Trinity is not the same as Tritheism, the worship of three gods (Kung 1987, pp. 90ff.; Watt 1978, pp. 21–2, 47–9; Basetti-Sani 1967, pp. 188–93). More specifically, the Unitarians, who also regard themselves as Christians, even reject any notion of the Trinity.

9. According to al-Baladhuri, the Prophet accepted *jizyah*, a kind of tax from the People of the Book. This was an indication of the status of people of *dhimmah*, from the Magians of Hajr, 'Umar al-Khattab from the Persians, and 'Uthman ibn 'Affan from the Berbers of North Africa (1966, p. 21) Subsequently in history, the *'ulama'* of some regions of the vastly enlarged Muslim domain further expanded the term 'people of *dhimmah'* to include the followers of other faiths not necessarily Semitic (al-Abidin 1986, p. 4). The *Shorter Encyclopaedia of Islam* states that 'in the 14th century a Muhammadan prince in India allowed the Chinese, against payment of *jizyah*, to keep up a pagoda on Muslim territory' and that 'the inner state of affairs in India brought it about that even veritable idolaters were considered as "people of *dhimmah*" (SEI 'People of the Book', p. 17). Al-Tabataba'i regarded the Zoroastrians as People of the Book (1973, 14, p. 538) and Abu'l-Kalam Azad (d. 1858) considered the Hindus as such (Hamidullah 1986, p. 4).

10. The expression 'Fourth World' is increasingly used to refer to those indigenous communities marginalized and oppressed in their own countries of origin, irrespective of the economic status of that country. These communities are also called 'first peoples' in the sense of having inhabited their lands before other communities settled there (Burger 1990).

11. The term *ummah* occurs nine times in the Meccan context and forty-seven times in that understood to be Medinan. It is used to refer exclusively to the socio-historical community of Muslims (2:143; 3:110), to 'a group of people' (from among the Muslims in 3:104 and from among the Christians in 5:66), community in the broad sense (6:108; 7:34; 10.47), to an individual (16:120–1). Qur'an 23:52 refers to the communities of all the prophets. For much of the Medinan period the term was used to describe 'the totality of individuals bound to one another irrespective of their colour, race or social status, by the doctrine of submission to one God' (Ahmad 1979, pp. 38–9). Looking at the way the term *ummah* has today acquired an exclusivist meaning, Ahmad says that 'the main difficulty in dealing with the history of ideas is that terms are more permanent than their definitions' (ibid. 1979, p. 39).

12. The other is Qur'an 5:69; 'Surely those who have faith and those who are Jews and the Sabeans and the Christians, whoever has faith in Allah and the Last Day and does good, they shall have no fear nor shall they grieve.' Since there is no significant difference in the exegetical treatment of these two texts, I have confined my reflections to interpretations of the first.

13. This theory is neatly supported by a lengthy account regarding the spiritual search of Salman al-Farsi (d. 658) before he encountered the Prophet. Salman was grieved at the inability of his deeply pious friends to embrace Islam, as they had died before hearing about his new faith (Ayoub 1984, I, pp. 110–12; McAuliffe 1991, pp. 105–9). According to several of the exegetes, this verse was occasioned by God's wish to console Salman. In one of the two narrations of this story, after informing Salman of the revelation of this verse, the Prophet is reported to have said: 'Whoever has died in the faith of Jesus and died in *islam* before he heard of me, his lot shall be good. But whoever hears of me today and yet does not assent to me shall perish' (al-Tabari 1954, I, p. 323).

Al-Shahrastani (d. 1153) discusses this problem at some length and substantiates the supercessionist theory on rational grounds. 'Islam abrogates all previous codes of which it is the perfection . . . if contemporary law is subject to constant alteration to meet changing conditions why is it impossible that laws given to one people at one time should be abrogated elsewhere at another time? The law corresponds to actions, and the active changes of death and life. Humankind's creation and annihilation, sometimes gradually, sometimes instantaneously, correspond to the legal changes of permitted and forbidden. If we consider the formation of man from his pre-embryonic beginning to his full stature we see that each progressed from code to code till the perfection of all codes was reached' (1934, pp. 158–9).

14. Al-Tabari includes Mujahid and al-Suddi in this 'group among the exegetes' who believed that the three categories of the Other applied to those who actually encountered Muhammad. The fact of a group with this opinion was, however, regarded as significant enough by al-Tabari for him to start his interpretation of this text with a refutation of those who argue that the verse relates to those who encountered Muhammad and for several others to devote attention to refuting it. (1954, I, p. 323)

15. Abu al-Futuh al-Razi and Khazin (n.d., 4, p. 135) are among those who hold this view while al-Baidawi (n.d., 4, p. 135) and al-Razi (1990, 3, p. 112) offer both committed followers of the Prophet and the hypocrites as possible meanings. Al-Razi cites two texts in support of the view that those who have faith can also be interpreted as the hypocrites': 5:41, ('those who say "we believe" with their mouths, but their hearts do not believe') and 4:136 ('O you who believe, believe in Allah') which he interprets as 'O you who believe with your tongues, believe with your hearts' (cited in McAuliffe 1991, p. 121).

16. The exegetes did not hesitate to name the converted individuals who are supposedly referred to in this text and in others. Thus, 3:199 ('Verily among the People of the Book are those who have faith . . .') is viewed as alternatively referring to the Christian Negus of Abyssinia and his associates, who, it is claimed, embraced Islam; 'Abd Allah ibn Salam, an early Jewish convert to Islam; and various groups such 'forty people from Najran', 'thirty from Abyssinia', 'eighty Romans' all of whom 'were following the din of 'Isa then they became Muslims', (al-Tabari n.d., 3, p. 173; al-Zamakhshari n.d., I, p. 459; al-Baidawi n.d. I, p. 656).

17. I have adopted the translation of Moosa (1988a, p. 9) who explains that shari'ah is a path with metaphysical implications while minhaj implies a practical way in which things are done. This distinction is also evident from al-Tabari's explanation of this verse that 'for every people among you we have made a way to the truth to believe in and a clear path to act upon' (1954, 6, p. 269). Interestingly, most of the exegetes do not deal here with the possible differences between shir'ah/shari'ah and minhaj, but between din and shari'ah. An exception is al-Razi who offers two opinions, including the following: 'shir'ah refers to shari'ah in a general way, whereas minhaj refers to a shari'ah of excellence; shari'ah is the origin of action while minhaj is a continuation on the path' (1990, 12, p. 13).

18. The Qur'an postulates that all of these scriptures originate from the same source, the Mother of the Book (13:39; 43:4) and that separately each constitutes only a portion of the Qur'an (2:231; 18:28; 29:45; 35:31), the Torah and the Gospels (4:44; 4:51).

19. I am indebted to Hamilton (1991) for the insights into the significance for religious pluralism of the qur'anic metaphor of competition in righteousness.

20. 'If a group or party arises which does not agree to the democratic rule and works to overthrow the government of the day by violent means in order to create a fascist social order wherein there is no room for democratic expression and exercise of opinion and power, that group cannot lay claim to those rights enjoined by a democracy' (Askari 1986, p. 328). Askari argues that the basis of this coexistence is a recognition of the superiority of pluralism and democracy. A group opposed to democracy and determined to violently overthrow a democratically elected government in order to create a fascist social order, he says, 'cannot lay claim to those rights enjoined by a democracy' (1986, p. 5). This analogy, extended to religious communities, according to him, means that 'the rights which religious communities have vis-à-vis one another should derive from a shared theology which . . . affirms religious diversity in order to give praise, in various ways and modes, to the One and the same Transcendent God' (ibid.).

6

REDEFINING COMRADES & OPPONENTS

INTERRELIGIOUS SOLIDARITY *for* JUSTICE

By God! As long as the ocean drenches wool we will be with the oppressed until they receive recompense for their rights and we see that all receive equal treatment.

(From the Oath of the Righteous, Ibn Sa'd 1967, 1, p. 145)

Pluralism Wedded to Liberation

As I showed in chapter 1, the discourse on religious pluralism among South African Muslims took place within a concrete struggle for liberation. We have seen how this struggle led to the employment of certain hermeneutical keys, invoked both as tools of liberation and as ways of approaching and understanding the Qur'an. Reflecting on the qur'anic texts with the use of these keys enabled progressive Islamists to develop a new appreciation of the Self and Other according to the Qur'an.

The fact that this redefinition took place within a concrete struggle for justice meant that the emerging theology of religious pluralism was intrinsically wedded to one of liberation. The vague liberal embrace of all forms of Otherness was thus avoided. While it was evident that the old theological categories of Self and Other were no longer tenable, if they ever were, the struggle against apartheid also taught the progressive Islamist that there were diverse forms of Otherness, some of which had to be opposed relentlessly. Within the Muslim community there were collaborators with tricameralism and within the oppressed black community there were those who made common cause with the apartheid regime. The embrace of Otherness was thus a qualified one, of the Other as comrade in arms.

In this embrace of the Other in solidarity, progressive Islamists drew theological support and affirmation from various paradigms of struggle in Islamic history and the Qur'an. This is evident from the   religio-political discourse in their sermons and publications, as discussed in chapter 1. Deriving support from the religious and just Other was affirmed by the sojourn of early Muslims in Abyssinia, while solidarity with the Other, religious or otherwise, was affirmed by the Exodus   paradigm.

Invoking the Exodus paradigm is based on the fact that the history of Islam is not confined to seventh-century Arabia and its environs. The Qur'an, as I have shown, insists on the acceptance of all the prophets who preceded Muhammad as authentic messengers of God and recounts some of their anguish, struggles and victories in detail. The phenomenon of Islamists resorting to pre-Muhammadan religio-historical paradigms can thus be said to be as old as reified Islam itself.

In this chapter I have two main objectives. The first is to show that the Qur'an does not prevent Muslims from working with others in a common cause to serve justice and righteousness. Those very texts that appear to be prohibiting this, if examined within their historical contexts, are in fact significant for a qur'anic hermeneutic of religious pluralism and liberation. The second is to show that the Qur'an and Muhammad's example encourage co-operation and solidarity across 'belief' lines for justice and righteousness and that this solidarity is not based on a vague and undefined desire for peace and quiet. Rather, it is based on a struggle against injustice and for the creation of a world wherein it is safe to be human and where people are freed from enslavement to man in order to worship God freely.

The Qur'an and *Wilayah* as Collaboration

In the first chapter we saw how the debate around interfaith solidarity against apartheid characterized much of South African Muslim discourse during the 1980s and how qur'anic texts were used by different sides of this debate to support their own perspectives. Here I reflect on the question of the qur'anic prohibition of alliances or relationships of affinity (*wilayah*) with the religious Other. The following text is one of several in the Qur'an prohibiting the *mu'minun* from taking Others as their allies:

O You who have attained to faith! Do not take the Jews and the Christians for your allies; they are but allies of one another; and whoever of you allies himself with them becomes, verily, one of them. Behold, God does not guide such evildoers. (5:51)

While this text prohibits the *wilayah* of the Jews and the Christians, else-where the prohibition applies to the *kafirun* (3:28; 4:139; 4:144), 'people who are not of your kind' (3:118), the hypocrites (4:89), 'such as mock at your *din*' (5:57), 'the enemies of God' (60:1), 'such as fight against you because of (your) *din*, and drive you forth from your homes, or aid (others) in driving you forth' (60:9), 'people whom God has condemned' (60:13) and 'your fathers and your brothers for friends if *kufr* is dearer to them than faith' (9:23–4). Related to this prohibition are the injunctions to seek the *wilayah* of God alone;[1] that of God, God and the *mu'minun*, (5:56); that of the *mu'minun* and those who went into exile (8:72–3) or that of the men and women of faith (9:70).

In addition to the South African experience of solidarity in the struggle against oppression, there are several seeming inconsistencies in the text and between the texts and early Muslim behaviour (including that of Muhammad) that necessitate a search for a contextual meaning of these texts. Firstly, several texts insisting that only God can be the protector and friend of the people of faith[2] are seemingly contradicted by a number of others stating that God and other *mu'minun* can also, and indeed ought to, be their allies (3:28, 118; 5:55; 9:16, 70). Then, in Qur'an 5:55 the type of *mu'min* whose *wilayah* is permitted is defined: 'those who fulfil their poor-due obligations and who establish prayer'.[3] This would exclude the generality of Muslims – those who follow what Rida described as 'ethnic Islam' – from such a relationship. Thirdly, elsewhere the Qur'an allows the most intimate of relationships, including that of matrimony (5:5) and asylum (5:82), between the People of the Book and the *mu'minun*. Moreover, Muhammad and his Companions maintained cordial personal relationships between themselves and various individuals and communities among the religious Other.[4] Finally, the early Muslims under the leadership of Muhammad had regularly entered into political and mutual defence agreements with the religious Other.

The text under discussion, Qur'an 5:51, like all those prohibiting Muslims from the *wilayah* of Others, is Medinan and reflects the religio-political tensions of that period. As I indicated in chapter 5, it is evident from the seemingly contradictory texts dealing with the religious Other that these reflect the various stages in the Muslim–Other relationship. A number of separate accounts have been offered by the exegetes regarding the particular circumstances around the revelation of this verse.

1. At the outbreak of hostilities between Banu Qaynuqa' and the Muslims, 'Abd Allah ibn Ubay, widely regarded as a prominent figure among the hypocrites, remained attached to Banu Qaynuqa'. He reportedly approached the Prophet, saying 'I am a person who fears the vicissitudes of time and shall not disavow the *wilayah* of my protectors' (al-Tabari 1954, 6, p. 275; al-Zamakhshari n.d., 1, p. 642). On the other hand, 'Ubadah ibn Samit and another person from Banu 'Awf ibn al-Khazraj, went to the Prophet, disavowed their similar relationship with the Banu Qaynuqa' and are reported to have said: 'We befriend God, His Prophet and the *mu'minun* and seek refuge in God and His Prophet from alliances with those *kuffar* and their allies' (ibid.). This verse was revealed to support the action of the latter and to denounce that of the former. 'God informs him [Ibn Ubay] that if he remains in solidarity with them and retains links with them then he [effectively] is among them in abandoning God and His Prophet' (al-Tabari 1954, 6, p. 275).

2. When Banu Qurayzah violated the agreement between them and God by writing to Abu Sufyan ibn Harb inviting him and the Quraysh to enter their strongholds, Muhammad sent Abu Lubabah ibn 'Abd al-Mundhir as an emissary to demand their surrender. When he departed, in a seeming act of sympathy with them, he pointed to his throat, indicating that they would be killed (Rida 1980, 6, p. 425; al-Tabari 1954, 6, p. 275).

3. Some of the Muslims corresponded with the Christians of Syria while others corresponded with the Jews of Medina, informing them of the activities and military plans of Muhammad 'so that they may benefit from their wealth, even if it was by way of borrowing money' (Rida 1980, 6, p. 425).

4. Al-Tabari (1956, 6, p. 276) says that, on the eve of the Battle of Uhud, a group of Muslims felt extremely anxious and feared that the *kuffar* would overpower them. Some of them indicated that they would join the Jews, seeking security with them and even become Jews, while others indicated that they would do so among the Christians in a part of Syria.

It should be noted that these various accounts of the event that occasioned this verse are generally characteristic of all the verses prohibiting the *wilayah* of the religious Other. The exegetes who have elaborated on the meaning of the term *wilayah* in this context differ as to whether it means formal alliances and agreements, more personal bonds or a combination of these. Rida and al-Zamakhshari interpret *wilayah* to mean 'the rendering of mutual assistance and alliances' (Rida 1980, 6, p. 425; al-Zamakhshari n.d., 1, p. 642). Al-Razi adds a more personalist dimension: 'relying upon their personal assistance and drawing close to them' (1990, 12, p. 18). Al-Tabataba'i goes to great lengths to insist that the personalist dimension, 'affectionate closeness', is the essence of its meaning. He, in fact, favours a meaning that removes any distinction between the partners in the *wilayah* relationship and fuses their personal and religious identities.[5] There has been some discussion around the employment of the singular form of the word, *wali*. Some have suggested that the *wilayah* of God, Muhammad and of the *mu'minun* really refers to a single relationship (al-Razi 1990, 12, p. 47; Rida 1980, 6, p. 441). Others, such as Nasr al-Din al-Baidawi (n.d., 11, p. 206), suggest that it is only the *wilayah* of God that is real and self-existing, while that of Muhammad and the *mu'minun* really emanates from the *wilayah* of God.[6]

The meaning of *wilayah* in the Qur'an is clearly not static. From the accounts of events that occasioned the revelation of the various texts dealing with *wilayah*, it is clear that the word is understood in at least three different senses: 1) personal links of affection; 2) agreements characteristic of Arab intertribal relations, or even relations between an individual and a tribe other than his own and; 3) a relationship of trust in God. While a clear distinction cannot always be drawn between these different meanings it is, nevertheless, important to appreciate the different applications of the term.

The word was never actively invoked in the South African context. However, two terms embody its socio-political and religious applications: collaboration and solidarity. While collaboration is defined in the *Shorter Oxford English Dictionary* as 'to co-operate' and a collaborator as 'someone who works in conjunction with another or others', in South Africa it had long since acquired a pejorative sense: to emerge from the community of the oppressed and to willingly participate in the socio-political structures of that oppression. Solidarity, defined as 'the fact or quality on the part of communities, etc., of being perfectly united or at one in some respect especially in interests, sympathy or aspirations', was how the relationship between the various components of the liberation struggle was described.

It is my submission that the Qur'anic injunctions against the *wilayah* of the *kuffar* relate to collaboration with the unjust and unrighteous Other and not solidarity with the exploited and marginalized Other. This interpretation is evident from the way the text prohibiting *wilayah* is circumscribed by a number of contextual and textual constraints.

The context of this verse within the chapter indicates that the central issue is not doctrinal; on the contrary, here, and elsewhere (Qur'an 3:22-5; 3:118-120; 5:57; 60:8-9), the prohibition of *wilayah* is preceded by an acknowledgement of religious diversity.

> Unto every one of you have We appointed a [different] law and way of life. And if God had so willed, He could surely have made you all one single community: but He willed it otherwise in order to test you by means of what He has vouchsafed unto you. Vie, then, with one another in doing good works! Unto God you all must return; and then He will make you truly understand all that on which you were wont to differ. (5:48)

From the context of the revelation, whichever of the putative occasions of revelation one may wish to consider, it is evident that the conditions under which the *wilayah* of the religious Other is denounced are those of hostility, war and physical threats to the survival of the community of believers. This is also true of all the other similar texts. In the words of Ansari, 'Every such verse relates without exception, only to those non-Muslims who were sworn enemies of Islam and whose active hostility towards Muslims had reached the highest limits' (1977, 2, p. 271). Within this context, engaging in a relationship of *wilayah* with the enemy is tantamount to betraying one's own. This is also shown by the frequent linking of these texts (e.g., 3:26-7, 5:51-60) to the activities of the hypocrites.[7]

Wherever the immediate context of warfare is missing, then the factor of relentless enmity towards the *mu'minun* is evident. At various other junctures the Qur'an is specific about the ways in which this enmity was manifested. The Qur'an prohibits the *mu'minun* from entering into alliances or having friendly relations with those who mock them and their beliefs (4:139; 5:57), who spare no effort to corrupt them and who rejoice in their misfortune. 'Vehement hatred has already come into the open from their mouths', says the Qur'an, and 'what their hearts conceal is yet worse' (3:118); they grieved at whatever good fortune occurred to the *mu'minun* and rejoiced at whatever evil overtook them (3:120); they yearned to see the *mu'minun* 'deny the truth even as they have denied it'

(4:89) and they preferred the penal system of pre-Islamic ignorance, which discriminated on the basis of tribal origin (5:50).[8] The enmity of those whose *wilayah* was denounced was not confined to the personal sphere. Among the reasons the Qur'an puts forward for denouncing the *wilayah* of the *kuffar* or that of the People of the Book is the fact that they actively engaged in the oppression of the *mu'minun*, drove them out of their homes and persecuted them on account of their faith (60:9).

It is evident from this that the *mu'minun* were instructed in a particular response to active hostility from the Other, rather than to the fact of Otherness or diversity. The context of hostility is specifically mentioned when the Qur'an instructs the *mu'minun* to avoid the company of 'those who deny the truth of God's messages and mock them . . . until they begin to engage in a different discourse' (4:138ff.). 'Now, whenever you meet such as indulge in (blasphemous) talk about Our messages,' says the Qur'an, 'turn thy back upon them until they begin to talk of other things' (6:68). This is also borne out in Qur'an 4:89 where the refusal to go into exile was seen as a sign of hypocrisy that would similarly exclude one from the *wilayah* of the *mu'minun*. Here the *mu'minun* were instructed to avoid the *wilayah* of other *mu'minun* who did not go into exile except in the case of someone who entered into an agreement with people with whom the *mu'minun* were connected by a treaty (4:90).

Given the vehemence with which the *wilayah* of the Other is generally denounced, one may assume that this is applicable to a situation of active hostility. In the words of Rida, 'these verses are clear proof that the prohibition is based on the enmity of people being at war with each other, not due to the existences of differences in *din* by itself as God has ordered all disputants to say: "You have your *din* and I have mine"' (1980, 6, p. 426). In one instance though, this prohibition does not occur within the context of war (5:57). In the absence of such a context and the citation of seemingly doctrinal differences one needs to consider the significance of the relationship between doctrine and praxis in society in general and that of Hijaz in particular. Furthermore, if the general import of the verse is considered, in the absence of the context of the hostilities of war, then one still finds that the prohibition of *wilayah* is circumscribed in several instances by qualifying phrases. This brings us to the question of textual qualification to the prohibition. While the prohibition of *wilayah* with the *kuffar* is characterized in the relevant texts, the Qur'an specifies four cases as exceptions to its prohibition. Firstly, such relationships should not be 'to the exclusion of the *mu'minun*' (3:28). Secondly, *wilayah* with the *kuffar* is permitted for the protection of the *mu'minun* (ibid.). Thirdly, it is acceptable to join a group with whom the *mu'minun* already have a non-aggression treaty (4:90). Fourthly, the prohibition does not apply to those who approach the *mu'minun* unwilling to fight them and their own people (ibid.).

The Exceptions to the Prohibition

The Mu'minun *Should Not be Excluded*

The phrase 'to the exclusion of the *mu'minun*' in Qur'an 3:28, may seem to imply that the Other may not be taken as one's friend or ally to the exclusion of the community of the faithful. However, this would be acceptable if the essential base of inspiration and support was that community. This qualification seems to highlight the significance of the sociological imperatives in the question of *wilayah*: Muhammad was also engaged in the task of building a social community, albeit on religious principles. Given that it was a community of faith and praxis, which people entered by choice, and that there was little by way of a common history, tradition, tribe, or class to cement their bonds, it was important that the new community be regarded as the essential base of support and inspiration.

Self-Defence May be an Objective

The expression *illa an tattaqu minhum tuqatan* has been translated in a variety of different ways:

> [Don't take them as your *awliya'*] but you should (instead) guard yourselves against them, guarding carefully. (Shakir, n.d., p. 78)

> [Don't take them as your *awliya'*] unless it be to protect yourselves against them in this way. (Asad 1980, p. 70; Yusuf 'Ali 1989, p. 134)

> [Don't take them as your *awliya'*] unless it be that you (are able to) guard against them. (Pickthall n.d., p. 57)

> [Don't take them as your *awliya'*] except if you fear a danger from them. (al-Hilali 1993, p. 80)

The classical commentaries favour the translations of Shakir and Asad, as is clear from the lengthy discourses on religious dissimulation that follows their brief explanations of the text (al-Zamakhshari n.d., 1, p. 351; al-Razi 1990, 8, p. 14).[9] Given the general context of hostility of this and other similar texts, the meaning of a somewhat expedient relationship favoured by al-Hilali, Asad, Yusuf 'Ali and Shakir is quite plausible.

During the 1980s some well-meaning Islamists in South Africa, along with some of the accommodationist clerics, reasoned along similar lines, that one may seek the *wilayah* of the People of the Book, or even of atheists, if this were to secure the long-term survival of Islam. The fundamentalist Islamists who argued along these lines differed only from the accommodationist clerics in making a strategic choice for security with the inevitably victorious masses, rather than with the collapsing regime. In view of the hermeneutical keys of justice elaborated upon in chapter 3, this unprincipled position is indefensible. People of faith participate in a struggle for justice because it is an expression of that faith; not to protect themselves or even to secure the survival of their faith.

Pickthall's translation is of greater relevance in the broader context of nurturing a fragile process of community building, the apparent context of the verse wherein this qualification features (5:28). In other words, the *wilayah* of the Other is acceptable on condition that one is able to guard against whatever is negative in the Other or detrimental to one's own community of faith and praxis.[10]

The Accountability of Those Connected to the Treaty Partners of the Mu'minun

The qualification in Qur'an 4:90 appears to apply to those Muslims who were unwilling or unable to go into exile to Medina when instructed to do so by Muhammad. In the preceding text those who did not wish to go into exile are asked to desist from taking those unwilling or unable to do so as their *awliya'*. Al-Razi says that the reference is to those Muslims who intended joining Muhammad but found this difficult. They sought asylum with a community who had a treaty with the Muslims until they could find a way to him.[11] The fact, though, that this text allows one group of Muslims to have a relationship with another group, not because of the bonds of a common religious identity, but because the second group has a political relationship with a group of another religious community, is significant. This points to the socio-political considerations underlying and informing the question of *wilayah* during the period of qur'anic revelation. The case for socio-political, rather than doctrinal, factors informing the question of *wilayah* is also affirmed if the text actually refers to the religious Other, as some have argued.[12]

Those Unwilling to Fight the Mu'minun and Their Own People

Here again one finds a difference of opinion regarding the referent of the text. The majority argue that it refers to the *kuffar*: 'God has ordered fighting the *kuffar* except if they are involved in a treaty or if they desist from killing, in which case it is not permissible to fight them (al-Razi 1990, 10, p. 230).[13]

However one interprets these qualifications to the prohibition of *wilayah*, the Qur'an is explicit about the fact that God does not forbid one from a relationship of compassion and justice with those who 'do not fight against you on account of [your] faith, and neither drive you forth from your homes' (60:8).

Who is the Self and Other in the *Wilayah* Rejected by the Qur'an?

The Qur'an is explicit about the motives that led some of the early Muslims, or those who identified with the community, into a relationship of *wilayah* with those who opposed Muhammad. In the attempt to develop a contextual theology of pluralism for liberation it is important to identify the basic motivation of those whose pursuit of *wilayah* with the Other was denounced, as well as the specific characteristics of that Other, and to relate these categories to the South Africa of the 1980s. In order to reflect on the qur'anic view of *wilayah* with the Other in a society characterized by the divisions of apartheid South Africa, two questions need to be addressed. How does the Qur'an describe the Other when it cautions the *mu'minun* against them? How does the Qur'an describe the Self seeking that *wilayah*?

The first characteristic of those whose *wilayah* is to be avoided is that they 'abuse the *din* of the *mu'minun* and mock the signs of God'. From the various accounts of the occasions of revelation that have been suggested for the texts referring to those who abused the *din* of the *mu'minun* (5:57) and mocked the signs of God (4:140), it is evident that these related to both verbal abuse[14] and an active disregard for living alongside the implications of faith. The Qur'an is emphatic about treating the religious beliefs of others, including that of the *mushrikun*, with sensitivity (6:108). What is being condemned in Qur'an 5:57 is the practice of insulting the beliefs of the *mu'minun*, in the same way that the Qur'an appealed to the *mu'minun* to desist from doing this to others. Given that *din* is essentially about transforming lives and society, this kind of competition in verbal declarations and mutual insults is anathema to it. Indeed, one may say that the mutual denunciation of each other's religious beliefs is often a form of compensation for the inability or refusal to live alongside all the implications of one's own, another form of taking one's faith as 'jest and play' (5:57).

In South Africa it was (and remains) characteristic of accommodation theology to engage in this kind of mocking of the faith. Furthermore, the mutual exchange of interreligious insults was characteristic of a particular form of accommodation theology, i.e. evangelism. Organizations such as Christ for All Nations and the International Islamic Propagation Centre, in varying degrees, consistently displayed support for the apartheid power structures whenever they paused in their onslaughts against the religious Other. On the other hand, as I showed in chapter 1, other non-Muslims committed to a theology of justice and compassion consistently showed a deep respect for the beliefs of Muslims. This was particularly the case when this belief was concretized in the daily struggles of people for justice. These non-Muslims were also willing to defend that respect publicly. As for the apartheid regime, even while it professed a sincere respect for religion, it consistently identified with and was sustained by accommodation theology, which remained contemptuous of any form of religion that sought to relate belief in God to compassion for all of God's people.[15]

Secondly, according to the Qur'an, the *mu'minun* should avoid those who yearn to see them deny the truth (4:89). The apartheid regime imposed various measures to enforce a system of racial segregation and was desperate for all South Africans to deny the truth of equality and non-racialism, and of a God concerned with all of creation, particularly the marginalized and oppressed. 'The truth', as I argued in previous chapters, was not so much about dogma or doctrine but about the implications of these in an oppressive and divided society.

The final characteristic of those whose *wilayah* must be avoided is that they oppress and persecute the *mu'minun* (60:9): 'It is only with regards to those who fought you on account of your religion and have driven you out of your homes, and help to drive you out, Allah forbids you to befriend them.' This verse is a reference to the early Muslims' forced removals from Mecca by a systematic process of persecution and harassment. The fact that this, as a sin, is mentioned immediately after lack of faith is significant, since forced removals are usually seen as an essentially political act. Here, once again, the Qur'an underlines the totality of life and the comprehensive nature of God's concern for *al-nas*.

The Group Areas Act, under which millions of people were unjustly and forcibly driven out of their homes, was perhaps the most vicious of the apartheid regime's laws. Enacted under the prayerful eye of the Dutch Reformed Church, it caused people to be uprooted from homes and land that had, in some cases, been inhabited by their ancestors for centuries. While the vast majority of the population refused to participate in the apartheid regime's various schemes to make them co-participants in their own oppression, a few were always found willing to collaborate. The refusal of a large number of Muslims to associate with those who collaborated with the apartheid regime was affirmed by the qur'anic reference to those 'who aid others in driving you from your houses'. It was thus not only the *wilayah* of the oppressors that the Qur'an condemned, but also relationships with the collaborators in oppression. This rejection of any association with the apartheid regime was also emphasized in another verse of the Qur'an: 'And lean not towards those who oppress, lest the fire should seize you and you will not find in God a friend or protector' (11:113). The vast majority of South Africans were not guilty of any of these crimes, neither were they in any position to inflict these crimes upon the Muslim community with whom they shared a common yolk of oppression.

One may argue that the Qur'an denounces the *wilayah* of the Other who oppress the Muslims on the basis of their faith and that, in apartheid South Africa, this was never the case. Furthermore, unlike the early Muslims, all South Africans were free to practise their faith. A United Democratic Front pamphlet suggests that a response to this question depends on what kind of faith one is dealing with.

Why were our mosques left untouched when they bulldozed District Six and Vrededorp out of existence? Why are we being offered more sites for graveyards by them? Why are we being allowed loudspeaker facilities to call others to worship?

Because they know that our call to prayer is no longer a call to struggle as it was in the time of Muhammad; that our mosques are no longer the centres of planning the struggle against the usurpation of power and that our graveyards no longer accommodate martyrs in the fight for justice!

Hence, when they offer us freedom to call to prayer, freedom to die a death of apathy and more graves to be buried in, then they also intend to bury the dynamic Islam of Muhammad! (UDF 1984, p. 19)

Those Who Sought the *Wilayah* of the Other

The various verses prohibiting the *wilayah* of the Other either allude to, or make explicit mention of, the motives of those who sought it. Furthermore, all the incidents cited as possible occasions of revelation suggest motives that may be classified as placing narrow self-interest above that of the community of faith and praxis; pursuing *'izzah* (honour and power); or identifying with narrow tribalism.

To consider first the motive placing self-interest above that of the community of faith and praxis: this is more specifically the motivation in the selected text (Qur'an 5:51, see page 181). Referring to those who sought the *wilayah* of the Other, Qur'an 5:52 says 'and yet you can see how those in whose hearts there is disease vie with one another for their goodwill, saying [to themselves], "We fear lest fortune turn against us" '.[16] This is also evident from the various accounts cited on page 182 by Rida, al-Tabari, al-Razi and al-Zamakhshari of the events that occasioned the revelation of this text.

In apartheid South Africa, the argument of collaboration with the Other 'lest fortune turns against us' was indeed common. This was an argument invoked by those who believed in the power of the apartheid regime, rather than in the ability of the masses to overcome it. Because the state and its institutions were the centres of political and economic power, rather than the various community or political organizations opposing them, it was also an argument used by those who desired to protect their often substantial financial stakes in the apartheid state.

Those who entered into a relationship of solidarity with the masses against the apartheid regime, on the contrary, made enormous sacrifices of whatever financial resources they had. They often opted out of established and financially lucrative careers for the financial uncertainty of life as political dissidents and the personal insecurity of living 'on the run'. Rather than choosing the *wilayah* of the powerful for security and protection against the vicissitudes of time, they chose the *wilayah* of the poor and marginalized and the concomitant long spells in detention and confrontation with tear-gas, quirts, bullets and even death.

The second motive for seeking the *wilayah* of the Other is the pursuit of power and glory. Denouncing those who choose the *kuffar* as *awliya'* instead of *mu'minun*, the Qur'an asks rhetorically: 'Do they look for power and glory at their hands? Lo! All power and glory belongs to God' (4:139). The general consensus of the exegetes on the word *kafirun* in this text is that it is a reference to some of the Jews, since Qur'an 4:137 is a direct allusion to them (al-Razi 1990, 11, p. 81). The kind of power the Qur'an suggests the hypocrites pursued in the *wilayah* with the *kuffar* is that which is characteristic of the politically, socially and economically powerful: a power that permeated the tribal and patriarchal social structures of pre-Islamic paganism. Muhammad and the early Muslims were at pains to avoid being absorbed into these leadership structures, because they militated against all that Islam represented. The kind of power Muhammad eschewed was that which meant being co-opted by the ruling class in order to lend credibility to them while the threat to their hegemony was being neutralized.[17]

In South African terms, one may say that it was the power that accompanied collaboration with the apartheid regime, its homeland system and its tricameral parliament. By contrast, there were those who sought a different kind of power, a simple dignity that comes from being human. This dignity was born from, and nurtured in, an ethos of resistance to oppression, and from activism in a struggle for liberation.

The third motive is the refusal to reject narrow tribalism. The attempts by the now disempowered Medinan power brokers to subvert the new order assumed different dimensions. One significant such dimension was the attempts to rekindle the flames of narrow tribalism that had so often threatened to consume pre-Islamic Arab society. Tribalism was the antitheses of this very fragile new-found unity based on the ideal of *tawhid*.[18] Some of the Jews in Medina, such as Shish ibn Qays, went to great lengths to revive tribal hostilities characteristic of pre-Islamic paganism (Lings 1983, p. 127; al-Zamakhshari n.d., 1, p. 393). The tribes, which now comprised the newly forged community of faith and praxis, were not always alert to these attempts at undermining their unity; nor were they fully aware of the extent to which tribal affinities might militate against this new-found and fragile unity. In at least one case, some of the *mu'minun* among Aws and Khazraj, both tribes that had entered the fold of Islam, came to blows with each other as a direct consequence of appeals to disregard their ideological unity in favour of their older tribal links. Muhammad was angered at this flare-up of hostilities between the Muslims. 'Do you appeal to the ethos of pre-Islamic pagan tribalism while I am in your midst?', he is reported to have chastised them (al-Zamakhshari n.d., 1, p. 393). It was in response to this event that the following instruction was issued to the *mu'minun* to avoid pursuing the *wilayah* of some of the People of the Book (al-Zamakhshari n.d., 1, p. 393; al-Razi 1990, 6, p. 422):

Say: O People of the Book! Why do you reject the signs of God? And God is a witness over what you do.

Say: O People of the Book! Why do you [endeavour to] bar those who have come to believe [in this divine writ] from the path of God by trying to make it appear crooked, when you yourselves bear witness [to its being straight]? For, God, is not unaware of what you do.

O you who have attained to faith! If you pay heed to some of the
People of the Book, they might cause you to renounce the truth after
you come have to believe [in it].

And how could you deny the truth when it is unto you that God's
message are being conveyed, and it is in your midst that His Apostle
lives? But he who holds fast unto God has already been guided onto
a straight way. (Qur'an 3:98–101)[19]

The contemporary equivalents of Shish ibn Qays are people whose ideology is rooted in racism and tribalism, and who continue to fan those
flames in order that their power bases remain intact. The apartheid state,
it needs be remembered, was not concerned with religious identity in
itself but utilized it to underpin its obsession with tribal and racial identities. It is the *wilayah* of the advocates of division based on lineage and
ethnicity, whatever labels – Muslim, Christian, Jewish or Hindu – they
may be wearing, against which the Qur'an cautions. In contrast, the section of the People of the Book with whom the progressive Islamists
entered into a *wilayah* were people with an intense commitment to bringing people together by destroying all that has separated Muslim from
Muslim, Christian from Christian and Muslim from Christian. In doing
so they gave expression to another form of wilayah, *wilayah* as solidarity.
For this solidarity they needed to look no further than the example of
Muhammad and the Qur'an.

Muhammad and Solidarity with the Oppressed

Given the Qur'an's own option for 'the people' in general and for the
oppressed in particular, in a context of oppression the highest form of
righteousness is praxis in the service of the wronged and exploited. The
idea of active and organized solidarity with the oppressed received
expression in Muhammad's life long before his prophethood.

This is evident both from his participation in what came to be known
as the Alliance of the Virtuous, and his own glowing references to it long
after he became a prophet. Ibn Sa'd (1967, 1, p. 144) narrates that a visiting Yemenite merchant had sold some expensive goods to a leading figure of the clan of Sahm in Mecca. The Sahmite refused to pay the agreed
price. Despite being a visitor in Mecca, without any allies to whom he
could turn for help, the merchant stood on the slope of Mount Qubays
and appealed to the Quraysh to ensure that justice was done. In
response, several tribes met in the home of 'Abd Allah ibn Jud'an. Here
they decided to found an alliance for the furtherance of justice and the

protection of the weak. They vowed that, at every act of oppression in Mecca, they would remain in solidarity with the wronged and exploited until justice was done, irrespective of whether the oppressors and exploiters were from among the Quraysh or not: 'By God as long as the ocean drenches wool we will be with the oppressed until they receive recompense for their rights and we see that they also receive equal treatment' (ibid.). In the end, the Sahmite was compelled to pay his debt. Muhammad, who had accompanied his uncles, Zubayr and Abu Talib, to the signing of the pact, later commented 'I was present in the house of 'Abd Allah ibn Jud'an at so excellent a pact that I would not exchange it for a herd of red camels; [the clans of] Hashim, Zuhrah and Taym swore to side with the oppressed till the sea drenched wool and if now, in Islam, I were summoned unto it, I would gladly respond' (ibid.).

The political dynamics of Hijaz altered dramatically with Muhammad's announcement of his prophethood and in Mecca the *mu'minun* themselves became the community that was wronged. In Medina the struggle for justice and a faith promising to secure it was taken further by a community consisting of the dispossessed and their supporters. Given that this community itself comprised the exiled and oppressed, one does not find any clear precedent in this period in Muhammad's life as a prophet. The incident narrated above, however, does indicate that Muhammad would not have been found wanting had such an occasion arisen.

The Exodus Paradigm of Solidarity

In chapters 2 and 3 I referred to the popularity of the Exodus paradigm among people of faith engaged in the struggle in South Africa. This paradigm has regularly been invoked in a broad spectrum of Muslim scholarship, ranging from the mystical and philosophical to the political. South African Islam though, appears unique in the use of the Exodus paradigm to invoke unambiguous support for solidarity with the marginalized and oppressed religious Other. The chapter of the Qur'an named 'Story', which deals with the Exodus paradigm, says the Call, 'explains relationships with the oppressed who do not lead Islamic or righteous lives' (Call of Islam 1987).

The Qur'an recounts the story of Moses and Pharaoh in several chapters, with different fragments scattered throughout them,[20] from the very early life of Moses in Egypt and exile, to his encounter with God at the burning bush, his engaging Pharaoh and his sorcerers and his demands that the Israelites be freed. The account continues with their subsequent liberation, the drowning of Pharaoh and his army, the rebelliousness and *kufr* of Israelites in the desert and God's revelation to Moses on Mount Sinai. Throughout all of this Moses has the companionship of his brother, Aaron. The account concludes with Moses' death as the Israelites are about to enter the Promised Land.

For present purposes, there is a single theme in the Exodus paradigm as recounted in the Qur'an: the active solidarity of God himself and of Moses with the religious or actively rejecting Other. Given that I am dealing with the question of solidarity with the marginalized and the suffering, my essential concern here is with the *kufr* or otherwise of Israelites prior to liberation and during their journey into the promised land. The following texts deal with this subject:

> But none save a few of his people declared their faith in Moses, [while others held back] for fear of Pharaoh and their great ones, lest they persecute them: for, verily, Pharaoh was mighty on earth and was, verily, of those who are given to excesses.
>
> And Moses said: 'O my people! If you believe in God, place your trust in Him – if you have [truly] surrendered yourselves unto Him!'
>
> Whereupon they answered: 'In God have we placed our trust! O our Sustainer, make us not a plaything for evildoing folk.' (10:83–5)
>
> And we brought the Israelites across the sea; and thereupon Pharaoh and his hosts pursued them with vehement insolence and tyranny, until [they were overwhelmed by the waters of the sea. And] when he was about to drown, [Pharaoh] exclaimed: 'I have come to believe that there is no deity save Him in whom the Israelites believe, and I am of those who surrender themselves to Him!' (10:90).

The Israelites' faith or lack of it is a rather unexplored theme in qur'anic exegetical literature. When the subject is dealt with in the Qur'an, as in these texts, then the exegeses tend to focus on some other related issue.[21] Despite the lack of attention to this question among the exegetes, there is consensus that, even before their liberation, the vast majority of Israelites did not have faith in Moses or in God. The exegetes suggest that this verse was revealed in order to console Muhammad, who also yearned for his own people to have faith in him. In the same manner that his people refused to believe in him, the Israelites refused to believe in Moses (al-Razi 1990, 17, p. 150; al-Nasafi n.d., 3, p. 277).

The Qur'an refers to a *dhurriyyah* as the only ones who had faith in Moses (10:83). This is interpreted as 'a small or insignificant number'

(Ibn 'Abbas, cited in al-Razi 1990, 17, p. 150; al-Nasafi n.d., 3, p. 277), 'their off-spring' (al-Zamakhshari n.d., 2, p. 364, al-Baidawi n.d., 3, p. 277) or a 'few of the youth' (Rida 1980, 11, p. 469).[22]

As for Moses' pleas to his people to place their trust in God if they are truly *muslims*, the exegetes argue that this is simply a plea and does not mean his people actually had faith (Rida 1980, 11, p. 470). The ones who prayed that they do not 'become a trial for the people who are oppressors' (Qur'an 10:85) and to be 'saved by your mercy from the people who are *kafirun*' (10:86) were the *dhurriyyah* who actually believed in Moses. In 10:90 Pharaoh talks about believing in the deity in whom the Israelites have faith. Ibn 'Abbas says Israelites, in this case, refers to the few companions of Moses who actually believed (n.d., 2, p. 282). Al-Razi, referring to the propensity of the Israelites towards idolatry, says that Pharaoh actually contributed to his destruction by his last minute proclamation of faith in the deity of the Israelites (al-Razi 1990, 17, p. 162).

The Qur'an frequently refers to the persistence of the *kufr* of the Israelites and their general recalcitrance throughout the journey to the Promised Land. Despite witnessing numerous miracles, including their own liberation, very few among them (26:67) really believed in Moses' call. Instead they sculpted an idol (2:51; 20:85–97) and, in speaking to Moses, they regularly referred to God as 'your Lord': 'Pray, then, to your Lord that He bring forth for us aught of what grows from the earth' (2:61). Their hearts were hardened, the Qur'an says, 'and became like rocks, or even harder' (2:74). On being asked to fight in defence of their freedom, they told Moses: 'Go forth, then, you and your Lord, and fight, both of you! We, behold, shall remain here' (5:24). They taunted Moses: 'we shall not believe you until we see God face to face' (2:55). Immediately after this, they are told by God to 'partake of the good things which We have provided for you as sustenance' (2:57). Despite rebelling yet again, they are still invited to 'enter this land and eat of its food as you may desire, abundantly' (2:58; 7:161). Nothing that came to the Israelites in terms of liberation and sustenance was as a consequence of their own faith: 'And had it not been for God's favour upon you and His grace, you would surely have found yourselves among the lost' (2:64).

The Themes of the Exodus Paradigm

There are several themes in God and Moses' dealings with Pharaoh and his supporters, on the one hand, and with the Israelites, on the other, that are very significant in proposing a hermeneutic of pluralism for liberation.

1. Neither God, nor Moses, abandoned the Israelites before they reached the Promised Land despite their recalcitrance in *kufr*.

2. An effective distinction was made in the response to the *kufr* of the Israelites and that of Pharaoh and his supporters.

3. Freedom was portrayed as a condition for the worship of God without necessarily leading to it.

4. During the period of slavery, Moses' prophetic responsibility was essentially to act in solidarity with the Israelites, rather than to preach to them.

5. Moses did not offer his people a balm to heal the wounds of oppression. Instead, he acted in solidarity with them in order to secure their liberation.

6. Solidarity with the Israelites meant taking sides against Pharaoh and his supporters.

7. Acting in solidarity with the oppressed and marginalized and against those whom the Qur'an describes as the *mutrafun* (ostentatious) or *mustakbirun* (arrogant) does not militate against the all-embracing grace of God or the universality of His prophets' mission.

In looking at each of these themes, I shall relate them to the quest for a theology which liberates in general and to apartheid South Africa and the struggle for liberation specifically.

Remaining with the Oppressed Despite their Non-Belief

Despite the vehemence and persistence of the *kufr* of the Israelites, neither God nor Moses abandoned them before they reached the sacred land. Moses, 'the Speech of God', is entrusted with the task of offering them his active and ongoing solidarity in the face of a tyrannical Pharaoh and their persistent and ever-growing *kufr* – *kufr* being manifested both as rejection and as ingratitude. It was this ingrate and rejecting people about whom the Qur'an on several occasions speaks as having been distinguished by God over others, (2:47; 5:20) because of the oppression they endured (2:49; 7:137).[23] To this community of exploited, with their propensity towards idolatry, God promises His grace and undertakes to establish them on the earth, to make them the leaders and to make them inheritors (28:5). The Israelites were 'saved from the awful calamity [of bondage], and God succoured them, so that [in the end] it was they who achieved victory' (37:115–6). Finally, they were placed in 'a most goodly abode' (10:93). In all of these we find a perfect example of God's unbounded and unqualified solidarity with those who are enslaved, marginalized and oppressed.

The Distinction Between Pharaoh's Kufr and that of the Israelites

There is a marked difference in the Qur'an's tone when commenting on the *kufr* of Pharaoh and that of the Israelites. The comment on the former is distinguished by a vehemence, that of the latter by a gentleness. One gets an unmistakable impression that, in the case of Pharaoh, the Qur'an deals with an incorrigible ingrate who has to pay a frightening price for elevating himself to godhood and oppressing others in the process (7:130). In the case of the Israelites, Moses pleads, reminds and cajoles rather than threatens or curses (7:138–41; 160–5). Qur'an 7:136–7 reflects this; in 7:136, referring to Pharaoh and his followers, the Qur'an says 'We took retribution from them . . . because they belied our verses and were heedless of them.' In direct contrast to this, the very next verse, referring to the Israelites, another rejecting and ingrate folk, says 'And we made the people who were oppressed to inherit the eastern parts of the land and the western parts thereof which we have blessed. Thus, the fair word of your Lord was fulfilled for the Israelites because of what they endured. And we destroyed completely all the great works and buildings which Pharaoh and his people erected' (7:137).

In both of these themes we see an overwhelming concern for the wronged and, in conditions of oppression, the primacy of liberative praxis over verbal affirmations of dogma because, in the words of Rida, 'there is no right greater than justice and no wrong worse than tyranny' (1980, 4, p. 45). Leonardo and Clodovis Boff, from the context of the struggles in Latin America, articulate the primacy of liberative praxis as follows: 'Today we accentuate the political aspect. In future under other conditions, it will surely be different. Who knows, in a classless society, perhaps the aspects of faith will then be most important . . . but in some other way' (Boff 1985, p. 104).

While the primacy of liberative praxis was never emphatically articulated in South African progressive Islamist discourse, a distinction was always made between the *kufr* of the oppressed and that of the regime. Exhorting the exploited and the wronged to intensify their militancy against the regime, the Call of Islam invoked Qur'an 48:29 '[Muhammad and the *mu'minun*] are severe towards the *kuffar*, gentle among themselves' (Call of Islam 1985, *Muslims Against the Emergency*, p. 1).

Freedom and Faith

Upon his return to Egypt after his long exile and first revelation, Moses' first words to Pharaoh were 'Behold, we bear a message from the

Sustainer of all the worlds: Let the Israelites go with us!' (Qur'an 26:16–17; 7:105). Whenever the conversation between Pharaoh and Moses is narrated in the Qur'an, one finds a continuous shifting between apparently this-worldly demands and those pertaining to the hereafter and to faith. Thus, Pharaoh's denial of God is linked to his own arrogance and claims to authority. Similarly, the *kufr* of the Israelites during the period of their enslavement is portrayed as a forced inability rather than a wilful refusal (al-Baidawi n.d., 3, p. 277; Rida 1980, 11, p. 469).

In South Africa those who identified with the oppressed similarly refused to distinguish between their commitment to Islam and their commitment to the liberation struggle. Instead, they viewed both commitments as strands in a single tapestry. Those who did distinguish between them, even if phrased as 'Islam and politics', in effect tacitly supported the oppressive status quo. Here we saw the interface between ideology and theology from both perspectives: the state invoking theology in the service of its ideology and the marginalized invoking theology as an extension of liberative ideology (Moosa 1989). Though liberation was always regarded as intrinsic to salvation, none of the progressive Islamists argued that socio-political liberation could ever be completely synonymous with salvation. Instead, faith and political solidarity were fused, without one being reduced to the other.

The Prophetic Responsibility Amidst Oppression

Nowhere in the qur'anic account of Moses' dealing with the Israelites during the period of enslavement in Egypt does one gain the impression that belief in a single God as dogma was a significant element. On the contrary, during this period Moses' prophetic responsibility was essentially to act in solidarity with the Israelites rather than preaching to them. They were only tried by God in freedom after they had inherited the earth (7:129); only then did the exhortations to faith come (20:82).

The South African experience drew one's attention to the tendency in accommodation theology to focus on dogma as a means of avoiding an overt liberatory political discourse even while, at a covert level, underpinning the dominant and oppressive ideological discourse. Thus, accommodationists preached Islam to the black masses while the masses were starving and fraternized with discredited Bantustan leaders in order to get permits to enter black areas for missionary activity. In response to this tendency, the progressive Islamists argued that the prophetic responsibility was to establish one's '*al-amin*-ness'[24] prior to any discussions about dogma or faith. The only way this '*al-amin*-ness' was going to be established was through active solidarity with the *mustad'afun fi'l-ard*.

Solidarity as Distinct from Charity

Moses, his slave origins notwithstanding, grew up in the bosom of Pharaoh's family amid royal splendour. It was, however, not this Moses who acted as the liberator of his people. He spent a long period in exile where he became an ordinary labourer, once again a part of the under-class of history (28:22–8). It was as a member of this class that he returned to be with his people. Once back in Egypt, he appealed to Pharaoh, not to improve the conditions of his people's slavery, but to let them go free. Moses' story with his people could have been otherwise: he could have remained with the 'ostentatious' and the 'arrogant' and uti-lized his position of influence to improve the lot of his people. However, because the entire Pharaonic system was based on injustice and corrup-tion, he chose the path of solidarity rather than that of charity.

In the South African context of the 1980s and the struggles in the townships, there was no need for Muslims to return to the oppressed and the marginalized, because they were an intrinsic part of them. Alluding to this shared marginalization and solidarity and its absence among the more affluent sectors of the Muslim community, the Call of Islam commented:

> In the townships Muslims and Christians depend on each other for survival. Some Muslims in other areas, in the absence of a real com-munity, try to compensate by speaking of 'Muslim interests', 'Islamic states' and 'our identity'. They feel they are Muslim when Ahmad Deedat attacks other religions. They have no time for toler-ance towards the *'nasara'* [Christians] or *'kaafirs'*. (Call of Islam 1987, p. 5)

In South Africa, particularly with the introduction of tricameralism, we also witnessed numerous government schemes to ease the burden of the exploited while maintaining the essentially discriminatory and unjust nature of the regime. In direct opposition to this, progressive Islamists chose solidarity with the oppressed, shared marginalization and a common struggle directed towards the actual, not seeming, removal of injustice. This implied an appreciation of the structural causes of poverty and human degradation and a commitment to eliminate these. 'Well-intended acts of charity', they argued, 'could be deceptive and militate against self-growth and the awareness of people's intrinsic dignity' (Call of Islam 1987, p. 9). The following quotation from a Call manual for its activists describes its views on how a naive awareness of poverty leads to a condescending 'assistentialism' that does not address the causes of human suffering.

We must go beyond giving a piece of bread to the little ones who knock on our doors . . . Saying 'yes' to them may make us feel good but does not solve the problem. One finds business people spending huge amounts on charity and it makes them feel very good. Nobody asks how come they have so much money . . . We must understand that if we choose solidarity with the poor that our option has a political character in so far as it means attacking structures and making decisions to take concrete actions to help specific classes. (1988, p. 33)

Solidarity with the oppressed, furthermore, implies a recognition of them as agents of their liberation with their own resources to draw on. The real question, as the Boff brothers point out, is 'what praxis will actually and not seemingly help?' (1985, p. 4)

Solidarity Against the Oppressor

The option for the weak has serious implications for the oppressor and the Qur'an does not avoid this. The fulfilment of the aspirations of the oppressed requires the realization of the fears of the oppressors. 'And We wish to bestow Our grace upon those who had been oppressed in the earth, to make them the rulers and to make them the inheritors, to establish them in the land. And We let Pharaoh, Haman and their supporters experience that which they feared,' (Qur'an 28:5–6). It is evident that throughout the Qur'an there is a Self that must be sustained and strengthened and an Other that must be relentlessly opposed, preferably through gentle discourse or, should this fail, by any other means. Moses was told to address Pharaoh in a gentle manner (20:44). When persuasion failed though, we see how, eventually, freedom for Israelites was contingent on Pharaoh's destruction (7:138). 'And thus were they vanquished there and then, and became utterly humiliated' (7:119) when God 'caused him and all who were with him to drown [in the sea]' (17:103). Such was 'what happened in the end to those spreaders of corruption!' (7:103).[25]

In South African Muslim liberatory discourse too, one finds distinctions made within the framework of the reinterpreted theological categories of *mu'min*, *muslim* and *kafir*. While the progressive Islamists did not articulate these distinctions at a public level it is evident that they refrained from using the term *kafir* to apply to the oppressed religious Other and withheld the appellation *muslim* from the collaborating religious Self.[26] Careful reflection on their rhetoric, though, reveals that all the qur'anic vituperation against the *kafir* was reserved for, and unleashed against, the apartheid regime and all its supporters, irrespective of their formal religious affinities. On the other hand, all the texts consoling, encouraging and exhorting the *mu'minun* and the *muslimun* were applied to the wronged, irrespective of their formal faith commitments, or even absence of them.

The categoric struggle against the oppressor Other is at odds with the lack of specificity that characterizes much liberal interreligious discourse, including that of Muslim liberals. This discourse, focusing on the language of peace and reconciliation, seeks to arrive at fundamental general ethical criteria that appeal to the common humanity of all, including that of the Pharaoh. While a theology of liberation remains rooted in the notion of the sacredness of all human beings, it would argue for specificity in any context of domination and subjugation. This specificity is particularly important when the vague affirmation of everyone's humanity – oppressor and oppressed – serves to arrest or to hamper the freedom, and therefore humanity, of both. In response to the question, 'Whose *humanum*?' I wish to echo the argument of Gustavo Gutierrez that 'the poor represent solidarity with humanity in the historical project of the quest for new ways of becoming human. To be in solidarity with the poor is not an option to be particular, but an option to be universal' (cited in Chopp 1989, p. 61).

The Universality of God's Concern

While the *humanum* is preferentially focused on the exploited, poor and marginalized, the struggle for liberation also affords the oppressor an opportunity to be free. 'To be with the oppressed', says the Call, 'means being against the oppressor – as oppressor. The struggle against the oppressor, supports the liberation of the oppressed and gives the oppressor the option to liberate him or herself and to become more human' (1988, p. 34) This is why Moses' message to Pharaoh is not confined to the liberation of Israelites, but also deals with the illusions of power and immortality that enslaved Pharaoh himself. It is precisely because of the universality of God's concern that options have to be exercised for some and against others. 'And if God had not enabled people to defend themselves against one another, corruption would surely overwhelm the earth: but God is limitless in His bounty unto all the worlds' (Qur'an 2:251).

I am in agreement with Gustavo Gutierrez, who argues that the poor and oppressed 'represent universal solidarity with all humanity in the historical project of the quest for new ways of becoming human' (cited in Chopp 1989, p. 61). The option of solidarity with the poor and oppressed, far from being an option for the particular, is really one for inclusivism and universality. There is no contradiction in God's being the Lord of humankind and His option for the downtrodden; it is in the option of the latter that the former finds expression. When a handful of people pursue ideological options and exploitative economic practices that prevent the vast majority of humankind from living out their full humanity, then those few also have their own humanity impaired in the process.

Conclusion: A Liberative Praxis

The texts dealing with the *wilayah* of the religious Other, when understood in their historical contexts, offer a radically different perspective to that which a casual and decontextualized reading renders. Far from preventing Muslims from entering into relationships of solidarity with the religious Other, they actually facilitate and inspire the progressive Islamists' pursuit of a hermeneutic that accommodates the religious Other and liberative praxis. In the Exodus paradigm, we see how this support for solidarity with the Other, though, was not limited to the religious Other, but also embraced those among the poor and downtrodden who actively rejected the religious beliefs of *islam*.

The context of this pluralism, though, was not a vague commitment to all forms of Otherness; indeed, some forms of Otherness are vehemently opposed and the Qur'an does not hesitate to encourage the severest forms of opposition to them. Instead, the Qur'an roots its own pluralism in a common struggle against oppression and injustice. Rather than a fashionable interfaith dialogue, we see an unarticulated solidarity with the marginalized and exploited that crosses narrow doctrinal lines. The basis of the pluralism being postulated in the Qur'an is, one may say, liberative praxis.

Notes

1. E.g., Qur'an 2:107; 4:45, 173; 6:14, 51; 7:3; 9:74, 116; 11:20, 113; 13:16, 37; 17:97; 18:26, 50, 102; 25:18; 29:22, 4; 32:4; 33:17; 39:3; 42:6, 9, 31; 45:19.
2. E.g., Qur'an 6:14; 11:20, 113; 13:16; 17:97; 18:50, 102; 25:18; 29:41; 39:3; 42:6, 9, 46.
3. Ibn 'Abbas, (n.d., 2, p. 186) in his explanation of this verse suggests that it is circumscribed by events in Medina at the time. The need to characterize a *mu'min* (believer) was, according to him, necessitated by the need to differentiate between them and the *munafiqun* who claimed to be Muslim, but were unenthusiastic about the Islamic injunctions such as the formal prayers and the poor due. (See also Rida 1980, 6, p. 441.)
4. The following account of one aspect of this personal relationship appears in al-Bukhari and Muslim: 'It is narrated about 'A'ishah that she said to 'Urwah: "My nephew! We [God's family] spent our days sometimes seeing three successive moons without the oven being lit in our houses." "How did you remain alive then?", 'Urwah asked. 'A'ishah replied: "We lived on dates and water. Indeed there were Christian neighbours of God who had some milk cattle. They [occasionally] sent him milk as a gift and he used to give some of it to us also"' (cited in

Nomani 1975, I, p. 277). An example of a warm communal relationship with the religious Other is that of the Muslims who sought asylum from the persecution of the Quraysh in the fifth year of Muhammad's prophethood among the Christians of Abyssinia. Here 'they were safe from the dangers of both apostasy and persecution' (Ibn Hisham n.d., 2, p. 146).

5. Citing al-Raghib, al-Tabataba'i argues that *wilayah* is the development of two elements to the level where nothing intervenes between them. This implies closeness in terms of space, religion, friendship, assistance and trust (n.d., 5, p. 368).

6. Al-Baidawi's opinion is interesting because it implies that there are two kinds of *wilayah*, which are not mutually exclusive.

7. Referring to Qur'an 3:27, al-Razi cites the opinion of Muqatil, who says that the verse was revealed about Hatib ibn Abi Balta'ah and others who befriended the Jews and the *mushrikun* and informed them of the war preparations of the Muslims, in the secret hope that the Jews would overpower Muhammad (al-Razi 1990, 7, p. 11; al-Tabataba'i n.d., 19, p. 234).

8. In his commentary on this text al-Razi (1990, 12, p. 16) supplies a lengthy account on the authority of Ibn 'Abbas regarding the deferential treatment of the Jewish nobility when engaging in extra-marital sexual relations as well as the question of disparity in blood money. The matter was referred to Muhammad by a group of distinguished Jews who undertook to abide by his judgment. However, they subsequently rejected the egalitarian path which he determined in his judgment. (See also al-Tabataba'i n.d., 5, pp. 357ff.; Rida 1980, 6, p. 422.)

9. Al-Zamakhshari, for example, explains this expression thus: 'Except that you have reason to fear them or some other reason necessitating being on your guard . . . The meaning of such *wilayah* is an apparent relationship while one's heart is firm on enmity and antagonism' (n.d., 1, p. 351).

10. It is important to note that organizations like the Call of Islam were, in addition to their affiliation, also entities existing in their own right. They had their own ideological training programmes and a host of other Islamic activities, which they conducted quite apart from their involvement with the religious Other. Thus, in these organizations, the debate did not centre on the permissibility of interfaith solidarity for justice, but on how best to protect one's faith and give expression to Islam within that relationship.

11. Some have argued that '*yasiluna*' refers to a blood relative. This opinion is considered weak because most of the people of Mecca were related to Muhammad 'despite the fact that the blood of the *kuffar* had become legitimate for them' (al-Razi 1990, 10, p. 229). Al-Razi also deduces a principle from this text that anyone who enters into an agreement with someone with whom the Muslims have entered into a treaty, is covered under the protection of that treaty.

12. Some of the exegetes have suggested that the people referred to in this text are the Aslamiyyun tribe with whom Muhammad had an agreement. At the time of his departure from Mecca, he took leave from Hilal bin 'Uwaymir al-Aslami and undertook 'never to harm him nor support anyone against him. Nor anyone in an alliance with him or who sought refuge with him' (al-Razi 1990, 10, p. 229). Ibn 'Abbas, on the other hand, says that the reference is to Banu Bakr ibn Ziyad Manah, while Muqatil says they are Khaza'ah and Khuzaymah ibn 'Abd Manah (ibid.).

13. Al-Isfahani has argued that an exception was made of those who did not fight Muhammad because they feared God; yet they were unable to fight the *kuffar* because they were related, or because they left their children and wives among them. They feared that if they fought them then their families would be attacked (al-Razi 1990, 10, p. 230).

14. Referring to Qur'an 5:57, ibn 'Abbas says that it refers to Rifa'ah ibn Zaid and Sumaid ibn al-Harth (n.d., 1, p. 528) who overtly displayed an allegiance to Islam but were subsequently found to be hypocrites. Some Muslims persisted in their fondness for these two despite their apparent *nifaq* (hypocrisy).

15. It is thus not a coincidence that the Durban-based International Islamic Propagation Centre and its founder, Ahmad Deedat, the world's most prominent Muslim evangelist, should also have displayed consistent public support for the KwaZulu homeland government

and its leader, Gatsha Buthelezi. This occurred at a time when progressive religious formations advocated non-collaboration with all the apartheid structures.

16. Al-Tabari narrates an account from Suddi that on the eve of Uhud (625) a group among the Muslims came under intense pressure and they feared that the *kuffar* would overpower them. One man told his companion: 'I shall connect with some of the Jews, seek my security from them and become a Jew with them, for I fear that the Jews would be victorious over us'. Another said: 'As for me, I shall connect to so-and-so among the Christians in a part of Syria, seek security among them and become a Christian' (1954, 6, p. 275).

17. This is evident from Muhammad's response to 'Utbah ibn Rabi'ah, an emissary from the Quraysh when the former was still in Mecca. 'Utbah is reported to have told Muhammad: 'You are in an honoured position in our tribe and possess a high status in our lineage. But you have introduced amongst our people a grave matter by which you have created dissension in our community, undermined our prudence, vilified our gods and religion and declared our forefathers unbelievers who are doomed to hell. Listen to me; I am going to offer you some options to consider so that you may accept some of them: O son of my brother, if you want money by this matter which you have brought unto us, we will collect for you of our money till you become the richest amongst us. And if you want honour, we will make you chief and overlord over us, deciding on nothing without you. And if you want dominion, we will make you a king over us' (Bashir 1978, pp. 154–6). Muhammad responded by reading from *Surahs Ha-mim* and *Fussilat* and then turned to 'Utbah: 'You have heard, O father of al-Walid, what you have heard. I will leave you with that' (ibid.).

18. The change that Islam had brought about in the basis of relationships is seen in the response of Muhammad ibn Maslamah when his tribe, Banu al-Nadir, expressed surprise that he could be the bearer of an ultimatum to them from the Muslims: 'Hearts have changed and Islam has wiped out old alliances', he is reported to have said (Rodinson 1980, p. 192).

19. The suggested *sabab al-nuzul* of this text has some profound implications for its meaning in an unjust and racially divided society. First, there is the idea that discrimination on the grounds of lineage, including racism, is *kufr*. Qur'an 3:99 speaks about 'a section from the People of the Book' who 'might cause you [the Muslims] to renounce the truth after you have come to believe [in it],' while 3:100 tells the believers that following the guidance of a section of the People of the Book will cause them to turn to *kufr* after *iman*. If this '*kufr* after *iman*' is the crime of tribalism after the universality of Islam, as is suggested by al-Zamakhshari (n.d., 1, p. 393), al-Razi (1990, 6, p. 422) and Rida (1980, 6, p. 441) then it follows that racism and tribalism is indeed *kufr* and the straight path is the path of universality and non-racialism. Second, faith or belief does not only pertain to the unseen or to dogma, but has everything to do with attitudes to other people. While the 'disbelief' that Aws and Khazraj fell prey to 'when the revelations are recited unto you and His messenger is in your midst' had nothing to do with dogma, it had everything to do with attitudes of cultural and tribal arrogance.

20. The most important of these are Qur'an 2:47–73; 7:103–62; 10:74–92; 20:9–98; 26:10–69; 27:7–14; 28:1–42.

21. A number of exegeses on Qur'an 10:90, for example, focus on the question of the non-acceptability of repentance at the time of death.

22. There has been some suggestion that the verse discussed here actually refers to the *dhurriyyah* of Pharaoh. All the exegetical works perused, however, while taking note of this suggestion, agree that the preposition 'his' in *dhurriyyah* from 'his people' refers to Moses, 'because it is the nearer of the two referents [i.e., Moses and Pharaoh] and because it is reported that those who believed in Moses were from among the Israelites' (al-Razi 1990, 17, p. 150).

23. As if to emphasize the point that this distinction is contingent upon a particular experience and not intrinsic to race or nationhood, the Qur'an immediately afterwards says that on the Day of Requital ties of blood will be of no avail. (See also Qur'an 2:122–3.)

24. First coined by Ebrahim Rasool, this term refers to the widely believed idea that Muhammad was referred to as *al-amin* (literally, 'the trustworthy', 'the credible') by the gen-

erality of the Quraysh long before his claims to prophethood. The term was often used in Call of Islam circles.

25. Islamic theology has never had any great need to justify an armed struggle. The legitimacy of the armed struggle against apartheid was seen as self-evident in progressive Islamic circles. The African National Congress, though, has always been at pains to point out that it only resorted to the armed struggle when all avenues of peaceful protest and negotiation had been closed by the apartheid regime (Mandela 1994, p. 61; Benson 1966, pp. 234–40).

26. There are several reasons why this was never clearly spelt out: the distaste for a controversy around dogma at a time when energies were needed for a concrete struggle, the enormous potential of such a controversy to alienate the majority of Muslims from the progressive Islamists, and the need to secure the support or lack of active opposition of the traditional clerics in the liberation struggle.

7

FROM *the* WILDERNESS to *the* PROMISED LAND

Never, never and never again shall it be that this beautiful land will experience the oppression of one by another and suffer the indignity of being the skunk of the world. The sun shall never set on so glorious a human achievement. Let freedom reign. God bless Africa!

Nelson Rolihlahla Mandela at his inauguration as president

From Confrontation to Negotiation

I nodded my head in somewhat condescending acknowledgement when Nazeem Louw told me that they had received a message from 'outside': not to worry, they would not sit out their full term in prison, they would be out sooner rather than later. It was in November 1988. I had just consulted with a number of combatants from Umkhonto we Sizwe, the military wing of the ANC, in prison. They were found guilty of terrorism and I was giving evidence for the defence in mitigation. 'These poor kids! How courageous and, simultaneously, so naive!'

Mercifully, I was the uninformed.

It was early in the morning of the second day of February 1990; Parliament was being opened and a short distance away a few hundred of us had gathered to demand the unbanning of the ANC and the release of all political prisoners. Some reporters came up to us, excitedly saying that De Klerk was about to announce exactly that. We were utterly bewildered. The march proceeded, the same placards were displayed and the prepared speeches were replaced with incoherent mutterings. No one had prepared us for freedom. In the words of Allister Sparks, 'there was a mixture of trauma, exhilaration, and disbelief as different groups struggled to come to terms with change so profound (1995, p. 9). The Call of Islam hailed the impending release of Nelson Mandela as a 'victory for the struggling masses of this country' (*Muslim Views*, March 1990, p. 4).

The following three years before the country's historic free and fair elections, and the subsequent two years leading to the adoption of a final constitution for a non-racial, non-sexist and democratic South Africa were going to be as tumultuous as ever; debates about Self and Other were going to re-emerge with a vengeance, this time fuelled by what 'they' are doing to 'us' in Iraq, later Bosnia, and even later, Chechnya. Could the theology of confrontation be converted into one of constructive negotiation with the regime? Those on the bus journeying to freedom, who truly understood what the journey to the stop called 'non-racialism' was all about knew that this was not the time to disembark. At the very least, there was another stop called 'non-sexism'. Who defended the humanizing of the religious and oppressed Other but now felt compelled to defend the dehumanizing of the gendered and equally oppressed Other? And in the shadows were the clerics, waiting to stake their claims for the patronage of a legitimate state, at long last giving expression to frustrated yearnings for institutional control over the lives of the believers.

Preparing for Freedom

From late 1990 it became evident that the apartheid regime was following a twin strategy of entering into negotiations with the ANC and all other parties while actively pursuing a programme of violence by proxy against their supporters throughout the country. Thus, the country witnessed a series of seemingly motiveless killings. Trains were stormed by armed masked men and passengers indiscriminately gunned down. The homes of alleged ANC supporters were attacked and the inhabitants murdered. Wakes at the funerals of these victims were stormed, perpetuating the cycle of violence. Even more horrific during this period were a number of massacres perpetrated by the police and army, or committed in their presence, often by armed men who entered the township under their escort.

While these events had the potential to throw South Africa into a long-drawn-out race war, they nearly always succeeded in focusing the minds of all the participants on the inevitability of a negotiated settlement. After six years of secret negotiations, fourteen months from the unbanning of the liberation movements, May 1991 saw the first round of ANC–Government talks. Mandela, ever the leader, opened the discussion:

I explained that the ANC had from its inception in 1912 always sought negotiations with the government in power. Mr De Klerk, for his part, suggested that the system of separate development had been conceived as a benign idea, but had not worked in practice. For that, he said, he was sorry and hoped that negotiations would make amends. It was not an apology for apartheid, but he went further than any NP [National Party] leader had. (Mandela 1994, p. 570)

If De Klerk were a theologian, then his theology would be appropriately described as one of accommodation. It was not a principled commitment to do the right thing. Until now there has been no sense that the man has understood the enormous pain he and his party caused, nor the havoc that they played with people's lives. It was just a project that did not quite work out; conditions had changed and they were going to do the useful thing. We shall see how much his attitude had in common with Muslim theology of accommodation.

The meeting produced what came to be known as the 'Groote Schuur Minute', committing both sides to a peaceful process of negotiations and the government to lifting the State of Emergency, which was still in effect. The ANC further called for the setting up of an interim government that would oversee the election of a Constituent Assembly to draw up a new constitution for the country.

In the Muslim community these 'talks about talks' were supported by most of the major organizations such as the MYM, Call and MJC. The single exception was Qibla, who continued engaging in the revolutionary rhetoric of the 1980s. In this they had allies in the Pan-Africanist Congress (PAC) and the Azanian People's Organization (Azapo), who argued for the formation of a united front to fight for a Constituent Assembly prior to any negotiations with the government. In the ranks of the ANC itself, disquiet was growing about the lack of unity among the oppressed and some sections of the PAC expressed concern about the inevitability of a negotiated settlement and their being politically marginalized. The ANC, past masters of 'broad church' politics under the slogan of 'maximum unity of the oppressed', and eternally confident of bringing as many players on board as possible, often with an unstated objective of co-opting them on to the organization's own agenda, mooted the idea of a united front against the apartheid regime. In November 1991 'socialists, Muslim activists and comfortable capitalists rubbed shoulders over three days at the historic Patriotic United Front Conference in Durban . . . to find common ground for a future democratic South Africa' (*Muslim Views*, November 1991, p. 1). This, the largest gathering of anti-apartheid forces, with only Azapo boycotting it, was jointly convened by the ANC and PAC. At the conclusion of the conference, the ANC and PAC announced a joint approach to the constitutional process and negotiations with the regime. The fact that all was not well in the erstwhile hardline camp was already evident at the conference when a letter from the external wing of the PAC was distributed. In it, the internal PAC was condemned for participating in the Patriotic Front. This internal dissension intensified and one month later the first earnest negotiations with the government about the New South Africa, the Convention for a Democratic South Africa (Codesa), commenced without the PAC, Azapo or the Inkatha Freedom Party (IFP).

Codesa created five working groups to prepare the way for a second round of more substantial talks scheduled for May 1992. These groups would examine questions of a free political climate, the future of the Bantustans, constitutional principles such as federalism and the installation of an interim government. The parties agreed that decisions would be taken by 'sufficient consensus' which, although undefined, meant agreement between the ANC and the government.

In these negotiations the common phenomenon of a disproportionately large Muslim presence was also evident, with nearly thirteen per cent of the participants from right across the political spectrum being Muslim, even if only in the cultural sense. One of Codesa's two chairs, selected from among the country's most respected judges, was Ismail Mohammed, also a Muslim and now the Republic's Chief Justice. Another significant event, albeit entirely symbolic, was the fact that Codesa did not commence with Christian prayers; instead representatives from a number of different faiths offered invocations. This was a clear break with the past when the only religious tradition of consequence for the state was the Dutch Reformed version of Christianity. It was, furthermore, an acknowledgement of the role of all religious communities in the struggle against the old order and an embrace of their contribution to the creation of a new society. All of this was televized live and there was much consternation among conservative religious groups at the equality of truths that it suggested. While this consternation was tempered in the minority communities; (it was, after all, a free and unexpected opportunity to show off one's own to the rest) the Afrikaans press was in full cry against the heresy of equating the triune God to the 'idols of the pagan Jews, Christians and Hindus'. The more 'serious' publications from these quarters ran lengthy debates on whether God is the same entity as Allah. For many deeply conservative Christians, De Klerk and the NP's inability to walk out during the prayers of other religions was the ultimate sign of betrayal.

Six weeks after the opening of Codesa, this incident featured prominently in right-wing electioneering in a by-election in Potchefstroom, a small university town in the north. The NP suffered an overwhelming defeat, prompting De Klerk to call a referendum of all white South Africans. They were asked whether they supported 'the continuation of the reform process . . . aimed at a new constitution through negotiation.' Sixty-nine per cent voted in favour and De Klerk returned to the negotiating table.

When Codesa 2 convened in May, De Klerk was not going to repeat the sin of listening to others praying and, immediately after the Christian prayers, slipped out of the hall, to return only when all invocations were completed. While he may have salvaged whatever remained of his reputation among conservative Christians, many Muslims were not amused.

> This was the NEW leader of the NEW National Party. All the leaders of the OLD National Party never recognized any other religion except their brand of Christianity. They didn't recognize Muslim marriages, inheritance, and they called our children illegitimate. Even under the NEW NATS they cannot listen to us praying. How can they still give us religious freedom? (Call of Islam 1994, *FW*, *Codesa 2 and the Duah*)

Codesa 2 collapsed after a few days, when it became clear that the NP rejected any notion of submitting to majority rule. Under the guise of 'power sharing', 'needs for checks and balances' and 'the negativity of simple majoritarianism', the NP countered every proposal to accede to the will of the people and demanded all sorts of vetoes for the white minority. Meanwhile, in a political organization proud of its roots in mass action and a trade union movement that viewed shop-floor displays of worker strength as essential to bolster wage demands during negotiation, numerous ANC activists and Cosatu trade unionists were growing restless with discussions behind closed doors seemingly leading nowhere.

June 16, 1992 saw the launch of a programme of rolling mass action, which included marches, defiance campaigns and strikes. The next night a group of IFP supporters emerged from their migrant labour hostels near the township of Boipathong, south of Johannesburg 'and in an orgy of slaughter hacked, stabbed and shot thirty-eight people to death in their homes. Among the dead were a nine-month-old baby, a child of four and twenty-four women, one of whom was pregnant' (Sparks 1995, p. 141).

Many residents insisted that they saw police escorting the attackers into the township and that white men in tracksuits directed the attacks.

Rejecting the government insistence that it was committed to peaceful negotiations and that it had no hand in the violence, the Call, quoting from the Qur'an, said: 'When it is said unto them: "Make not mischief on the earth", they said: "why, we only want to make peace". Of surety, they are the ones who make mischief' (Call of Islam n.d., *We can't trust the NATS*, p. 1). The unshakable conviction among the vast majority of South Africans was that so-called 'Black-on-Black' violence was part of a carefully orchestrated political strategy of the apartheid regime in its dying days, intended to weaken the ANC and it supporters. This is borne out today with virtually every scrap of evidence to emerge in front of the country's Truth and Reconciliation Commission.[1]

The ANC and Cosatu continued with their programme of strikes and marches throughout August and September 1992. One such march into Bisho, the capital of the Ciskei Bantustan, led to the massacre of twenty-nine people. The escalating violence forced the ANC and the government to renew their negotiations. This resulted in a 'Record of Understanding' whereby both parties agreed to establish an independent body to review police actions and to create a single elected Constitutional Assembly (CA) that would negotiate a new constitution and serve as a transitional legislature. A subsequent negotiation session in December agreed on a five-year government of national unity with a multi-party cabinet and the creation of a Transitional Executive Council.[2]

In April 1993 talks reconvened, with the IFP and PAC also present, and in June a date was set for the country's appointment with destiny: our first free and democratic elections on 27 April 1994. In November an interim constitution, guaranteeing all citizens the right to equality irrespective of race, religion, gender or sexual orientation, was adopted by multi-party talks with an interim government in place soon thereafter.

The Political Challenges

The social and political challenges presented to Muslims by a society pregnant with non-racialism, non-sexism and democracy were formidable. Given that the dominant issue in the period before the elections was the question of Muslim participation therein and the old issue of joining forces with the *kuffar*, for many only temporarily buried under the tidal wave of resistance to apartheid.

The first significant opportunity for the question of solidarity with the religious Other to emerge after 2 February 1990 was at the National Muslim Conference (NMC) in May of that year. Convened by the Call, this, the largest representative gathering of South African Muslims in the country's history, was intended to 'reach out to as many Muslims as possible across the political and strategic spectrum' and was attended by more than six hundred delegates. Issues covered in discussions and workshops reflected the way the conveners had succeeded in relating their religious commitment to the here and now: attitudes to negotiations with the apartheid regime, Muslim Personal Law (MPL), the protection of Muslim institutions and freedom of religion, the right of all to shelter, a living wage, and a decent health system, the environment ('Will the reverence which Islam has for the earth and the environment in general be respected in a free South Africa?') and Muslims' relationship with the state and the religious Other.

The Call, unambiguously aligned with the ANC, which was then preparing to negotiate with the government, had clearly intended the conference to be the mechanism whereby most, if not all, Muslims would be drawn into this process. Qibla, the PAC, the New Unity Movement (NUM) and Azapo had by then already rejected negotiations as a 'sellout' and had called for a Constituent Assembly where the oppressed would chart out their own future. Achmat Cassiem, explaining subsequently why Qibla rejected negotiations with the regime, said:

Can a thief draw up a legitimate will to let his children inherit his stolen property . . .? Peaceful co-existence between oppressors and oppressed does not feature on the agenda of the oppressed, and especially not on that of Muslims. We cannot . . . direct any of our legitimate demands to an illegitimate government. Is this too difficult to understand? . . . too difficult to digest? Or is it the sacrifices that follow this understanding, which are too great to bear? (*Muslim Views*, March 1991, p. 5)

Fatima Meer, one of the most formidable Muslim women in the liberation struggle, in an address at the inaugural session of the conference, responded to the political argument against negotiations in the following vein:

Those who have opposed the talks between the ANC and the government had totally misread the situation . . . Some of the *mustad'afin* [oppressed] have been thrown into a cycle of suicidal violence. They have become blinded and lost sight of their target and have become victims of their own anger . . . It is irresponsible if this is perceived as revolution. The time for reasoning has come. It is our duty to support the negotiations with all our heart and soul. (*Muslim Views*, May 1990, p. 9)

At the conference itself, the demonizing of the religious Other was alive and well in the form of the persistent interventions of the Murabitun,[3] who argued that exclusively Islamic solutions were the only way to solve the problems of the Muslims and that a *kafir* entering into negotiations with another *kafir* is of no consequence to Muslims. Particularly offensive to this group was an address delivered by Albie Sachs, a Jewish Communist and presently Judge in the Constitutional Court whose right hand had been blown off in a bomb sent by the apartheid regime. Sachs, nevertheless, received a standing ovation.

Clearly, living side by side along with the religious Other, even being oppressed along with them, was not sufficient to convert everyone to the cause of coexistence, let alone an appreciation of religious Otherness. Reflecting on the use of the term *kafir* by the Murabitun to demonize others at the NMC, Abdul Rashied Omar, formerly president of the MYM and currently *imam* of the Claremont Main Road Mosque, said:

> Despite the integrative nature of Muslim practice, [much of] their ideological discourse continues to be couched in exclusivistic terms. This is best symbolized in the pejorative or derogatory usage of the Arabic term *kafir* . . . it is an emotionally laden term skilfully manipulated by conservative Muslims to conjure up extreme hatred and abhorrence of non-Muslims.
>
> Anti-apartheid Muslim groupings which champion the cause of a religio-pluralistic post-apartheid South Africa will no doubt have a massive task in transforming parochial theological perspectives which beset their constituency. If, however, they are serious about building an apartheid-free South Africa they have no choice but to face up to this challenge. (*Al-Qalam*, December 1991, p. 11)

The extent of this challenge referred to by Omar was evident in the response of *The Majlis* and some sections of the Muslim community when rioting broke out in the Eastern Cape city of Port Elizabeth after a rally protesting against high rents. A number of shops, some owned by Indian Muslims, were attacked and a church whose minister was a prominent collaborator with the apartheid regime, was set alight. *The Majlis* called for *jihad* against the 'barbaric *kuffar* . . . in these times of anarchy, strife and corruption' (10 (11), p. 7). Battle plans were drawn up in the event of an invasion of their mosque. These plans would see the women and their weapons, 'be it an axe in hand' (ibid.), huddling in the basement, with the armed men guarding the windows and doors. Three-inch-thick steel bars were erected at all entry points, to the mosque, including windows, and these have remained in place until today. Reinforcements, among whom it was rumoured were veterans of the Afghanistan war against the Soviets, were called from the north of the country and 'were openly walking around in Port Elizabeth with rifles and strings of bullets slung over their shoulders' (*Muslim Views*, February 1991, p. 16). Hassan Solomon, referring to *The Majlis'* frenzied call to arms against the *mustad'afun* on the one hand and its regular denunciation of the armed struggle against apartheid, on the other, said 'Their jihad against the poor, weak and the deprived of the oppressed are conducted through the barrel of the gun whilst jihad against an oppressive regime should be done through the "proper channels"' (ibid.).

In the same way that numerous God-fearing right-wing Afrikaners found it impossible to see any distinction between their class, ethnic and cultural identities on the one hand, and their religious beliefs on the other, it did not occur to these warriors that there were 'many [black] Muslims from the townships involved in the rioting' (ibid.). Despite their blanket demonizing of all Blacks as *kuffar*, there were still those among the ranks of the *mustad'afun* who continued in their attempts to reach out to them. 'It is high time', wrote Adam Jack, a leading Muslim from a nearby black township, 'that they realized that they are also victims of apartheid. Being outcast would be the result of their own living in isolation and failing to recognize the issues . . . The time has come for them to rid themselves of the infamous mentality that worries about the length of beards when all is burning around them' (*Muslim Views*, January 1991, p. 12).

The ability of the oppressed Muslim who is relatively new to reified Islam to display a far more profound and humane appreciation of the faith than those who are what Rashid Rida described as 'ethnic Muslims' was also reflected in the letter pages of *Muslim Views*. Writing in defence of the local cleric who had denounced the calls for the release of a Muslim political prisoner, a certain Y. Abrahams said:

> The munafiks [hypocrites] in our town who just make all the trouble . . . want to change our deen [religion] and say Muslims must go to the townships and help the black koeffaar [unbelievers] and to tell our children to fight and make trouble agenst the government . . . What have we Muslims to do with all these things. Let us leave this politics and other business to the koeffaar . . . Let them take the dunja [this world] and let us not forget our iebaadaat [rituals] works and we will take the aagira [hereafter]. (*Muslim Views*, October 1991)

215

Responding to Abrahams, Fatima Sibeko, a black Muslim woman, probably new to reified Islam, advised:

> My Muslim brother, please learn the real Islam and take it to the black people of this country. Why are we only good for you as customers in your shops, as servants in your homes, but not as fellow oppressed and fellow Muslims? We have been dehumanized for very long now, and it will be through Islam that [we] will be liberated. Not the 'American Islam' the Islam which says pray, fast, perform hajj [pilgrimage] and keep quiet. NO! I am talking about the Islam the Prophet Muhammad practised, the Islam that stood for justice, peace and love. In that order. (*Muslim Views*, November 1991)

As the new South Africa was slowly taking shape and fears of the unknown under a government of the unknown were escalating, increasing numbers of Muslims sought refuge in comforting but none the less glib and simplistic religious responses, as is evident from some of the political developments leading up to the elections. In terms of the present work, the two most significant of these were the debate on the Islamicity or otherwise of participating in a multi-party democracy and the formation of two religiously based parties in the Muslim community to contest the elections.

To Vote or Not to Vote?

Those who argued against Muslim participation in the April 1994 general elections were, broadly speaking, those who invoked religious rhetoric and Qibla, whose position derived from an unfathomable *mélange* of religious, party political, strategic and idiosyncratic considerations.[4] The Murabitun and the Majlisul Ulama of the Eastern Cape were at least coherent in their unambiguous denunciation of any participation in *kuffar* politics: 'Voting has no relevance to the establishment of Islam as an existential reality', said Tariq Samarqandi from the Murabitun in a letter to *Muslim Views* (September 1993). 'The Western system of voting', said the Majlisul Ulama, 'is not permissible for Muslims. The masses lack the understanding for appointing a government. A variety of lowly and worldly motives influence them to vote. The government in Islam is a single individual who possesses the ability to rule according to the *shari'ah*. He is appointed by the Brains of the nation, not by masses of ignoramuses' (*The Majlis* 11 (4), p. 1). Who exactly 'the Brains' are, alas, was left unexplained!

Ebrahim Rasool, then national secretary of the Call and treasurer of the ANC in the Western Cape, articulated this flight into the safe havens of obscurantist blustering as follows:

> As we edge towards the 'New South Africa', as we re-grapple and come to terms with issues which previously were rejected in an uncomplicated manner, as fears and insecurities seek their salvation from future contestants for power, a confusion of identities emerges. In the case of the Muslim community, the confusion is an interplay of religious, ethnic and class identities, they draw on each other, they justify each other, and they put on the garb most socially acceptable. This garb is religion.
>
> While fear of losing your business through nationalization is a class fear, it is more acceptable to express it in terms of being Islamic/un-Islamic. Fear of black majority rule may, at root, be ethnic, yet it is more acceptable to express it in terms of whether elections or multi-party democracy is Qur'anically justified. (*Al-Qalam*, January 1992)

Which Ship to Board?

While the nature of religio-political discourse had shifted fundamentally, the political choices of those who had decided to participate in the electoral process were, nevertheless, very significant indicators of the relationship between ideology and theology. At a national level, the MYM called on Muslims to 'Vote for the ANC or PAC' while in the Cape they used the same posters and stickers after pasting over the words 'or PAC'. Both positions could be distilled from a document to which both the Call and the MYM were party. The 'Muslim Declaration of April 27 Elections' is a remarkable document that reflects the sentiment of all the progressive Muslim forces on the eve of the elections (see Appendix Two). This declaration, drawn up by Na'eem Jeenah, the secretary general of the MYM and the late Haroon Patel,[5] was the outcome of discussions of the Muslim Forum on Elections, formed in the middle of 1993 and comprising about thirty Muslim organizations. It reads in part:

> We believe that an historic opportunity exists in the 27 April national elections for a constituent assembly to deliver unto our land and its people a just political, economic, social and religious dispensation . . . It affords all South Africans an opportunity to free ourselves from oppression and institutionalized discrimination on the basis of race, ethnic or gender identity.
>
> When voting, choose wisely and according to your own conscience, and be mindful of the hopes and aspirations of the majority of the poor and oppressed in our country. Also remember the history of struggle for justice and the upliftment of the masses of our people.

Decades of apartheid rule has left many scars on our land. All around us there is unemployment, poverty, inequality, broken families, crime and human misery.

A future democracy must mean more than just a vote every now and then. It must allow us to play a meaningful role in the day to day decision-making in our society. It must lead to improvement in the quality of life for all South Africans – not only the rich and powerful ... It must create conditions for human and spiritual development ... It must uphold basic human rights and respect the varied religious codes and customs of all South Africans ...

We therefore commit ourselves to contributing to the spiritual rebuilding and well-being of all South Africans. (*Al-Qalam*, March 1994, p. 7)

The Call, not unexpectedly, called for an ANC vote. Acknowledging the shift in terrain, it said that

throughout the Election Campaign we should refrain from using emotive, specialized religious terms like *halal* [permissible] and *haram* [prohibited] to get support for one party or the other. This does not mean that it is acceptable to vote for the NP . . . Those contemplating support for the NP do so based on fears which we understand, but cannot condone. Those fears are based in racial stereotypes and apartheid propaganda. Muslims are required to rise above such stereotypes. The Call has decided to campaign for people to vote ANC. [This is] the only real way for this country to build justice, democracy, non-racialism and peace. (*Muslim Views*, December 1993, p. 8)

The position of the Durban-based Islamic Propagation Centre (IPC) headed by the world famous Muslim evangelist, Ahmed Deedat, was particularly interesting. There is no record of Deedat or his organization ever having pronounced a word against apartheid other than within the context of Muslim–Christian polemics; 'Christianity was responsible for it and Islam has all the answers'. While locally, and in private, he was scathing of the involvement of Muslims in the struggle against apartheid,[6] abroad he complained about the fact that the 'international Jewish media were deliberately obscuring the role which Muslims are playing in the struggle.'

The IPC did not take any position during the elections; it merely assisted the conservative and deeply feared IFP of Gatsha Buthelezi, held responsible for the overwhelming amount of so-called Black-on-Black violence, to raise some funds in the Middle East (*Muslim Views*, April 1994, p. 13). More ingeniously, the IPC littered the lampposts of the

KwaZulu–Natal Province with slogans saying 'Islam For Peace', the first letter of each word enlarged and in bold. And just in case the viewers missed the connection, the posters were all in full-blown IFP colours. As far as Deedat's theology and the mission to which he had devoted an entire lifetime was concerned, Buthelezi, an Anglican, was destined for hell because he did not embrace reified Islam. All of this was of little consequence: the solidarity of the right wing was alive and well.

Voting for Double Reward – Here and the Hereafter!

An Islamic Party (IP) was launched in Cape Town late in 1990 under the leadership of a local school teacher, Naushad Omar. Although it evoked some publicity then, little was heard of it until the election campaign, by which time it was largely overshadowed by the African Muslim Party (AMP), formed by a group of prominent businessmen in Johannesburg and Pretoria a few weeks before the elections. While both of these parties campaigned in the Cape, only the AMP functioned at a national level.

In line with all other such ideological formations in the world, from the right wing of the Republican Party in the United States to the religious groups currently sharing power in the Israeli government, they advocated a combination of puritanical moral (read 'sexual') views and a fierce commitment to a free market economy. In a lecture at the University of the Western Cape, Omar said that the party advocated 'the economic policy of free-enterprise – a free market system with private property rights' (*UWC Bulletin*, 4 April 1991, p. 4). The manifestoes of these parties were simple reproductions of texts from the Qur'an, mostly without any elaboration. 'The Qur'an is our constitution' was the stock response to any further enquiries. 'This party is for your *halaal* [permissible] vote. We are anti-abortion on demand, anti-homosexual, anti-casinos, anti-communist and anti-gambling' read the manifesto of the Islamic Party and their posters declared that one would be rewarded in the hereafter if one voted for them.

Neither of these parties achieved a sufficient number of votes in the election to win a single seat in parliament where seats were allocated to parties on a proportional basis. Despite their inability to attract any significant Muslim support, their very emergence was sufficient to raise the temperature of Muslim political discourse. The progressive Muslims' response to these parties and the way they dealt with questions of religious morality is fascinating, and provides much insight into how the Qur'an continued to shape or underpin political discourse in the circles of progressive Islam. The basic thrusts of these responses rotated around three issues: the lack of political and moral credibility of the figures involved in the Muslim parties; the appropriateness of voting for the religious Other and the need to embrace the just Other even if the Other's agenda does not coincide with that of reified Islam.

In reply to a question asking whether it was not sufficient to know that the candidates of these parties were Muslim in order to vote for them, the Call said:

> The struggle against apartheid had taught us only too well that there are Muslims and 'muslims'. Is the one who went to jail in the struggle for justice exactly the same as the one who quietly sat by and did not raise a finger or a shout when we were uprooted from our homes? The Qur'an itself is clear that Allah has raised the *mujahidin* (fighters) above the *qa-idin* (the ones who remain seated) . . . Your commitment during the eighties **does** matter because it is a reflection of the kind of Islam that you believe in. (Call of Islam 1994, *Thinking of Voting for an Islamic Party?*, p. 1)

The fallacy of a common Muslim identity which could unite behind a single party on the basis of a simple Muslim label was exposed by Essa al-Seppe, education officer of the MYM, who described the AMP as a 'wasted effort in the struggle for democracy'.

> Islam **is** the common binding factor, but Islam in South Africa depends on where you are located on the apartheid landscape . . . Generalized language about 'the interests of Muslims' must not dull our senses about the geographical realities of apartheid, which influence attitudes towards race and class. The hierarchy of privilege and affluence has its corollary in the hierarchy of suffering, not only in terms of the Black–White divide, but also in terms of the Muslim–Muslim divide, born Muslim–convert Muslim divide, Indian–Malay–Coloured–African–Muslim divide . . . [Muslims can be organized as Muslims but] on the basis of true Islam and not Islam nurtured under the Group Areas Act – a type of Islam that silently endorsed apartheid socialization and articulated a theology of accommodation.' (*Al-Qalam*, March 1994, p. 6)

A question raised in conservative religious circles, as well as among a number of ordinary Muslims, was whether one can vote for a 'non-believer'. 'This is the polite version of the question,' ventured the Call. 'The cruder version used by some Muslims more privately is "I will not be ruled by *Kaffirs*, meaning blacks"'.

The early Muslims were sent to be protected by a Black Christian ruler. The *Nabi* [Prophet] said to the first group they should go to a land where 'A king rules without injustice, a land of truthfulness . . .' In South Africa it is people like Nelson Mandela who went to jail for justice and truth . . . We must not judge by colour or religion. We must judge by justice and freedom of religion. (Call of Islam 1994, *Must Muslims Vote for a Muslim Party?*)

Their experience in the liberation struggle had taught them that religion can mean anything to just about anyone. It is thus not surprising that in this response we see the elevation of the principles of justice and freedom of religion above those of generalized and unqualified religion.

In a masterful display of contextual hermeneutics, the Call used the qur'anic narration of what is usually presented as a sad tale with a happy ending, in a manner that affirms the need to put one's own religious beliefs unconditionally at the service of the suffering and the hungry. The story is that of the Prophet Joseph, and given the remarkable way it reflects the core of the ideas of this book, it is presented here in full:

Nabi Yusuf: Minister of Justice

The trials and tribulations of Nabie Yusuf [Prophet Joseph] is so valuable as lessons for all time that the Qur'an has a whole chapter dedicated to explaining his story. He was thrown in a pit by his brothers, sold to a passing caravan, thrown in a jail for refusing to be seduced and forgotten there. If there is a Prophet that went through all different forms of imprisonment then it is Nabi Yusuf. And through all of this, he remained steadfast and unshaken.

While in prison, a messenger of Firoun [the Pharaoh] of Egypt came to relate to him a dream Firoun had. Being able to interpret dreams through the will of Allah, he could see drought and famine in the future of Egypt. On hearing his interpretation, Firoun released him. Nabie Yusuf then asked the king to put him in charge of the store houses so that he may save the country from starvation and poverty. He wanted to use the seven fat years to help the country through the seven lean years. In the end he helped the country avert national disaster and could then bring his family into Egypt. This was in the time before the evil Firoun of Nabie Moosa [the Prophet Moses].

But why is this story so important in the Qur'an? What are we to learn from it today? What are we to gather from Nabi Yusuf's attitude after having been in prison for so long? Nabie Yusuf did not say Firoun must resign first before he saved the country. He did not say first unite. He did not say first become Muslims. Why did he become minister in a kingdom that worshipped the sun instead of

221

Allah? Why did he not say that Firoun must first believe in Islam and its values before he, Nabie Yusuf will save his country? Why did he not ask to be made king and rule the entire country in Allah's way? No, Nabie Yusuf realized that saving people from hunger and starvation was what Allah wanted him to do. And that's what he did.

This story with all its details has important lessons for Muslims in South Africa and the oppressed in general.

Muslims have come to South Africa under much the same circumstances as Nabie Yusuf. We came either as slaves or indentured workers. We were imprisoned, oppressed, exploited and discriminated like the majority in the land. For the first time we will have a legitimate government. That government will not be Muslim. Some of its values will not even have sanction in the Qur'an. But as Muslims we have, by the grace of Allah, the capacity to help this country avoid starvation and hunger. Like Nabie Yusuf we must do our best and build a new country. We must draw on our Islam, our Qur'an and our history and seize the opportunity before us. We cannot ask that everybody be Muslim before we act. We must make our contribution because of the strong sense of justice and because of the inspiration we get from Nabie Yusuf. (May Allah bless him). (Call of Islam 1994, *FW, Codesa 2 and the Duah*, p. 6)

The Social Challenges

I remember during the early 1980s speaking at public meetings with a deep sense of excitement about the inevitable death of apartheid and the rise of a new dawn, telling people: 'Can you imagine that *we* are the generation responsible for the death of apartheid; that *we* are going to slay the monster of racial arrogance; that *we* are going to be the first South Africans in 350 years who are going to live in a non-racial, non-sexist and democratic homeland?' Difficult as it was to sustain this belief at times, we did it.

The elections took place over a period of three days, from 26 to 28 April 1994. I found myself in the rural areas, having been deployed by the ANC to help sort out some problems at the polling stations. On my rounds, I came across one that was relatively deserted – only about two hundred people. I joined a queue of farm labourers, among the most exploited of the oppressed. Armed with my ballot paper and a pencil I entered the polling booth. I couldn't believe it. Here I was. I paused and thought of Yusuf Akhalwaya, our twenty-one-year-old brother and comrade in the Call, in WCRP and in Umkhonto we Sizwe. He had died in a bomb blast a mere two months before the unbanning of the liberation movements and the release of Mandela, and only one year after his marriage. Yusuf, was this what you gave your life for? This for which you left behind a tiny daughter, Raisa?

I thought of the pain our country had endured in its long march to freedom, the loneliness of exile, of detention without trial, the political murders, the dispossession, the sighs of the tired and the exploited factory and farm workers, the months of living on the run like a fugitive, the attacks by police dogs, the clandestine pamphleteering . . . all for a single mark with a cheap little lead pencil!

The ANC won with 62.65 % of the national vote, followed by the NP with 20.4%. The African Christian Democratic Party, the counterpart of the Muslim religious parties, had less than 0.5% but managed to secure two seats in the new Parliament. Both the AMP and the IP were flattened. Twenty-three of the four hundred new Members of Parliament, including three Cabinet Ministers, came from Muslim backgrounds. Among them were several who were also deeply committed to Islam. Ebrahim Rasool was appointed as the local Minister of Health and Social Welfare in the Western Cape. Two other Cabinet Ministers come from Hindu backgrounds and the new Speaker of Parliament, Frene Ginwala, is a Zoroastrian.

Less than two weeks later Nelson Mandela was inaugurated as our country's president. In the three days immediately following the event he visited a church, a mosque and a synagogue to underline his commitment to religious pluralism and to inclusivity. The New South Africa was truly going to belong to all of its people. I viewed the inaugural events along with some fellow students at the Philosophische Theologische Hochschule in Frankfurt am Main in Germany. Here I had been pursuing research in biblical hermeneutics for nearly a year. No one knew anything about my background, except that I was a Muslim and from South Africa. At one point a huge banner came on to the screen 'The Call of Islam salutes President Mandela'. 'Do you know that organization?' someone asked. I muttered 'Yes', cried silently and slipped away.

Back to South Africa . . .

Three contexts supply a useful background within which to examine the way Muslims responded to the social challenges of a post-apartheid South Africa in the wilderness. First, internationally, the Gulf was in flames and the 'Great Satan', the USA, was leading Muslim armies in a war against other Muslims. Bosnia, and much later Chechnya, joined Kashmir and Palestine on the growing list of causes which we feel passionately about. Yet they only serve to highlight our impotence and the insurmountable chasm between our indomitable illusions about being the best of people, with all the solutions to all of humankind's problems, and the reality of a ceaseless victimhood in which we are despised as refugees whose dreams cannot transcend a green card to enter the belly of the 'Great Satan'. Second, locally, the police state founded on Calvinist puritanism had disintegrated. The collapse of a state that required gambling dens and easily available sex in the so-called independent Bantustans, providing relief at close proximity while simultaneously permitting the illusion of your own righteousness, led to the general liberalization of South African society. Crime escalated, drugs were more freely available than ever before. Yesterday's 'prostitutes' became today's 'sex workers' and *Scope*, a popular magazine that featured female nudes with their star-capped nipples, died to make way for the 'real stuff'. Third, if the long-drawn-out and often, of necessity, secretive negotiations alienated the most seasoned of activists, then this sense of disengagement was much more acutely felt among ordinary politically aware people. For years, anti-apartheid activists had defined their existences and even theologies in terms of the enemy. Now Pharaoh, however despised, had become a negotiation partner. This left many an activist bewildered and organizations such as the Call, the MSA and the MYM in a state of disarray. This is a situation from which they have still not fully recovered, and, in the case of the Call, it is probably fatal. Only Qibla, never having had much of an interest in reality, remained on course in their *cul-de-sac*.

Marching into the Laager: Occasionally Even Side by Side

Marching, first popularized by the UDF in the late 1980s, became the most common form of public expression of Muslim sentiment after 2 February 1990. All over the country, including in the most conservative little towns, Muslims took to marching. The plight of the Muslims in Bosnia, Kashmir and Palestine was the object of many of these marches and thousands participated in them. The embassies of the United States and of Israel bore the brunt of Muslim anger. The USA, particularly, was bitterly denounced for intervening (Iraq and Somalia) and for not intervening (Bosnia). Demonstrations for international Muslim causes were, of course, not uncommon in the 1980s. The major difference is that then the MYM and the Call always insisted on relating those causes to the struggle in South Africa. In fact, these causes were often invoked in order to utilize Muslim indignation at the oppression of Muslims in other parts of the world, to bring about a greater awareness of the suffering of all of the oppressed, especially of their fellow South Africans. The Call, in particular, displayed immense acumen in transforming virtually any international or local event that could potentially demonize the religious Other, into a demonstration of broad religious solidarity against all forms of dehumanization, whoever the victims might be. Thus Jews were invited to speak on the oppression of Palestinians and prominent Christian Reformed theologians were invited to speak at meetings to denounce the Dutch Reformed Church for describing Islam as a false religion. (And Muslim speakers used the same opportunity to denounce other Muslims who regularly heaped abuse upon the Christian faith.)

The rhetoric characterizing the demonstrations of the last period is unmistakably fundamentalist. When the religious Other was not explicitly excluded from the messages on the placards or in speeches, they were excluded from the form of the demonstrations. Jews were invariably equated with blood-sucking Zionists and Christians with imperialists. The following excerpt from a pamphlet issued during this period is one such example:

Allah, Most Gracious and Wise, says:
O ye who believe! Take not the Jews and the Christians for your friends and your protectors: They are but friends and protectors to each other. And he amongst you that turns to them for friendship is of them. Verily Allah guideth not a people unjust.' Qur'an (5:54)

The world's greatest evils today are zionism and imperialism. It is against these evils that Allah is warning us: the Jew with his bigoted zionist racism and the exploitative selfish capitalism and the world devouring and dehumanizing imperialist in the name of Christianity. The moment we seek to entrench their value system and seek their protection by NEGOTIATING pacts with them, Allah unambiguously states that we are for them and that HE will not guide us. Quite clearly, the Qur'an prohibits the believers from entering into any form of alliances, economic, political or military with zionism and imperialism because they are unjust and because they will not fail to corrupt the believers (Qibla n.d., *One Solution, Islamic Revolution*, p. 1.)

Equally popular, although often attracting a different crowd, were the marches against drugs, crime and the various manifestations of what is viewed as the descent of South African society into an immoral abyss. These marches culminated in the meteoric rise of People Against Drugs and Gangsterism (Pagad) in the second half of 1996. A number of factors were responsible for the escalating crime rate and the rapidly changing social mores, especially in the urban areas. These included the loosening of the reins of the police state; the general opening up of our borders, allowing in rather undesirable elements; the pervasive disrespect for the law and mistrust of its enforcers engendered by apartheid; the general cheapening of human life under apartheid (and, more specifically, through its hit squads, which could indiscriminately kill scores of mourners at funerals) and the growing unemployment and poverty.

These marches ranged from small ones, attracting a few hundred, protesting against the opening of a tote in a local area, to thousands demonstrating against the proliferating presence of drug peddlers, dubbed 'merchants'. 'Push out the Drug Pushers!' 'Kill the merchants before they kill us!' and 'No to the Tote' were some of the slogans doing the rounds. These marches culminated in the rather dramatic events which dominated the Muslim community's public profile towards the latter part of 1996, the formation of Pagad and the killing of a prominent gang leader, Rashaad Staggies. Subsequent marches by Pagad have also resulted in the deaths of an alleged drug dealer and of Achmat Najaar, a Pagad member, in November during one of their public demonstrations.

Pagad, a Qibla-inspired initiative against drugs and gangsterism, organized a series of marches to the homes of alleged drug dealers. Twenty-four ultimatums were delivered to the alleged dealers to stop their activities or to 'face the mandate of the community'. During one such march in August, Staggies, a notorious gang leader, was doused with petrol and burnt to death. This event, televised across the world, conjured up images of a blood-thirsty Islam hell-bent on imposing its morality on all and sundry. While there were few who shed tears for the death of someone who had brought ruin to many families, there was a deep sense of disquiet about the barbarity of the method.

Radio 786 in the Cape, one of the numerous community radios operating in the wake of the government's liberalization of the airwaves, was, and is, controlled by Qibla and became an important means of popularizing their message and mobilizing Muslims towards their causes. With Qibla's militancy blunted by engagements with their ideologyless allies in the newly formed Islamic Unity Convention, and their radio being compelled to conform to the somewhat liberal standards of the Independent Broadcasting Authority, a number of their more militant elements have moved sideways to form the core of Pagad. They have done this while remaining under the ideological guidance and inspiration of Achmat Cassiem and retaining control over Radio 786.

For the vast majority of ordinary, even if armed, participants in these marches and rallies, Pagad represented the gut response of a community exasperated with the, at best, seeming inability of the police to address the escalating crime levels or, at worst, active police collusion with the drug lords and gangsters. Initially, the group appeared to be rather disparate with several and often conflicting, or no, ideological perspectives, all buried under the wave of emotionalism and belief in essentialist notions of an ahistorical truth encapsulated in an Islam which consistently defies intellectual scrutiny.

The early stages of the Pagad drama in Cape Town saw a myriad of seeming discordant voices coming from its leadership. On one day they could be 'willing to die tonight' for the 'One Solution, Islamic Revolution' option and on the next they could be 'sensible, ordinary community people who are fed up with drugs' and who dismiss the idea of an Islamic state as 'laughable'. For me, this reflected the tension between the genuine leadership position being exercised from a safe distance, probably for security and strategic reasons, and the ostensible one which was exposed to the public and, incidentally, had not had a historical or ideological relationship with Qibla.

These discordant voices also reflect the convergence of a number of different strands among sections of the Cape Muslim community, although there was no coherent distinction between them, and one can simultaneously belong to more than one strand. We have the Africanists who believe that the PAC sold out by participating in the 1994 elections and that the state is essentially illegitimate; the morally outraged who believe that the values of a liberal democratic state is repugnant to human decency and subversive of all religious values; and there are those who believe that there is only one solution for South Africa and the world, an 'Islamic' revolution along the lines of the Iranian experience. At all of these levels the discourse is essentially an anti-state one which feeds on deeply felt community concern. As one of Pagad's members recently told me, 'This [the current Pagad-inspired activity] is the true meaning of "the people shall govern"'.

When confronted with the fact of Muslims being only 1.32% of the population and the seeming absurdity of an Islamic option for the country, Pagad members will respond with the qur'anic text 'How many a time hath a small force not vanquished a large force with the permission of God?'. As for the will of the people and the democratic state, their response is that the majority cannot determine what is true and what is false, the Qur'an does so. When confronted with the fact that the Qur'an does not sanction killing by fire as was the case with Staggies, nor does it sanction bypassing the rule of law in a just state, nor does it support the death penalty for drug pushing, the Qur'an is neatly side-stepped and Pagad has to resort to 'the community' – back to the majority – as the key to legitimize their activity.

True to the nature of absolutist formations which inevitably erode their own base with the deluded and 'truth-possessing' Self becoming fewer and fewer while the demonized Other grows larger and larger, Pagad split into two groups with mutual recrimination and excommunication flying thick and fast.

The Pagad, their marches and their 'Kill the Merchant! Kill!' chants are reflective of a number of instinctive and often simplistic responses and solution to crime and violence in our society. The rise of the liberal democratic state which upholds the human rights of all, including criminals and gangsters, has been heavily criticized by a large section of the population and they have called for the return of the death penalty. The rise of the liberal democratic state has certainly loosened the reins of the state and many of the police are still paralysed about what goes and what does not in the new South Africa. Furthermore, while the state now guarantees all kinds of rights to its citizens, we have not seen a commitment to protect the lives and property of those citizens, arguably the state's primary function. The problem, however, is not the liberal democratic state itself, nor is the solution a return to totalitarianism with its slogans of death to all dissidents and social delinquents. The problem is rooted in the apartheid regime and the accompanying destruction of any sense of morality, along with the growth of a self-centred utilitarian culture where people just see themselves and their own needs.

We are, however, dealing with the South African nation, a nation which turned all predictions of a drawn-out, bloody and dirty race war on its head. The people of our land refused to adjust to decades of enforced discrimination and doggedly pursued their own agenda of liberation. The point I want to make is that, while in the long run, only a vast improvement in our socio-economic position will bring about a fundamental change in the crime situation, we are not entirely powerless and can do an enormous amount to turn things around. For this, all of us – victims and perpetrators – need the willingness to own the problem and a determined bid to be a part of a humane solution, one that will not see the remedy aggravating the disease. This means a refusal to divide the world into 'them' and 'us'. Subsequent to the death of Staggies, we saw events in the working-class areas of Mannenberg and Valhalla Park where hundreds of people joined the gangsters in their display of community support and demonstrated the extent to which the gangsters are an organic part of the community. Similarly, with Pagad, it is not the 'them' Iranian or Libyan influence at work, as much of the media speculated, but, in large measure, another organic part of our community giving vent to their anger at the seeming inability or unwillingness of the state to move against those wreaking havoc with our lives.

Some of our public responses to drugs and gangsterism really reflect on us as the prisoners of deep-seated anger and bitterness who have fallen prey to the most atavistic and primordial revenge response seen in a long time. We have, in fact, become victims who have internalized the cheapening of the human spirit which the apartheid system had so desperately sought – just when we thought that the beast had been slain we find that it had entered our innards. Desperate to exorcize the beast, we find an enemy 'out there' in the shape of gangsters and drug merchants against whom we direct our venom without fully appreciating the source of the venom. There may well be an enemy out there, as many a victim of gangsterism and drugs may testify, but that is only part of the story; we are the Siamese twins to whom yesterday's regime gave birth and the cake cannot now be unbaked, nor the sugar separated from the flour. Drug merchants require customers; gangsters require customers to buy their stolen merchandise – here lies the rub. Blame the collapse of sexual morality on the freedom with which sex workers go about their business, if you will, but it takes two, well, at least two, to tango.

A refusal to recognize the way Selfhood is tied up to the despised Other and that the seat of the venom is the Self is dangerous because if we do not come to terms with its presence, then we will be engaged in an eternal search for external entities on which to unleash it. 'Where are we going to clean up next?' becomes a driving quest. Yet venom is like acid; it does more harm to the vessel in which it is stored than to the object on which it is poured.

The simplistic solutions offered by the marchers and their organizers alienated those who saw the rise in crime as a reflection of larger socio-economic issues. While they were welcomed when they did participate in these marches, their banners were not as *Muslim Views* reported. 'Residents expressed disappointment with a group of people who joined the march with political banners. They stated that while one of the contributing factors to the drug problem could have been apartheid, that the group should rather have joined the march with strong anti-drug banners' (*Muslim Views*, April 1990, p. 4)

While the simplistic solution of 'kill all peddlers' was the one most commonly offered by the organizers of these marches, this was not without exception. Lufi Omar of the Salt River Anti-Drug Coordinating Council argued that the marches and meetings ought not to be a 'personal war' against merchants. 'In actual fact, the opposite is true. They are part and parcel of the community, you cannot wish them away . . . we are not against peddlers *per se* but rather their activities and the problems arising therefrom' (*Muslim Views*, April 1991, p. 4). Maliqalim Simone, a Muslim academic, also argued that given that we were just emerging from an apartheid society, which was prescriptive, one should guard against imposing similar solutions on peddlers (*Muslim Views*, May 1991, p. 8). These, however, were unheeded noises in a wilderness of self-righteousness on the part of a people who insisted on seeing the problem as the eternally Other and the solutions in the elimination of that Other. One day it is the 'Great Satan', the next 'Zionism', the following the 'merchant'. The fact of Otherness as a condition for selfhood was sardonically reflected in the comment of 'merchant' addressed to a man watching an anti-drug march. He replied: 'Let them march today as they please. I see a number of my customers among this lot and I know that by this evening they'll be back.'

The second major focus of the marches was the consequences of the liberalization of South African society on capital punishment and on personal, more specifically sexual, morality. De Klerk had placed a moratorium on capital punishment in 1992 and in May 1995 all eleven judges of the Constitutional Court, including Ismail Mohammed, unanimously declared that the death penalty was unconstitutional in terms of section 9 of the Bill of Rights, which upholds the right of every citizen to life, as well as under section 10, which upholds the right to human dignity. Both of these clauses were retained in the final draft of the constitution adopted in March 1996 by the Constitutional Assembly, despite hundreds of thousands of petitions and numerous marches in support of the death penalty. Some time later that month a crowd of more than a hundred, mostly Qibla supporters, some brandishing guns, invaded the house of the Minister of Justice, Dulla Omar, in protest at the abolition of the death penalty.

Despite the seemingly explicit qur'anic sanction, even prescription, of the death penalty and the wave of support for it among the vast majority of Muslims, there were several significant Muslim voices who argued for its abolition. Omar, himself a Muslim, took the path of caution and argued that 'According to Muslim Law, one must look at the crime and punishment within the broader context of the system of justice and this entire system must be in line with Muslim values. Where justice does not conform to such values the use of the death penalty is inappropriate' (*Muslim Views*, June 1995, p. 1). Similarly the Call argued that

> While Muslims have every right to articulate the Islamic view of personal morality, it is important to understand that this is part of a comprehensive Islamic moral-ethico world view. In the same way

that one does not demand the amputation of thieves in a poverty ridden society one cannot insist on capital punishment as the norm in a society which is not governed by the laws and values of Islam. The Shari'ah injunctions and Islamic morality are parts of a whole. To isolate the rules from their context and argue for their artificial transplantation into a non-Islamic society is to reduce an entire world view to a set of punishments. (Call of Islam 1994, *Must Muslims Vote for a Muslim Party?* p. 1)

Avoiding any reference to the Qur'an, and freed from any organizational discipline, I argued in my column in a local daily that the justification for capital punishment 'in the face of overwhelming evidence that it does not deter seems to be rooted in most atavistic, primordial and revenge cords in people.' 'Surely such responses', I said, 'have little or no place in a civilized society'. If the 'advocates for the death penalty argue that this is the retribution that society must exact for murder then why do we then not rape rapists? Simply because deep down we realize that something of our humanness will be severely impaired, that there is something abominable about stooping to the level of the lowest among us.'

What the vast majority of ordinary citizens, especially those living in the cities, found most disconcerting about the direction of the new South Africa was the public face of a new sexual explicitness. Sex services were being freely advertised in the newspapers and those soliciting or procuring sex business on the streets were no longer harassed or prosecuted. The possession and sale of pornographic material by and to adults was allowed. Until then, all of these things had been intrinsic to life in South Africa but society could somehow pretend that they did not exist. Furthermore, the interim as well as the most recent version of the constitution, which was passed by the Constitutional Assembly with an overwhelming majority, outlawed discrimination on the grounds of religion, race, sex and sexual orientation. The extent of the changes in social climate in South Africa was witnessed at the Beijing Conference on women. Here, South Africa, geographically and politically aligned with Africa and the rest of the developing nations, which have in their ranks the most conservative Muslim and Catholic states, became the darling of Western countries and lesbian groups because the provisions of the interim constitution were way ahead of even the most liberal Western democracies. It is the only constitution in the world that explicitly protects sexual preference and South Africa is the only country in Africa that legalizes abortion on demand up to fourteen weeks of pregnancy. 'Unlike many African countries which allow discriminatory customary laws to take precedence over written laws in matters such as ownership and inheritance, the South African Constitution stipulates that the Bill of Rights overrides traditional practices.' (*Mail and Guardian*, 15–21 November 1995, pp. 18–19) 'South Africa', said Nkosazana Zuma, the Minister of Health and leader of the country's delegation in Beijing, 'has experienced the worst form of discrimination that any country can ever experience and we will make sure that no one is ever discriminated against on the basis of individual preference regardless of how any other country sees the issues' (ibid.) In a controversy with Muslim countries over whether girls and boys should have equal inheritance rights, South Africa vowed to stand firm. 'The issue is non-negotiable', said Geraldine Moleketi-Fraser, the Minister of Welfare and Human Development and another delegate to Beijing (ibid).

A curious but not unexpected phenomenon became rather common in the responses of both conservative Muslims and Christians to these profound changes. Although they insisted that the religious Other was eternally damned, except through embracing Islam or accepting Jesus Christ as personal saviour, they, nevertheless, embraced each other like long-lost brothers. Thus, one saw the Anti-Tote Action Committee being formed to protest against the building of a tote next to a church in Belgravia. The secretary, a Muslim, announced that more than a thousand signatures had been collected at mosques and churches in the area (*Muslim Views*, April 1991, p. 31). More insidious was the co-operation between Muslims in the African Muslim Party and right-wing Christians in the African Christian Democratic Party and the Christian Voice, organizations whose leaders were actively engaged in supplying Renamo with weapons against Frelimo in the Mozambican war of liberation. Here, Muslims and Christians who opposed interfaith solidarity against apartheid worked hand in hand in the Forum Against Abortion on Demand 'to teach people about morality' (*Al-Qalam*, November 1994, p. 4). Two thousand Muslims and Catholic protesters marched against abortion in Pretoria in April 1995 and the MJC joined the newly formed Moral Standards Commission to oppose pornography and abortion on demand (*Muslim Views*, April 1995, p. 4).

An editorial in *Muslim Views*, never particularly renowned for acknowledging virtue in the religious Other, reflected a curious combination of religious arrogance and expedience in a newly discovered acknowledgement of the authenticity of other religious paths.

> Muslims are the custodians of morality and cannot tolerate the audacious onslaught against Islam presently and overtly taking place in the form of ungodly Bills to be passed at an unprecedented rate.

Those who fight against the laws of Allah cannot be considered as believers nor as friends of the *ummah*. The Qur'an – in which divine laws decrees social and governmental arbitration differentiates between believers and unbelievers.

It is not only Muslims who abhor Satanistic laws, but also Christians, Jews, Hindus, Buddhists and Others. The Qur'an quotes them [sic] as believers and People of the Book if their beliefs are based on divine scripture (*Muslim Views*, editorial, April 1995, p. 4)

Freedom, which very few Muslims had bargained for, was clearly a package deal and so they utilized their new-found freedom to march in order to curb the freedom of others, including those who had fought for freedom long before these Muslims took to the streets. 'It is a pity', said the Call of Islam,

that those who were in the shadows when the people of this country suffered severely under apartheid are now holding up the banner of Islam. The early Muslims did not wait for better days, staying in the shadows until Qureish calmed down. Where were they then and why do they come out only now? Only they know. While waiting for better days they hid in the shadow of their *masjid* [mosque], their surgeries, their institutes, and even in the shadow of Navy ships while the army and their third force generals were killing in the townships. Why did the guardians of morality wait for better days before speaking up? Did they not always believe in the morality of Islam or was the Qur'an silent before 1994? The Prophet said that the greatest jihad is to speak the truth in the face of a tyrant. Why did they wait for others to kill the tyrant and then use the freedom of speech that others fought for to speak. Sincere people do not wait for better days when it is safe to oppose something which they believe is wrong. Now we must ask ourselves whether insincere people should be allowed to fly the flag of Islam on our behalf? (Call of Islam 1994, *Must Muslims Vote for a Muslim Party?* p. 1)

While conservative Muslims spoke about a 'a tug of war between freedom and morality' (*Muslim Views*, June 1995, p. 10) others viewed freedom and democracy as manifestations of morality and spoke about the need to embrace 'moral pluralism.'

While the vast majority of Muslims feel strongly about issues of personal sexual morality such as abortion and alcohol (admittedly not strongly enough to actually live alongside the injunctions of Islam in this regard) it is important to remember that some of these norms are peculiar to Islam. Can we really expect a government representing the people of this country to implement laws which are peculiar to us and our world view. What if environmentalists insist that, by their standards of morality, eating meat is an evil and asks the government to ban the eating of meat throughout the country? What if the government listen to animals rights activists and declare that the Islamic way of slaughtering animals is cruel? Where does it stop? (Call of Islam 1994, *Must Muslims Vote for a Muslim Party?*, p. 1)

While the progressive Muslims did not avoid the *shari'ah* discourse on abortion – even making significant contributions to the debate – they argued that, 'there are more pressing issues on the national agenda [than abortion] that need urgent attention in the process of reconstruction. Chief among these are the gross unemployment, poverty, homelessness, educational crisis, and poor health care' (*Al-Qalam*, March 1994, p. 14). Tahir Sitoto, then national president of the MYM, deplored the selective morality of the conservative Muslims, which 'confines morality to sexual matters only' and said that 'in the South African context the most moral action is to work for the upliftment of the deprived and oppressed masses of our country' (ibid).

Believers (Somewhat Haggard) in the Future

It is clear from much of the above that progressive Muslims were not lagging behind in responding to the challenges presented by other Muslims. The question is whether there was anything more to them and their programme in this period, beyond this?

While both the Call and the MYM played a crucial role in some of the key issues of the Muslim relationship with the state and the religious Other, that were going to shape Muslim life in the new South Africa, their presence and influence as viable organizations with an organized leadership and coherent programme have been in gradual decline since the unbanning of the liberation movements and the release of political prisoners. While the MYM is still very much alive, even if not always well, in the Cape one can safely write out a death certificate for the Call, without any fear of the corpse protesting.[7] From quite early on in the negotiation period both of these organizations were shadows of their former selves and, in the case of the Call, their programmes hardly ever went beyond dressing up ANC policy and negotiating tactics in qur'anic wrapping. This is not to suggest that they were selling a product in whose manufacture they had no share. On the contrary, a number of Call activists and other committed Muslims joined the ANC. Ebrahim Rasool became its Western Cape treasurer and, later, elections co-ordinator and subsequently a number of others came to play significant roles in various levels of government. Furthermore, the ANC, as I shall indicate further on, persisted along a path of principled commitment to many of the values of progressive Islam. However, the internal quiet and ongoing reflections on the Qur'an – communitarian exegesis – and the emphasis on the personal growth of the engaged interpreter which characterized its work before the unbanning of the liberation movement were missing.

Reflecting this changing scenario was the emergence of the Claremont Main Road Mosque as the new heart of progressive Islam. Here one could come as an activist or spectator, be a fully paid-up member or slip in and out unobtrusively, enjoy a variety of intellectually stimulating sermons or just savour the quiet of a safe haven. Whereas before, progressive Islam had seemed to be all over the place, particularly in working-class areas: now it was concentrated in a mosque.

The reasons for its diminishing organizational presence are diverse and intrinsically linked to the dramatic political developments unfolding in the country. First, in the changed political situation choices still had to be made. However, with the fuel supplied by the presence of an unmistakable Pharaoh gone, what were previously viewed as purely moral imperatives were now reduced to 'politics'. For a while this could still correctly be described as 'liberation politics' but the inevitable transformation into party politics, however strong the emphasis on redressing past injustices, could not be delayed indefinitely. While there is nothing intrinsically ignoble about such politics, they simply do not have the moral appeal of a liberation struggle. All progressive organizations experienced enormous difficulty in sustaining their programmes and the interest of their members.[8] While, along with all progressive organizations, the Call 'lost' a number of leadership figures to government, numerous individuals found it impossible to make the political adjustments required by the new situation. Others walked away in quiet disgust at the rapid appearance of three-piece suits and the pace at which the incoming ruling class was switching from Volkswagens and Minis to BMWs and Mercedes Benz.

The MYM had a much longer history than the Call, a sound internal financial base (reflecting also its middle-class orientation), a greater sense of being an organization, a clearer affinity with the International Islamic Movement and greater emphasis on normative, even if enlightened, Islam. The Call of Islam, on the other hand, far more of a movement than an organization, was too intrinsically wedded to the vicissitudes of struggle for liberation for it to survive a free South Africa as an organization. It is also regrettable that despite the common ground between the two organizations, particularly in the Cape, their co-operation never went beyond a joint response to a few short-term issues.[9]

I would tentatively venture a third reason for the diminishing presence of progressive Islam: the loss of charismatic leadership figures. The Muslim community seem to display a penchant for such figures and while both the Call and the MYM claimed an aversion to 'leaderism' and an affinity with collegial leadership, both were, nevertheless, led by such figures during the 1980s. I had resigned as National Co-ordinator of the Call of Islam in February 1990 and from the organization itself in October of that year, after a series of rather bruising encounters over, amongst other matters, 'incompatible understandings of organizational accountability'. Early in 1991, the MYM also experienced a major change in its leadership when the terms of office of both its national director and national president, Mawlana Ebrahim Moosa and Imam Abdul Rashied Omar respectively, came to an end. They were also religious leadership figures officiating at mosques. This kind of leadership is, of course, by its very nature in tension with the vision of progressive Islam, which asks that everyone become a subject of history and desires partners in struggle and pursuit of truth, rather than leaders and followers.

The impact of the ideas of the Call and the MYM, and even their occasional organizational presence, continued to be felt in two significant developments in the overall process of rethinking Islam within the context of religious pluralism and for liberation during this period: the reaching of a historic interfaith consensus of the vision and demands of all religious groups in the country, and the struggle for gender equality.

In May 1988 the World Conference on Religion and Peace (WCRP) organized a consultation in Soweto on the subject of 'Believers in the Struggle for Justice and Peace'. Subsequently, in the wake of the momentous changes occurring in South Africa, Albie Sachs at the NMC in May 1990 called for a national conference of religious leaders to discuss the future of religion–state relations in a post-apartheid South Africa. The Call, the key mover behind the NMC, was also WCRP's most significant ally in the Muslim community; indeed, its national secretary was simultaneously in the full-time employment of WCRP as its national co-ordinator. It was in response to this call that WCRP hosted a major conference titled 'Believers in the Future'.

The themes of both conferences consciously had twin meanings, suggesting both that people of religious faith were dealing with the question of justice and peace and the future, and that people had faith in justice and peace and the future. The organizers were also at pains to explain that the description of themselves as believers did not exclude those who did not subscribe to any religious faith but who were committed to the creation of a just social order in South Africa. The conference itself reiterated that 'the rights of religious people to practise their religion may never be exalted over the rights of other people not to practise any religion . . . and that religious people have much to learn from people variously identified as agnostics, atheists, or secular humanists about the creation of a just and peaceful society' (Kritizinger 1991a, p. ix).[10]

The conference was attended by about 350 delegates and opened by Ali Mazrui, a prominent Kenyan Muslim scholar, who also delivered the sixth Annual Desmond Tutu Peace Lecture. A number of keynote addresses were delivered by various religious leaders. Albie Sachs, by then emerging as one of the most brilliant and critical thinkers in the ANC, gave a paper on the relationship between religion and state in a democratic South Africa. Sachs advocated the option of a state 'which is secular, tolerant and accepting of the deep importance religion has for millions of South Africans while religious communities should be free to organize their own worship as they please and be encouraged to take part in the life of the nation' (Sachs 1991, p. 37). To be secular, he said, 'does not mean to be anti-religious, but rather that there is no official religion, no favouring of any particular denomination, and no persecuting of or any discrimination against non-believers' (ibid., p. 39). Referring to the religious 'insistence on an ethical basis for personal conduct, the spirit of service and community' and the way 'the poetical and mystical visions of the holy books have entered the world views of most South Africans', he said: 'These are powerful points of reference for the creation of a new united South Africa in which national life is enriched by religious diversity and religious organizations transform themselves and become more spiritual and more truly South African as they help transform the country' (ibid., p. 42).

In a well-reasoned response, Abdul Rashied Omar articulated a position from the perspective of progressive Islam. Given the propensity for the leadership of organized religious minorities to insist joyfully on religious pluralism for their own traditions, while repressing dissent within their own ranks, Omar appealed for an acknowledgement and acceptance of what he described as 'intrinsic pluralism'. 'Not only is there a need for us to acknowledge the plurality of religious traditions that pervade the South African landscape, but even more importantly, we need to incorporate pluralism in our very notion of religious tradition. Applying this to the Islamic tradition, we need to understand that there is no one monolithic Islam in South Africa. There are diverse articulations . . . frequently locked in fierce rivalry in their claims to be the privileged orthodox and authentic voice of Islam in South Africa' (Omar 1991, p. 50).

In the light of this 'intrinsic pluralism', Omar cautioned against the state insisting on dealing only with a single entity among competing ones. This caution, I shall later show, subsequently became crucial for the question of gender equality and Muslim Personal Law. Omar, further-more, appealed to religious people to avoid becoming the accommoda-tion theologians of the new South Africa, 'the African National Congress at prayer' (ibid) and advocated a position described as 'positive neutrality *vis-à-vis* all political parties of a future democratic South Africa'. Finally, he raised the crucial question of discrimination in the name of religion: 'How will it [the state] deal with religious organizations and individuals who persist in articulating and practising discrimination and bigotry in a new South Africa, subtly cloaking it in religious garb?' (ibid., p. 52).

While the conference itself was valuable in articulating the concerns and hopes of religious people in a new South Africa, its most significant outcome was the decision to respond positively to Albie Sachs' appeal to the religious community to draw up a 'religious charter which would embrace all the rights expected in a new post-apartheid South Africa' (Sachs 1991). What followed was the most remarkable consultative process religion in South Africa had ever experienced. A WCRP work-shop, comprising twenty-five representatives from different religious groups, met in June 1992 and produced an initial draft based on feed-back from a number of regional interfaith and single faith conferences. For a further six months the draft was widely circulated and debated in synagogues, mosques, universities, colleges, temples and in WCRP semi-nars. *Al-Qalam* and *Muslim Views* ran regular 'updates' which dealt extensively with the various critiques and amendments which a large number of Muslim community meetings, academics and activists were producing, as well as denunciations of the entire idea and process.[11]

This process culminated in a National Interfaith Conference held in Pretoria in November 1992. Attended by 150 representatives from diverse religious communities throughout the country, the 'Declaration on Religious Rights and Responsibilities' was adopted after three days of debate (see Appendix Three). The preamble to the declaration acknowl-edged the diversity of religious commitments, expressed regret about the way 'religion has been used to contribute to the oppression, exploitation and suffering of people', paid homage to 'the courageous role played by many religious people in upholding human dignity, justice and peace in the face of repression and division' and expressed its belief that religious communities 'can play a role in redressing past injustices and the reconstruction of society'. The declaration itself affirmed freedom of conscience – including the freedom of accepting or changing religious affiliation,[12] the equality of all religious communities before the law, and the rights to religious education, access to public media, recognition of systems of customary law, propagation of teachings and the observance of holy days.

A wide spectrum of Muslim organizations were present, the widest spectrum of Muslims ever to meet under one roof. 'It is ironic', commented a Muslim delegate, 'that it took an interfaith meeting to bring such diverse Muslim groups together, not even the National Muslim Conference had all those organizations represented' (*Al-Qalam*, November 1992, p. 3). Another delegate said: 'There was a common purpose in the Muslim delegation. We were there to level the playing field . . . For too long has a particular brand of one religion been officially favoured. Thus as Muslims we attempted to infuse as much of an Islamic world view as possible into the declaration . . . our objective was to make real gains for Muslims as a community in a post-apartheid South Africa' (ibid.). This historic exercise in grassroots religious consultation reflected the best in the democratic ethos, making words such as 'mandates', 'consultation', 'accountability' and 'transparency' an indispensable part of progressive political currency. Once again, even if unknowingly, the struggle for freedom was teaching religion a thing or two about human dignity and the need to involve people in the decisions which would affect their lives.

There were, however, two major problems in the composition of the Muslim delegations: there wasn't a single black person among the twenty-six present and there were only two women. It was the marginalization of women, reflected in the latter problem, which ensured that the co-operation achieved among the Muslims at the conference was going to be rather short-lived. The next phase of the South African *jihad* had begun: women, the other component of the *mustad'afun*, were now demanding their liberation.

The Gender *Jihad*

There are several significant reasons for the prominent part that the struggle for gender equality plays in South Africa. As I showed in chapter 1, numerous groups inside South Africa had contributed to the struggle for freedom. Carrying their multiplicity of identities – Muslim, Rastafarian, feminist, coloured, trade unionist, liberal, gay, young person, business person, conservative – the vast majority of South Africans were skilfully mobilized under various constituencies within the national democratic struggle, for the broader objective of the liberation struggle. The fact that many of these individuals were simultaneously organized at more than one level of identity meant that the other dimensions, with their own unique agendas, were seldom neglected, even if they were of little immediate consequence for the struggle. In the Call, for example, activists organized as Call members with a peculiarly Islamic agenda, which they nurtured in their meetings. This shaped their input at the second level, that of UDF–ANC activism. This was also the case with feminists, who recognized that, although women were oppressed as gendered beings, they were also part of a national liberation struggle in which very many did not appreciate the significance of the struggle for gender equality. Engaging in the struggle for national liberation, and invoking landmarks in that struggle, such as the march of thousands of women against the pass laws to the Union Buildings in Pretoria in August 1956, they used every opportunity to drive home the relationship between sexism and racism.

Secondly, the South African struggle had the immense advantage of a formidable international solidarity movement, the like of which no other political cause has known. The activists in these movements, largely based in North America and Europe, were essentially people who had identified racism as but one of a number of socio-ideological forces that they believed dehumanized people, and which had to be relentlessly opposed. Among the other such forces were consumerism, sexism, homophobia, the arms industry and the destruction of the environment. Freed from the concerns about the next meal for their own kids, they could actually think about the survival of the white rhino. While they did not place all of these concerns on the agenda of the numerous South African activists with whom they interacted, it was inevitable that the latter would be influenced and would even identify with the issues, which would otherwise have been seen as divisive or diversionary.

The Call has, since its inception, been committed to a radical challenging of the position of women in Islam and has consistently focused on the specificity of women's oppression and patriarchal relations within the family and society. The very first item under the heading 'What is our Line?' (i.e., ideological position) in the organization's information brochure is about women and states:

> We believe in the equality of men and women and in the liberation of women from [jurisprudential] legacies pertaining to the period of Muslim decline. We believe that our country will never be free until

its women are also free from oppressive social norms. Women must focus on the rights being withheld from them today rather than basking in the knowledge that the Prophet Muhammad (PBUH) had in fact stipulated these rights. (Call of Islam 1984, p. 2)

The Call undertook a consistent critique of the traditionalist interpretation of the role of women in Islam and regularly denounced the fact that 'for far too long Muslim men have treated women as they treat their beards; the more control they have over women, the greater they judge their faith to be' (Call of Islam n.d., *Women Arise! The Qur'an Liberates You!*'). In line with its own earlier reformist agenda, the MYM has also always been concerned, even if rather condescendingly in its early stages, with the religious marginalization of women.

In the period preceding the elections, and well thereafter, progressive Islam found a new focus for much of its activity and campaigns in the issue of gender discrimination. In fact, in the case of the Call, it may even be said that this was the single issue with which they have dealt independently of the short-term political demands of the liberation movement. The MYM, describing women as 'the most oppressed sector in South Africa', and arguing that 'Muslim women, despite the qur'anic position regarding the liberation of women are oppressed even within the Muslim community by Muslims themselves' (*Muslim Views*, August 1990, p. 11), initiated a number of programmes focusing on gender equality. This included the formation of a Gender Desk, the organizing of a number of seminars, courses and public conferences on the position of Muslim women, a rethinking of the *shari'ah* provisions regarding women and a campaign for women to pray in mosques.[13] A perusal of the contents of the Muslim newspapers and pamphlets after 2 February 1990 shows that, other than the more explicit political developments and the role of Muslims therein, gender equality was the single most debated issue.

Two major developments reflected all the tensions between the old and new South Africas and the fault lines between a principled progressive Islam: and a simplistically anti-apartheid Islam; the formation and collapse of the Muslim Personal Law Board (MPLB) and the controversy around the delivery of a sermon by a woman in the Claremont Main Road Mosque.

Muslim Personal Law: Legitimizing the Illegitimate?

MPL had for long been a carrot dangled in front of Muslims to encourage them to become more fully a part of a particular political party's agenda. Towards the end of 1985 the apartheid regime, through the South African Law Commission, called for proposals in this regard. These were, in varying degrees, entertained for discussion by the clerical bodies, the Islamic Council of South Africa and the Association of Muslim Attorneys and Lawyers. Given that these moves were initiated in the tricameral parliament, the Call and the MYM argued that MPL should never be used as a means of co-opting Muslims in their own oppression and protested at the lack of consultation with the community. At the National Conference of Muslims in May 1990 and during the election campaign in 1994 this emerged as the most significant demand of Muslims, and one to which Mandela personally promised to accede.

The apartheid regime never recognized Muslim marriages, other than for purposes of taxation, and all Muslims born from such unions were regarded as 'illegitimate'. While marriage and divorce are but one dimension of MPL,[14] it is understandable that the lack of recognition in this specific area should be viewed as particularly offensive. Furthermore, the chaotic and manifestly unjust way MPL was, and still is, administered led to widespread support for its regularization. 'Today', said Ebrahim Moosa,

> we are saddled with a Muslim clergy whose obsession with the letter of the law – rather than its spirit – rendered . . . MPL redundant and obsolete. Instead of bringing about justice to parties concerned in personal law disputes, it has the opposite effect . . . An unscrupulous husband can for a paltry sum divorce his wife at the hands of an equally unscrupulous clergyman or marry another female to satisfy his hedonistic impulse (Moosa 1988b, p. 1)

Wives had no recourse to civil protection: in the event of a divorce the wife usually ended up without a roof over her head, even when the house was jointly purchased. When the husband died without leaving a will his parents and/or siblings were his only legal heirs. Nor were men under any legal obligation to provide maintenance to their former wives in the case of abandonment or divorce.

It is thus not surprising that many South African Muslims viewed the introduction of MPL as their share of the 'New South Africa cake'. Yet this cake contained some ingredients clearly incompatible with the traditional interpretations of MPL: non-sexism and guarantees of non-discrimination. For Muslims who had for long fought for the marginalized and the oppressed, to now succumb to interpretations of the shari'ah that perpetuated the subjugation of women, was tantamount to legitimizing the illegitimate.

The matter of both MPL and African Traditional Law had evoked considerable controversy in the multi-party talks that followed the breakdown of Codesa. The Congress of Traditional Leaders (Contralesa) demanded that customary law be excluded from a Bill of Rights and be exempt from the gender equality guarantee of the proposed Bill of Rights. Contralesa, furthermore, argued 'that communities subject to customary law and traditional authority (i.e., rural communities) should remain exclusively subject to such authority'. Muslim clerics, not unsurprisingly, indicated their support for these proposals 'in so far as it applies to Muslim women' (*Al-Qalam*, October 1993, p. 1). At the other side of the spectrum, one saw the tension between an indomitable belief in gender equality and an equally stubborn persistence, more accurately, a desperate hope, that this was compatible with the Qur'an. Acknowledging the need for customary and religious law to be recognized by civil law, Shamima Shaikh of the MYM, echoing the view of progressive Muslims throughout the country, nevertheless argued that customary or religious law 'cannot be exempted from the Bill of Rights and be allowed to perpetuate inequalities. To even consider excluding any sector of society from being covered by the Bill of Rights is an injustice and makes a mockery of the Bill' (ibid.). Fatimah Hujaij from the Call said that she recognized the absolute equality of men and women *as sanctioned by the Qur'an* (emphasis mine) and said that the Call had submitted to the multi-party talks 'that they recognize this right as sanctioned by the Qur'an . . . and not endorse these [Contralesa] recommendations as they deny women equality with men' (ibid.). Others showed a finer appreciation for the tensions inherent in MPL and the Bill of Rights. At a subsequent seminar Soraya Bosch pleaded for a review of Islamic law to bring it into line with the current transformation in South Africa. Ebrahim Moosa identified areas of these tensions and Rasool called for 'the mobilization and empowerment of Muslim women to ensure that they play a leading role in the implementation of MPL' (ibid., p. 4).

The MPL Board, initiated by a number of Muslim ANC Members of Parliament, was inaugurated in August 1994 with a fifteen-member executive committee consisting of clerics from a number of different organizations, including the MJC as well as representatives from the MYM and the Call. One of the Call's delegates and a Member of Parliament, Fatimah Hujaij, was elected as one of the vice-presidents in a reserved slot and Ebrahim Moosa as assistant secretary general. The very first meeting of the MPL Board after its inauguration laid bare all the tensions. One observer described it as a 'war zone' (*Al-Qalam*, March 1995,

p. 1), between progressive Islam and the conservative clerics. Much of the discussion centred around the agenda and procedure of the meeting itself, the question of mandates and representativeness and the structure of the board that ensured a veto for the clergy in all essential matters.

The secretary general of the MPL Board had, without authorization, made two submissions to the Constitutional Assembly on behalf of the board, calling for the establishment of *shari'ah* courts, the appointment of Muslim judges to the existing judiciary and for five clerical organizations to have the authority to decide on the dissolution of Muslim marriages. The most contentious submission though, was that MPL be exempt from constitutional challenge and the Bill of Rights. The Call and the MYM opposed both the process and the contents of the submission. They demanded structural changes, whereby the cleric organizations would not have effective sole control of the board and women would be represented in larger numbers (only six out of eighty members were women) and they pleaded for an end to the vilification of some board members by others. A few weeks later, a two-paragraph letter signed by its president, Nazim Mohammed, and the secretary general was received by all the board members, informing them of its dissolution in terms of a resolution signed by a majority of its membership. Moosa described the dissolution as 'a sign of cowardice and the inability of the alleged '*ulama*' groups to deal with the problems faced by SA Muslims' (ibid.).

The clerics had been for years reluctant openly to demand recognition by the apartheid state and felt that their time, too, had arrived. With the introduction of MPL, to be administered by them, they would be accorded a much-longed-for legal authority role. With issues such as the husband's right to unilateral divorce, polygamy, and gender differentiated or discriminatory inheritance to be decided by an all-male clergy, the progressive Muslims argued that the clergy's project was simply about the further disempowerment of victims (women) and the legal empowerment of male authority.

With the MPL Board up in smoke, the disparate Muslim forces were free to argue their own positions in discussions with the Minister of Justice and proposals to the Constitutional Assembly. The way the wind was blowing became evident at a hearing before a sub-committee of the Constitutional Assembly in May 1995, attended by nearly two hundred religious leaders and academics. The chair, Fatimah Hujaij, an ANC MP from the Call, opened the hearings by inviting proposals and arguments on gender, religion and morality 'which are consistent with other aspects of the constitution'. As one of the Muslims who addressed the session, I argued against the elevation of any cultural or religious community and its traditions over that of another by exempting their laws from the Bill of Rights: 'Should the state advantage one group over another, including religious over non-religious, then it would violate the ethos of justice which brought it into being' (*Al-Qalam*, May 1995). Even the official MJC speaker, in a clear departure from his organization's position, argued for MPL 'which was consistent with women's rights' (ibid.). Virtually all of the Muslim interventions from the floor argued for the subjection of MPL to the proposed Bill of Rights. Shoaib Omar, secretary of the defunct MPL Board and the legal expert of conservative Islam in South Africa, intervened once to take issue with Ebrahim Moosa's pleas for 'moral pluralism'. After the lunch break most of the conservative clerics failed to return.

In October 1996, the Constitutional Assembly adopted the final draft of the country's constitution. Not only did all the equality clauses survive the onslaughts of hundreds of thousands of petitions and numerous marches, but they emerged extended and even more firmly entrenched in two significant ways. Firstly, while the equality clause in the Interim Constitution only had a vertical effect, i.e., between the state and its citizens, it was now extended to the horizontal level, where all persons, private companies and employees were also compelled to uphold these rights. Secondly, in the Interim Constitution, legislation recognizing systems of religious personal and family law was insulated from challenge under the Bill of Rights. Section 9 of the final draft, which reads as follows, undermines this caveat so thoroughly as to render it meaningless:

1. Everyone is equal before the law and has the right to equal protection and benefit of the law.
2. Equality includes the full and equal enjoyment of all rights and freedoms. To promote the achievement of equality, legislative and other measures designed to protect or advance persons, who are disadvantaged by unfair discrimination may be taken.
3. The state may not unfairly discriminate directly or indirectly against anyone on one or more grounds, including race, gender, pregnancy, marital status, ethnic or social origin, colour, sexual orientation, age, disability, religion, conscience, belief, culture, language and birth.
4. No other person may unfairly discriminate directly or indirectly against anyone on one or more grounds in terms of subsection 3.
5. Discrimination on one or more grounds listed in subsection 3 is unfair unless it is established that the discrimination is fair.

Women: The Day Coming Down Meant Going Up!

Amina Wadud-Muhsin, an eminent Muslim academic and theologian from the USA, was in South Africa to attend an international conference on 'Islam and Civil Society'. On Friday, 11 August 1994 she took to the rostrum in front of the pulpit at the Claremont Main Road Mosque and delivered what was, for all intent and purpose, a sermon. While several women had, in fact, previously addressed men in mosques in South Africa, this was the first time that it was on the occasion of the congregational prayers on a Friday. Although it preceded the more formal ritual of a rehearsed Arabic sermon, in the religious *imaginaire* of Muslims it was every bit as significant as the sermon itself.[15] The mosque was packed and the mood, rather than curious, was euphoric and celebratory. The women, many clad in black with only their faces and hands exposed, had until that day usually worshipped upstairs. Now they came down, sat in space normally reserved for men, separated by a piece of rope, and never went back again.[16]

More committed to consciously transforming gender roles in the community rather than seeking publicity and conscious of the major rupture with tradition, the organizers perhaps deliberately downplayed the significance of the event by insisting that it was 'only a pre-sermon lecture'. The extent of this rupture was, however, clearly recognized by the MJC and its supporters. The following Friday a large crowd gathered at the nearby *al-Jamiah* Mosque in Stegmann Road from where they marched to the Main Road Mosque. Here, after some of them had had their firearms discovered by newly installed metal detectors and had been disarmed, one of the leaders was invited to give a talk on their opposition to a woman speaking at a mosque. Without further incident they returned to the Stegmann Road Mosque, where the congregational prayers were being delayed. In February 1995 a crowd of a few hundred, led by the chair of the MJC, Ebrahim Gabriels, made a violent but unsuccessful attempt to disrupt the Annual General Meeting of the mosque and to unseat the *imam* and the mosque committee. Amid the brandishing of firearms and the assaulting of several female members of the congregation, the situation returned to calm after it had been agreed that all protesters would be able to apply for membership of the mosque and, if accepted, allowed unhindered participation in the following AGM.

This abortive attempt to take control of the Claremont Main Road Mosque led to another huge controversy in the community, all of it dutifully reported in the local and national press. In response to several death threats, the *imam* of the mosque (and national vice-president of WCRP), 'Abdul Rashied Omar, said: 'These threats are not new, we can deal with it much better now after going through the anti-apartheid struggle. [For us] the liberation struggle includes the issues of race, class and gender' (*Al-Qalam*, August 1994, p. 2)

The MJC, not wanting to be seen as the key instigators of the violence against what was widely regarded as a human rights issue in the new South Africa, initiated a short-lived Forum of Muslim Theologians to wage its battles against 'mosques that wanted to allow women to address congregations in the mosque' (ibid.). The Claremont Main Road Mosque, keen to elicit the support of as many non-congregants as possible, launched the equally short-lived Campaign Against Religious Intolerance, which I spearheaded.

In what is clearly reflective of the mosque's commitment to a comprehensive sense of justice towards the demonized Other, the following months saw more women and Christian clerics addressing the Friday congregation. By far the most moving initiative, though, was the address of an HIV positive Muslim woman from Singapore. Sitty Dhiffy, a young mother, contracted the disease from her husband in 1991 and since then both he and her eighteen-month-old son have died.

> We must acknowledge that HIV and Aids infect everybody and is no longer considered only a gay disease. I and my other Muslim friends need support from our own Muslim community. We cannot survive alone. The Muslim community must talk about Aids. Aids is just another disease like cancer. We must help people get rid of this social stigma. Let us talk about oppression, love, happiness and discrimination. We need to put aside our own personal judgements and just open our eyes and our hearts (Dhiffy 1995, p. 2)

Many of us wept openly, for Sitty, for our own ignorance, for the many Muslims who cling to their own prejudices and their yearnings for control, for those who are so terrified of shedding their negative images of the Other – images that succeed not only in blocking out the Other but also in imprisoning the Self. Ebrahim Rasool spoke for the entire congregation in his response to Dhiffy's talk, saying:

> Aids knows no colour, gender, sex, religion or age and there had to be Muslims willing to brave the tide of bigotry to reach out to those who also had a right to the infinite mercy of Allah . . . Muslims have to be a lot more introspective on the question of Aids. Creating external enemies to justify the sores within our own community was

not the way to cope with Aids. We have to recognize our own faults and in doing so become infinitely more human to those vulnerable and marginalized around us. (*Muslim Views*, December 1995, p. 3)

Nazim Mohammed, president of the MJC, in his denunciation on radio of the Wadud-Muhsin sermon was correct when he argued that the debate on women speaking in mosques was connected to similar debates in Christianity and Judaism. The conservative clerics have clearly recognized the implicit and unstated objectives of the progressive Muslims: women officiating in all worship ceremonies in mosques as an intrinsic part of human rights and gender equality. 'Where will it all lead?', the conservatives ask and point to the West where 'moral chaos reigns' in Other religion. The progressives have hitherto avoided this question and just point to the 'inherently immoral nature of gender discrimination'.

Far more significant than the interreligious connection in this debate, though, is the South African 'struggle' connection. Organizations such as the Call and the MYM have been deeply committed to the struggle against apartheid and have been very active in the many debates that have shaped our country's Bill of Rights and its constitution. Alongside most of the progressive forces in the country, they have made the connection between the struggle against the dehumanization of racialism and that of gender oppression. The struggle has, furthermore, taught them that people's humanity is in large measure given meaning to the extent that they, especially the marginalized, are empowered and, on the other hand, the powerful, even the religious ones, are disempowered.

Conclusion: Progressive Islam Imprisoned in a Mosque?

A seemingly trivial incident during the course of the board's second and last meeting captured all the tensions between not only the approach of conservative Islam and progressive Islam, but also between a simplistic anti-apartheid religious rhetoric and a principled progressive commitment to oppose all forms of discrimination. Nazim Mohammed, formerly a patron of the UDF, leader of the MJC and chair of the meeting, who takes much pride in his putative stands against apartheid, announced 'a presidential decree' that women without headscarves would not be allowed into the meeting. In the first place, while a number of Muslim clerics were, in varying degrees, supportive of the liberation struggle, they clearly understood liberation in a rather simplistic sense, as meaning an end to racialism rather than the empowering of all sections of the marginalized. Indeed, for many of them it really meant the dawn of an era when they could exercise power over others with the unashamed support of state structures.[17] Secondly, those who merely supported 'the struggle' as opposed to those who waged the struggle, were simply incapable of making any connection between racism and sexism as two forms of the denial of basic human rights, and nor did all those who waged the struggle make these connections.[18] These connections between racism and sexism, the product of ongoing engagement with the qur'anic text and of solidarity with women, were only made by those who were part of ongoing communitarian exegesis, the circles of praxis and reflection. Moreover, what a number of observers described as 'meaningless bickering' was, in fact, the outcome of radically different approaches to doing theology and approaching the word of God. The words 'consultation', 'transparency', 'accountability' and 'mandates' stood in stark contrast to 'presidential decrees'; Rosieda Shabodien speaks of the board's workings being 'replete with undemocratic procedures, opaqueness and barely concealed exclusion of progressives from decision-making' (1995, p. 17). Under the cover of the struggle, progressive men and women had shifted from essentialist and absolutist notions of knowledge owned by 'qualified repositories', all of whom were men. 'The people' – *al-nas* – had arrived. What the anti-apartheid cleric had simplistically believed to be a clever use of several verses from the Qur'an, as bullets in an anti-apartheid arsenal, was something much more profound. 'The people shall govern' was no empty slogan; *al-nas* were determined to have a share in the construction of meaning and to do so in terms of their own perspectives from the underside of history and the gender pile, and from a principled commitment to human rights.[19] Finally, the insistence of the progressives on the invoking of context along with texts, indicated that the boundaries between texts and context were no longer tenable. Others such as Hassan Solomon, who thought that the cake could still be unbaked, argued that 'the role of women [is a matter] of law based on *nusus* [sacred texts] and should be debated in that context' and that they 'will find it disturbing if the *nusus* are replaced by secularist/modernist trends' (*Al-Qalam*, June 1992, p. 15). They failed to appreciate the fact it was not a question of secularism or modernism replacing the text, but one of a stubborn, even if inexplicable, belief in a text, inseparably wedded to an equally stubborn commitment to justice. While the Call says that 'we must unleash a debate on the question of women so that equality and freedom become achievable', it hastens to add that 'this debate need not depart from the pages of the Qur'an at all for within these pages there is sufficient evidence to suggest that Muslim women can and must play a full role in our society' (Call of Islam n.d., *Women Arise! The Qur'an Liberates You!*, p. 1).

With no contemporary model of liberation in minority situations, progressive Muslims were compelled to engage in *ad hoc* theologizing. Very little of this progressive theology was ever really embraced by the clerics or the community at large. The purely utilitarian employment by the clergy of 'struggle texts', usually supplied by the Call, excluded possibilities of an internal modernization or search for contextuality. The vast majority of Muslims have not begun to think through all of these issues, although the lives of ordinary Muslim women are filled with horrendous tales of wife battering, sexual abuse, and wife abandonment, as the social workers in the offices of the MJC will readily testify. Many are convinced that the redress of all their pain is located within traditional notions of the male being the sultan in the home and that they merely require a gentle sultan who observes Islamic morality. How connected to ordinary women and their concerns are these progressive Muslims? Will this be another case of the masses cheering while their liberators are being fed to the lions? This growing distance between progressive Islamists and ordinary Muslims was also seen in responses to the anti-drug marches and marches in solidarity with the Muslims oppressed elsewhere. While progressive Islam in the 1980s was manifested on the streets, in townships, in church halls, mosques and in a plethora of organizations, it now seems to be located in the portals of academia and in a single mosque. The extent of the broader influence of its congregants is formidable in academia, politics, the mass media and education. However, these domains are not essentially the home turf of a progressive theology, which has praxis in active and shared solidarity with the marginalized. While the gender *jihad* and the very humane and crucial extension of the concept of the *mustad'afun* into the area of those afflicted with Aids can correctly be regarded as such solidarity, its lapse into a middle-class discourse entirely unconnected to the concerns of the poor ought to be a matter of deep concern to progressive Muslims.

We thus find that not only is the country in the wilderness, but so is progressive Islam. In many ways the Western Cape remains fertile ground for the nurturing of progressive Islam. Despite the present wilderness there remain a number of indicators that a local theology of liberation, which must embrace the quest for comprehensive human rights and religious pluralism, may still see its Promised Land. Some of these indicators are the legacy of the MYM and CIF of the early 1960s, the assertiveness of women, the presence of strong and often progressive mosque committees, the liberative experience of the 1980s, the pleasant coexistence with the religious Other, the growing intellectual interest in Islam at progressive universities and the generally enlightened atmosphere which characterizes this area.

Equally significant for the future of progressive Islam in this part of the world is the fact that Islam will continue to be shaped and reshaped by South Africa, a new South Africa, which is in some ways the product of a contempt as well as a deep reverence for religion – a contempt for all expressions of religion that fostered and justified racial discrimination, exclusivism, exploitation and oppression. Conversely, the new South Africa came about through the active labour of numerous men and women who, moved by their indomitable faith in a just God, sought to give active expression to the dream of country wherein all of God's people would be fully human and fully alive. It is this reverence for all of God's people, what the Quakers call 'that of God in all of us', that is the highest religious value the new constitution seeks to uphold, when it insists that equality for all human beings cannot be subjected to exclusivist and discriminatory interpretations of religious or traditional law.

Notes

1. The Truth and Reconciliation Commission under the leadership of the Archbishop Emeritus of Cape Town, Desmond Tutu, is a government-appointed but completely independent body to uncover the truth of the political crimes of the apartheid era. While it has the power to decide on individual amnesty, it may also refer matters to the Attorney General for prosecution.

2. This was giving effect to an idea first mooted by the late Joe Slovo, the then chair of the South African Communist Party that a 'sunset clause' be included to give the NP and the largely racist civil service a period to acclimatize to democracy.

3. Founded by 'Abd al Qadir al-Murabit, a member of the Darqawi Sufi order, the group adheres to a strict perspective of Islam as they believe it was lived out in the city of Medina during the life of Muhammad and recorded in the works of Anas ibn Malik (d. 795), one of the four scholars upon whose views Sunni jurisprudence is based. The group advocates 'supremacy of the Law of Allah above all man-made laws. To strive (jihad) in the way of Allah in establishing Deen, to be compassionate amongst themselves, to be firm against Kufr' (Muslim Views, February 1992, p. 4). Although a rather small group, they have been organizing in South Africa, particularly among black Muslims, since 1984.

4. Despite the fact that Achmat Cassiem, the Qibla leader, appeared at the Western Cape launch of the PAC manifesto during the election campaign and the widespread perception of their mutual affinity (Muslim Views, November 1993, p. 8), in a rather confusing set of advertisements in a local daily, Qibla appeared to call for a boycott of the elections. Asked what role Qibla envisaged playing in the new South Africa, a Qibla spokesperson responded that 'any revolutionary movement worthy of the name pursues the ideal of a just social order. The "new South Africa" is a figment of the oppressor's imagination. The struggle for justice continues unabated' (ibid.). Cassiem's response to a direct question about their relationship with the PAC was also not very helpful to anyone interested in some clarity: 'The question is an improper one' said he, 'because in a country which has oppressors and oppressed the question should rather be: "What is my relationship with the oppressed people?"' (Al-Qalam, December 1991, p. 7)

5. Haroon was one of South Africa's most committed activists and a brilliant political analyst. He died in a car accident in May 1994 at the age of 34, just a month after the birth of a South Africa to which he had devoted his entire life from the age of fourteen.

6. This is based on personal conversations Mr Deedat had with me in 1984.

7. In May 1996, a pamphlet titled *Tafakkur* with the Call's logo appeared, calling upon Muslims to vote for the ANC in the local government elections. The fact that such a message did not come in the name of the Call and that the pamphlet itself was not the product of the Call, indicates its demise in the Cape. In the northern province of Gauteng one still finds an organizational entity under the name of the Call of Islam. Its chair, theoretically also National chair of the Call, Dr Yusuf Salogie, is one of the founders of the Call in that area. They meet 'from time to time' and are engaged in what seems to be a very innovative housing project for the disadvantaged. A number of them are local councillors and one a Member of Parliament. While they are seemingly united in their support for the ANC, the discordant voices emerging from them on a number of other issues such as MPL or the role and presence of women in mosques gives an impression of an ideologically disparate group.

8. This was of course also true for foreign funders and, in the case of the Call, had a significant negative impact on the administrative infrastructure.

9. There were several unsuccessful attempts to initiate some sort of joint organizational programme between the MYM and the Call during 1994 and 1995. The Call, misjudging the durability of its struggle pedigree and burdened with a misplaced political arrogance, played the difficult suitor. The Call also misread the leadership orientation of the MYM and overestimated the modernist, as opposed to liberative, element therein. Two elements which would have made such a merger a rather messy one at a national level are the conservative nature of the MYM in KwaZulu-Natal and of the Call in Gauteng.

10. Klippies Kritzinger, the editor of the conference proceedings, illustrates the point by telling a wonderful story about beginning a new day. The disciples of a Jewish rabbi were debating the question of when exactly daylight begins. One ventured: 'It is when you can see the difference between a sheep and goat in the distance.' Another suggested: 'It is when you can see the difference between a fig tree and an olive tree at a distance.' And so it went on. When they eventually asked the Rabbi for his view, he said: 'When one human being looks into the face of another and says: "This is my sister" or "This is my brother", then the night is over and the day has begun.' (Kritzinger 1991a, pp. ix–x)

11. Qibla, noting that the idea emerged from Albie Sachs, a Jew and a Communist, denounced it as a Zionist and Communist plot. (*Al-Qalam*, 1992, 'A different kind of debate', November, pp. 4–5) On the other side of the spectrum, the Ibadur Rahman Study Group, based at the Claremont Main Road Mosque, took the final declaration so seriously that it conducted a series of five seminars to discuss it.

12. This is particularly significant given the traditional Muslim point of view that apostates should be jailed for three days during which all-out attempts should be made to have them recant, failing which they are to be killed. The presence of representatives of virtually all of the country's traditional cleric organizations made this acceptance all the more remarkable. Alternatively, and probably more correctly, it could be a statement of the complete absence of any sense of mandates, accountability or report-backs that characterized these organizations.

13. Although it is quite common for all the mosques in the Cape to have facilities for women worshippers, this is not the case in the northern parts of the country.

14. Other aspects include matrimonial property, laws of succession, guardianship, custody and adoption, maintenance and public trusts.

15. I am unaware of such an event having occurred in the world of Islam. *Al-Qalam* claimed that the event was historic in the world of Islam and the *Jami'atul Ulama* of Natal said that they viewed 'this practice, which is unprecedented in the entire history of Islam since the time of the Prophet,' with 'alarm and great concern' (*Al-Qalam*, August 1994).

16. Since that occasion a rather small congregation has taken an even greater leap in the

gender *jihad*. In the northern province of Gauteng up to twenty people meet on Fridays and have an entirely non-discriminatory congregational prayer. Although separated on two sides of the prayer area with the men on one side and, next to them, the women, who often preach and lead the prayers. During the month of Ramadan they have also been meeting, with women, more often than not, leading the prayers.

17. The similarities between the IFP of Buthelezi and the Muslim clergy bodies, particularly the MJC, both traditional entities drawing strength from leaders rather than 'the people' in this regard are fascinating in a number of respects. Both genuinely believe that they were significant players in the struggle against apartheid, a perception at variance with everyone outside their ranks. It was however not the new South Africa and contributing to it that they found challenging, but the struggle to secure the best stakes in it for themselves. The similarity extends into the realm of negotiations. Leon Wessels, a leading NP negotiator, speaks about the differences between the IFP and the ANC during the multi-party talks leading to the country's first elections: 'We would arrive at a bilateral meeting with the ANC, and they would be well prepared . . . always properly mandated, and would always find a spirit of compromise, of seeking solutions . . . This was not the situation with Inkatha. They would listen, they would not always be mandated properly. They couldn't explore ideas with us. Sometimes they read a lecture that sounded as though it had been written by Buthelezi, attacking all our people' (cited in Sparks 1995, pp. 187–8). Of course it was far from merely a question of organizational or personal style. It was the tension between preaching and conversing, participatory decision making and decrees, the old and the new, between tradition and renewal.

18. Two of the Muslim male ANC Members of Parliament, both with impeccable struggle pedigrees, were among the most consistent supporters of the conservative positions. Another irony was the fact that those who came on the Friday following Wadud-Muhsin's sermon to protest at the Claremont Main Road Mosque gathered at the Stegmann Road Mosque and returned there afterwards for the delayed congregational prayers. This is the same mosque where the martyred Imam Abdullah Haron had officiated. The mosque was also one of the few where the congregants could receive an interminable diet of anti-apartheid rhetoric during the 1980s.

19. The inability of the clerics and others to make the connections between their vocal commitments to human rights and their theology was also evidenced in the area of apostasy. Equally visible was the inability of many Islamists, including myself, who were deeply committed to the struggle for justice, to understand all the implications of such a commitment. In South Africa it was thus not surprising that many clerics and Islamists were vocal against apartheid yet supported the call to kill Salman Rushdie on the grounds of apostasy. A considerable number of rank-and-file Call and MYM members also supported the call for Rushdie's assassination. This led to serious tensions within these organizations. The kind of argumentation commonly heard around the Ahmadiah–Qadiani issues, a putatively heretical group ('If this were a Muslim country then they would have had to be killed after a three-day period within which to recant'), similarly, betrayed the inconsistencies in most Muslim opinion regarding human rights. It seems to be a worthwhile commodity for most Muslims as long as it is one to be acquired for oneself and not to be bestowed on others. Given the minority position of Muslims in South Africa the concern for the status of the religious Other or apostates understandably never progressed beyond the ideological–cultural discourse of interfaith solidarity and the socio-religious effects of 'mingling with the religious Other'.

CONCLUSION

In order to know whether God and Sunyata might, after all, have something in common, we must not only pray and meditate together, but we must first act together with and for the oppressed.

(Knitter 1987, p. 188)

In South Africa the reflections on the Qur'an's position regarding relationships with the Other and interreligious co-operation, and later the question of gender equality, assumed conscious and dynamic dimensions within the framework of liberative praxis. The inverse of this is also true: opposition to this solidarity and the hermeneutical reflections based on it came from those who espoused political quietism. In a situation of manifest injustice, political quietism is really tantamount to collaboration with injustice. When such collaboration was not overt, then affinities with the ideological discourse of the apartheid regime were certainly evident in the appeals of conservative theologians to avoid *fitnah* (disorder), to obey the political authorities, to identify with the lesser of the two evils (i.e., with apartheid rather than communism) and to hold on to the known, in this case, sexist and exclusivist clerical theology, rather than the unknown of communitarian theological reflections on the qur'anic text.

Reflections on qur'anic hermeneutics took place within a context that has a number of significant implications. There was an obvious contest between meaning as a weapon of liberation for all the oppressed and marginalized and the defence, even if under the guise of apolitical theology, of an unjust socio-economic system. It is these implications that are now considered, in an attempt to draw the various sub-themes together with the overall theme of this work; qur'anic support for a theology of religious pluralism in the service of the marginalized and exploited. I have shown that the Qur'an supports solidarity with both the religious

254

and areligious Other who is oppressed and marginalized. The hermeneutical method of arriving at such a conclusion is equally significant. This support is only discerned by those actually engaged in a struggle for liberation, who seek the guidance of the Qur'an based on their liberative praxis. In the words of the Qur'an, 'as for those who strive hard in Our cause, We shall most certainly guide them on to the paths that lead unto Us' (29:69).

Firstly, all readings of any text are necessarily contextual. If the word of God is at all interested in being heard and actualized, as all Muslims would insist, then the Qur'an has to be contextual. The difference about a specific hermeneutic is that it is consciously located within a particular context and, based on that context, geared towards a particular quest. This is how Moosa and Rasool respectively, both key thinkers among progressive Islamists in South Africa, express this commitment to contextuality:

> It becomes absolutely essential to discover the will of that Sustainer. Overriding all this is the need to discover that will in a contextual sense. We must know what the norm – the 'ought' to be – is in terms of our objective situation in South Africa as well as at a global level. (Moosa 1987a, pp. 3–4)

> Any attempt to understand the Qur'an has to firmly root its bias in the reality in which it finds itself. In our case, we have to work, not in a vacuum, but in the South African reality, a reality which is fundamentally *jahili* [a combination of ignorance and arrogance] where we see the flagrant disregard for the dictates of Allah when Allah says: Allah created the heavens and the earth for just ends in order that each soul may find its just recompense and none be wronged. (Rasool 1983)

The universality of the Qur'an, far from being subverted by the contextualization of its message is, in fact, at the basis of it. This universality is located in the willingness of the faithful to hear the Qur'an speaking to them in terms of their deepest and most painful reality at all times, and in hearing that message in terms of what the text proclaims to be the author's will for humankind. It is in the synthesis of suffering and God's will that the meaning of the Qur'an's universal applicability lies for a divided and exploitative society, not in a single of these two elements.

From the Exodus paradigm we have seen that, whatever the overall divine scheme for humankind, the bestowal of grace upon and the empowerment of the oppressed are the first stated aspects of this divine will. This means that the marginalized and oppressed are hermeneutically privileged; they are favoured to arrive at a more correct understanding of the text, because the author identifies with them. The inverse of this is also true: those who are active participants in the socio-economic structures of oppression, even if they regard themselves as believers, are excluded from this privilege. This privileged position notwithstanding, the experience of the oppressed, however significant and consuming, is not the sole measure of the veracity of the text. God has a broader will for humankind and the Qur'an also deals with this. In chapter 6 we saw how the Israelites worked at subverting their own liberation. The phenomenon of a revolution consuming its own children is also a common one, thus the importance of viewing the hermeneutical keys elaborated upon in chapter 3 as a composite whole. It is in embracing all of these keys that one can also prevent the gender *jihad* from becoming a purely middle-class phenomenon.

Secondly, while the commitment to a conscious location of the interpreter is evident in the statements by Rasool and Moosa cited above, equally unmistakable is the notion that a South African context necessarily implies that the purpose of interpretation is the transformation of an unjust society. The Qur'an has a specific message for God's people who live (or die, as may have been the case in apartheid South Africa, or in other oppressive societies) within a specific context. Without any significant awareness of what their Latin American Christian comrades in liberation theology were engaged in, progressive Islamists in South Africa, nevertheless, shared with them the belief that 'only by standing with the poor and by focusing our interpretive lens through the poor may we, too, adequately experience and interpret history. The first step is taken: we stand with the poor in the underside of history; from here we seek to understand human existence' (Chopp 1989, p. 48). Progressive Islamists consistently argued that only within a commitment to liberation and concrete solidarity with the marginalized could one meaningfully understand the word of God. This is not to say that such a reading of the Qur'an in a context of oppression is the only way of reading it and that meaning thereby discovered is the only meaning; it is simply to insist this is the only meaningful reading of a text coming from a God who is concerned with justice for all humankind.

Such a commitment to justice also means a refusal to hold any person or community hostage to the past of a community carrying the same name, or with which the individual identifies. Nor can we hold people hostage to arbitrarily imposed religious categories of exclusion that were revealed in a specific historic context. The rethinking of theological categories such as *iman, islam* and *kufr,* far from being abstract theological musing, is thus firmly grounded in this quest for justice.

Thirdly, the Qur'an bears testimony to the idea that it is a book of understanding through praxis, rather than one of doctrine and dogma. This is not to suggest that it does not deal with doctrine. Rather, it asks that doctrine, which it outlines in very broad terms, be experienced and detailed in praxis. Muhammad's own journey into and during prophethood was reflective of this. As an inhabitant of pre-Muslim Hijaz, with its many gods, its injustices, and tribal warfare, struggling to witness for justice and reconciliation, Muhammad existed before the Qur'an and its doctrinal content became a factor in his life and struggles. The first phase of Muhammad's prophetic experience was his initial social awareness, the accompanying distress at the manifold social sicknesses in Meccan society and in the active involvement with his community. Known as 'the credible', long before he experienced revelation, he had established an image as one deeply concerned with, and involved in, the affairs of his people. It was the agonizing reflections on those experiences that saw him embarking on long retreats in the caves of the Mount of Light. The revelation encountered here was the second phase of his journey into prophethood. The Qur'an may have existed prior to that, as the orthodoxy hold, but what is of social consequence is that it reached Muhammad at the second stage of his own evolution into prophethood. Praxis preceded theory and when theory unfolded, it did so in terms of the reality experienced by Muhammad and the people to whom he was sent.

The South African experience taught the progressive Islamist that liberative praxis in solidarity with the oppressed is the initial act of understanding the Qur'an. The fact that all of the oppressed did not share their religious commitment, furthermore, meant that this solidarity was also the initial act of 'understanding' the religious Other. In chapter 1 I showed how this 'understanding' deliberately avoided the Interfaith Forum where dialogue was confined to middle-class discussions on the finer matters of faith, in isolation from liberative praxis. The position of the progressive Islamist in South Africa finds an echo in the belief of M. M. Merton that 'the common response to the problems of humanization of existence in the modern world, rather than any common religiosity is the most fruitful point of entry for a meeting of faiths at the spiritual depth in our time' (cited in Knitter 1987, p. 186.).

In conditions of oppression and exploitation, any meaningful interreligious encounter has to be rooted in the struggles of ordinary people.

It cannot be reduced to theological discourses or polemics, although it may embrace them. South Africans of all faiths committed to the vision of a non-racial, non-sexist and democratic society have had no alternative but to have a dialogue with each other while engaged in confrontation with the Pharaonic Other. Trust among these religionists materialized only when they were jointly seen to be where the poor suffer and struggle. This dialogue had little or no relation to purposes of merely understanding each other or societal harmony.

When religionists committed to pluralism fail or refuse to recognize that all human responses and refusals to respond are located within a socio-political context, then 'understanding', *de facto*, becomes an extension of the dominant ideological status quo characterized by injustice and exploitation and the reduction of people to commodities. Interfaith 'understanding', in such a context, becomes little more than co-option to strengthen the overall ideological framework of the powerful.

Within the context of the enormous injustice suffered by people all over the world, the South African example is a powerful argument for the moral imperative to disturb the peace. In the world today, interfaith solidarity for a just and human world is a far greater requirement than interfaith dialogue. It is good for us to understand the Other, to know about their beliefs and to understand where they come from. It is, however, only on the battlefield for human dignity for all of God's people, for freedom and justice, that we shall see and experience the point of our faith and what it actually does for us in our lives.

Finally, the liberation of the Qur'an and that of theology are parallel processes. Interreligious solidarity against apartheid gives credence to the argument of Paul Knitter, a North American scholar of religion and liberation, that 'if the religions of the world, can recognize poverty and oppression as a common problem, if they share a common commitment to remove such evils, they will have the basis for reaching across their incommensurabilities and differences in order to hear and understand each other and possibly be transformed in the process' (1987, p. 186).

Within the South African struggle for liberation and justice we have seen how 'believers from different traditions can experience together and yet differently that which grounds their resolves, inspires their hopes and guides their actions to overcome injustice and promote unity' (ibid., p. 186). The hermeneutical notions emerging from the synthesis of solidarity and reflections on the Qur'an were a guide for further liberative praxis. However they also contributed to the transformation, and even liberation, both of the Islamist and of the Qur'an from the prison of a contextual dogma and fossilized unjust deprecations of the Other. Referring to this transformation in the MYM in the mid-1980s, Ebrahim Moosa speaks about 'a watershed event', which 'coincided with an initial moment where an unfamiliar and difficult discourse was used . . . [and] the aghast-looking faces when "epistemology", "worldview" and "hermeneutics" were spoken of' (Moosa 1990, p. 28).

> It meant that new questions were to be asked; familiar and accepted assumptions would be questioned; in short, it meant a new way of thinking, speaking and experiencing. What was previously 'obvious' to many of us was no longer accepted. Did not the Prophet question the 'obvious' assumptions of Makkah and Madinah? He questioned what seemed to many to be 'obvious'. He questioned the 'obvious-ness' of slavery, exploitation, idolatry, etc. And resistance was sure to come! (Ibid.)

We have seen how the progressive Islamists in South Africa succeeded in establishing new attitudes to the Qur'an as a book of liberative guidance, despite the vituperative denunciations by the conservative clerics. The latter correctly viewed these new attitudes as part of a broader movement against the professionalization of Islam by those who were also the upholders of acquiescence – if not collaboration – with an unjust socio-political status quo. This engagement in the struggle alongside others has in significant measures transformed the way Islam, the Qur'an and Islamic theology are perceived by many in the Muslim community. While abortion, the abolition of the death penalty by the country's Constitutional Court and gender equality are currently among the key issues being debated, the liberative spirit characterizing much of this dis-course is a significant example of how approaches to Islam and the Qur'an were humanized by the liberation struggle.

For Muslims the Qur'an is alive, in that it seeks to reach them as they struggle not only to cope with the madness of humankind in our day and age, but also to seek ways of effectively challenging the madness. That this be done side by side with others who are equally threatened by it goes without saying; that Muslims have the inspiration and encourage-ment to do so from the basis of the Qur'an has, I hope, been proven in the preceding pages.

The heurism inherent in the kind of theology done on these pages is unavoidable. Anyone who engages in the contemporary discipline of hermeneutics knows that there are no guarantees of being theologically absolutely correct. I do, however, know that those who claim to have such guarantees have not done anything to address the causes of starvation, exploitation and racial strife in our land. Indeed, more often than not, they have been a part of the problem. I understand and acknowledge that some of the issues raised in this book have opened doors without any indication as to where they may be leading. This is but reflective of my own ignorance.

Where does one draw the line in one's endeavours to rethink tradition, theological categories and the meaning of the Qur'an? While post-modernity does not acknowledge boundaries, the Qur'an does; it speaks about the limits of God that ought not to be transgressed, or even approached (2:187, 229, 230). Where do notions of equality and justice stop, if they do stop anywhere? Women leading the congregational prayers? A Hindu priest conducting a marriage ceremony in a mosque? In fact, one may go further and ask 'Why have any kind of marriages, at all?' Isn't that too defined a relationship, too confined a union for post-modernity? How do the religious rituals of Islam relate to a theology of pluralism?

Pluralism itself is not without ideology, but is intrinsically related to a discourse founded and nurtured in critical scholarship which, in turn, functions as an extension of areligious – even anti-religious – Western scholarship. This scholarship is not physically limited to the West, but is an extension of an entire cultural system which is not without hegemonic interests over the so-called under-developed world. Is a commitment to pluralism, even if for the downtrodden, not paradoxically also buying into neo-colonialism?

Pluralism goes beyond tolerating differences and focuses on valuing them and being enriched by it. Does this include *shirk* in its classical forms, such as ancestor veneration in African Traditional Religions? What does Hinduism and its multiple gods have to teach Muslims? How different is post-modernity, with its absence of boundaries, overlapping gods, and million ideas, from *shirk*?

Perhaps it is instructive to return to an argument of Francis Schussler-Fiorenza, invoked in chapter 2 in my critique of Arkoun:

> To take into account the historical, cultural and political conditions about the demise of biblical authority is to view the scriptures historically but to view unhistorically both ourselves and our views on scriptures. Descriptions about the demise of biblical authority are as much autobiographical statements as they are objective descriptions. (1990, p. 15)

The hermeneutic of suspicion that we apply to conservative interpretations of the qur'anic text also applies to us; we require as much rethinking and scrutiny as the theological categories of exclusion and inclusion.

These are but some of the many issues that we know little about and need to address. It is not going to be easy. What we do know is that our world has become small and the dangers threatening it, multifarious. There is no conspiracy directed specifically against Islam; there are frightening mechanisms available to ensure the destruction of humankind. Humankind, especially the marginalized and oppressed, need each other to confront these dangers and the challenges of liberation. Let us hope that, because of, and not despite, our different creeds and worldviews, we are going to walk this road side by side. Let us hope that we will be able to sort out some of the theological issues whilst we walk the road. If not, then at least we will get another opportunity after we have ensured our survival and that of our home, the earth.

In the midst of all of this praise of tentativeness and heurism there is a certainty that I embrace. The struggle for justice, gender equality and the re-interpretation of Islam so that it legitimates and inspires a comprehensive embrace of human dignity is one to which I am deeply committed. My own humanity is intrinsically wedded to this struggle in its various forms. While the struggle for gender equality is about justice and human rights for women, it cannot be regarded as a women's struggle any more than the battle against anti-Semitism is a Jewish struggle, or that of non-racialism a struggle belonging to Blacks, or that of religious pluralism one belonging to Western academics. All of us, whether in our offices, bedrooms, kitchens, mosques or boardrooms participate in the shaping of the cultural and religious images and assumptions that oppress or liberate the Other, and thus ourselves.

APPENDIX ONE

POLLSMOOR MAXIMUM PRISON,
P/B X 4, TOKAI, 7966
4 3 85

D220/82:NELSON MANDELA

Dear Sheikh Gabier,
As a member of the Methodist Church of South Africa I was baptised and brought up as a Christian, educated in Christian schools and, at an early age, I developed a strong attachment to the Christian faith.

During my long term of imprisonment I and my fellow prisoners received tremendous support and encouragement from the Christian Churches. The new trend that the Church, as opposed to ~~indiv~~ the isolated actions of individual clergymen, should be in the forefront of the struggle for self expression and justice, and the elevation of Blacks (i.e. Africans, Coloureds and Indians) to positions of authority in the Church have, in terms of our unique situation, turned Christianity into a militant doctrine, and the institution itself into a powerful force and natural ally of all those who are involved in that struggle. These developments have made the Church more aware of the evils of lack of opportunity, poverty and malnutrition and as a result, more acceptable to the masses of our people.

Until I was 23 years of age I lived, like most of us in those days, in a homogeneous social environment. Although I knew vaguely of the existence of other religions, I never even seriously thought about them. Then in the early forties I found myself working closely with members of other population groups, and discovered that these religions were as great as and, in some cases, even older than Christianity, with equally magnificent achievements in the field of human rights, education and welfare. I found that men like Maulvi Cachalia, Nana Sita and a host of others were fine and forceful personalities as eminent for virtue as any Christian. I must add that it was Maulvi Cachalia who first outlined to me the basic tenets of Islam and the history and achievements of the University of Deoband.

Later I became an admirer of Dr Abdurahman, the far-sighted pioneer who raised the question of Black unity with unrivalled dedication as far back as the twenties. I never met Imam Haroun but heard many good things about him. Imam Bassier visited us regularly on Robben Island and, at the time of my transfer to this place, his services were enjoying ever-growing support. Having listened to him there, I consider it regrettable that there should be no Moslem priest visiting us in this prison. The support we got as prisoners from the Christian Churches was not greater than the support and encouragement we were given by our Moslem and Hindu communities.

I should have indicated that my 1962 African Tour opened my eyes even wider and I gained a deeper insight into the principles and influence of Islam on our continent. Although I have no authentic statistics on the matter, my three months tour of the Arab States in North Africa from Egypt to Morocco, and my visits to Mali, Guinea and Nigeria gave me the impression that on this continent there were more Moslems than Christians.

But I must return to the domestic scene and inform you that on the Island I literally harassed the Commanding Officer for permission to visit Sheikh Mautura's kramat. Permission was granted only in 1977. That is the day which I will not easily forget. Symbols and monuments, especially those which represent great movements or national heroes, can move one beyond words. My fellow prisoners and I spent more than an hour in the shrine and we came out feeling proud and happy that we were able to pay our respects to so great a fighter as Sheikh Mautura.

Unfortunately, there was nobody among us who was well-versed in Islam to explain to us the significance of the articles, signs and symbols inside and outside the kramat. Our knowledge would have been considerably enriched.

In conclusion, I want to point out that there are two evils which have confronted society right down the centuries. These are wars, on the one hand, and lack of opportunity and disparities in wealth, on the other. Those whose primary concern is the elimination of these evils tend to judge all ideas, spiritual and otherwise, and all social institutions on the extent to which they contribute towards the removal of these evils. In my current situation, I cannot express myself fully and frankly, except to let you know that I consider the Moslem Judicial Council to be fully committed to the elimination of these evils. This is the reason why the MJC is an inspiration to us all. Fondest regards to you, Sheik Najar and to all the members of the MJC.

Yours sincerely

NR Mandela

APPENDIX TWO

In the Name of Allah, Most Gracious, The Dispenser of Grace

Muslim Forum Declaration on the April Elections

The following declaration was drawn up by the Muslim Forum on Elections, and followed months of consultation nationally on the issue of a Muslim response to the April General Elections.

The Forum was formed in the middle of last year and brought together about thirty Muslim organisations to discuss the elections. The process of consultation finally ended in an agreement on a strategic orientation for the forum, and this declaration. Organisations that have supported the process and endorse this declaration include: *Muslim Youth Movement of South*

Africa, Call of Islam, Muslim Students Association, Islamic Council of South Africa, Islamic Medical Association, Central Islamic Trust, various Mosque jamaats, Muslim Judicial Council, Muslim Front (Western Cape), Natal Regional Elections Coordinating Committee, Soweto Muslim Association, Kagiso Muslim Trust, Islamic Foundation of the North, South African National Zakah Fund

Preamble

For the first time in South Africa we are to have real and meaningful elections. Historically our people have suffered in various ways under a racist-capitalist apartheid state. Who can forget how we were removed from our homes and dumped in inferior areas at the whim of the state; how our people had to carry passes all the time; how our mosques were desecrated by soldiers; how our children were regarded as illegitimate because our country was governed as a "Christian National" state and our marriages were not recognised....

We believe that an historic opportunity exists in the 27 April 1994 national elections for a constituent assembly to deliver unto our land and its people a just political, economic, social and religious dispensation. These elections are the first step towards achieving democracy in our society.

It affords all South Africans an opportunity to free ourselves from oppression and institutionalised discrimination on the basis of race, ethnic or gender identity.

It holds out the possibility for national reconciliation, peace and social development, rather than continuing social conflict and the horrific prospect of a devastating civil war.

Our Call to South Africans

We call on all South Africans, and Muslims in particular, to vote and to participate fully in the forthcoming elections.

Prepare yourself for the electoral process by acquiring a valid identity document and by developing a proper understanding of the voting procedure. Assist other people in this process.

When voting choose wisely and according to your conscience, and be mindful of the hopes and aspirations of the majority of the poor and oppressed in our country. Also remember the history of those who have perpetrated gross injustices against our people. Support those who have a history of struggle for justice and the upliftment of the masses of our people.

Ensure that the party you vote for has a history of commitment to and supports the following Islamic principles:

* **The right to religious freedom and association**
* **Upholding the dignity of all human beings, irrespective of race, gender, tribe, etc.**

- Working for a clean, transparent administration with a code of conduct for people in authority
- A spirit of shura (consultation) with all the people of our country
- Subjection to muhasabah (accountability) to all the people
- Redressing land and economic imbalances, and striving for a just order
- Striving to make available to all people educational, health and social security opportunities equitably
- Protection of the earth and environment as an amanah (trust) to humanity.

Our Call to Political Leaders

We call on the leaders and members of all liberation movements and political parties to give peace a chance and to work for the establishment of justice. Commit yourselves fully to the transitionary process, and accept the outcome of the April 27 elections.

Defend the right to free association. Stamp out political intolerance, war talk and violence, and encourage a culture of tolerance and the dignity of all human beings.

Allow the electoral process to unfold smoothly and peacefully, and ensure that there is free political activity in all areas.

The Future

Decades of apartheid rule has left many scars on our land. All around us there is unemployment, poverty, inequality, broken families, crime and human misery.

A future democracy must mean more than just a vote every now and then. It must allow us to play a meaningful role in the day-to-day decision-making in our society; it must lead to an improvement in the quality of life for all South Africans – not only the rich and powerful. It must create conditions for human and spiritual development.

It must uphold basic human rights and respect the varied religious codes and customs of all South Africans.

We therefore commit ourselves to contributing to the spiritual rebuilding and well-being of all South Africans.

Issued by the Muslim Forum on Elections, PO Box 42608,
Fordsburg, 2033. (011)839-1771

APPENDIX THREE

DECLARATION ON RELIGIOUS RIGHTS AND RESPONSIBILITIES

WE WHO SUBSCRIBE TO THIS DECLARATION

a) understand, for the purpose of this declaration, a religious community to mean a group of people who follow a particular system of belief, morality and worship, either in recognition of a divine being, or in the pursuit of spiritual development, or in the expression of a sense of belonging through social custom and ritual;

b) recognise that the people of our continent, Africa, belong to diverse religious communities;

c) regret that in South Africa religion has sometimes been used to justify injustice, sow conflict and contribute to the oppression, exploitation and suffering of people;

d) acknowledge the courageous role played by many members of religious communities in upholding human dignity, justice and peace in the face of repression and division.

e) are convinced that our religious communities can play a role in redressing past injustices and the construction of a just society.

THEREFORE

f) affirm the rightful and lawful existence of diverse religious communities and call upon the state to recognise them and guarantee their autonomy;

g) call upon religious communities to promote spiritual and moral values, reconciliation and reconstruction, in accordance with their own teachings;

AND AFFIRM THAT

1 PEOPLE SHALL ENJOY FREEDOM OF CONSCIENCE

1.1 All persons shall be free to have and give expression to a system of values or religious beliefs and practices of their choice, and no-one shall be coerced into accepting or changing his/her religious affiliation.

1.2 Everyone should respect and practise tolerance towards other people whatever their religious beliefs, provided that the expression of religion shall not violate the legal rights of others.

2 RELIGIOUS COMMUNITIES SHALL BE EQUAL BEFORE THE LAW

2.1 The state shall uphold the equality of all religious communities before the law, not identifying with or favouring any, but shall consult and cooperate with religious communities in matters of mutual concern.

2.2 Religious communities, singly, jointly or collectively, shall have the right to address that state and enter into dialogue on matters important to them.

2.3 The state shall uphold the professional confidentiality of people who exercise a leadership function in religious communities concerning any information acquired in the course of their religious duties.

2.4 There shall be no discrimination on the basis of religious affiliation in employment practices, except where religious affiliation is an essential job qualification.

3 RELIGIOUS COMMUNITIES HAVE MORAL RESPONSIBILITIES TO SOCIETY

Religious communities should, in accordance with their particular teachings,

3.1 educate their communities in spiritual and moral values and promote these in society;

3.2 direct energies, talents and resources towards the service of their fellow human beings;

3.3 direct their land resources to the benefit of the landless;

3.4 remain self-critical at all times and strive to eliminate discrimination based on gender, race, language or social status in their own structures and among their members;

3.5 critically evaluate all social, economic and political structures and their activities;

3.6 ensure that people who exercise a leadership function in religious communities follow the dictates of their conscience to avoid conspiring or colluding to violate the public good or the legal rights of others.

4 PEOPLE HAVE THE RIGHT TO RELIGIOUS EDUCATION

4.1 Parents, guardians and religious communities have the primary responsibility for the faith development of their children, and parental consent is required in all matters pertaining to their religious instruction and worship in schools.

4.2 The decision about whether or not to offer religious education in state schools shall be made by each local school community.

4.3 Schools that offer religious education may choose single-faith instruction in each of the religions represented in the school, or in the study of world religions, or both.

4.4 In the case of a single-faith curriculum, school communities should ensure that suitably qualified persons from religious communities give religious instruction to their own adherents.

4.5 Religious communities shall be entitled to establish and maintain their own educational institutions at all levels.

4.6 Such institutions shall have the right to financial support by the state, provided that they comply with the academic norms laid down by the educational authorities.

5 PEOPLE IN STATE INSTITUTIONS SHALL ENJOY RELIGIOUS RIGHTS

5.1 Members of the security forces, prisoners, as well as patients and residents in state institutions, shall have the right to observe the requirements of their religions.

5.2 Such persons shall have access to spiritual care from their own religious communities.

6 RELIGIONS HAVE THE RIGHT TO PROPAGATE THEIR TEACHINGS

6.1 The propagation of religious teachings should be done with respect for people of other religious communities, without denigrating them or violating their legal rights.

6.2 Such propagation should not take unfair advantage of anyone on the basis of age, physical and mental weakness, economic need or any other vulnerability.

7 RELIGIOUS COMMUNITIES SHALL HAVE ACCESS TO THE PUBLIC MEDIA

7.1 Every religious community shall have reasonable access to the publicly-owned communications media and the right to establish its own.

7.2 To ensure such reasonable access and to avoid misunderstanding and intolerance, the broad religious spectrum of society should be represented on all boards responsible for religious media.

8 THE STATE SHALL RECOGNISE SYSTEMS OF FAMILY AND CUSTOMARY LAW

8.1 The state shall grant legal status to systems of family and customary law of religious communities with regard to marriage and its dissolution, the support of dependents and succession.

8.2 The state shall recognise persons from all religious communities as marriage officers.

8.3 Marriage and dissolutions contracted under family or customary law should be registered with the appropriate civil authorities.

8.4 People whose family or customary law has been granted legal status may also have legal recourse to the civil authorities on issues of family law.

8.5 In the case of the dissolution of a marriage, recourse may be sought in civil law after the avenues of family or customary law have been reasonably utilised.

9 THE HOLY DAYS OF RELIGIOUS COMMUNITIES SHALL BE RESPECTED

9.1 Authorities and employers shall make reasonable allowances for people from all religious communities to observe their religious holidays and days or times of worship.

10 RELIGIOUS INSTITUTIONS MAY OWN PROPERTY AND BE EXEMPT FROM TAXES

10.1 Local authorities shall set aside adequate land for religious purposes, such as worship, burial and cremation and shall respect the religious integrity of these sites.

10.2 Such land shall be allocated to religious communities in terms of the needs of the local population.

10.3 Assets, religious objects or symbols imported, and funds received by religious communities for worship, education and works of mercy shall be exempt from taxation, and donations or bequests for the above purposes shall be tax-deductible.

AFFIRMATION

We, the signatories to this declaration,

* convinced that there is an urgent need for all religious communities and the state to accept and implement the principles in this declaration;

* trusting that this will contribute to better relations between the state and religious communities and between religious communities themselves;

* recognising that these principles will function within the framework of a Bill of Rights;

hereby commit ourselves to implement this declaration and appeal to all religious communities to promote these principles everywhere.

A National Inter-Faith Conference, held in Pretoria on 22-24 November 1992 under the auspices of WCRP-SA, adopted this declaration on Religious Rights and Responsibilities. It is the result of two years of discussion and consultation among the religious groups, and is hereby presented to all religious communities and individuals for endorsement.

IF YOU ACCEPT THE DECLARATION, PLEASE RETURN THE ATTACHED POSTCARD. IF YOU ARE UNABLE TO ENDORSE IT, PLEASE RESPOND BY EXPLAINING TO US THE REASONS WHY YOU DISAGREE.

On the basis of the Declaration, the National Inter-Faith Conference also proposed the following clause on religious freedom to be included in a future Bill of Human Rights for South Africa. This clause, together with the Declaration, will be presented to the writers of a new South African constitution for their consideration.

PROPOSED CLAUSE FOR THE BILL OF HUMAN RIGHTS

1. All persons are entitled:
    1.1 to freedom of conscience,
    1.2 to profess, practice, and propagate any religion or no religion,
    1.3 to change their religious allegiance;

2. Every religious community and/or member thereof shall enjoy the right:
    2.1 to establish, maintain and manage religious institutions;
    2.2 to have their particular system of family law recognised by the state;
    2.3 to criticise and challenge all social and political structures and policies in terms of the teachings of their religion.

GLOSSARY

'adl
Maintaining a balance, justice

ahl al-kitab
People of the Book, usually employed for Jews and Christians

Ansar
Literally, 'helpers', used for the host community in Medina who welcomed Muhammad and the exiles from Mecca

Ash'arite
Follower of school of thought in Muslim theology which held that the Qur'an is uncreated. They opposed rationalism and were supportive of notions of predetermination

ayah (pl. ayat)
Literally, 'sign', used to denote a qur'anic verse

batil
False, falsehood

dar al-harb
'The abode of war', a country in which the lives of Muslims are threatened, or which is at war with Muslims. For many traditional Muslim constitutional lawyers, a place which is not *dar al-Islam*

dar al-Islam
A country where the laws of Islam are applied or a Muslim government rules

dhimmi (pl. ahl al-dhimma)
One of the People of the Book, living in a Muslim state, under its protection

dhurriyyah
Literally, 'following', 'offspring'

din (pl. adyan)
Faith, religion, reckoning

fiqh
Literally, 'intelligence', 'knowledge'. Term given to Islamic jurisprudence

fitnah
Disorder, usually insurrection or rebellion

fitrah
Natural

functionalism
The idea that the value of a text is related to the role and function which it plays in the life and activities of the reader

hadith
Tradition, religious or profane, conveying a saying or action of Muhammad

hajj
The pilgrimage to Mecca

halal
Permissible for consumption

halqah (pl. halaqat)
Literally, 'circle', a study group

hijrah
Muhammad's departure to Medina, the starting point of the Muslim calendar

'Id al-Fitr
The Festival of Charity, celebrating the end of Ramadan, the month of fasting

i'jaz
Literally, 'incapacitation', usually refers to the inimitability of the Qur'an

ijtihad
Creative intellectual effort, applying principles of Islamic jurisprudence to new problems

imam
Literally, 'leader'. In Sunni Islam, the prayer leader

iman
Faith, belief

injil
Revelations to Jesus

'izzah
Honour, glory, strength

jahiliyyah
A state of ignorance or arrogance, usually denoting pre-Islamic Arab society

jinsiyy
Ethno-cultural

kafir (pl. kafirun, kuffar)
Literally, 'ingrate', usually 'unbeliever'

kalam
Literally, 'speech'. Scholastic theology

kufr
Literally, 'ingratitude', usually 'unbelief'

lawh al-mahfuz
Literally, 'the protected tablet', believed to be the sacred realm where the Qur'an was located before its earthly manifestation as revealed scripture

mihnah
Literally, 'trial'. The Mu'tazillite inquisition and persecution, extending from 833, of those refusing to acknowledge the createdness of the Qur'an

minhaj
Path, method

mujahid
Someone engaged in *jihad*

mu'min (pl. mu'minun)
A person of faith, conviction, usually 'believer'

munafiq (pl. munafiqun)
Hypocrite

mushrik (pl. mushrikun)
Associationist, believer in a deity other than God

mustad'afun fi'l ard
'Oppressed of the earth', marginalized and exploited

mustakbirun
Literally, 'the arrogant ones'

Mu'tazilite
Follower of school of thought in Islamic theology which insisted on the createdness of the Qur'an. They upheld rationalism as a source of knowledge and rejected predetermination as inconsistent with divine justice

nas
People as a sociological entity

naskh
Abrogation

nifaq
Hypocrisy

qist
Equity

sabab al-nuzul (pl. asbab al-nuzul)
Occasion of revelation, event connected to the revelation, of a particular qur'anic text

sahabah
The Companions of Muhammad

salah
The five daily prayers at pre-scribed times, which are obligatory for Muslims

shari'ah
Literally, 'path', the religious law of Islam

shirk
Associating others with God

sunnah
The example of Muhammad, prophetic precedent

tadrij
Gradualism, progressive revelation

tafsir
Interpretation, exegesis of the Qur'an

taqwa
Awareness of accountability to God, piety

tawhid
The absolute oneness of God

tawrat
The revelations to Moses

ta'wil
Interpretation, elaboration

'ulama' (sing. *'alim*)
Literally, 'scholars', used for tradi-tional scholars in Islam and loosely for those who perform religious duties

'ulum al-qur'an
Traditional qur'anic studies

ummah
Community

'urf
Custom, local usage

usul al-fiqh
Principles and bases of Islamic jurisprudence

usul al-tafsir
Principles of exegesis

wali (pl. *awliya'*)
Friend, comrade, ally, guardian

wilayah
Friendship, comradeship, alliance, guardianship

zakah
Tax, amounting to 2.5% of wealth accumulated over a year and given to the needy

BIBLIOGRAPHY

'Abd al-Baqi, Muhammad Fuad. 1945. Al Mu'jam al-Mufahras. Cairo: Dar al-Kutub.

'Abd al-Ra'uf, Muhammad. 1967. Some Notes on the Qur'anic Use of the Terms *Islam* and *Iman*. *The Muslim World* 57 (2) pp. 94–102.

Al-Abidin, Zain. 1986. Introduction, *Journal Institute of Muslim Minority Affairs* 7 (2) pp. 3–6.

Abu Zaid, Nasr Hamid. 1993. *Mafhum al-Nass: Dirasah fi 'Ulum al-Qur'an*. Cairo: al-Hai'ah al-Masriyyah al-'Ammah li'l-Kitab.

Ahmad, (Jullandri), Rashid. 1968. Quranic Exegesis and Classical *Tafsir*. *Islamic Quarterly Review* 12 (1) pp. 71–119.

Ahmad, Barakat. 1979. *Muhammad and the Jews: A Re-Examination*. New Delhi: Vikas Publishing House.

Ahmad, Shaikh Mahmud. 1979. *Social Justice in Islam*. Lahore: Institute of Islamic Culture.

Aitken, Richard. 1991. Did Those Mortal Beings Imagine that Allah Talked with the Quakers' God: Reflections on a Woodbrookean Conversation. Paper delivered at President's Seminar, Selly Oak Colleges, September.

Akhtar, Shabbir. 1991. An Islamic Model of Revelation. *Islam and Muslim–Christian Relations* 2 (1) pp. 95–106.

Al-Albani, Nasir al-Din. 1979. *Silsilah al-Ahadith al-Da'ifah wa'l-Mawdu'ah*. Beirut: al-Maktab al-Islami.

Ali, Ameer. 1974. *The Spirit of Islam*. London: Chatto and Windus.

Ali, Muhammad. 1990. *The Religion of Islam*. Michigan: Ahmadiyya Anjuman Isha'at Islam.

'Ali, Yusuf. 1989. *The Holy Qur'an: Text, Translation and Commentary*. The New Revised Edition. Washington DC: Amanah Corporation.

Amra, Muhammad. 1986. Give Islam to the Oppressed, *Al-Qalam*, June, p. 14.

Ansari, Fazl al-Rahman. 1977. *The Qur'anic Foundations and Structure of Muslim Society*. 2 vols. Karachi: Bawany.

The Argus. 1983. 16 June.

— 1988. Muslims' Duty to Fight Oppression. 10 November, p. 1.

Arkoun, Mohammad. 1987a. *The Concept of Revelation: From the People of the Book to the Societies of the Book*. Claremont, CA: Claremont Graduate School.

— 1987b. *Rethinking Islam Today*. Washington: Centre for Contemporary Arab Studies.

— 1988. The Concept of Authority in Islamic Thought: *'La Hukma illa li-llah'*, in *Islam, State and Society*, ed. K. Ferdinand and M. Mozaffer. London: Curzon Press. Pp. 53–73.

— 1990. *Al-Fikr al-Islami: Naqd wa Ijtihad*, tr. Hashim Salih. London: Dar al-Saqi.

Asad, Muhammad. 1980. *The Message of the Qur'an*. Gibraltar: Dar al-Andalus.

Askari, Hassan. 1986. Christian Mission to Islam: A Muslim Response. *Journal of International Muslim Minority Affairs* 7, pp. 314–29.

Ayalon, Amy. n.d. From Fitna to Thawra, in *Studia Islamica* 66, pp. 147–74.

Ayoub, Mahmoud. 1984. *The Qur'an and Its Interpreters*. 2 vols. Albany: State University of New York Press.

— 1985. A Muslim Appreciation of Christian Holiness. *Islamochristiana* 11, pp. 91–8.

— 1989. Roots of Muslim–Christian Conflict. *Muslim World* 79 (1) pp. 25–45.

— 1991. Islam Between Tolerance and Acceptance. *Islam and Christian–Muslim Relations* 2 (2) pp. 171–81.

Azami, Mohammad. 1978. *Studies in Early Hadith Literature*. Indiana: American Trust Publications.

Al-Badawi, Fawzi. 1991. Mulahazat hawla Manzilah al-Adyan ghair al-Islamiyyah fi'l-Fikr al-Islami al-Mu'assir. *Islamochristiana* 17.

Al-Baidawi, Nasr al-Din Abu Sa'id 'Abd Allah ibn 'Umar. n.d. *Majmu'ah min al-Tafasir*. Beirut: Dar Ihya' al-Turath al-'Arabi. 6 vols.

Al-Baladhuri, Ahmad ibn Yahya. 1966. *Futuh al-Buldan*, tr. Phillip K. Hitti as 'The Origin of the Islamic State'. Beirut: Dar al-Kutub.

Basetti-Sani, Julius. 1967. For a Dialogue Between Christians and Muslims. *Muslim World* 57 (2) pp. 126–37 and 57 (3) pp. 186–96.

Bashir, Zakaria. 1978. *The Meccan Crucible*. London: Federation of Students Islamic Societies.

Bell, Richard. 1970. *Introduction to the Qur'an*, ed. and rev. W. Montgomery Watt. Edinburgh: Edinburgh University Press.

Benson, Mary. 1966. *The Struggle for a Birthright*. London: Penguin.

Bickford-Smith, V. 1989. The Emergence of Coloured Political Organizations and The Question of Coloured Identity in Cape Town 1875–1902. Unpublished paper presented at 'Cape Slavery – and After' conference, University of Cape Town, August.

Binder, Leonard. 1988. *Islamic Liberalism: A Critique of Development Ideologies*. Chicago and London: University of Chicago Press.

Boeseken, A. J. 1964. *Simon Van der Stel en sy Kinders*. Cape Town: Nasou.

Boff, Leonardo and Clodovis. 1985. *Salvation and Liberation: In Search of a Balance Between Faith and Politics*. New York: Orbis Books.

Botha, P. W. 1987. *Partners in Terror*. Parow: CTD Book Printers.

Braaten, Carl. 1966. *History and Hermeneutics*. Philadelphia: Fortress.

Bradlow, M. Adil. 1984. United Democratic Front: An Islamic Critique. Unpublished paper.

— 1985. Islam, the Colonial State and South African History: The 1886 Cemetery Uprising. BA (Hons.) thesis, University of Cape Town.

— 1987. Exploring the Roots of Islam at the Cape in the Eighteenth Century: State, Hegemony and Tariqah.

Postgraduate seminar paper, University of Cape Town.

Bradlow, F. R. and Cairns, M. 1978. *Origins of the Early Cape Muslims*. Cape Town: A. A. Balkeria.

Buckley, J. J. 1990. The Hermeneutical Deadlock Between Revelationists, Textualists, and Functionalists. *Modern Theology* 6 (4) pp. 325–39.

Al-Bukhari, Muhammad bin Isma'il. 1893. *Sahih al-Bukhari*, ed. 'Abd al-Fattah 'Abd al-Hamid Murad. Cairo: Maktabah al-Jumhuriyyah al-'Arabiyyah.

Bultmann, Rudolf. 1955. *Essays, Philosophical and Theological*. London: SCM Press.

Burger, Julian. 1990. *The Gaia Atlas of First Peoples*. London: Gaia Books.

Burton, John. 1977. *The Collection of the Qur'an*. Cambridge: Cambridge University Press.

Call of Islam. 1984. Introductory Brochure. Benoni: Call of Islam

— 1985. *Eid Mubarak*. 2 (4) p. 1.

— 1985. *All Blacks Out!!!* 2 (5) p. 1.

— 1985. *Muslims Against the Emergency*. 2 (6) p. 1.

— 1985. *Unite for Justice*. 2 (7) p. 1.

— 1985. *We Fight On*. 2 (10) p. 6.

— 1985. *Interfering with the Sanctity of Islam* (formerly *What Have We Done?*) 2 (12) p. 2.

— 1985. The Review of Faith. Unpublished manual.

— 1987. On Relationships with Other Groups. Internal unpublished document.

— 1988. *The Struggle*, ed. F. Esack. Johannesburg: Call of Islam.

— 1994. *FW, Codesa 2 and the Duah* 11 (4) p. 2.

— 1994. *Must Muslims vote for a Muslim Party?* 11 (5).

— 1994. *Thinking of Voting for an Islamic Party*. April.

— n.d. *We Can't Trust the NATS*.

— n.d. *Women Arise! The Qur'an Liberates You!*

Cantwell-Smith, Wilfred. 1963. *Modern Islam in India*. Lahore: Sh. Muhammad.

— 1980. The True Meaning of

Scripture: An Empirical Historian's non-Reductionist Interpretation of the Qur'an. *International Journal of Middle Eastern Studies* 11, pp. 487–505.

— 1991. *The Meaning and End of Religion.* New York: Mentor Books.

The Cape Lantern. 1889. The Malays and their Revolt. 9 November, p. 6.

The Cape Standard. 1943. Athlone Calls for a Boycott of the Coloured Affairs Committee. 4 May, p. 3.

The Cape Times. 1882. Religion Superior to the Law. 2 September, p. 3.

— 1886. The Malays and the Cemeteries. 19 January, p. 3.

— 1925. First Muslim Congress in South Africa. 18 June, p. 10.

Charfi, Abdelmajid. 1980. Christianity in the Qur'an: Commentary of al-Tabari. *Islamic Culture* 6, pp. 105–148.

Chidester, David. 1991. *Shots in the Streets: Violence and Religion in South Africa.* Boston: Beacon Press.

Chopp, Rebecca, S. 1989. *The Praxis of Suffering.* New York: Orbis Books.

Cragg, Kenneth. 1971. *The Event of the Qur'an: Islam and Its Scripture.* London: George Allen and Unwin.

— 1985. *The Pen and the Faith: Eight Modern Muslim Writers and the Qur'an.* London: George Allen and Unwin.

Da Costa, Y. 1990. The Spatial Origins of the Early Cape Muslims, and the Diffusion of Islam to the Cape Colony. *Journal for Islamic Studies* 10, pp. 45–67.

Dangor, Sulaiman. 1991. The Muslim Community in South Africa. *Al-'Ilm* 11, pp. 65–74.

Davids, Achmat. 1980. *The Mosques of the Bo-Kaap.* Athlone: South African Institute of Arabic and Islamic Research.

— 1981. Politics and the Muslims of Cape Town: An Historical Survey, in *Studies in the History of Cape Town,* ed. Christopher Saunders et al. 5 vols. Cape Town: Department of History, University of Cape Town. Vol. 4, pp. 174–220.

— 1984. The Revolt of the Malays: A Study of the Reactions of the Cape Muslims to the Smallpox Epidemics of Nineteenth-Century Cape Town, in *Studies in the History of Cape Town,* ed. Christopher Saunders et al. 5 vols. Cape Town: Department of History, University of Cape Town. Vol. 5, pp. 55–87.

— 1985. *The History of the Tana Baru.* Cape Town: Committee for the Preservation of the Tana Baru.

— 1989. The Role of Afrikaans in the History of the Cape Muslim Community, in *Afrikaans en Taalpolitiek: 15 Opstelle,* ed. Hans du Plessis and Theo du Plessis. Johannesburg: Huam Opvoeding. Pp. 37–59.

De Blij, H. J. 1969. South Africa. *Islam in Africa.* New York: Van Nostraud. Pp. 243–9.

De La Hunt, Rose. 1984. The Man on the Hill. *Odyssey* August–September, pp. 6–11.

Dehlawi, Shah Wali Allah. 1952. *Hujjat Allah al-Balighah.* Cairo: Dar al-Kutub al-Hadithah. 2 vols.

— 1966. *Al-Fawz al-Kabir fi 'Usul al-Tafsir.* Karachi: Qadimi Kutub Khana.

Dhiffy, Sitti. 1995. *Being HIV Positive.* Claremont: Claremont Main Road Mosque.

Dutch Reformed Church. 1986. Verslag: Algemene Sinodale Sendingommissie. Unpublished report.

Engineer, Ali Asghar. 1982. On Developing Liberation Theology in Islam. *Islam and the Modern Age* 13 (2) pp. 101–25.

Esack, Farid. 1986. Bericht uit de gevangeniscel, in *Vu Magazine,* February.

— 1988a. Interview in *The Jews of South Africa: What Future?.* eds Tippi Hoffman and Alan Fischer. Johannesburg: Southern Book Publishers. Pp. 122–33.

— 1988b. Three Islamic Strands in the South African Struggle for Justice. *Third World Quarterly* 10 (2) pp. 473–98.

Fakhry (Pen name of columnist). 1961. In *Islamic Mirror,* March.

Al-Faruqi, Isma'il Raji. 1962. *Tawhid: Its Implications for Thought and Life.*

Kuala Lumpur: International Institute of Islamic Thought.

Faruqi, I. Hl Azad. 1983. Coalescence of Universalism and Particularism in the Qur'an. *Islam and the Modern Age* February, pp. 27–40.

Ferguson, Duncan S. 1986. *Biblical Hermeneutics: An Introduction*. London: SCM Press.

Gadamer, Hans Georg. 1992. The Historicity of Understanding, in *The Hermeneutics Reader*, ed. K. Meuler-Volmer. New York: Continuum. Pp. 261–7.

Gifford, Paul. 1988. *The Religious Right in Southern Africa*. Harare: Jongwe.

— 1989. Theology and Right Wing Christianity. *Journal of Theology for Southern Africa* 69, pp. 28–39.

Glasse, C. (ed.) 1989. *Concise Encyclopedia of Islam*. London: Stacey International.

Goldfield, Y. 1993. The Development of Theory on Qur'anic Exegesis in Islamic Scholarship. *Studia Islamica* 67, pp. 5–27.

Goldziher, Ignaz. 1970. *Die Richtungen der Islamischen Koranauslesung*. Leiden: Brill.

Graham, A. William. 1977. *Divine Word and Prophetic Word in Early Islam*. The Hague and Paris: Mouton.

— 1980a. The Qur'an as Spoken Word, in *Approaches to Islam in Religious Studies*, ed. R. C. Martin. Tucson: University of Arizona Press. Pp. 23–40.

— 1980b. Those Who Study and Teach the Qur'an, in *Proceedings of the International Congress for the Study of the Qur'an, Canberra 1980*, ed. A. H. Johns. Canberra: Australia National University. Pp. 9–28.

— 1984. The Earliest Meaning of 'Qur'an'. *Die Welt des Islams* 23–24, pp. 361–77.

Greyling, Chris. 1980. Schech Yusuf, The Founder of Islam in South Africa. *Journal for the Study of Religion in South Africa* 1 (1) pp. 9–23.

Gross, Selwyn O. P. 1990. Religious Pluralism in Struggles for Justice. *New Blackfriars* 71 (841) pp. 377–86

Gutierrez, Gustavo. 1973. *A Theology of Liberation: History, Politics and Salvation*, tr. and ed. C. Inda and J. Eagleston. New York: Orbis Books.

Haddad, Yvonne. 1974. The Conception of the Term *Din* in the Qur'an. *The Muslim World* 64 (2) pp. 114–23.

Hamidullah, M. 1986. Relations with Non-Muslims. *Journal for Muslim Minorities Institute* 7, p. 1-4.

Hamilton, Ernest. 1991. The Olympics of Good Works: Exploitation of a Qur'anic Metaphor. *The Muslim World* 81 (1) pp. 72–81.

Hampson, A. R. 1934. The Mission to Moslems in Cape Town. *The Moslem World* 26, pp. 271–77.

Hanafi, Hassan. 1988. *Theory and Practice of Liberation at the End of the XXth Century*. Brussels: International Foundation for the Rights and Liberation of Peoples.

Hassan, Ahmad. 1965. The Theory of *Naskh*. *Islamic Studies* 4 (2) pp. 181–200.

Hassan, Riffat. 1986. The Basis for a Hindu–Muslim Dialogue and Steps in That Direction from a Muslim Perspective, in *Religion, Liberty and Human Rights in Nations and in Religions*, ed. Leonard Swidler. Philadelphia: Ecumenical Press. Pp. 125–41.

Hermansen, Marcia K. 1985. Shah Wali Allah of Delhi's *Hujjat Allah al-Balighah*: Tensions Between the Universal and the Particular in an Eighteenth-Century Islamic Theory of Religious Revelation. *Studia Islamica* 63, pp. 143–57.

Al-Hilali, Muhammad Taqi-ud Din. 1993. *Interpretation of the Meanings of the Noble Qur'an in the English Language*. Riyadh: Maktabah Dar al-Salaam.

Ibn 'Abbas, 'Abd Allah. n.d. *Majmu'ah min al-Tafasir*. Beirut: Dar al-Ahya al-Turath al-'Arabi.

Ibn 'Arabi, Muhiyy al-Din. n.d. *Tafsir Ibn 'Arabi*. 2 vols. Beirut: Dar al-Sadir.

Ibn Fudi, 'Uthman. 1978. *Bayan Wujub al Hirjan ala'l 'ibad*, tr. and ed. F. H. El Masri. Khartoum and Oxford: n.p.

Ibn Hanbal, Ahmad. 1978. *Musnad al-Imam Ahmad bin Hanbal,* ed. 'Abbas Ahmad al-Baz. 6 vols. Mecca: Dar al-Baz li al-Nashr wa al-Tawzi'.

Ibn Hazm, Abu Muhammad 'Ali. n.d. *Al-Muhalla.* 11 vols. Cairo: Dar al Fikr.

Ibn Hisham, 'Abd al-Malik. n.d. *Sirah Rasul Allah.* 4 vols. Cairo: n.p.

Ibn Maja, Muhammad ibn Yazid. 1979. *Al-Maqasid al-Hasanah fi Bayan Kathir min al-Ahadith al-Mushtahar 'ala al-Sunnah,* ed. Muhammad ibn Abd al-Rahman al-Sakhawi. 4 vols. Beirut: Dar Al-Kutub al-'Ilmiyyah.

Ibn Manzur, Muhammad ibn Mukarram. n.d. *Lisan al-'Arab.* 6 vols. Cairo: Dar al-Kitab al-Masri.

Ibn Sa'd, Abu 'Abd Allah Muhammad. 1967. *Kitab al-Tabaqat al-Kabir,* tr. and ed. S. Moinul Haq. 2 vols. Karachi: Pakistan Historical Society Publications.

Ibn Taymiyyah, Taqiyy al-Din. 1905. *Al-Jawab al-Sahih li Man Badala Din al-Masih.* 4 vols. Cairo: Matba'at al-Nil.

— 1924. *Al-Rasa'il al-Muniriyyah.* 2 vols. Cairo: n.p. Vol. 1, p. 236.

Irfani, Shuroosh. 1983. *Revolutionary Islam in Iran: Popular Liberation or Religious Dictatorship?* London: Zed Publications.

Izutsu, Toshihiko. 1966. *Ethico-Religious Concepts in the Qur'an.* Montreal: McGill University Press.

Jafri, S. H. M. 1980. Particularity and Universality of the Qur'an with Special Reference to the Term *Taqwa,* in *Proceedings of the International Congress for the Study of the Qur'an, Canberra 1980,* ed. A. H. Johns. Canberra: Australia National University. Pp. 113–29.

Al-Jawziyyah, Ibn Qayyim. 1895. *I'lam al-Muwaqqi'in.* 2 vols. Delhi: n.p.

— 1953. *Al-Turuq al-Hukmiyyah fi al-Siyasat al-Shar'iyyah.* Cairo: n.p.

Jeffreys, K. M. 1937. In *Cape Naturalist.* June.

— 1938. In *Cape Naturalist.* July.

— 1939. Sheikh Joseph at the Cape, in *Cape Naturalist.* July.

Jeppie, M. S. 1987. 'Historical Process and the Constitution of Subjects: I. D, Du Plessis and the Reinvention of the "Malay" ', BA (Hons) thesis, University of Cape Town.

— 1988. I. D. Du Plessis and the 'Re-Invention' of the 'Malay'. Unpublished paper for Africa Seminar, University of Cape Town. September.

Johns, A. H. 1990. Let My People Go! Syed Qutub and the Vocation of Moses. *Islam and Christian–Muslim Relations* 1 (2) pp. 143–70.

The Kairos Document. 1985. Braamfontein: The Kairos Theologians.

Khalifah, Hajji. 1835. *Kashf al-Zunun 'an 'Asamiy al-Kutub wa'l-Funun,* ed. G. Flugel. Leipzig: n.p.

Khazin, 'Ala al-Din 'Ali. n.d. *Majmu'ah min al-Tafasir.* Beirut: Dar al-Ahya al-Turath al-'Arabi.

Knitter, Paul F. 1987. 'Towards a Liberation Theology of Religion', in *The Myth of Christian Uniqueness,* ed. John Hick and Paul F. Knitter. Maryknoll, NY: SCM Press. Pp. 178–200.

Kollisch, Maximilien. 1867. The Musselman Population of the Cape of Good Hope. *Les Deux Mondes.* Constantinople: Levant Herald Office.

Kritzinger, J. N. J. 1980. Islam as Rival to the Gospel in Africa. *Missionalia* 8 (3) pp. 89–104.

— 1991a. Introduction to 'Believers in the Future', ed. J. N. J. Kritzinger, *Proceedings of National Interfaith Conference on Religion–State Relations.* Cape Town: World Conference on Religion and Peace. Pp. vii–x.

— 1991b. A Contextual Christian Theology of Religions. *Missionalia* 19 (3) pp. 215–31.

Kung, Hans. 1987. The Dialogue with Islam as One Model. *Muslim World* 77, pp. 80–95.

Kunstlinger, David. 1935. Islam, 'muslim', 'aslama' im Kuran. *Rocznik Orjentalistyczny* 9, pp. 128–37.

Lane, E. W. 1980. *Lane's Arabic–English Lexicon.* Beirut: Librairie du Liban.

Le Roux, C. du P. 1989. Hermeneutics:

Islam and the South African Context. *Journal for Islamic Studies* 9, pp. 48–54.

— 1990. Hermeneutics: Islam and the South African Context. *Journal for Islamic Studies* 10, pp. 23–31.

Lewis, Gavin. 1987. *Between the Wire and the Wall: A History of South African 'Coloured' Politics.* Cape Town: David Phillip.

Lidzbarsky, Mark. 1922. Salam und islam. *Zeitschrift für Semistik und Verwandte Gebiete* 1, pp. 85–96.

Lings, Martin. 1983. *Muhammad: His Life Based on the Earliest Sources.* London: George Allen and Unwin.

Lodge, Tom and Nasson, Bill. 1991. *All, Here, and Now: Black Politics in South Africa in the 1980s.* London: Hurst.

Lubbe, G. J. A. 1988. Interfaith Dialogue in South Africa, in *Believers in the Struggle,* ed. J. N. J. Kritzinger. Johannesburg: World Conference of Religion and Peace.

— 1989. The Muslim Judicial Council: A Descriptive and Analytical Investigation. Ph.D. thesis, University of South Africa, Pretoria.

MacIntyre, Alisdaire. 1988. *Whose Justice? Which Rationality?* London: Duckworth.

Madelung, Wilferd. 1985. The Origins of the Controversy Concerning the Creation of the Qur'an, in *Religious Schools and Sects in Medieval Islam.* London: Variorum Reprints. Pp. 504–25.

The Majlis. n.d. They are Astray. 7 (2) p. 8.

— n.d. Participation in Kuffar Politics. 8 (9).

— n.d. 10 (11) p. 7.

— n.d. 11 (4) p. 4.

Mandela, Nelson. 1994. *Long Walk to Freedom.* Randburg: Macdonald Purnell.

Martin, Richard. 1982. Understanding the Qur'an in Text and Context. *History of Religions* 21 (4) pp. 361–84.

Mawdudi, Abul A'la. 1988. *Towards Understanding the Qur'an,* tr. and ed. Z. I. Ansari. Leicester: Islamic Foundation.

McAuliffe, J. M. 1991. *Qur'anic Christians: An Analysis of Classical and Modern Exegesis.* Cambridge: Cambridge University Press.

McDonough, Sheila. 1971. *Iman* and *Islam* in the Qur'an. *Iqbal Review* 12, pp. 81–8.

Meer, Fatima. 1969. *Portrait of Indian South Africans.* Durban: Avon House.

Mofokeng, Takatso. 1990. Black Theology in South Africa: Achievements, Problems and Prospects, in *Christianity in South Africa,* ed. Martin Proezesky. Bergvlei: Southern Book Publishers. Pp. 37–54.

Moosa, Ebrahim. 1987a. *Tarbiyyah:* Working Paper One, *Proceedings of General Assembly, Kimberley, 1987.* Gatesville: Muslim Youth Movement.

— 1987b. Theological Method and Hermeneutics: An Islamic Response to David Tracy's Theology of Pluralism: Towards a Critical Islamic Hermeneutic. MA term paper, University of Cape Town.

— 1988a. Application of Muslim Personal Law in South Africa. MA thesis, University of Cape Town.

— 1988b. Muslim Personal Law in South Africa – Quo Vadis. *Al-Qalam,* February, pp. 1–2.

— 1989. Muslim Conservatism in South Africa. *Journal of Theology for Southern Africa* 69, pp. 73–81.

— 1990. 'Appendix A: Cape Regional Report' in Muslim Youth Movement of South Africa General Assembly Report. (Internal MYM Document) Pp. 28–9.

Moosa, Shabbir. 1990. MYMSA Structure and Programme for 1990. *Proceedings of MYMSA General Assembly 1990.* Pp. 14–17

Mosala, Itumeleng. 1986. The Use of the Bible in Black Theology, in *The Unquestionable Right to Be Free,* ed. J. Mosala and B. Tlhlagale. Johannesburg: Skotaville.

Muslim, Hajjaj ibn. 1960. *Al-Jami al-Sahih.* Cairo: Sharika Maktabah wa Mataba'ah Mustafa al-Babi al-Halabi.

Muslim News. 1961. Muslims Demand Freedom. 31 March, pp. 1–4.

— 1961. True Christians Reject Attack on Islam. 29 September, p. 1.

— 1964. The Impetuosity of Youth. 31 July, p. 1.

Muslim Views. 1990. March, p. 4.

— 1990. April, p. 4.

— 1990. May, p. 9.

— 1990. August, p. 11.

— 1991. January, p. 12.

— 1991. February, p. 16.

— 1991. March, p. 5.

— 1991. April, pp. 4, 31.

— 1991. May, p. 8.

— 1991. October.

— 1991. November.

— 1992. February, p. 4.

— 1993. September.

— 1993 November, p. 8.

— 1993. December, p. 8.

— 1994. April, p. 13.

— 1995. April, p. 4.

— 1995. June, pp. 1, 10.

— 1995. December, p. 3.

Muslim Youth Movement. 1978. *Mode of Religious and Spiritual Training in Four Phases.* Evolved by MYM for its members. Durban: Muslim Youth Movement of South Africa. 24 December–1 January.

— 1983. Minutes and Reports on Proceedings and Recommendations of First Islamic Workers' Forum 21–23 October. Pietermaritzburg: Muslim Youth Movement of South Africa.

— 1986. The Dutch Reformed Church Report on Islam and Muslims in Africa & the Impact of Islam in South Africa. Durban: Impress.

— 1987. *Proceedings and Papers: Third Cape Regional Assembly,* 28–29 November. Saldanha Bay: Muslim Youth Movement of South Africa.

Muslim–Christian Research Group. 1989. *The Challenge of Scriptures,* tr. Stuart E. Brown. Maryknoll, NY: Orbis Books.

An-Na'im Abdullahi Ahmed. 1990. *Towards an Islamic Reformation: Civil Liberties, Human Rights and International Law.* New York: Syracuse University Press.

Nait-Belkacem, M. K. 1978. The Islamic Concept of Social Justice, in *The Challenge of Islam,* ed. Altaf Gauhar. London: Islamic Council of Europe. Pp. 134–52.

Al-Nasafi, 'Abd Allah ibn Ahmad ibn Mahmud. n.d. *Majmu'ah min al-Tafasir.* Beirut: Dar al-Ahya al-Turath al-'Arabi.

Naude, J. A. 1985. Islam in South Africa: A General Survey. *Journal of the Institute of Muslim Minority Affairs* 6 (1) pp. 21–33.

Newby, Gordon, D. 1988. *History of the Jews of Arabia: From Ancient Times to their Eclipse Under Islam.* Columbia: University of South Carolina Press.

Al-Nimr, 'Abd al-Mun'im. 1983. *'Ulum al-Qur'an al Karim.* Beirut: Dar al-Kitab al-Lubnani.

Nöldecke, Theodore et al. 1909–38. *Geschichte des Qorans.* 3 vols. Leipzig: Dieterich'se Verlagsbuchhandlung.

Nomani, Mohammad Manzoor. 1975. *Meaning and Message of the Traditions,* tr. Mohammad Asif Kidwai. 3 vols. Lucknow: Academy of Islamic Research and Publications.

Omar, 'Abdur Rashid. 1987. Presidential Report presented at MYM National Executive Meeting, Benoni, September. Durban: Muslim Youth Movement.

— 1991. Demonizing the 'Other': Tracing the Etymological links between Kafir and Kaffir. Unpublished paper, University of Cape Town.

Palmer, Richard E. 1969. *Hermeneutics: Interpretation Theory in Schleiermacher, Dilthey, Heidegger, and Gadamer.* Evanston: Northwestern University Press.

Patton, W. M. 1897. *Ahmad ibn Hanbal and the Mihnah.* Leiden: Brill.

Pickthall, Marmaduke. n.d. Holy Qur'an with English Translation. Karachi: Taj Company.

Pipes, Daniel. 1989. Whodunit? *Atlantic Monthly.* May, pp. 18–24.

Al-Qalam. 1980. January.

— 1984. February.

__ 1985. The Struggle in South Africa. March, p. 8.

— 1986. Right to Lead. January, p. 8.

— 1986. Proclaim the Social Gospel of Islam. August, p. 2.

— 1991. December, pp. 7, 11.

— 1992. January.

— 1992. June, p. 15.

— 1992. A Different Kind of Debate. November, pp. 3–5.

— 1993. October, pp. 1–4.

— 1994. Muslim Forum Declaration on the April Elections. March, pp. 6, 7, 14.

— 1994. August, p. 4.

— 1994. November, p. 4.

— 1995. March, p. 1.

— 1995. May.

Qibla. n.d. *Arise and Bear Witness.* Athlone: Qibla.

— n.d. *Dimensions of the Kalimah.* Claremont: Qibla.

— n.d. *Martyrdom is Victory.* Athlone: Qibla. p. 1.

— n.d. *Neither Oppressed, Nor Oppressor Be!* Athlone: Qibla.

— n.d. *One Solution, Islamic Revolution.* Gatesville: Qibla.

Qutb, Sayyid. 1954. Al-'Adalah al Ijtima 'iyyah fi-'I-Islam. Cairo: Dar al-Shuruq.

— 1967. *Fi Zilal al-Qur'an.* 8 vols. Beirut: Dar al-Ahya al-Turath al-'Arabi.

Rahman, Fazlur. 1958. *Prophecy in Islam: Philosophy and Orthodoxy.* Chicago: University of Chicago Press.

— 1966. *Islam.* London: Weidenfeld and Nicholson.

— 1970. Revival and Reform in Islam, in *The Cambridge History of Islam,* ed. P. M. Holt et al. Cambridge: Cambridge University Press. Vol. 2, pp. 632–56.

— 1976. Some Issues in the Ayub Khan Era, in *Essays on Islamic Civilisation,* ed. D. P. Little. Leiden: E. J. Brill.

— 1982a. *Islam and Modernity: Transformation of an Intellectual Tradition.* Chicago: University of Chicago Press.

— 1982b. Approaches to Islam in Religious Studies. Review Essay in *Islam and the History of Religions: Perspectives on the Study of a Religious Tradition,* ed. Richard C. Martin. Berkeley: Berkeley University. Pp.

189–202.

— 1982c. Islam's Attitude Towards Judaism. *Muslim World* 72 (1) pp. 1–13.

— 1983. Some Key Ethical Concepts of the Qur'an. *Journal of Religious Ethics* 2 (2) pp. 170–85.

— 1986a. The Prophet's Society as the Ideal for Contemporary Muslims. *Journal for Islamic Studies* 6, pp. 40–53.

— 1986b. Interpreting the Qur'an. *Inquiry.* May, pp. 45–9.

— 1988. Translating the Qur'an. *Religion and Literature* 20 (1) pp. 23–30.

Rasool, Ebrahim. 1983. The Role of Muslim Students' Publications in South Africa Today. Unpublished presentation at first 'Ilm Book Exhibition and Seminar, 17 July.

— 1987. Unpublished sermon, University of Cape Town, October.

— 1988a. Interview in *Jews in South Africa: What Future?,* ed. Tippi Hoffman and Allan Fischer. Johannesburg: Southern Book Publishers. Pp. 108–21.

— 1988b. Muslims Mobilize. *New Era.* March, 33–4.

Al-Razi, Abu'l-Hasan Sayyed Muhammad (Compiler). 1979. *Peak of Eloquence: Nahjul Balaghah – Sermons, Letters and Sayings of Imam Ali (A. S.),* tr. Askari Jafery. Bombay: Islamic Seminary for World Shia Muslim Organizations.

Al-Razi, Fakhr al-Din. 1990. *Tafsir al-Fakhr al-Razi.* 32 vols. Mecca: al-Maktabah al-Tijariyyah.

Reventlow, H. G. 1986. *Problems of Biblical Theology in the Twentieth Century.* London: SCM Press.

Ricoeur, Paul. 1981a. *Essays on Biblical Interpretation,* ed. Mudge Lewis. London: SPCK.

— 1981b. *Hermeneutics and the Human Sciences,* tr. and ed. by John Thompson. Cambridge: Cambridge University Press.

Rida, Muhammad Rashid. 1980. *Tafsir al-Manar.* Beirut: Dar al-Ma'rifah. 12 vols.

Ringgren, Helmer. 1949. *Islam, Aslam*

and Muslim. Lund: CWK Gleerup.

Rippin, Andrew. 1988a. The Exegetical Genre *Asbab al-Nuzul*: A Bibliographical and Terminological Survey. *Bulletin of the School of Oriental and African Studies* 48, pp. 1–15.

— 1988b. The Function of *Asbab al-Nuzul* in Qur'anic Exegesis. *Bulletin of the School of Oriental and African Studies* 51, pp. 1–20.

Riter. 1983. Ideological Warfare. *Muslim News.* 12 September, pp. 2, 14.

Robinson, James. 1964. *The New Hermeneutic.* New York: Harper and Row.

Robson, James. 1954. 'Islam' as a Term. *Muslim World* 44 (1) pp. 101–9.

Rodinson, Maxime. 1980. *Muhammad.* New York: Pantheon Books.

Royster, James. 1987. Configurations of *Tawhid* in Islam. *Muslim World* 77 (1) pp. 28–42.

Sachs, A. 1991. To Believe or Not to Believe, in Kritzinger, J. N. J. (ed.), Believers in the Future. Proceedings of National Interfaith Conference on Religion–State Relations. Cape Town: World Conference on Religion and Peace.

Al-Said, Labib. 1975. *The Recited Qur'an: A History of the First Recorded Version,* tr. and adapted Bernard Weiss, M. A. Rauf and Morroe Berger. Princeton: The Darwin Press.

Saunders, J. J. 1982. *The History of Medieval Islam.* London: Routledge & Kegan Paul.

Al-Sawwaf, Mujahid Muhammad. 1979. Early *Tafsir*: A Survey of Qur'anic Commentary up to 150 A. H., in *Islamic Perspectives: Studies in Honour of Sayyid Abul 'Ala Mawdudi,* ed. Khurshid Ahmad and Z. I. Ansari. Leicester: Islamic Foundation. Pp. 135–46.

Sayyidain, K. G. 1972. Islam's Quest for Religious Unity. *Islam and the Modern Age* 3 (4) pp. 1–21.

Schleifer, Abdullah. 1982. Jihad: Sacred Struggle in Islam. *Islamic Quarterly.* 28 (1) pp. 118–31.

Schussler-Fiorenza, Francis. 1990. The Crisis of Scriptural Authority, Interpretation and Reception. *Reception* 2 (2) pp. 15–26.

Segundo, Juan Luis, S. J. 1991. *The Liberation of Theology.* New York: Orbis Books.

Shabodien, Rosieda. 1995. Muslim Personal Law: Progressive or Conservative? *Agenda* 25. Pp. 16–20.

Al-Shafi'i, Muhammad. 1973. *Ma'arif al-Qur'an.* Karachi: Idarah al Ma'arif. 8 vols.

Shafiq, Muhammad. 1984. The Meaning of *Ra'y* and the Nature of its Usage in Islamic Law. *Islamic Studies* 23 (1) pp. 21–31.

Al-Shahrastani, Muhammad 'Abd al-Karim. 1934. *Nihayat al-Iqdam fi 'Ilm al-Kalam.* Tr. and ed. Alfred Guillaume. Oxford: n.p.

— 1961. *Al-Milal wa al-Nihal,* ed. Muhammad Sayyid Kailani. 2 vols. Beirut: Dar al-Ma'rifah.

Shakir, M. H. n.d. Translation of the Qur'an-e-Majid. Qum: Ansariyan Publications.

Shari'ati, Ali. 1980. *Marxism and other Western Fallacies.* Berkeley: Mizan Press.

Shell. R. C. 1984. Islamic Conversion at the Cape, 1808–1915. *Studies in the History of Cape Town,* ed. Christopher Saunders et al. 5 vols. Cape Town: Department of History, University of Cape Town. Vol. 5, pp. 1–46.

— n.d. The Development of the Military Duties of the Malays: 1642-1846, The Maardycker–Malay Loyalty and the Toleration of Islam at the Cape. BA (Hons.) coursework, University of Cape Town.

The Shorter Encyclopaedia of Islam. 3rd edition, 1944. Leiden: Brill.

Smith, Jane. 1975, *A Historical and Semantic Study of the Term 'Islam' as seen in a Sequence of Qur'an Commentaries.* Montana: University of Montana Press.

Solomon, Hassan. 1985. What is the *Ummah* to do? *Muslim News,* August, pp. 3–6.

— n.d. Bind Us Together. Transcript of speech. Cape Town: Call of Islam Records.

Spencer-Trimingham. 1979. *Christianity Among the Arabs in Pre-Islamic Times*. London: Longman.

Stott, John. 1984. *Issues Facing Christians Today: A Major Appraisal of Contemporary Social and Moral Questions*. Hants: Marshalls, Morgan and Scott.

Al-Suyuti, Jalal al-Din. 1987. *Al-Itqan fi 'Ulum al-Qur'an*. 2 vols. Beirut: Maktab al-Thaqafiyyah.

Al-Tabari, Abu Ja'far Muhammad ibn Jarir. 1879–1890. *Tarikh al-Rusul wa'l-Muluk*, ed. M. J. de Goeje et al. 15 vols. Leiden: Brill.

— 1954. *Jami' al-Bayan 'an Ta'wil Ay al-Qur'an*, ed. Mahmud Muhammad Shakir. Cairo: Mustafa al-Babi al-Halabi, Dar al-Kutub. 12 vols.

Al-Tabataba'i, Muhammad Hussain. 1973. *Al-Mizan fi Tafsir al-Qur'an*. Qum: Al- Hawzah al-'Ilmiyyah. 21 vols.

Talbi, Mohamed. 1981. A Community of Communities: The Right to be Different and the Paths to Harmony. *Encounter* 77, p. 114.

— 1985. Religious Liberty: A Muslim Perspective. *Islamochristiana* 11 pp. 99–113.

Taleghani, Sayyid Mahmud. 1982. *Society and Economics in Islam*, tr. R. Cambell. Berkeley: Mizan Press.

Tayob, Abdulkader. 1990. Muslims' Discourse on Alliance Against Apartheid. *Journal for the Study of Religion* 3 (2) pp.31–47.

Thompson, Leonard. 1985. *The Political Mythology of Apartheid*. New Haven: Yale University Press.

Al-Tirmidhi, Abu 'Isa Muhammad ibn Surah. 1990. *Shama'il al-Tirmidhi*, tr. Muhammad bin 'Abdurahman Ebrahim. Johannesburg: Dar al-Nasr.

Tracy, David. 1987. *Plurality and Ambiguity: Hermeneutics, Religion, Hope*. San Francisco: Harper and Row.

Troll, Christian, W. 1987. The Qur'anic View of Other Religions: Grounds for Living Together. *Islam and the Modern Age* 18 (1) pp. 5–19.

Al-'Umari, Akram Diya'. 1991. *Madinan Society at Time of the Prophet*. Tr. Huda Khattab. 2 vols. Herndon, Virginia: Institute of Islamic Thought.

United Democratic Front. 1984. *Islam and the New Deal in UDF*. Area Committee Handbook. Observatory: LOGRA. Pp. 16–24.

UWC Bulletin. 1991. 'Islamic Party is against socialism'. 4 April, p. 4.

Vahidduddin, Syed. 1983. The Islamic Experience in Contemporary Thought, in *Islam in India: Studies and Commentaries*, ed. C. W. Troll. Vol. 3. Delhi: Chanakya.

Wansbrough, J. 1977. *Quranic Studies: Sources and Methods of Scriptural Interpretation*. Oxford: University Press.

Watt, W. Montgomery. 1950. Early Discussions About the Qur'an. *Muslim World* 60 pp. 20–39; 50 pp. 28, 97–105.

— 1953. *Muhammad at Medina*. Oxford: Clarendon Press.

— 1969. *Islamic Revelation in the Modern World*. Edinburgh: Edinburgh University Press.

— 1978. Thoughts on Muslim–Christian Dialogue. *Hamdard Islamicus* 1 (1) pp. 1–52.

— 1991. *Muslim–Christian Encounters: Perceptions and Misperceptions*. London: Routledge.

Wijoyo, Alex Soesilo. 1982. The Christians as Religious Community According to the Hadith. *Islamochristiana* 8, pp. 83–105.

Wilson, Francis and Ramphele, Mamphela. 1989. *Uprooting Poverty: The South African Challenge*. Cape Town: David Phillip.

Worldview. 1984. *Iqbal to Shariati: A Worldview*. August.

Ye'or, Bat. 1985. *The Dhimmi: Jews and Christians Under Islam*. London and Toronto: Associated University Press.

Al-Zamakhshari, Abu al-Qayyim Mahmud ibn 'Umar. n.d. *Al-Kashshaf 'an Haqa'iq Ghawamid al-Tanzil*. Beirut: Dar al-Kutub al-'Arabi. 4 vols.

INDEX